Praise for the second
Marketing Metrics

'The most comprehensive and authoritative guide to defining, constructing and using the metrics every marketer needs today. It's a book I keep handy on my shelf and refer to frequently'.

JIM LECINSKI, VICE PRESIDENT, AMERICAS CUSTOMER SOLUTIONS, GOOGLE

'Marketers know that they must use metrics. The key – which this book addresses superbly – is which metrics to use and how to use them'.

ERV SHAMES, CHAIRMAN, WESTERN CONNECTICUT HEALTH NETWORK; FORMER PRESIDENT AND CEO, BORDEN, INC. AND STRIDE RITE CORPORATION

Praise for the first edition of *Key Marketing Metrics*

'Measurement is critical to the health of any business, and Key Marketing Metrics "highlights key" tools and techniques across many measurement landscapes – from the consumer, to the sales force, to the ever-changing media environment. It's a "must-read" for any business leader who wants to optimize the way they measure business activities and results in order to grow their business'.

KIMBERLEY B. DEDEKER, VICE PRESIDENT, GLOBAL CONSUMER AND MARKET KNOWLEDGE, PROCTER & GAMBLE

'Why read Key Marketing Metrics? Because better metrics lead to better decisions, which lead to better outcomes. This book does a superb job of helping marketers, and all executives, understand which metrics to use and how to use them'.

ERV SHAMES, FORMER CEO, KRAFT FOODS

'Why was this book not written earlier? Key Marketing Metrics presents an excellent compendium of the metrics you really need to know, along with a structural framework that ties them together and helps you steer your business successfully'.

DR HANS-WILLI SCHROIFF, VICE PRESIDENT, MARKET RESEARCH/BUSINESS INTELLIGENCE, HENKEL

'Marketing is being challenged, as never before, to be accountable. This book, by describing metric options and their risks, will help address this challenge'.

DAVID AAKER, AUTHOR OF *BRAND PORTFOLIO STRATEGY*

'*Measurement is central to our business discipline. What gets measured matters, and having the right measures is key.* Key Marketing Metrics *provides an insightful compilation of what to measure and how to measure it for today's marketing-savvy executives'.*
GLENN RENWICK, CEO OF THE PROGRESSIVE CORPORATION (PROGRESSIVE DIRECT℠ AND DRIVE® INSURANCE FROM PROGRESSIVE)

'*Marketing, as a function, is under increasing pressure to develop business-oriented metrics to justify marketing mix investments.* Key Marketing Metrics *offers clear advice on how to develop common marketing metrics that are relevant and accessible to both marketing and non-marketing decision makers'.*
ANIL MENON, VICE PRESIDENT, MARKETING, SYSTEMS AND TECHNOLOGY GROUP, IBM

Key marketing metrics

Pearson

At Pearson, we have a simple mission: to help people make more of their lives through learning.

We combine innovative learning technology with trusted content and educational expertise to provide engaging and effective learning experiences that serve people wherever and whenever they are learning.

From classroom to boardroom, our curriculum materials, digital learning tools and testing programmes help to educate millions of people worldwide – more than any other private enterprise.

Every day our work helps learning flourish, and wherever learning flourishes, so do people.

To learn more, please visit us at **www.pearson.com/uk**

NEIL T. BENDLE
PAUL W. FARRIS
PHILLIP E. PFEIFER
DAVID J. REIBSTEIN

Key marketing metrics

The 50+ metrics every manager needs to know

Third edition

Pearson

Harlow, England • London • New York • Boston • San Francisco • Toronto • Sydney • Dubai • Singapore • Hong Kong
Tokyo • Seoul • Taipei • New Delhi • Cape Town • São Paulo • Mexico City • Madrid • Amsterdam • Munich • Paris • Milan

PEARSON EDUCATION LIMITED
Kao Two
Kao Park
Harlow CM17 9SR
United Kingdom
Tel: +44 (0)1279 623623
Web: www.pearson.com/uk

Original edition, entitled MARKETING METRICS, 4th edition, by BENDLE, NEIL; FARRIS, PAUL; PFEIFER, PHILLIP; REIBSTEIN, DAVID published by Pearson Education, Inc., Copyright © 2021. UK edition © Pearson Education 2021.

UNITED KINGDOM edition published by PEARSON EDUCATION LTD, Copyright © 2021.

This edition is manufactured in The United Kingdom and is authorized for sale only in UNITED KINGDOM AND EUROPE.

The rights of Paul W. Farris, Neil T. Bendle, Phillip E. Pfeifer and David J. Reibstein to be identified as authors of this work have been asserted by them in accordance with the Copyright, Designs and Patents Act 1988.

ISBN: 978-1-292-36086-7 (print)
      978-1-292-36087-4 (PDF)
      978-1-292-36088-1 (ePub)

British Library Cataloguing-in-Publication Data
A catalogue record for the print edition is available from the British Library

Library of Congress Cataloging-in-Publication Data
Names: Bendle, Neil T., author.
Title: Key marketing metrics : the 50+ metrics every manager needs to know
   / Neil T. Bendle, Paul W. Farris, Phillip E. Pfeifer, David J.
   Reibstein.
Description: Third edition. | New York : Pearson, 2021. | First edition
   entered under: Marketing metrics. 2006. | Includes bibliographical
   references and index.
Identifiers: LCCN 2020054744 (print) | LCCN 2020054745 (ebook) | ISBN
   9781292360867 (paperback) | ISBN 9781292360874 (pdf) | ISBN
   9781292360881 (epub)
Subjects: LCSH: Marketing research. | Marketing--Mathematical models.
Classification: LCC HF5415.2 .M35543 2021 (print) | LCC HF5415.2 (ebook)
   | DDC 658.8/3--dc23
LC record available at https://lccn.loc.gov/2020054744
LC ebook record available at https://lccn.loc.gov/2020054745

10 9 8 7 6 5 4 3 2 1
25 24 23 22 21

Cover design by Michelle Morgan, At the Pop Ltd.

Print edition typeset in 9.25/12pt Helvetica Neue LT W1G by SPi Global
Printed by Ashford Colour Press Ltd, Gosport

NOTE THAT ANY PAGE CROSS REFERENCES REFER TO THE PRINT EDITION

*We dedicate this book to our students, colleagues,
and consulting clients, who convinced us that
a book like this would fill a real need.*

Contents

Acknowledgments

We hope this book will be a step, however modest, toward clarifying the language, construction, and meaning of many of our important key marketing metrics. If we have succeeded in making such a step, we owe thanks to a number of people.

Jerry Wind reviewed our initial concept and encouraged us to set our sights higher. Rob Northrop, Simon Bendle, and Vince Choe read early drafts and gave valuable feedback on the most important chapters. Eric Larson, Jordan Mitchell, Tom Disantis, and Francisco Simon helped develop material for important sections and provided their research skills. Gerry Allan and Alan Rimm-Kauffman allowed us to cite liberally from their materials on customers and internet marketing. We thank Valerie Redd and Kelly Brandow for their help in designing, testing, and administering the survey of the metrics that senior marketing managers use to monitor and manage their businesses.

Marc Goldstein and Lynn Selhat combined business savvy with deft editing touches that improved the readability of almost every chapter. Kim Spenceley, Chris Zahn, Paula Lowell, Lori Lyons, and the production team also made significant improvements in moving from a raw manuscript to the book in your hands.

Erv Shames, Stu James, and Richard Johnson have collaborated on our "Management by the Numbers" online tutorials. That work helped us set the stage for this volume. Finally, we thank Emily, Kate, Donna, and Sarah, who graciously tolerated the time sacrificed from home and social lives for the writing of this book.

For the previous edition, we would also like to thank Raymond Pirouz and Liz Gray for sharing their opinions and expertise in respect to online marketing.

Thanks to Dr. Manuel Garcia-Garcia, Neuroscience Director, Nielsen and Adjunct Associate Professor, NYU Stern School of Business, and Neuroscience UVA student Pasha Davoudian for their invaluable guidance and assistance with the section on neuro-marketing.

For the third edition, we would like to add our thanks to those who have shared their ideas and suggestions, such as Samuel Franssens, Raymond Pirouz, Bob Robicheaux, and Bruno Aeschbacher.

About the authors

Neil T. Bendle is an Associate Professor of Marketing at the Terry College of Business, University of Georgia. He holds a PhD from the Carlson School of Management, University of Minnesota, and an MBA from Darden. He has been published in journals such as *Marketing Science, MIT Sloan Management Review, Management Science,* and the *Journal of Consumer Research.* He has experience in marketing management, consulting, business systems improvement, and financial management. He was Director of Finance of the British Labour Party before entering academia.

Paul W. Farris is Landmark Communications Professor Emeritus of the Darden Graduate Business School, University of Virginia. Previously he was on the faculty of the Harvard Business School and worked in marketing management for Unilever. Professor Farris's research has produced award-winning articles on retail power, the measurement of advertising effects, and marketing budgeting. He has published many articles in journals such as the *Harvard Business Review, Journal of Marketing, Journal of Advertising Research,* and *Marketing Science.* He is currently developing improved techniques for integrating marketing and financial metrics and is coauthor of several books, including *The Profit Impact of Marketing Strategy Project: Retrospect and Prospects.* Farris's consulting clients have ranged from Apple and IBM to Procter & Gamble and Unilever. He has also served on boards of manufacturers and retailers and as an academic trustee of the Marketing Science Institute.

Phillip E. Pfeifer, Richard S. Reynolds Professor Emeritus of Business Administration at the Darden Graduate Business School, specializes in direct/interactive marketing. He has published a popular MBA textbook and more than 40 refereed articles in journals such as the *Journal of Interactive Marketing, Journal of Database Marketing, Decision Sciences,* and the *Journal of Forecasting.* In addition to writing academic articles and a textbook, Mr. Pfeifer was a prolific case writer, having been recognized in 2004 as the Darden School's faculty leader in terms of external case sales and in 2008 with a Wachovia Award for Distinguished Case Writer. His teaching has won student awards and has been recognized in *Business Week's* "Guide to the Best Business Schools."

Dr. David J. Reibstein is the William S. Woodside Professor and Professor of Marketing at the Wharton School, University of Pennsylvania. Dave has been on the Wharton faculty for more than two decades. He was the Vice Dean of the Wharton School and Director of the Wharton Graduate Division. In 1999–2001, Dave took a leave of absence from academia to serve as the Executive Director of the Marketing Science Institute. He previously taught at Harvard and was a Visiting Professor at Stanford, INSEAD, and ISB (in India). Dave was the Chairman of the American Marketing Association. He was the host of a radio show, "Measured Thoughts with Dave Reibstein," on SiriusXM Radio. He has more than 50 articles published in top journals and has consulted and/or presented in more than 30 countries. He has presented his research at the World Economic Forum in Davos, Switzerland.

Foreword

Despite its importance, marketing is one of the least understood, least measurable functions at many companies. With sales force costs, it accounts for 10% or more of operating budgets at a wide range of public firms. Its effectiveness is fundamental to stock market valuations, which often rest upon aggressive assumptions for customer acquisition and organic growth. Nevertheless, many corporate boards lack the understanding to evaluate marketing strategies and expenditures. Most directors—and a rising percentage of Fortune 500 CEOs—lack deep experience in this field.

Marketing executives, for their part, often fail to develop the quantitative, analytical skills needed to manage productivity. Right-brain thinkers may devise creative campaigns to drive sales but show little interest in the wider financial impact of their work. Frequently, they resist being held accountable even for top-line performance, asserting that factors beyond their control—including competition—make it difficult to monitor the results of their programs.

In this context, marketing decisions are often made without the information, expertise, and measurable feedback needed. As Procter & Gamble's Chief Marketing Officer has said, "Marketing is a $450 billion industry, and we are making decisions with less data and discipline than we apply to $100,000 decisions in other aspects of our business." This is a troubling state of affairs. But it can change.

In an article in *The Wall Street Journal*, I called on marketing managers to take concrete steps to correct it. I urged them to gather and analyze basic market data, measure the core factors that drive their business models, analyze the profitability of individual customer accounts, and optimize resource allocation among increasingly fragmented media. These are analytical, data-intensive, left-brain practices. Going forward, I believe they'll be crucial to the success of marketing executives and their employers. As I concluded in the *Journal*:

> Today's boards want chief marketing officers who can speak the language of productivity and return on investment and are willing to be held accountable. In recent years, manufacturing, procurement and logistics have all tightened their belts in the cause of improved productivity. As a result, marketing expenditures account for a larger percentage of many corporate cost structures than ever before. Today's boards don't need chief marketing officers who have creative flair but no financial discipline. They need ambidextrous marketers who offer both.

In *Key Marketing Metrics*, Bendle, Farris, Pfeifer, and Reibstein have given us a valuable means toward this end. In a single volume, and with impressive clarity, they have outlined the sources, strengths, and weaknesses of a broad array of key marketing metrics. They have explained how to harness those data for insight. Most importantly, they have explained how to act on this insight—how to apply it not only in planning campaigns but also in measuring their impact, correcting their courses, and optimizing their results. In essence, *Key Marketing Metrics* is a key reference for managers who aim to become skilled in both right- and left-brain marketing. I highly recommend it for all ambidextrous marketers.

JOHN A. QUELCH
LEONARD M. MILLER UNIVERSITY PROFESSOR AND VICE PROVOST, UNIVERSITY OF MIAMI;
AND DEAN, MIAMI HERBERT BUSINESS SCHOOL

Foreword to the third edition

At Google, we had a saying we used quite frequently: "Data beats opinion." This mantra inspired us to constantly think about how we could increase the ratio of fact to speculation. What do we *actually* know versus what do we only *think* we know? The best approach we found was to determine our key performance indicators and then measure how we were doing against them on a regular basis. This allowed us to optimize and expand those programs that were working, while pulling back on those that were not.

In today's hyper-competitive business landscape, most marketers are compelled to take a similar approach. No longer can marketers rely on conventional wisdom, rules of thumb, or intuition that may have been sufficient in the past.

The challenge, however, for all marketers is knowing *what* to measure and exactly *how* to measure it.

That's where *Key Marketing Metrics* comes in. In its first two editions, I've found it to be the most comprehensive and authoritative guide to defining, constructing, and using the metrics every marketer needs today. It's a book I keep handy on my shelf and refer to frequently.

As marketing continues to rapidly evolve, *Key Marketing Metrics* continues to stay at the cutting edge. This third edition updates and adds more detail on a number of the key metrics, including brand metrics and ROI. Given the increasing importance of online and social metrics, this new edition now dedicates a chapter to them that is separate from traditional advertising metrics. Herein you will also find a section about the metrics for the emerging area of neuro-marketing.

In our experience at Google, marketers who move with speed, make their messages highly relevant, and use data (it beats opinion!) are best positioned for success with today's buyers and modern media vehicles. I therefore heartily recommend *Key Marketing Metrics* as the foundation of the data portion of this three-pronged recipe for marketing success!

JIM LECINSKI
CLINICAL ASSOCIATE PROFESSOR OF MARKETING, NORTHWESTERN UNIVERSITY,
AND FORMER VICE-PRESIDENT OF CUSTOMER SOLUTIONS AT GOOGLE

Introduction

Data-based marketing swept through the business world and was followed by the era of big data. Measurable performance and accountability have become the keys to marketing success. However, even now, few managers appreciate the range of metrics by which they can evaluate marketing strategies and dynamics. Fewer still understand the pros, cons, and nuances of each.

In the early years of the millennium, we recognized that marketers, general managers, and business students needed a comprehensive, practical reference on the metrics used to judge marketing programs and quantify their results. This book was the result and seeks to provide that reference. This is now the third edition of the book, and we continue to wish our readers great success using this book to improve their understanding of marketing.

1.1   What is a metric?

A metric is a measuring system that quantifies a trend, dynamic, or characteristic.[1] In virtually all disciplines, practitioners use metrics to explain phenomena, diagnose causes, share findings, and project the results of future events. Throughout the worlds of science, business, and government, metrics encourage rigor and objectivity. They make it possible to compare observations across regions and time periods. They facilitate understanding and collaboration.

1.2   Why do you need metrics?

"When you can measure what you are speaking about, and express it in numbers, you know something about it; but when you cannot measure it, when you cannot express it in numbers, your knowledge is of a meager and unsatisfactory kind: it may be the beginning of knowledge, but you have scarcely, in your thoughts, advanced to the stage of science."

Lord Kelvin, Popular Lectures and Addresses (1891–1894)[2]

Lord Kelvin, a British physicist and the manager in charge of laying the first successful transatlantic cable, was one of history's great advocates for quantitative investigation. In his day, however, mathematical rigor had not yet spread widely beyond the worlds of science, engineering, and finance. Much has changed since then.

Today, numeric fluency is a crucial skill for every business leader. Managers must quantify market opportunities and competitive threats. They must justify the financial risks and benefits of their decisions. They must evaluate plans, explain variances, judge performance, and identify leverage points for improvement—all in numeric terms. These responsibilities require a strong command of measurements and of the systems and formulas that generate them. In short, they require metrics.

Managers must select, calculate, and explain key business metrics. They must understand how each is constructed and how to use it in decision making. Consider the following, more recent quotes from management experts:

"…every metric, whether it is used explicitly to influence behavior, to evaluate future strategies, or simply to take stock, will affect actions and decisions."[3]

"If you can't measure it, you can't manage it."[4]

1.3 Marketing metrics: opportunities, performance, and accountability

Marketers are by no means immune to the drive toward quantitative planning and evaluation. Marketing may once have been regarded as more an art than a science. Executives may once have cheerfully admitted that they knew they wasted half the money they spent on advertising, but they didn't know which half. Those days, however, are gone.

Today, marketers must understand their addressable markets quantitatively. They must measure new opportunities and the investment needed to realize them. Marketers must quantify the value of products, customers, and distribution channels—all under various pricing and promotional scenarios. Increasingly, marketers are held accountable for the financial ramifications of their decisions. Observers have noted this trend in graphic terms:

"For years, corporate marketers have walked into budget meetings like neighborhood junkies. They couldn't always justify how well they spent past handouts or what difference it all made. They just wanted more money— for flashy TV ads, for big-ticket events, for, you know, getting out the message and building up the brand. But those heady days of blind budget increases are fast being replaced with a new mantra: measurement and accountability."[5]

1.4   Choosing the right numbers

The numeric imperative represents a challenge. In business and economics, many metrics are complex and difficult to master. Some are highly specialized and best suited to specific analyses. Many require data that may be approximate, incomplete, or unavailable.

Under these circumstances, no single metric is likely to be perfect. For this reason, we recommend that marketers use a portfolio or "dashboard" of metrics. By doing so, they can view market dynamics from various perspectives and arrive at "triangulated" strategies and solutions. In addition, with multiple metrics, marketers can use each as a check on the others. In this way, they can maximize the accuracy of their knowledge.[6] They can also estimate or project one data point on the basis of others. Of course, to use multiple metrics effectively, marketers must appreciate the relations between them and the limitations inherent in each.

When this understanding is achieved, however, metrics can help a firm maintain a productive focus on customers and markets. They can help managers identify the strengths and weaknesses in both strategies and execution. Mathematically defined and widely disseminated, metrics can become part of a precise, operational language within a firm.

Data availability and globalization of metrics

A further challenge in metrics stems from wide variations in the availability of data between industries and geographies. Recognizing these variations, we have tried to suggest alternative sources and procedures for estimating some of the metrics presented in this book.

Fortunately, although both the range and type of marketing metrics may vary between countries,[7] these differences are shrinking rapidly; the inter-country differences have shrunk considerably since the first edition of this book. Ambler and colleagues,[8] for example, report that performance metrics have become a common language among marketers and that they are now used to rally teams and benchmark efforts internationally.

1.5   What are we measuring?

Measuring marketing is highly challenging. For example, marketers generally agree that a firm's brand is a key marketing asset, but different marketers all have subtly different views of what is meant by a brand. It is hard to measure something when you don't know what exactly you are trying to measure. We, therefore, suggest that the first thing marketers need to establish is a clear definition of what they are trying to measure.

Watt and van den Berg distinguish theoretical and operational definitions in a way that we find useful:

"Concepts represent the 'real world' phenomena being explained by the theory. The scientific method requires that the nature of these concepts be unambiguously communicated to others. This requirement mandates the creation of theoretical definitions....Concepts must also be objectively observed. This requires that we create operational definitions, which translate the verbal concepts into corresponding variables which can be measured."[9]

The same authors differentiate constructs from concepts, arguing that the former are even more abstract than concepts and cannot be directly observed. They use "source credibility" as an example of a construct that comprises concepts such as expertise, status, and objectivity. Of course, constructs can also be operationalized in a number of ways.

To see what this means, note that marketing has a number of basic ideas that capture real-world phenomena; let us call these *concepts*. These basic ideas are very important to marketers and can be explained—and even formally defined—verbally. These concepts are, however, not the same as metrics. For example, loyalty is a critical concept for many marketers, but my idea of loyalty may differ from yours. Is loyalty demonstrated when I visit a grocery store every week? What if that grocery store is the only one I can easily get to? In that case, I might not feel loyal to the store, but I still visit it every week. Someone else might feel highly loyal to the same store but live much further away and only be able to visit irregularly. Which, if any, of these consumers are loyal?

We must make concrete our abstract concept of loyalty by providing an operational definition, a precise specification in numeric terms of what exactly we mean. This allows us to create metrics to keep track of how a firm is performing against the operational definitions specified. This book aims to improve measurement validity—how well you translate your ideas into numbers; we do not seek to provide new ways of looking at marketing or argue which concepts are more important than any others.

Some common ways of translating concepts into metrics are shown in Table 1.1.

Keeping a clear distinction between concepts, operational definitions, and metrics is surprisingly hard. In any given marketing team or organization, one can expect to see a certain level of confusion. We hope our book helps reduce this confusion and promote a common language, but we are realists. Indeed, we are happy to acknowledge that we also make mistakes and inadvertently refer to metrics by the name of the concept. We are trying to be clear but please contact Neil Bendle if you see areas where we can improve (just in case there is a fourth edition).

Table 1.1 Common metrics used to track important concepts

Concept	Metric(s)
Loyalty	Share of Requirements (SOR)
Distribution	All Commodity Volume (ACV), Total ACV
Market Concentration	Three-Firm Concentration Ratio, Herfindahl Index

There will continue to be healthy (or at least vigorous) debates in marketing on what *should* be meant by various theoretical concepts and constructs. However, at the level of measurement and reporting, we believe that the field should be striving for consistency, accuracy, and reliability that allow us to at least understand what other people mean, even if we disagree with what they are suggesting. No shared understanding can happen without clear operational definitions. Providing these definitions is the primary focus of the Common Language Marketing Dictionary. The aim of this project is to improve the measurement of marketing, specifically making measurement in the discipline more consistent. It has been undertaken by MASB (Marketing Accountability Standards Board, www.themasb.org), along with MSI (Marketing Science Institute, www.msi.org), ANA (Association of National Advertisers, www.ana.net), and AMA (American Marketing Association, www.ama.org). We encourage readers to learn more about, and support, the initiative, which can be accessed at marketing-dictionary.org. We add a special plea to any professors reading the book to encourage your students to use the Common Language Marketing Dictionary (for example, by adding a link in any syllabi).

1.6   Value of information

An almost infinite number of metrics could be calculated. Even the most quantitative marketer will recognize that having more calculations doesn't always help make better decisions. Thus, one question a marketer may want to start with is "When is a metric useful?"

A classic distinction is between data versus information versus knowledge. Data are what we have a profusion of in the world of big data. Data are in raw form and doesn't tell us anything without being manipulated in some way. Information is data that has been converted into something that can be used by a human reader. Ideally, information gets converted into knowledge when a user understands and internalizes the information. Thus, one way of thinking about the value of information is whether it creates knowledge or not. Data that are simply being stored are not currently valuable but often has the potential to be valuable if approached in the right way. How can we extract the information from the data we have? (Clearly marketers should ensure that they have legal and ethical rights to use the data in this manner. Consent is usually a key consideration, but discussing law and ethics is beyond the scope of this book.)

One way to increase the value of information is to make it easier for users to convert it to knowledge. To do this, we recommend considering how the information you have extracted, such as the metrics you have calculated, can be presented in a user-friendly way. There are now many companies, such as Tableau software (www.tableau.com), that specialize in translating information into visual representations. Such visual depictions are an excellent aid to allowing users to more easily extract the message from the information you provide them.

An alternative way of thinking about the value of information is whether the information helps take an action. Information is valuable only if it allows us to make better decisions. To cast this in terms of metrics, a metric's value arises from its ability to improve our decisions in some way. Note that this is a very pragmatic approach, as the value of the metric depends upon what the user can do with the result. A chief marketing officer (CMO) might find estimates of the value of the brand she controls invaluable when arguing for increasing the marketing budget with her C-suite colleagues. A more junior marketer, however, may feel that he can't impact brand value in any significant way, so knowing this number is of no value to him. The more junior marketer can, however, impact whether the product is on the retailers' shelves and so may find distribution measures invaluable.

A related point is that people sometimes equate the value of information with the range of possible alternatives that the metric can take. Knowing the precise number for a metric that swings wildly can be very informative and thus valuable. If the metric never changes significantly, knowing its precise reading at any given point is unlikely to be very valuable. For example, information on the sales of a fashion item where consumer reaction is unpredictable can be exceptionally valuable for stock planning. Estimates for items with more predictable sales (such as matches) are less valuable because knowing the precise sales number is less likely to change the inventory order you would make without the more refined sales estimate. For items with very stable sales, your estimate based upon last year is likely to be good regardless of whether you calculate the precise metric for this year.

Testing is a critical component of marketing plans, but where should you spend your testing budget? What gives you the most information for your money? Scott Armstrong notes that this depends upon what you are trying to achieve.[10] Sometimes you will want to emulate much academic research and drill down into a very specific topic. This can lead to very consistent estimates, also known as being "reliable." This means every time you measure, you get a similar result because you measure exactly the same thing each time you measure. In everyday life, the electronic scale that weighs you every morning is reliable, and you generally get the same result if nothing changes. This approach makes sense if it is critical for you to be very precise and if small changes in a metric would radically alter your plans.

More often, however, you aren't sure you are measuring the right thing. You want to know how the firm is performing generally, but you have a less-than-perfect understanding of what performance means exactly. You might be interested in your general health rather than your precise weight. Your weight is likely to be connected to your general health but is far from the complete picture. In such situations, you are interested in whether the measures you are using are valid and whether the measures accurately capture what you want them to capture. To assess validity, you are likely to want multiple measures, in which case you will spread your testing budget across a wider range of tests and will be more tolerant of conflicting results. To assess your health, you might look at your weight, your blood pressure, your blood sugar, the ease of your breathing, etc. These will sometimes point in different directions, but put together they give a more comprehensive picture than fixating upon a single metric—however reliably the single metric can be measured.

To have valid estimates of hard-to-define concepts, such as performance, we often recommend a variety of tests and the use of multiple metrics. As we will discuss in Chapters 13 and 14, it is often possible to have one metric look very good while the true value of the company is destroyed. Testing multiple different areas and assessing different metrics may give you a less precise picture (it is less reliable) but is much less likely to miss a major problem (it is more valid).

1.7   Mastering metrics

Being able to "crunch the numbers" is vital to success in marketing. Knowing which numbers to crunch, however, is a skill that develops over time. Toward that end, managers must practice the use of metrics and learn from their mistakes. By working through the examples in this book, we hope our readers will gain both confidence and a firm understanding of the fundamentals of quantitative marketing. With time and experience, we trust that you will also develop an intuition about metrics and learn to dig deeper when calculations appear suspect or puzzling.

Ultimately, with regard to metrics, we believe many of our readers will require not only familiarity but also fluency. That is, managers should be able to perform relevant calculations on the fly—under pressure, in board meetings, and during strategic deliberations and negotiations. Although not all readers will require that level of fluency, we believe it will be increasingly expected of candidates for senior management positions, especially those with significant financial responsibility. We anticipate that a mastery of quantitative marketing will become a means for many of our readers to differentiate and position themselves for career advancement in an ever-more-challenging environment.

1.8   Where are the "top ten" metrics?

Working on this book, we received many requests to provide a short list of the "key" or "top ten" marketing metrics. The intuition behind this request is that readers (managers and students) want to be able to focus their attention on the "most important" metrics.

Although some readers may have enjoyed reading the earlier editions from cover to cover, it is safe to say that none of the authors has had that pleasure. We view the book as a reference book—something to keep on the shelf and use when confronted with a new or less familiar metric. The list of metrics covered is therefore long so as to be useful for those occasions. It is not intended to be a guide to the X number of metrics you must apply to monitor marketing. It is this view of the book as a reference guide that helps explain why we do not rate or rank the long list of metrics. We see you pulling the book from the shelf as needed rather than us pushing our preferred metrics upon you.

Specifically, the reasons for us not providing the short list of "really important" metrics are as follows.

First, we believe that any ranking of marketing metrics from most to least useful should depend on the type of business under consideration. Thus, what metrics you prefer depend upon what you need them for. For example, marketers of business-to-business products and services that go to market through a direct sales force don't need metrics that measure retail availability or dealer productivity.

Second, even what might begin as a short list tends to expand rapidly as metrics come in matched sets. For example, if customer lifetime value is important to your business (let's say, financial services), then you are also likely to use measures of retention and acquisition costs. The same notion applies to retail, media, sales force, and internet traffic metrics. If some of these are important to you, others in the same general categories are likely to be rated as useful, too.

Third, businesses don't always have access (at a reasonable cost) to the metrics they would like to have. Inevitably, some of the rankings presented will reflect the cost of obtaining the data that underlie the particular metrics. Some metrics may be interesting to know but are not worth considering if they cost more to obtain than the value of the information and insight they provide. The size of the organization thus matters. Small organizations may use metrics that are cheaper to obtain, whereas larger organizations are more likely to be able to realize the full value from expensive, proprietary, or custom-created metrics. The same goes for stages in the product life cycle. Managers of newly launched products often have different concerns and metrics to monitor them than do managers of mature products.

Fourth, we believe that some metrics currently ranked lower by managers will ultimately prove to be very useful when managers fully understand the pros and cons of a particular metric. For example, for many years, advocates for Economic Value Added (EVA) have argued it is the "gold standard" of profitability metrics, but when we discuss it with many managers, it ranks far below other financial performance measures, such as Return on Investment (ROI). We believe one reason for the low ranking of EVA is that this metric is less applicable at the "operating level" than for overall corporate performance. So even within the same business, depending on where a manager sits in the organization, some metrics are more relevant than others. Also, like EVA, many metrics that we have included are relatively new to marketing, and many managers don't understand them well or know how they might be relevant to their particular business. Customer Lifetime Value is another metric that is gaining acceptance but is still unfamiliar to many managers. If all these metrics were perfectly understood, there would be no need for a book of this type.

We included the results of our survey of marketing managers in the previous edition of this book so that readers could learn what metrics other managers thought were potentially useful. However, we became less convinced that the survey results were useful because metric use and understanding remain an awfully long way from where we want them to be. In the second and third editions, we have not included the survey and have instead used the space to explore more metrics.

Here we simply note the key points from the survey. For one thing, managers value the profit-related metrics Net Profit, ROI, and Margin most highly, even though these metrics have less to do with day-to-day marketing decisions. We presume this is because those are the metrics they are asked about by the people who control budgets. Customer Satisfaction was the most popular "non-financial" metric. Sales-related metrics, such as Sales Total, also proved popular.

1.9   What is new in the third edition?

The third edition of this book has significant changes. In addition to reviewing and clarifying the text from the previous edition, we have included a number of major additions.

First, we now have a dedicated focus on sponsorship metrics, which we have included in Chapter 10. How much firms benefit from sponsorship is a topic that is both fiendishly difficult to measure and also critical for many of them. One need only think of how much Visa, Coke, and various beer companies invest in their partnerships. Sponsorship is often a strategic decision involving large commitments of resources over extended periods of time, such as when naming a stadium or sponsoring a golf or tennis tournament. We hope that this new edition will positively contribute to bringing more standardization and accountability to sponsorship so marketers can feel more confident in their investments.

Second, we have added sections in Chapter 12 on the interface among financial markets, accounting, and marketing metrics. We have provided this information for marketers who are involved in C-suite decisions or who hope to be in the future. Chapter 12 outlines difficulties in assessing the impact of marketing on the ultimate financial objectives of a publicly listed for-profit firm. We also note challenges marketers face in using financial accounting data for their decisions.

Third, in the years since the first edition of this book was published, "omni-channel" has become a major marketing concept. In a new section, we outline how marketers can measure their activities where there are multiple channels and sources of communication that consumers may access as part of a single purchase decision. We look at channel dependencies, how search and distribution interact, and online distribution metrics. We have broken off distribution measures from sales and created a new Chapter 7 featuring the new metrics.

Fourth, a completely new section of the book outlines changes that have occurred in the world of marketing metrics and accountability. We note progress that is being made by MASB on creating more discipline in marketing measurement. We highlight work by the International Organization for Standardization (ISO) at a multi-country level to improve brand evaluation.

Finally, in addition to these major changes, we have added some individual metrics such as Return on Advertising Spend.

We very much hope you enjoy this new edition of *Key Marketing Metrics*.

1.10 New developments in the world of marketing metrics

Since the first edition of this book was published, there has been considerable progress in the world of marketing metrics. This section of the book outlines some of these developments and mentions some bigger issues related to the topic.

MASB

The Marketing Accountability Standards Board (MASB) is an independent body that aims to set standards for marketing accountability (see themasb.org). MASB was launched in 2007 from "The Boardroom Project," with the involvement of a number of major figures in the world of marketing accountability, including Meg Blair (founding President of The ARS Group) and Dave Stewart (President's Chair in Marketing and Law at Loyola Marymount University and former editor of the *Journal of Marketing* and the *Journal of the Academy of Marketing Science*).

Three of your authors (Paul, Dave, and Neil) have been heavily involved in MASB. Indeed, earlier editions of this book have had an influence on the Common Language Marketing Dictionary, a project of MASB that seeks to standardize marketing language (see marketing-dictionary.org). We see this as a major contribution to standardizing marketing. We hope managers and educators will encourage those they deal with to use terms that are widely recognized. The Common Language Marketing Dictionary is an evolving repository of marketing terms. Please share ideas for terms and edits of dictionary items with MASB or one of us.

MASB has a YouTube channel (www.youtube.com/c/masbmarketingaccountabilitystandardsboard) that houses videos explaining key marketing accountability-related topics. Please view these videos if you are interested in more information about topics related to marketing accounting.

MASB is also involved in discussing the way marketing is presented in financial accounting, with the ultimate aim of improving the reporting of marketing's contribution to firm performance and generating greater accountability for marketing.

ISO 20671: Brand Evaluation — Principles and Fundamentals

One of MASB's key roles has been to represent the United States (under the delegated authority of the American National Standards Institute [ANSI]) at the ISO with respect to brand measurement. In 2019, the group launched ISO 20671: Brand Evaluation — Principles and Fundamentals. Anyone who works with brands should read this standard, which contains best practice advice on brand evaluation and management. (For more details, see www.iso.org/standard/68786.html). This standard includes the key advice that firms should hold regular brand audits.

SASB

The Sustainability Accounting Standards Board (SASB) has had considerable success in developing company reporting — specifically with respect to sustainability. SASB's concentration on sustainability issues means the organization experiences many similar issues to those faced by accountable marketers. One area of overlap is that measures adopted in financial accounting tend to avoid harder-to-assess values or values involving long time frames. This means financial accounting leaves a more limited picture of the firm and its sustainability both in the sense of the firm "being green" and the firm being run with a long-term mindset (such as investing in the brand). For more information on SASB, see www.sasb.org.

Organization of the text

This book is organized into chapters that correspond to the various roles played by marketing metrics in enterprise management. Individual chapters are dedicated to metrics used in promotional strategy, advertising and sponsorship, and distribution, for example. Each chapter is composed of sections devoted to specific concepts and calculations.

We present these metrics in a sequence that may appear somewhat arbitrary, but there is a rationale behind it. In organizing this text, we have sought to strike a balance between two goals: (1) to establish core concepts first and build gradually toward increasing sophistication and (2) to group related metrics in clusters, helping our readers recognize patterns of mutual reinforcement and interdependence. In Figure 1.1, we offer a graphical presentation of this structure, demonstrating the interlocking nature of all marketing metrics—indeed of all marketing programs—as well as the central role of the customer.

The central issues addressed by the metrics in this book are as follows:

- *Chapter 2, "Share of hearts, minds, and markets":* Customer perceptions, market share, and competitive analysis
- *Chapter 3, "Margins and profits":* Revenues, cost structures, and profitability
- *Chapter 4, "Product and portfolio management":* Metrics behind product strategy, including measures of trial, growth, cannibalization, and brand equity
- *Chapter 5, "Customer profitability":* The value of individual customers and relationships
- *Chapter 6, "Sales force management":* Sales force organization, performance, and compensation

Figure 1.1 Marketing metrics: marketing at the core of the organization

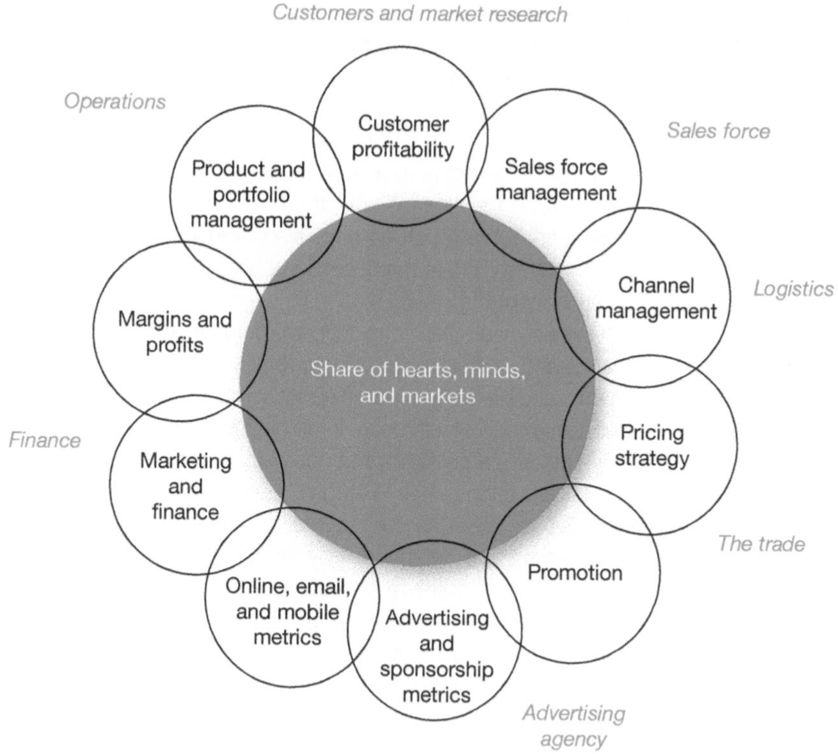

Customers and market research

Operations

Customer profitability

Product and portfolio management

Sales force

Sales force management

Channel management

Logistics

Margins and profits

Share of hearts, minds, and markets

Finance

Marketing and finance

Pricing strategy

The trade

Online, email, and mobile metrics

Promotion

Advertising and sponsorship metrics

Advertising agency

- *Chapter 7, "Channel management":* Distribution coverage and logistics
- *Chapter 8, "Pricing strategy":* Price sensitivity and optimization, with an eye toward setting prices to maximize profits
- *Chapter 9, "Promotion":* Temporary price promotions, coupons, rebates, and trade allowances
- *Chapter 10, "Advertising and sponsorship metrics":* The central measures of advertising coverage and effectiveness, including reach, frequency, rating points, and impressions; models for consumer response to advertising; and sponsorship-relevant metrics
- *Chapter 11, "Online, email, and mobile metrics":* Specialized metrics for web-based, mobile, and email campaigns
- *Chapter 12, "Marketing and finance":* Financial evaluation of marketing programs
- *Chapter 13, "The marketing metrics x-ray and testing":* The use of metrics as leading indicators of opportunities, challenges, and financial performance
- *Chapter 14, "System of metrics":* Decomposing marketing metrics into component parts to improve measurement accuracy, add managerial insight into problems, and assist marketing model building

Components of each chapter

As shown in Table 1.2, the chapters are composed of multiple sections, each dedicated to specific marketing concepts or metrics. Within each section, we open with definitions, formulas, and a brief description of the metrics covered. Next, in a passage titled "Construction," we explore the issues surrounding these metrics, including their formulation, application, interpretation, and strategic ramifications. We provide examples to illustrate calculations, reinforce concepts, and help readers verify their understanding of key formulas. That done, in a section titled "Data sources, complications, and cautions," we probe the limitations of the metrics under consideration and potential pitfalls in their use. Toward that end, we also examine the assumptions underlying these metrics. Finally, we close many sections with a brief survey section titled "Related metrics and concepts."

In organizing the text in this way, our goal is straightforward: Most of the metrics in this book have broad implications and multiple layers of interpretation. Doctoral theses could be devoted to many of them—and have been written about some. In this book, however, we want to offer an accessible, practical reference. If the devil is in the details, we want to identify, locate, and warn readers against him but not to elaborate his entire demonology. Consequently, we discuss each metric in stages, working progressively toward increasing levels of sophistication. We invite our readers to sample this information as they see fit, exploring each metric to the depth that they find most useful and rewarding.

With an eye toward accessibility, we have also avoided advanced mathematical notation. Most of the calculations in this book can be performed by hand, on the back of the proverbial envelope. More complex or intensive computations may require a spreadsheet. Nothing further should be needed.

Table 1.2 Major metrics list

Section	Metric	Section	Metric
Share of hearts, minds, and markets		3.5	Marketing Spending
2.1	Revenue Market Share	3.6	Contribution per Unit
2.1	Unit Market Share	3.6	Contribution Margin (%)
2.2	Relative Market Share	3.6	Break-Even Sales
2.3	Brand Development Index	3.7	Target Volume
2.3	Category Development Index	3.7	Target Revenues
2.4–2.6	Decomposition of Market Share	*Product and portfolio management*	
2.4	Market Penetration	4.1	Trial
2.4	Brand Penetration	4.1	Repeat Volume
2.4	Penetration Share	4.1	Penetration
2.5	Share of Requirements	4.1	Volume Projections
2.6	Usage Index	4.2	Year-on-Year Growth
2.7	Hierarchy of Effects	4.2	Compound Annual Growth Rate (CAGR)
2.7	Awareness	4.3	Cannibalization Rate
2.7	Top of Mind	4.3	Fair Share Draw Rate
2.7	Ad Awareness	4.4	Brand Equity Metrics
2.7	Knowledge	4.5	Conjoint Utilities
2.7	Consumer Beliefs	4.6	Segment Utilities
2.7	Purchase Intentions	4.7	Conjoint Utilities and Volume Projections
2.7	Purchase Habits		
2.7	Loyalty	*Customer profitability*	
2.7	Likeability	5.1	Customers
2.8	Willingness to Recommend	5.1	Recency
2.8	Customer Satisfaction	5.1	Retention Rate
2.9	Net Promoter	5.2	Customer Profit
2.10	Willingness to Search	5.3	Customer Lifetime Value
2.11	Neuro-Marketing	5.4	Prospect Lifetime Value
Margins and profits		5.5	Average Acquisition Cost
3.1	Unit Margin	5.5	Average Retention Cost
3.1	Margin (%)	*Sales force management*	
3.2	Channel Margins	6.1	Workload
3.3	Average Price per Unit	6.1	Sales Potential Forecast
3.3	Price per Statistical Unit	6.2	Sales Goal
3.4	Variable and Fixed Costs	6.3	Sales Force Effectiveness

Section	Metric	Section	Metric
11.7	Value of a Like	12.2	Return on Investment (ROI)
11.8	Downloads	12.3	Economic Profit (aka EVA®)
11.9	Average Revenue per User	12.4	Payback
11.10	Email Metrics	12.4	Net Present Value (NPV)
Marketing and finance		12.4	Internal Rate of Return (IRR)
12.1	Net Profit	12.5	Marketing Return on Investment
12.1	Return on Sales (ROS)		(MROI)
12.1	Earnings Before Interest, Taxes, Depreciation, and Amortization (EBITDA)	12.6	Financial Market Measures
		12.7	Combined Market and Accounting Measures

Reference materials

Throughout this text, we have highlighted formulas and definitions for easy reference. We have also included outlines of key terms at the beginning of each chapter and section. Within each formula, we have used the following notation to define all inputs and outputs:

$—(Dollar Terms): A monetary value. We have used the dollar sign and "dollar terms" for brevity, but any other currency, including the euro, yen, dinar, or yuan, would be equally appropriate.

%—(Percentage): Used as the equivalent of fractions or decimals. For readability, we have intentionally omitted the step of multiplying decimals by 100 to obtain percentages.

#—(Count): Used for such measures as unit sales or number of competitors.

R—(Rating): Expressed on a scale that translates qualitative judgments or preferences into numeric ratings. Example: A survey in which customers are asked to assign a rating of "1" to items that they find least satisfactory and "5" to those that are most satisfactory. Ratings have no intrinsic meaning without reference to their scale and context.

I—(Index): A comparative figure, often linked to or expressive of a market average (for example, the consumer price index). Indices are often interpreted as percentages.

Further reading

Abela, Andrew, Bruce H. Clark, and Tim Ambler. (2004). "Marketing Performance Measurement, Performance, and Learning," working paper.

Ambler, Tim, and Chris Styles. (1995). "Brand Equity: Toward Measures That Matter," working paper No. 95-902, London Business School, Centre for Marketing.

Armstrong, J. Scott. (1974). "Eclectic Research and Construct Validation," in Jagdish N. Sheth (Ed.), *Models of Buyer Behavior: Conceptual, Quantitative, and Empirical* (pp. 3–14), Harper & Row.

Barwise, Patrick, and John U. Farley. (2003). "Which Marketing Metrics Are Used and Where?" Marketing Science Institute working paper.

Clark, Bruce H., Andrew V. Abela, and Tim Ambler. (2004). "Return on Measurement: Relating Marketing Metrics Practices to Strategic Performance," working paper.

Hauser, John, and Gerald Katz. (1998). "Metrics: You Are What You Measure," *European Management Journal*, 16(5), 517–528.

Kaplan, R. S., and D. P. Norton. (1996). *The Balanced Scorecard: Translating Strategy into Action*, Harvard Business School Press.

Watt, James H., and Sjef van den Berg. (1995). *Research Methods for Communication Science*, Allyn & Bacon.

Share of hearts, minds, and markets

2

Key concepts covered in this chapter:

- Market share
- Relative market share
- Market concentration
- Brand development index (BDI)
- Category development index (CDI)
- Penetration
- Share of requirements
- Usage index
- Awareness, attitudes, and usage (AAU)
- Customer satisfaction
- Willingness to recommend
- Net promoter
- Willingness to search
- Neuro-marketing

Introduction

"...Walmart now has about 15% of total retail sales in grocery, home furnishings, electronics, apparel, sporting goods, general merchandise and office suppliers, and has been adding an average of about $10.6 billion in incremental sales per year. In grocery, Walmart dominates with a 23% share, about 2.5 times the next largest retailer. It's also winning in e-groceries, with 17% of consumers saying they ordered from Walmart.com last year, compared with 15% in 2017."[1]

It is common for businesspeople to discuss market share, as illustrated above. At first glance, market share appears to involve a relatively simple calculation: "us/ (us + them)." But think more deeply, and this simple calculation raises a host of questions. Who, for example, does "them" refer to? That is, how broadly do we define our competitive universe? Which units are used? Where in the value chain do we capture our information? What time frame will maximize our signal-to-noise ratio? In a metric as important as market share, and in one as closely monitored for changes and trends, the answers to such questions are crucial. In this chapter, we will address them and also introduce key components of market share, including penetration share, usage index, and share of requirements.

Probing the dynamics behind market share, we'll explore measures of awareness, attitude, and usage—major factors in the decision-making process by which customers select one brand over another. We'll discuss customer satisfaction with products and dealers, the quantification of which is growing in importance among marketing professionals. Finally, we'll consider metrics measuring the depth of consumer preference and satisfaction, including customers' willingness to search (that is, go to another store) if a brand is unavailable and their disposition to recommend that brand to others. Increasingly, marketers rely on these as leading indicators of future changes in share.

	Metric	Construction	Considerations	Purpose
2.1	Revenue Market Share	Sales revenue as a percentage of market sales revenue.	Scope of market definition. Channel level analyzed. Before/after discounts. Time period covered.	Measure of competitiveness.
2.1	Unit Market Share	Unit sales as a percentage of market unit sales.	Scope of market definition. Channel level analyzed. Time period covered.	Measure of competitiveness.

	Metric	Construction	Considerations	Purpose
2.2	Relative Market Share	Brand market share divided by largest competitor's market share.	Can use either unit or revenue shares.	Assesses comparative market strength.
2.3	Brand Development Index	Brand sales in a specified segment, compared with sales of that brand in the market as a whole.	Can use either unit or revenue sales.	Regional or segment differences in brand purchases and consumption.
2.3	Category Development Index	Category sales in a specified segment, compared with sales of that category in the market as a whole.	Can use either unit or revenue sales.	Regional or segment differences in category purchases and consumption.
2.4 2.5 2.6	Decomposition of Market Share	Penetration Share * Share of Requirements * Usage Index.	Time period covered.	Calculation of market share. Competitive analysis. Historical trends analysis. Formulation of marketing objectives.
2.4	Category Penetration	Purchasers of a product category as a percentage of total population.	Based on population. Therefore, unit/revenue consideration not relevant.	Measures category acceptance by a defined population. Useful in tracking acceptance of new product categories.

	Metric	Construction	Considerations	Purpose
2.4	Brand Penetration	Purchasers of a brand as a percentage of total population.	Based on population. Therefore, unit/revenue consideration not relevant.	Measures brand acceptance by a defined population.
2.4	Penetration Share	The ratio of brand penetration to category penetration.	Also the percentage of category buyers who bought the brand. A component of the market share formula.	Comparative acceptance of the brand within its category.
2.5	Share of Requirements	Brand purchases as a percentage of total category purchases by buyers of that brand.	Purchases can be either units or revenues.	Level of commitment to a brand by its existing customers.
2.6	Usage Index	The ratio of average category purchases of customers of the brand to the overall average category purchases per category customer.	Can be used with both unit or revenue sales.	Measures relative usage of a category by customers of a specific brand.
2.7	Hierarchy of Effects	Involves awareness; attitudes, beliefs; importance; intentions to try; buy; trial, repeat purchase.	Strict sequence is often violated and can be reversed.	Set marketing and advertising objectives. Understand progress in stages of customer decision process.

	Metric	Construction	Considerations	Purpose
2.7	Awareness	Percentage of total population that is aware of a brand.	Is this prompted or unprompted awareness?	Consideration of who has heard of the brand.
2.7	Top of Mind	First brand to consider.	May be subject to most recent advertising or experience.	Saliency of brand.
2.7	Ad Awareness	Percentage of total population that is aware of a brand's advertising.	May vary by schedule, reach, and frequency of advertising.	One measure of advertising effects. May indicate "stopping power" of ads.
2.7	Knowledge	Percentage of population with knowledge of product, recollection of its advertising.	Not a formal metric. Is this prompted or unprompted knowledge?	Extent of familiarity with product beyond name recognition.
2.7	Consumer Beliefs	Customers'/consumers' view of product, generally captured via survey responses, often through ratings on a scale.	Customers/consumers may hold beliefs with varying degrees of conviction.	Perception of brand by attribute.
2.7	Purchase Intentions	Probability of intention to purchase.	To estimate probability of purchase, aggregate and analyze ratings of stated intentions (for example, top two boxes).	Measures pre-shopping disposition to purchase.

▶

	Metric	Construction	Considerations	Purpose
2.7	Purchase Habits	Frequency of purchase. Quantity typically purchased.	May vary widely among shopping trips.	Helps identify heavy users.
2.7	Loyalty	Measures include share of requirements, willingness to pay premium, willingness to search.	"Loyalty" itself is not a formal metric, but specific metrics measure aspects of this dynamic. New product entries may alter loyalty levels.	Indication of base future revenue stream.
2.7	Likeability	Generally measured via ratings across a number of scales.	Often believed to correlate with persuasion.	Shows overall preference prior to shopping.
2.8	Willingness to Recommend	Generally measured via ratings across a 1–5 scale.	Nonlinear in impact.	Shows strength of loyalty, potential impact on others.
2.8	Customer Satisfaction	Generally measured on a 1–5 scale, in which customers declare their satisfaction with brand in general or specific attributes.	Subject to response bias. Captures views of current customers, not lost customers. Satisfaction is a function of expectations.	Indicates likelihood of repurchase. Reports of dissatisfaction show aspects that require improvement to enhance loyalty.

Metric		Construction	Considerations	Purpose
2.9	Net Promoter	Percentage of customers willing to recommend to others less the percentage unwilling to recommend the product or service.	Requires a survey of intentions.	Some claim it to be the single best metric for marketers.
2.10	Willingness to Search	Percentage of customers willing to delay purchases, change stores, or reduce quantities to avoid switching brands.	Hard to capture.	Indicates importance of distribution coverage.
2.11	Neuro-marketing Measures	Technological advances have allowed marketers to gain greater insight into how consumers think.	Requires expertise and sometimes expensive equipment.	Can help illuminate reactions that consumers find hard to verbalize.

2.1   Market share

Purpose: key indicator of market competitiveness.

Market share is an indicator of how well a firm is doing against its competitors. This metric, supplemented by changes in sales revenue, helps managers evaluate both primary and selective demand in their market. That is, it enables them to judge not only total market growth or decline but also trends in customers' selections among competitors.

Market share is the percentage of a market (defined in terms of either units or revenue) accounted for by a specific entity.

$$\text{Unit Market Share (\%)} = \frac{\text{Unit Sales (\#)}}{\text{Total Market Unit Sales (\#)}}$$

$$\text{Revenue Market Share (\%)} = \frac{\text{Sales Revenue (\$)}}{\text{Total Market Revenue (\$)}}$$

Unit Market Share is also known as Volume Share. Revenue Market Share is also known as Value Share. Marketers need to be able to translate sales targets into market share because this will demonstrate whether forecasts can be attained by growing the market or by capturing share from competitors. The latter will almost always be more difficult to achieve. Market share is closely monitored for signs of change in the competitive landscape, and it frequently drives strategic or tactical action.

Generally, sales growth resulting from primary demand (total market growth) is less costly and more profitable than that achieved by capturing share from competitors. Conversely, losses in market share can signal serious long-term problems that require strategic adjustments. Firms with market shares below a certain level may not be viable. Similarly, within a firm's product line, market share trends for individual products are considered early indicators of future opportunities or problems.

Construction

Market share: The percentage of a market accounted for by a specific entity.

Unit market share: The units sold by a particular company, as a percentage of total market sales, measured in the same units.

$$\text{Unit Market Share (\%)} = \frac{\text{Unit Sales (\#)}}{\text{Total Market Unit Sales (\#)}}$$

This formula, of course, can be rearranged to derive either unit sales or total market unit sales from the other two variables, as illustrated in the following:

$$\text{Unit Sales (\#)} = \text{Unit Market Share (\%)} * \text{Total Market Unit Sales (\#)}$$

$$\text{Total Market Unit Sales (\#)} = \frac{\text{Unit Sales (\#)}}{\text{Unit Market Share (\%)}}$$

> **Revenue market share:** This differs from unit market share in that it reflects the prices at which goods are sold. In fact, a relatively simple way to calculate relative price is to divide revenue market share by unit market share (see Section 8.1).

$$\text{Revenue Market Share (\%)} = \frac{\text{Sales Revenue (\$)}}{\text{Total Market Sales Revenue (\$)}}$$

As with the unit market share, this equation for revenue market share can be rearranged to calculate either sales revenue or total market sales revenue from the other two variables.

Data sources, complications, and cautions

Market definition is never a trivial exercise: If a firm defines its market too broadly, it may dilute its focus. If it does so too narrowly, it will miss opportunities and allow threats to emerge unseen. To avoid these pitfalls, as a first step in calculating market share, managers should define the served market in terms of unit sales or revenues for a specific list of competitors, products, sales channels, geographic areas, customers, and time periods (for example, "Among grocery stores, we are the revenue market share leader in sales of frozen Italian food entrées in the Northeastern U.S.").

Data parameters must be carefully defined: Although market share is likely the single most used marketing metric, there is no generally acknowledged best method for calculating it. This is unfortunate, as different methods may yield not only different computations of market share at a given moment but also widely divergent trends over time. The reasons for these disparities include variations in the lenses through which share is viewed (units versus dollars), where in the channel the measurements are taken (shipments from manufacturers versus consumer purchases), market definition (scope of the competitive universe), and measurement error. In the situation analysis that underlies strategic decisions, managers must be able to understand and explain these variations.

We illustrate the complexities involved in quantifying market share by looking at the competitive dynamics in the automobile industry and at General Motors in particular:

"With market share sliding in the first two months of the year, from 27.2% to 24.9%—the lowest level since a two-month strike shut the company down in 1998—GM as a whole expects a net loss of $846 million the first quarter."[2]

Reviewing this statement, drawn from *Business Week* in 2005, a marketing manager might immediately pose a number of questions:

- Do these figures represent unit (autos sold) or revenue (dollar) market shares?
- Does this trend hold for both unit and revenue market shares at GM?

- Was revenue market share calculated before or after rebates and discounts?
- Do the underlying sales data reflect factory shipments, which relate directly to the manufacturer's current income statement, or sales to consumers, which are buffered by dealer inventories?
- Does the decline in market share translate to an equivalent percentage decrease in sales, or has the total market size changed?

Managers must determine whether a stated market share is based on shipment data, channel shipments, retail sales, customer surveys, or some other source. On occasion, share figures may represent combinations of data (a firm's actual shipments, for example, set against survey estimates of competitors' sales). If necessary, managers must also adjust for differences in channels.

The time period measured will affect the signal-to-noise ratio: In analyzing short-term market dynamics, such as the effects of a promotion or a recent price change, managers may find it useful to measure market share over a brief period. Short-term data, however, generally carry a low signal-to-noise ratio. By contrast, data covering a longer period will be more stable but may obscure important recent changes in the market. Applied more broadly, this principle also holds in aggregating geographic areas, channel types, or customers. When choosing markets and time periods for analysis, managers must optimize for the type of signal that is most important.

Potential bias in reported shares: One way to find data for market sizing is through surveys of customer usage (see Section 2.7). In interpreting these data, however, managers must bear in mind that shares based on reported (versus recorded) sales tend to be biased toward well-known brands.

Related metrics and concepts

> Served market: The portion of the total market for which a firm competes. This may exclude geographic regions or product types. In the airline industry, for example, as of early 2020, Ryanair did not fly to the United States. Consequently, the United States would not be considered part of its served market.

2.2   Relative market share and market concentration

Purpose: to assess a firm's or a brand's success and its position in the market.

A firm with a market share of 25% would be a powerful leader in many markets but a distant number two in others. Relative market share offers a way to benchmark a firm's or a brand's share against that of its largest competitor, enabling managers to compare relative market positions across different product markets.

Relative market share indexes a firm's or a brand's market share against that of its leading competitor.

$$\text{Relative Market Share (I)} = \frac{\text{Brand's Market Share (\%)}}{\text{Brand's Largest Competitor's Market Share (\%)}}$$

Market concentration, a related metric, measures the degree to which a comparatively small number of firms account for a large proportion of the market.

These metrics are useful in comparing a firm's or a brand's relative position across different markets and in evaluating the type and degree of competition in those markets.

Relative market share gains some of its significance from studies—albeit controversial ones—suggesting that major players in a market tend to be more profitable than their competitors. This metric was further popularized by the Boston Consulting Group (BCG) in its famous matrix of relative share and market growth (see Figure 2.1).

Figure 2.1 The BCG matrix

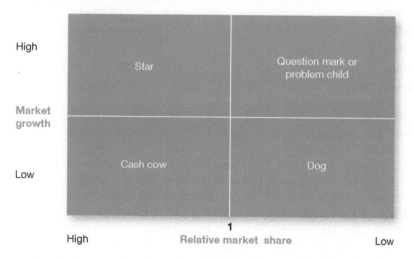

In the BCG matrix, one axis represents relative market share—a surrogate for competitive strength. The other represents market growth—a surrogate for potential. Along each dimension, products are classified as high or low, and each is placed in one of four quadrants. In the traditional interpretation of this matrix, products with high relative market shares in growing markets are deemed stars, suggesting that they should be supported with vigorous investment. The cash for that investment may be generated by cash cows, products with high relative shares in low-growth markets. Problem child products may have potential for future growth but hold weak competitive positions. Finally, dogs have neither strong competitive position nor growth potential.

Construction

$$\text{Relative Market Share (I)} = \frac{\text{Brand's Market Share (\%)}}{\text{Brand's Largest Competitor's Market Share (\%)}}$$

Relative market share can also be calculated by dividing brand sales (#, $) by largest competitor's sales (#, $) because the common factor of total market sales (or revenue) cancels out.

Example The market for small urban cars consists of five players (see Table 2.1).

Table 2.1 Market for small urban cars

	Units sold (thousands)	Revenue (thousands)
Zipper	25	€375,000
Twister	10	€200,000
A-One	7.5	€187,500
Bowlz	5	€125,000
Chien	2.5	€50,000
Market Total	50.0	€937,500

In the market for small urban cars, managers at A-One want to know their firm's market share relative to its largest competitor. They can calculate this on the basis of revenues or unit sales.

In unit terms, A-One sells 7,500 cars per year. Zipper, the market leader, sells 25,000. A-One's relative market share in unit terms is thus 7,500/25,000, or 0.30. We arrive at the same number if we first calculate A-One's share (7,500/50,000 = .15) and Zipper's share (25,000/50,000 = .50) and then divide A-One's share by Zipper's share (.15/.50 = .30).

In revenue terms, A-One generates €187.5 million in car sales each year. Zipper, the market leader, generates €375 million. A-One's relative market share in revenue terms is thus €187.5m/€375m, or 0.5. Due to its comparatively high average price per car, A-One's relative market share is greater in revenue than in unit terms.

Market concentration: The degree to which a relatively small number of firms accounts for a large proportion of the market. This is also known as the concentration ratio. It is often calculated for the largest three or four firms in a market. The eight-firm concentration ratio is also popular.[3]

Three- (Four-) firm concentration ratio: A metric that is the total (sum) of the market shares held by the leading three (four) competitors in a market.

Example In the small urban car market, the three-firm concentration ratio is composed of the market shares of the top three competitors: Zipper, Twister, and A-One (see Table 2.2).

Table 2.2 Market share—small urban cars

	Units sold (thousands)	Unit share	Revenue (thousands)	Revenue share
Zipper	25.0	50%	€375,000	40.0%
Twister	10	20%	€200,000	21.3%
A-One	7.5	15%	€187,500	20.0%
Bowlz	5.0	10%	€125,000	13.3%
Chien	2.5	5%	€50,000	5.4%
Market Total	50.0	100%	€937,500	100%

In unit terms, the three-firm concentration ratio is 50% + 20% + 15% = 85%. In revenue terms, it is 40% + 21.3% + 20% = 81.3%.

Herfindahl Index: A market concentration metric derived by adding the squares of the individual market shares of all the players in a market. As a sum of squares, this index tends to rise in markets dominated by large players.

Example The Herfindahl Index dramatically highlights market concentration in the small urban car market (see Table 2.3).

On a unit basis, the Herfindahl Index is equal to the square of the unit market share of Zipper ($50\% \wedge 2 = 0.25$), plus that of Twister ($20\% \wedge 2 = 0.04$), plus those of A-One, Bowlz, and Chien = 0.325.

On a revenue basis, the Herfindahl Index comprises the square of the revenue market share of Zipper (40% ^ 2 = 0.16), plus those of all its competitors = 0.2661.

Table 2.3 Calculation of the Herfindahl Index for small urban cars

	Units sold (thousands)	Unit share	Squared share	Revenue (thousands)	Revenue share	Squared share
Zipper	25.0	50%	0.25	€375,000	40%	0.16
Twister	10	20%	0.04	€200,000	21%	0.0455
A-One	7.5	15%	0.0225	€187,500	20%	0.04
Bowlz	5.0	10%	0.01	€125,000	13%	0.0178
Chien	2.5	5%	0.0025	€50,000	5%	0.0028
Market Total	50.0	100%	0.325	€937,500	100%	0.2661

As demonstrated by the Herfindahl Index, the market for small urban cars is slightly more concentrated in unit terms than in revenue terms. The reason for this is straightforward: Higher-priced cars in this market sell fewer units.

Note: For a given number of competitors, the Herfindahl Index would be lowest if shares were equally distributed. In a five-firm industry, for example, equally distributed shares would yield a Herfindahl Index of 5 * (20% ^ 2) = 0.2.

Data sources, complications, and cautions

As ever, appropriate market definition and the use of comparable figures are vital prerequisites for developing meaningful results.

Related metrics and concepts

Market share rank: The ordinal position of a brand in its market, when competitors are arranged by size, with 1 being the largest.

Share of category: This metric is derived in the same manner as market share but is used to denote a share of market within a certain retailer or class of retailers (for example, mass merchandisers).

2.3 Brand development index and category development index

> The brand development index (BDI) quantifies how well a brand is performing within a specific group of customers, compared with its average performance among all consumers.
>
> $$\text{Brand Development Index (I)} = \frac{\text{Brand Sales to Group (\#,\$) / Households in Group (\#)}}{\text{Total Brand Sales (\#,\$) / Total Households (\#)}}$$
>
> The category development index (CDI) measures the sales performance of a category of goods or services within a specific group, compared with its average performance among all consumers.
>
> $$\text{Category Development Index (I)} = \frac{\text{Category Sales to Group (\#,\$) / Households in Group (\#)}}{\text{Total Category Sales (\#,\$) / Total Households (\#)}}$$
>
> The brand and category development indexes are useful for understanding specific customer segments relative to the market as a whole. Although defined here with respect to households, these indexes could also be calculated for customers, accounts, businesses, or other entities.

Purpose: to understand the relative performance of a brand or category within specified customer groups.

The brand and category development indexes help identify strong and weak segments (usually demographic or geographic) for particular brands or categories of goods and services. For example, by monitoring the category development index (CDI), marketers might determine that Midwesterners buy twice as many country music CDs per capita as Americans in general, while consumers living on the East Coast buy fewer than the national average. This would be useful information for targeting the launch campaign for a new country music performer. Conversely, if managers found that a particular product had a low brand development index in a segment that carried a high CDI for its category, they might ask why that brand suffered relatively poor performance in such a promising segment.

Construction

$$\text{Brand Development Index} - \text{BDI (I)} = \frac{\text{Brand Sales to Group (\#,\$) / Households in Group (\#)}}{\text{Total Brand Sales (\#,\$) / Total Households (\#)}}$$

The brand development index (BDI) is a measure of brand sales per person or per household within a specified demographic group or geography, compared with its average sales per person or household in the market as a whole. To illustrate its use, one might hypothesize that sales per capita of Ben & Jerry's brand ice cream would be greater in the brand's home state, Vermont, than in the rest of the country. By calculating Ben & Jerry's BDI for Vermont, marketers could test this hypothesis quantitatively.

Example Oaties is a minor brand of breakfast cereal. Among households without children, its sales run 1 packet per week per 100 households. In the general population, Oaties' sales run 1 packet per week per 80 households. This translates to 1/100 of a packet per household in the childless segment, versus 1/80 of a packet in the general populace.

$$\text{BDI} = \frac{\text{Brand Sales/Households}}{\text{Total Brand Sales/Households}}$$

$$. = \frac{1/100}{1/80} = 0.8$$

Oaties performs slightly less well in the childless segment than in the market as a whole.

$$\text{Category Development Index (I)} = \frac{\text{Category Sales to Group (\#,\$) / Households in Group (\#)}}{\text{Total Category Sales (\#,\$) / Total Households (\#)}}$$

Similar in concept to the BDI, the CDI demonstrates where a category shows strength or weakness relative to its overall performance. By way of example, Boston enjoys high per-capita consumption of ice cream. Bavaria and Ireland both show higher per-capita consumption of beer than Iran.

Data sources and complications

In calculating BDI or CDI, a precise definition of the segment under study is vital. Segments are often bounded geographically, but they can be defined in any way for which data can be obtained.

Related metrics and concepts

CDI has been applied to retail organizations. In such an application, it measures the extent to which a retailer emphasizes one category versus others.

$$\text{Category Development Index (I)} = \frac{\text{Retailer's Share of Category Sales (\%)}}{\text{Retailer's Total Share of Market (\%)}}$$

The use of CDI to assess category emphasis by particular retailers is very similar to the category performance ratio (see Section 7.1).

2.4   Penetration

Penetration is a measure of brand or category popularity. It is defined as the number of people who buy a specific brand or a category of goods at least once in a given period, divided by the size of the relevant market population.

$$\text{Market Penetration (\%)} = \frac{\text{Customers Who Have Purchased a Product in the Category (\#)}}{\text{Total Population (\#)}}$$

$$\text{Brand Penetration (\%)} = \frac{\text{Customers Who Have Purchased the Brand (\#)}}{\text{Total Population (\#)}}$$

$$\text{Penetration Share (\%)} = \frac{\text{Brand Penetration (\%)}}{\text{Market Penetration (\%)}}$$

$$\text{Penetration Share (\%)} = \frac{\text{Customers Who Have Purchased the Brand (\#)}}{\text{Customers Who Have Purchased a Product in the Category (\#)}}$$

Often, managers must decide whether to seek sales growth by acquiring existing category users from their competitors or by expanding the total population of category users, thereby attracting new customers to the market. Penetration metrics help indicate which of these strategies would be most appropriate and help managers monitor their success. These equations might also be calculated for usage instead of purchase.

Construction

Penetration: The proportion of people (households) in the relevant population who bought (at least once in the period) a specific brand or a category of goods.

$$\text{Market Penetration (\%)} = \frac{\text{Customers Who Have Purchased a Product in the Category (\#)}}{\text{Total Population (\#)}}$$

$$\text{Brand Penetration (\%)} = \frac{\text{Customers Who Have Purchased the Brand (\#)}}{\text{Total Population (\#)}}$$

Whereas market share focuses on the sales of a product (either units or dollars), penetration focuses on the number of buyers.

Example In the previous month, 500 of the 10,000 households in the panel purchased Big Bomb Flea Fogger, and 750 bought any kind of flea fogger, including Big Bomb.

Big Bomb's Brand Penetration = 500/10,000 = 5%

Flea Fogger Category Penetration = 750/10,000 = 7.5%

Big Bomb's Penetration Share = 500/750 = 66.67%

It is not surprising that in a given month, only 7.5% of the panel bought flea spray. The expected penetration is a combination of how often the product is bought and the length of the time period. The longer the time period, the higher will be the calculated penetration.

Penetration share can be thought of as the share of category households that bought the brand. Thus, a brand's penetration share can never be greater than one. When households buy multiple brands, however, penetration shares will sum to more than one.

$$\text{Penetration Share (\%)} = \frac{\text{Brand Penetration (\%)}}{\text{Market Penetration (\%)}}$$

Decomposing market share

Market share can always be calculated as the product of three components: penetration share, share of requirements (defined in Section 2.5), and usage index (defined in Section 2.6.).

$$\text{Market Share (\%)} = \text{Penetration Share (\%)} * \text{Share of Requirements (\%)} * \text{Usage Index (I)}$$

This decomposition is useful in that it identifies three ways to improve market share: sell to more people, achieve a higher share of your customer's purchases, or get your customers to use more of the category. Although this is true by definition, in practice the three components rarely move independently.

This decomposition works for both revenue and unit share, depending on whether share of requirements is calculated using units or dollars.

There are four variables in this decomposition, and (as in any equation) it can be used to find the fourth if the other three are known. In subsequent sections, we will give equations for each component in terms of market share and the remaining two components.

$$\text{Penetration Share (\%)} = \frac{\text{Market Share (\%)}}{[\text{Usage Index (I)} * \text{Share of Requirements (\%)}]}$$

Example Eat Wheats brand cereal has a market share in Urbanopolis of 6%, a usage index of 0.75, and a share of requirements of 40%. From these data, we can calculate the penetration share for Eat Wheats brand cereal in Urbanopolis:

$$\text{Penetration Share} = \frac{\text{Market Share}}{\text{Usage Index} * \text{Share of Requirements}}$$

$$= \frac{6\%}{0.75 * 40\%} = \frac{6\%}{.30} = 20\%$$

Data sources, complications, and cautions

The time period over which a firm measures penetration will have a significant impact on the result. For example, even among the most popular detergent brands, many are not purchased weekly. As the time period used to define penetration becomes shorter, brand penetration declines. In contrast, although penetration share will be more volatile for shorter periods, it will not necessarily be lower.

Related metrics and concepts

Active customers: Customers (people, households, accounts) who have purchased the brand (category) in the current time period. When these are counted, this gives Total Number of Active Customers.

Note that any count of active customers will likely be less than the total number of customers because the latter includes customers who have bought previously but not in the current period. This is discussed in more detail in Section 5.1 (recency).

Active customers may also be expressed as a percentage of the total population. To do so divide the number of active customers by the total number of people in the population. (When assessed at a brand level, this percentage is equivalent to brand penetration).

Ever-tried: Customers who have purchased the brand at any time (see Section 4.1 for more on trial.) This is equivalent to the term "penetration." Ever-tried customers who are not active are sometimes referred to as former customers (if there is little chance they will buy in the future) or simply inactive customers (if there is a good chance they will buy in the future.) Ever-tried may be expressed as a percentage of the population. To do so divide the number of customers who have ever tried by the total number of customers in the population.

Acceptors/accepters: Customers who research indicates are willing to buy the brand; the opposite of rejectors.

2.5 Share of requirements

Share of requirements, also known as share of wallet, is calculated solely among buyers of a specific brand. Within this group, it represents the percentage of purchases within the relevant category, accounted for by the brand in question.

$$\text{Unit Share of Requirements (\%)} = \frac{\text{Brand Purchases (\#)}}{\text{Total Category Purchases by Brand Buyers (\#)}}$$

$$\text{Revenue Share of Requirements (\%)} = \frac{\text{Brand Purchases (\$)}}{\text{Total Category Purchases by Brand Buyers (\$)}}$$

Many marketers view share of requirements as a measure of loyalty. This metric can guide a firm's decisions on whether to allocate resources toward efforts to expand a category, to take customers from competitors, or to increase share of requirements among its established customers. Share of requirements is, in essence, the market share a brand enjoys within a market narrowly defined as the people who have purchased that brand.

Purpose: to understand the source of market share in terms of breadth and depth of consumer franchise as well as the extent of relative category usage (heavy users/larger customers versus light users/smaller customers).

Construction

Share of requirements: **A given brand's share of purchases in its category, measured solely among customers who have purchased that brand. Also known as share of wallet.**

When calculating share of requirements, marketers may use either dollars or units.

$$\text{Unit Share of Requirements (\%)} = \frac{\text{Brand Purchases (\#)}}{\text{Total Category Purchases by Brand Buyers (\#)}}$$

$$\text{Revenue Share of Requirements (\%)} = \frac{\text{Brand Purchases (\$)}}{\text{Total Category Purchases by Brand Buyers (\$)}}$$

The best way to think about share of requirements is as the market share enjoyed by a brand among the customers who buy it.

Example In a given month, the unit purchases of AloeHa brand sunscreen ran 1,000,000 bottles. Among the households that bought AloeHa, total purchases of sunscreen came to 2,000,000 bottles.

$$\text{Share of Requirements} = \frac{\text{AloeHa Purchases}}{\text{Category Purchases by AloeHa Customers}}$$

$$= \frac{1,000,000}{2,000,000} = 50\%$$

Share of requirements is also useful in analyzing overall market share. As previously noted, it is part of an important formulation of market share.

Market Share = Penetration Share * Share of Requirements * Usage Index

Share of requirements can thus be calculated indirectly by decomposing market share.

$$\text{Share of Requirements (\%)} = \frac{\text{Market Share (\%)}}{[\text{Penetration Share (\%)} * \text{Usage Index (I)}]}$$

Example Eat Wheats brand cereal has a market share in Urbanopolis of 8%. The usage index for Eat Wheats in Urbanopolis is 1. The brand's penetration share in Urbanopolis is 20%. On this basis, we can calculate Eat Wheats' share of requirements in Urbanopolis.

$$\text{Share of Requirements} = \frac{\text{Market Share}}{(\text{Usage Index} * \text{Penetration Share})}$$

$$= \frac{8\%}{(1 * 20\%)} = \frac{8\%}{20\%} = 40\%$$

Note that in this example, market share and usage index must both be defined in the same terms (units or revenue). Depending on the definition of these two metrics, the calculated share of requirements will be either unit share of requirements (%) or revenue share of requirements (%).

Data sources, complications, and cautions

> **Double jeopardy:** As mentioned earlier, the three components of market share do not move independently in practice. In an empirical observation labeled "double jeopardy," brands with lower market share almost invariably have lower penetration share and lower share of requirements. The name "double jeopardy" captures the notion that low-share brands are punished twice for their lower share. Not only do fewer households buy them but also those buying households buy less of them (lower share of requirements).

Double jeopardy is a very real and pervasive phenomenon. One implication is that improvements in market share will be accompanied by improvements in both penetration and share of requirements. It is also true that brands appear to vary more with respect to penetration than share of requirements—which has led others to argue that it is better to try to increase penetration (sell to more households) than to increase the loyalty of the brand's current customers. We do not endorse that argument.

One explanation for double jeopardy is that low-share brands do not get broad distribution. Thus, it is more difficult for the few customers who prefer them to find and buy them, and share of requirements suffers. In this way of thinking, it is market share that leads to both penetration and share of requirements.

There is also a purely statistical explanation for double jeopardy that we will describe at the end of Section 2.6.

Related metrics and concepts

> Sole usage percentage: The proportion of a brand's customers who bought only that brand's product and did not buy from competitors. Sole users are a combination of extremely loyal customers, customers with limited access to brands, and customers who just happened to buy one unit during the period. Sole users are also known as purely loyals. Among sole users, a brand's share of requirement is, by definition, 100%.

$$\text{Sole Usage (\%)} = \frac{\text{Customers Who Buy Only the Brand in Question (\#)}}{\text{Total Brand Customers (\#)}}$$

> Number of brands purchased: During a given period, some customers may buy only a single brand within a category, whereas others buy two or more. In evaluating loyalty to a given brand, marketers sometimes compare the average number of brands purchased by brand customers to the average number purchased by all customers in the category.

Example Among 10 customers for cat food, 7 bought the Arda brand, 5 bought Bella, and 3 bought Constanza. One does not need to know the pattern of overlap across these customers to calculate the average number of brands per cat food customer. It is 15 brand purchases (7 + 5 + 3) per 10 customers, yielding an average of 1.5 brands per customer.

A Bella brand manager noted that of his firm's 5 customers, 3 bought only Bella, whereas 2 bought both Arda and Bella. None of Bella's customers bought Constanza. Thus, the 5 Bella customers made 7 brand purchases (1 + 1 + 1 + 2 + 2), yielding an average of 1.4 (that is, 7/5) brands per Bella customer. Compared to the average category purchaser, who buys 1.5 brands, Bella buyers are slightly more loyal.

> Repeat rate: The percentage of brand customers in a given period who are also brand customers in the subsequent period.
>
> Repurchase rate: The percentage of customers for a brand who repurchase that brand on their next purchase occasion.

Confusion abounds in this area. In these definitions, we have tried to distinguish a metric based on calendar time (repeat rate) from one based on "customer time" (repurchase rate). In Chapter 5, "Customer profitability," we will describe a related metric, retention, which is used in contractual situations in which the first non-renewal (non-purchase) signals the end of a customer relationship. Although we suggest that the term *retention* be applied only in contractual situations, you will often see repeat rates and repurchase rates referred to as *retention rates*. Due to a lack of consensus on the use of these terms, marketers should not rely on the names of these metrics as perfect indicators of how they are calculated.

As with penetration, the interpretation of repeat rate depends on the time period covered. The shorter the time period, the lower will be the repeat rate. One minus the repeat rate is sometimes called the turnover rate.

2.6 Usage index

> The usage index is a relative measure that indicates how heavily the customers of a given brand use the product category.
>
> $$\text{Usage Index (I)} = \frac{\text{Average Total Purchases in Category by Brand Customers (\#,\$)}}{\text{Average Total Purchases in Category by All Customers for That Category (\#,\$)}}$$
>
> or
>
> $$\text{Usage Index (I)} = \frac{\text{Market Share (\%)}}{[\text{Penetration Share (\%)} \ast \text{Share of Requirements (\%)}]}$$
>
> The usage index, also called the weight index, yields insight into the source of volume and the nature of a brand's customer base.

Purpose: to define and measure whether a firm's consumers are "heavy users."

The usage index answers the question "How heavily do our customers use the category of our product?"

Construction

> **Usage index:** The ratio of the average category usage for the customers of a brand to the average category usage of all customers.

The usage index can be calculated on the basis of units or dollars.

$$\text{Usage Index (I)} = \frac{\text{Average Total Purchases in Category by Brand Customers (\#,\$)}}{\text{Average Total Purchases in Category by All Customers for That Category (\#,\$)}}$$

Example Over a period of one year, the average shampoo purchases by households using Shower Fun brand shampoo was six 15-ounce bottles. During the same period, average shampoo consumption by households using any brand of shampoo was four 15-ounce bottles.

The usage index for households buying Shower Fun is therefore 6/4, or 1.5. Customers of Shower Fun brand shampoo bought more shampoo than average.

As previously noted, market share can be calculated as the product of three components: penetration share, share of requirements, and usage index (see Section 2.4). Consequently, we can calculate a brand's usage index if we know its market share, penetration share, and share of requirements, as follows:

$$\text{Usage Index (I)} = \frac{\text{Market Share (\%)}}{\text{Penetration Share (\%)} * \text{Share of Requirements (\%)}}$$

This equation works for market shares defined in either units or dollars, as long as the construction of share of requirements and usage index matches. Comparing a brand's dollar usage index to its unit usage index, marketers can determine whether the brand purchasers pay more (less) per category unit.

Data sources, complications, and cautions

The usage index does not indicate how heavily customers use a specific brand, only how heavily they use the category. A brand can have a high usage index, for example, meaning that its customers are heavy category users, even if those customers use the brand in question to meet only a small share of their needs.

Understanding double jeopardy and usage index

In the previous section we described an empirical generalization called double jeopardy. Brands with lower share are punished twice in that they sell to fewer people (lower penetration) who buy them less frequently (lower share of requirements). Before jumping to conclusions about the marketing strategy implications of double jeopardy, however, it is important to understand the statistical explanation for double jeopardy.

Double jeopardy is a natural consequence of two things:

- How the component metrics are defined—with customers of a brand being defined as all households that bought the brand during the period.
- How households behave—as households often buy multiple brands within a given period for inexplicable reasons.

To illustrate, consider a market with three brands (A, B, and C) serving ten households with unit sales for the period given in Table 2.4.

Table 2.4 Household brand purchase counts example

Household	A	B	C	Total
1	10	0	0	10
2	10	0	0	10
3	10	0	0	10
4	10	0	0	10
5	10	0	0	10
6	10	0	0	10
7	0	10	0	10
8	0	10	0	10
9	0	10	0	10
10	0	0	10	10

The category summary metrics paint a clear picture of this ten-household market. All households were loyal to a single brand, and all households bought the same number of units. The 60/30/10 share split exactly matches the brands' penetrations (PENs) of 60%, 30%, and 10%, respectively (see Table 2.5).

Table 2.5 Sample summary metrics

Summary Metric	A	B	C
Share of Market	0.6	0.3	0.1
Penetration	0.6	0.3	0.1
Share of Requirements	1.0	1.0	1.0
Usage Index	1.0	1.0	1.0

But now let us add an 11th household that is a heavy, but indiscriminate, buyer purchasing 12 units of A, 6 units of B, and 2 units of C (see Table 2.6).

Table 2.6 Sample household brand purchase counts after adding a new customer

Household	A	B	C	Total
1	10	0	0	10
2	10	0	0	10
3	10	0	0	10
4	10	0	0	10
5	10	0	0	10
6	10	0	0	10
7	0	10	0	10
8	0	10	0	10
9	0	10	0	10
10	0	0	10	10
11	12	6	2	20

We contend that the presence of this multiple-brand buyer doesn't really change our view of the relative loyalties enjoyed by the three brands. Brand C got a 10% share of the ten loyal households and also a 10% share of not-so-loyal household 11. Brand C performed exactly as one might expect.

But look at the new category summary statistics shown in Table 2.7.

Table 2.7 Sample summary metrics after adding a new customer

Summary Metric	A	B	C
Share of Market	0.600	0.300	0.100
Penetration	0.636	0.364	0.182
Usage Index	1.048	1.146	1.375
Share of Requirements	0.900	0.720	0.400

The penetration metrics have all gone up a bit and now sum to something greater than one because household 11 is counted as a customer of each of the three brands. A consequence of this double counting and the fact that household 11 was a heavy category user is that all three usage indices are greater than one. In our experience, this is often the case. Heavy-using households tend to buy several brands (which makes sense), and we end up with usage indices that are all greater than one.

It also makes sense that the presence of household 11 causes share of requirements to decrease for all three brands. But the important observation is that the decrease in share of requirements is much greater for the small-share brand simply because it is the small-share brand, and heavy-user household 11 has a bigger influence on its summary statistics. (Household 11 is 1/2 of brand C's customers but only 1/7 of brand A's.) The result is double jeopardy caused by the presence of household 11 and the fact that household 11 gets counted as a customer of all three brands. Although this is appropriate in one sense (household 11 *is* a customer for all three brands) and allows our market share decomposition to hold, it affects the behavior of share of requirements and usage index metrics in a way that makes them challenging to interpret. Certainly for us, share of requirements is a less-than-perfect measure of the concept of loyalty.

Related metrics and concepts

See also the discussion of brand development index (BDI) and category development index (CDI) in Section 2.3.

2.7 Awareness, attitudes, and usage (AAU): metrics of the hierarchy of effects

> Studies of awareness, attitudes, and usage (AAU) enable marketers to quantify levels and trends in customer knowledge, perceptions, beliefs, intentions, and behaviors. In some companies, the results of these studies are called *tracking data* because they are used to track long-term changes in customer awareness, attitudes, and behaviors.
>
> AAU studies are most useful when their results are set against a clear comparator. This benchmark may comprise the data from prior periods, different markets, or competitors.

Purpose: to track trends in customer attitudes and behaviors.

Awareness, attitudes, and usage (AAU) metrics relate closely to what has been called the Hierarchy of Effects, an assumption that customers progress through sequential stages from lack of awareness, through initial purchase of a product, to brand loyalty (see Figure 2.2). AAU metrics are generally designed to track these stages of knowledge, beliefs, and behaviors. AAU studies also may track "who" uses a brand or product—in which case customers are defined by category usage (heavy/light), geography, demographics, psychographics, media usage, and whether they purchase other products.

Figure 2.2 Awareness, attitudes, and usage: hierarchy of effects

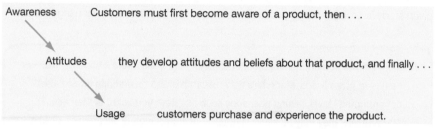

Awareness   Customers must first become aware of a product, then . . .

     Attitudes   they develop attitudes and beliefs about that product, and finally . . .

           Usage   customers purchase and experience the product.

Information about attitudes and beliefs offers insight into the question of why specific users do or do not favor certain brands. Typically, marketers conduct surveys of large samples of households or business customers to gather these data.

Construction

Awareness, attitudes, and usage studies feature a range of questions that aim to shed light on customers' relationships with a product or brand (see Table 2.8). For example, who are the acceptors and rejecters of the product? How do customers respond to a replay of advertising content?

Table 2.8 Awareness, attitudes, and usage: typical questions

Type	Measures	Typical questions
Awareness	Awareness and knowledge	Have you heard of Brand X? What brand comes to mind when you think "luxury car"?
Attitudes	Beliefs and intentions	Is Brand X for me? On a scale of 1 to 5, is Brand X for young people? What are the strengths and weaknesses of each brand?
Usage	Purchase habits and loyalty	Did you use Brand X this week? What brand did you last buy?

Marketers use answers to these questions to construct a number of metrics. Among these, certain "summary metrics" are considered important indicators of performance. In many studies, for example, customers' "willingness to recommend" and "intention to purchase" a brand are assigned high priority. Underlying these data, various diagnostic metrics help marketers understand *why* consumers may be willing—or unwilling—to recommend or purchase that brand. Consumers may not have been aware of the brand, for example. Alternatively, they may have been aware of it but did not subscribe to one of its key benefit claims.

Awareness and knowledge

Marketers evaluate various levels of awareness, depending on whether the consumer in a given study is prompted by a product's category, brand, advertising, or usage situation.

Awareness: The percentage of potential customers or consumers who recognize—or name—a given brand. Marketers may research brand recognition on an "aided" or "prompted" level, posing questions such as "Have you heard of Mercedes?" Alternatively, they may measure "unaided" or "unprompted" awareness, posing questions such as "Which makes of automobiles come to mind?"

Top of mind: The first brand that comes to mind when a customer is asked an unprompted question about a category. The percentage of customers for whom a given brand is top of mind can be measured.

Ad awareness: The percentage of target consumers or accounts who demonstrate awareness (aided or unaided) of a brand's advertising. This metric can be campaign or media specific, or it can cover all advertising.

Brand/product knowledge: The percentage of surveyed customers who demonstrate specific knowledge or beliefs about a brand or product.

Attitudes

Measures of attitude concern consumer response to a brand or product. Attitude is a combination of what consumers believe and how strongly they feel about it. Although a detailed exploration of attitudinal research is beyond the scope of this book, the following are some key metrics in this field.

Attitudes/liking/image: A rating assigned by consumers—often on a scale of 1–5 or 1–7—when survey respondents are asked their level of agreement with propositions such as "This is a brand for people like me" or "This is a brand for young people." A metric based on such survey data can also be called "relevance to customer."

Perceived value for money: A rating assigned by consumers—often on a scale of 1–5 or 1–7—when survey respondents are asked their level of agreement with such propositions as "This brand usually represents a good value for the money."

Perceived quality/esteem: A consumer rating—often on a scale of 1–5 or 1–7—of a given brand's product when compared with others in its category or market.

Relative perceived quality: A consumer rating—often on a scale of 1–5 or 1–7—of brand product compared to others in the category/market.

Usage

Measures of usage concern such market dynamics as purchase frequency and units per purchase. They highlight not only what was purchased but also when and where it was purchased. In studying usage, marketers also seek to determine how many people have tried a brand. Of those, they further seek to determine how many have "rejected" the brand and how many have "adopted" it into their regular portfolio of brands.

In measuring usage, marketers pose questions such as "What brand of toothpaste did you last purchase?" and "How many times in the past year have you purchased toothpaste?" and "How many tubes of toothpaste do you currently have in your home?" and "Do you have any Crest toothpaste in your home at the current time?"

In the aggregate, AAU metrics concern a vast range of information that can be tailored to specific companies and markets. They provide managers with insight into customers' overall relationships with a given brand or product.

Data sources, complications, and cautions

Sources of AAU data include

- Warranty cards and registrations, often using prizes and random drawings to encourage participation.
- Regularly administered surveys, conducted by organizations that interview consumers via telephone, mail, web, or other technologies, such as handheld scanners.

Even with the best methodologies, however, variations observed in tracking data from one period to the next are not always reliable. Managers must rely on their experience to distinguish seasonality effects and "noise" (random movement) from "signal" (actual trends and patterns). Certain techniques in data collection and review can also help managers make this distinction:

- *Adjust for periodic changes in how questions are framed or administered.* Surveys can be conducted via mail or telephone, for example, among paid or unpaid respondents. Different data-gathering techniques may require adjustment in the norms used to evaluate a "good" or "bad" response. If sudden changes appear in the data from one period to the next, marketers are advised to determine whether methodological shifts might play a role in this result.

- *Try to separate customer from non-customer responses; they may be very different.* Causal links among awareness, attitudes, and usage are rarely clear-cut. Though the hierarchy of effects is often viewed as a one-way street, on which awareness leads to attitudes, which in turn determine usage, the true causal flow might also be reversed. When people own a brand, for example, they may be predisposed to like it.

- *Triangulate customer survey data with sales revenue, shipments, or other data related to business performance.* Consumer attitudes, distributor and retail sales, and company shipments may move in different directions. Analyzing these patterns can be challenging but can reveal much about category dynamics. For example, toy shipments to retailers often occur well in advance of the advertising that drives consumer awareness and purchase intentions. These, in turn, must be established before retail sales. Adding further complexity, in the toy industry, the purchaser of a product might not be its ultimate consumer. In evaluating AAU data, marketers must understand not only the drivers of demand but also the logistics of purchase.

- *Separate leading from lagging indicators whenever possible.* In the auto industry, for example, individuals who have just purchased a new car show a heightened sensitivity to advertisements for its make and model. Conventional wisdom suggests that they're looking for confirmation that they made a good choice in a risky decision. By helping consumers justify their purchase at this time, auto manufacturers can strengthen long-term satisfaction and willingness to recommend.

Related metrics and concepts

Likeability: Because AAU considerations are so important to marketers, and because there is no single "right" way to approach them, specialized and proprietary systems have been developed. Of these, one of the best known is the Q Scores rating of "likeability." A Q Score is derived from a general survey of selected households, in which a large panel of consumers share their feelings about brands, celebrities, and television shows.[4]

Q Scores rely upon responses reported by consumers. Consequently, although the system used is sophisticated, it is dependent on consumers understanding and being willing to reveal their preferences.

Segmentation by geography, or geo-clustering: Marketers can achieve insight into consumer attitudes by separating their data into smaller, more homogeneous groups of customers. One well-known example of this is Prizm. Prizm assigns U.S. households to clusters based on zip code,[5] with the goal of creating small groups of similar households. The typical characteristics of each Prizm cluster are known, and these are used to assign a name to each group. "Golden Ponds" consumers, for example, comprise elderly singles and couples leading modest lifestyles in small towns. Rather than monitor AAU statistics for the population as a whole, firms often find it useful to track these data by cluster.

2.8   Customer satisfaction and willingness to recommend

Customer satisfaction is generally based on survey data and expressed as a rating. For example, see Figure 2.3.

Figure 2.3 Ratings

Very dissatisfied	Somewhat dissatisfied	Neither satisfied nor dissatisfied	Somewhat satisfied	Very satisfied
1	2	3	4	5

Within organizations, customer satisfaction ratings can have powerful effects. They focus employees on the importance of fulfilling customers' expectations. Furthermore, when these ratings dip, they warn of problems that can affect sales and profitability.

Another important metric related to satisfaction is willingness to recommend. When a customer is satisfied with a product, he or she might recommend it to friends, relatives, and colleagues. This can be a powerful marketing advantage.

Purpose: customer satisfaction provides a leading indicator of consumer purchase intentions and loyalty.

Customer satisfaction data are among the most frequently collected indicators of market perceptions. Their principal use is twofold:

- Within organizations, the collection, analysis, and dissemination of these data send a message about the importance of tending to customers and ensuring that they have positive experiences with the company's goods and services.

- Although sales or market share can indicate how well a firm is performing *currently*, satisfaction is perhaps the best indicator of how likely it is that the firm's customers will make further purchases *in the future*. Much research has focused on the relationship between customer satisfaction and retention. Studies indicate that the ramifications of satisfaction are most strongly realized at the extremes. On the scale in Figure 2.3, individuals who rate their satisfaction level as "5" are likely to become return customers and might even evangelize for the firm. Individuals who rate their satisfaction level as "1," by contrast, are unlikely to return. Further, they can hurt the firm by making negative comments about it to prospective customers. Willingness to recommend is a key metric related to customer satisfaction.

Construction

> **Customer satisfaction:** The number of customers, or percentage of total customers, whose reported experience with a firm, its products, or its services (ratings) exceeds specified satisfaction goals.
>
> **Willingness to recommend:** The percentage of surveyed customers who indicate that they would recommend a brand to friends.

These metrics quantify an important dynamic. When a brand has loyal customers, it gains positive word-of-mouth marketing, which is both free and highly effective.

Customer satisfaction is measured at the individual level, but it is almost always reported at an aggregate level. It can be, and often is, measured along various dimensions. A hotel, for example, might ask customers to rate their experience with its front desk and check-in service, with the room, with the amenities in the room, with the restaurants, and so on. In addition, in a holistic sense, the hotel might ask about overall satisfaction "with your stay."

Customer satisfaction is generally measured on a five-point scale (see Figure 2.4).

Figure 2.4 A typical five-point scale

Very dissatisfied	Somewhat dissatisfied	Neither satisfied nor dissatisfied	Somewhat satisfied	Very satisfied
1	2	3	4	5

Satisfaction levels are usually reported as either "top box" or, more likely, "top two boxes." Marketers convert these expressions into single numbers that show the percentage of respondents who checked either a "4" or a "5." (This term is the same as that commonly used in projections of trial volumes; see Section 4.1.)

Example The general manager of a hotel in Quebec institutes a new system of customer satisfaction monitoring (see Figure 2.5). She leaves satisfaction surveys at checkout. As an incentive to respond, all respondents are entered into a drawing for a pair of free airline tickets.

Figure 2.5 Hotel customer survey response

	Very dissatisfied	Somewhat dissatisfied	Neither satisfied nor dissatisfied	Somewhat satisfied	Very satisfied
Score	1	2	3	4	5
Responses (200 useable)	3	7	40	100	50
%	1.5%	3.5%	20%	50%	25%

The manager collects 220 responses, of which 20 are unclear or otherwise unusable. Among the remaining 200, 3 people rate their overall experience at the hotel as very unsatisfactory, 7 deem it somewhat unsatisfactory, and 40 respond that they are neither satisfied nor dissatisfied. Of the remainder, 50 customers say they are very satisfied, while the rest are somewhat satisfied.

The top box, comprising customers who rate their experience a "5," includes 50 people or, as a percentage, 50/200 = 25%. The top two boxes comprise customers who are "somewhat" or "very" satisfied, rating their experience a "4" or "5." In this example, the "somewhat satisfied" population must be calculated as the total usable response pool, less customers accounted for elsewhere; that is, 200 – 3 – 7 – 40 – 50 = 100. The sum of the top two boxes is thus 50 + 100 = 150 customers, or 75% of the total.

Regardless of the scale used, the objective is to measure customers' perceived satisfaction with their experience of a firm's offerings. Marketers then aggregate these data into a percentage of top-box responses.

In researching satisfaction, firms generally ask customers whether their product or service has met or exceeded expectations. Thus, expectations are a key factor behind satisfaction. When customers have high expectations and the reality falls short, they will be disappointed and will likely rate their experience as less than satisfying. For this reason, a luxury resort, for example, might receive a lower satisfaction rating than a budget motel—even though its facilities and service would be deemed superior in "absolute" terms.

Data sources, complications, and cautions

Surveys constitute the most frequently used means of collecting satisfaction data. As a result, a key risk of distortion in measures of satisfaction can be summarized in a single question: Who responds to surveys?

Response bias is endemic in satisfaction data. Disappointed or angry customers often welcome a means to vent their opinions. Contented customers often do not. Consequently, although many customers might be happy with a product and feel no need to complete a survey, the few who had a bad experience might be disproportionately represented among respondents. Most hotels, for example, place response cards in their rooms, asking guests, "How was your stay?" Only a small percentage of guests ever bother to complete those cards. Not surprisingly, those who do respond probably had a bad experience. For this reason, marketers can find it difficult to judge the true level of customer satisfaction. By reviewing survey data over time, however, they may discover important trends or changes. If complaints suddenly rise, for example, that may constitute early warning of a decline in quality or service. (See number of complaints in the following section.)

Sample selection may distort satisfaction ratings in other ways as well. Because only *customers* are surveyed for customer satisfaction, a firm's ratings may rise artificially as deeply dissatisfied customers take their business elsewhere. Also, some populations may be more frank than others or more prone to complain. These normative differences can affect perceived satisfaction levels. In analyzing satisfaction data, a firm might interpret rating differences as a sign that one market is receiving better service than another, when the true difference lies only in the standards that customers apply. To correct for this issue, marketers are advised to review satisfaction measures over time *within the same market*.

A final caution: Because many firms define customer satisfaction as "meeting or exceeding expectations," this metric may fall simply because expectations have risen. Thus, in interpreting ratings data, managers may come to believe that the quality of their offering has declined when that is not the case. Of course, the reverse is also true. A firm might boost satisfaction by lowering expectations. In so doing, however, it might suffer a decline in sales as its product or service comes to appear unattractive.

Related metrics and concepts

Trade satisfaction: Founded on the same principles as consumer satisfaction, measures the attitudes of trade customers.

Number of complaints: The number of complaints lodged by customers in a given time period.

2.9 Net promoter[6]

> Net promoter is a measure of the degree to which current customers will recommend a product, service, or company.
>
> Net Promoter Score (I) = Percentage of Promoters (%)
> − Percentage of Detractors (%)
>
> Net promoter is claimed to be a particularly useful measure of customer satisfaction and/or loyalty.

Purpose: to measure how well the brand or company is succeeding in creating satisfied, loyal customers.

Net Promoter Score[®7] (NPS) is a registered trademark of Frederick F. Reichheld, Bain & Company, and Satmetrix that is a particularly simple measure of the satisfaction/loyalty of current customers. Customers are surveyed and asked (on a ten-point scale) how likely they are to recommend the company or brand to a friend or colleague. Based on their answers to this single question, customers are divided into several categories:

- **Promoters:** Customers who are willing to recommend the company to others (who gave the company a rating of "9" or "10").
- **Passives:** Satisfied but unenthusiastic customers (ratings of "7" or "8").
- **Detractors:** Customers who are unwilling to recommend the company to others (ratings of "0" to "6").

High NPSs generally mean that a company is doing a good job of securing its customers' loyalty and active evangelism. Low and negative NPSs are important early warning signals for the firm. Because the metric is simple and easy to understand, it provides a stable measure companies use to motivate employees and monitor progress.

Construction

The Net Promoter Score (NPS) is created by subtracting the percentage of detractors among current customers from the percentage of promoters among current customers.

Net Promoter Score (I) = Percentage of Promoters (%)
− Percentage of Detractors (%)

For example, if a survey of a company's customers reports that there were 20% promoters, 70% passives, and 10% detractors, the company would have an NPS of $20 - 10 = 10$.

Data sources, complications, and cautions

Although the trademarked NPS asks a specific question, uses a scale up to 10, and defines promoters, passives, and detractors in a particular way, it is easy to imagine other versions of NPS-like metrics that differ with respect to the wording of the question, the scale used (1–5 rather than 0–10), and the definitions (and labels) of the resulting groups of responders. The defining features of NPS are that it is constructed from responses to a question about willingness to recommend and is a net measure found by subtracting the fraction unwilling to recommend from the fraction willing to recommend and leaving out those in the middle.

The same NPS can indicate different business circumstances. For instance, an NPS of 0 can indicate highly polarized customers with 50% promoters and 50% detractors, or it can indicate a totally ambivalent customer base with 100% passives. Getting the NPS may be a good way of starting a discussion about customer perceptions of a brand. As it is an average of current customers' responses, managers must drill down to the data to understand the precise situation their business faces.

This score in specific circumstances can generate results that could mislead a manager who is not being careful. For example, consider a company whose current customers are 30% promoters, 30% detractors, and 40% passives. This company's NPS is an unimpressive 0 because $30\% - 30\% = 0$.

Now suppose that a new competitor steals two-thirds of the company's detractors, and because these detractors immediately defect to the new competitor, they cease to be customers of the company. The NPS is remeasured.

Promoters are now 30% / (100% − 20% = 80%) = 37.5% of the customers that remain.

Passives are now 40% / (100% − 20% = 80%) = 50% of the customers that remain.

Detractors are now only (30% − 20% = 10%) / (100% − 20% = 80%) = 12.5% of the customers that remain.

The NPS is now 37.5% − 12.5% = a very healthy-looking 25.

The defection of the most vulnerable and unhappy customers led directly to an increase in NPS. Managers should make sure they fully understand what has happened.

While benchmarking is often a useful exercise, it is inappropriate to directly apply this measure across categories. Some products are in categories that are more likely to gain engagement, both positive and negative, than others.

A high Net Promoter Score, while generally desirable, does invite the question whether the company is properly monetizing the value it is providing to the consumer. The easiest way to develop a high NPS is to provide a highly valued product to customers for free. Why wouldn't they be happy to recommend you? While there might be strategic reasons for situations like this to be acceptable to the company in the short or medium term, it probably wouldn't be a viable long-term strategy.

The NPS is calculated from survey data. As such, it may suffer from the problems common to most surveys, and the results should be interpreted in light of other data, such as sales trends. Is increased customer satisfaction leading to increased sales? If so, fine; if not, why not?

Although the NPS has received much attention and relatively rapid adoption, it has also been the target of significant criticism. Consultant Timothy Keiningham and his coauthors claim that the benefits of the measure have been overstated relative to other measures of loyalty and satisfaction.[8,9]

2.10   Willingness to search

Although many metrics explore brand loyalty, one has been called the "acid test." That is,

Willingness to Search (%) = Percentage of Customers Willing to Delay
Purchases, Change Stores, or Reduce
Purchase Quantities to Avoid Switching Brands

This metric can tell a company much about the attitudes of its customers and whether its position in the market is likely to be defensible against sustained pressure from a competitor.

Purpose: to assess the commitment of a firm's or a brand's customer base.

Brand or company loyalty is a key marketing asset. Marketers evaluate aspects of it through a number of metrics, including repurchase rate, share of requirements, willingness to pay a price premium, and other AAU measures. Perhaps the most fundamental test of loyalty, however, can be captured with a simple question: When faced with a situation in which a brand is not available, will customers search further for it (that is, go to another store), or will they substitute the best available option?

When a brand enjoys loyalty at this level, its provider can generate powerful leverage in trade negotiations. Often, such loyalty will also give providers time to respond to a competitive threat. Customers will stay with them while they address the threat.

Loyalty is grounded in a number of factors, including

- Satisfied and influential customers who are willing to recommend the brand
- Hidden values or emotional benefits, which are effectively communicated
- A strong image for the product, the user, or the usage experience

Purchase-based loyalty metrics are also affected by whether a product is broadly and conveniently available for purchase and whether customers enjoy other options in its category.

Construction

> **Willingness to search:** The likelihood that customers will settle for a second-choice product if their first choice is not available. Also called "accept no substitutes."

Willingness to search represents the percentage of customers who are willing to leave a store without a product if their favorite brand is unavailable. Those willing to substitute constitute the balance of the population.

Data sources, complications, and cautions

Loyalty has multiple dimensions. Consumers who are loyal to a brand in the sense of rarely switching may or may not be willing to pay a price premium for that brand or recommend it to their friends. Behavioral loyalty may also be difficult to distinguish from inertia or habit. When asked about loyalty, consumers often don't know what they will do in new circumstances. They may not have accurate recall about past behavior, especially in regard to items with which they feel relatively low involvement.

Furthermore, different products generate different levels of loyalty. Few customers will be as loyal to a brand of matches, for example, as to a brand of baby formula. Consequently, marketers should exercise caution in comparing loyalty rates across products. Rather, they should look for category-specific norms.

Degrees of loyalty also differ between demographic groups. Older consumers have been shown to demonstrate the highest loyalty rates.

Even with these complexities, however, customer loyalty remains one of the most important metrics to monitor. Marketers should understand the worth of their brands in the eyes of the customer—and of the retailer.

2.11 Neuroscience measures[10]

> In this section, written with the help of Dr. Manuel Garcia-Garcia and Pasha Davoudian, we discuss important methods of studying consumers made possible by advances in neuroscience technology and outline the biometrics associated with them that are being applied in marketing.
>
> **Electroencephalography (EEG)**
> **Functional Magnetic Resonance Imaging (fMRI)**
> **Facial Action Coding System (FACS)**
> **Eye Tracking**
> **Skin Conductance Response**

> **Heart Rate**
>
> **Electromyography (EMG)**
>
> These techniques are often used, for example, to improve the effectiveness of advertising.

Purpose: obtain deeper insights into consumer behavior.

Consumers do things for reasons they do not fully understand and cannot articulate. Surveys only reveal what people can or care to tell us and are subject to post hoc rationalization (that is, making up a reason for actions that sounds plausible but only after the decision was made). Surveys thus have limitations. The good news is that technological advances have allowed marketers to gain greater insight into how consumers react, especially preconciously or non-consciously. We have a better understanding of how consumers view visual advertisements and even which parts of the consumer's brain are active when deciding between alternatives. Many companies provide specialist consultancy services to help marketers benefit from these new techniques.

Current research in cognitive neuroscience suggests that decision making is less deliberate than once thought and instead relies heavily on early emotional responses. Traditional market research methods, such as focus groups and surveys, are unable to assess consumers' initial, preconscious reactions. Consumer neuroscience methods can reveal insights into early emotional responses to help us better understand these reactions and so give a unique insight into consumer behavior.

Construction

We consider four of the most important measures used in trying to understand consumer reactions. These are classified here by the technology rather than the measure, as the choice of technology is generally the way that marketers will encounter the metrics.

Electroencephalography (EEG)

EEG is a technique that involves taking surface readings from electrodes embedded in headgear. The electrodes pick up voltage fluctuations within the brain and can pin down activity to an area of the brain.

> *An EEG measures brain waves in terms of Hertz (frequency) and micro-voltage (amplitude).*

EEGs are useful for exploring such things as a consumer's immediate response to an advertisement. EEGs allow a better understanding through rapid monitoring of general brain activity. This removes the subjectivity that is present in many assessments of marketing (such as surveys of consumer attitudes).

This approach can assess the consumer's attentional effort. This captures two different ideas:

- **Top-down attention:** Voluntary attentional focus
- **Bottom-up attention:** Involuntary responses, often to the novel, rewarding, or threatening

When properly interpreted, marketing applications include giving insight into branding and advertising effects. In advertising, an EEG can provide a measure of attention from the changes in certain brain-wave patterns over regions of the brain. The strengths of brands and the types of associations held about a brand can also be assessed based on the activity the brand generates in the consumer's brain.

Functional magnetic resonance imaging (fMRI)

fMRI involves the consumer entering a scanning machine that is large, expensive, and non-portable. Although the technique is non-invasive, it is an artificial environment, and entering the scanner presents challenges to those who suffer from claustrophobia.

The consumer will usually be shown stimuli and his or her brain responses monitored. This process can be effective at visualizing brain processes at fine spatial resolution.

fMRI measures blood-oxygen-level-dependent (BOLD) brain tracking that resolves activity to the micrometer scale per second.

When showing the results, the intensity of activity in the consumer's brain is color coded to indicate relative brain activity. Red normally depicts high brain activity and blue lower brain activity. Thus, we see which areas of the brain were most active when the individual was seeing certain stimuli. A researcher might then talk about areas associated with emotional reactions being more active when the consumer was shown one brand than another. One interesting example is the "Pepsi Challenge" study. This identified brain regions that attracted greater blood flow when brand associations were triggered.[11,12]

Facial action coding system (FACS)

Facial coding involves attempting to identify the consumer's mood/reaction through his or her facial movements. There is no single unit of measurement. The system employs numerous facial action unit characterizations along with related general head and specific subfacial movements. Users are trained to identify these through "reading" data output. Automatic classification of observable facial expressions can be done by several software programs, some of which can be implemented through webcams, with more or less reliable results.

This technique may help to identify a person's underlying mood or reaction to a stimulus—reactions that otherwise might not be explicitly expressed, such as the subtle facial movements that correlate with particular mindsets or attitudes. Facial coding can be used to analyze consumer reactions to proposed product features or to choose between different versions of an advertisement. One can consider how consumers respond emotionally to a brand or even use the technique as part of an autopsy to determine why a marketing campaign failed.

An example of facial coding being used in marketing is the work of Thales Teixeira and his colleagues.[13] These researchers examined the surprise and joy of consumers who were viewing a series of online advertisements. They used facial coding software to fit a virtual facial mask on the consumers who were watching the advertisements and measured deviations from the baseline to measure the emotions being experienced. For example, smiles were detected from deviations related to the corners of the lips. The emotions were then linked to what the consumer was paying attention to at the time. The emotions were also linked to whether the consumers clicked past a given advertisement or watched it. By using such an approach, a marketer can get a clearer view of the emotions consumers experience when seeing an advertisement and so design advertisements to better gain the consumers' attention and sustain the consumers' interest.

Eye tracking

Eye tracking provides a real-time record of where visual attention is directed. It can also show how pupil dilation changes. This measure is a useful indicator of emotional arousal.

Small, high-resolution video cameras are placed near, but without obstructing, the consumer's eyes. A small non-invasive light guides the camera to track what is being viewed, and other cameras capture related information. Typically studies are run on stationary subjects, but additional hardware can be employed to track a subject's gaze when moving.

Eye-tracking measures include fixations per second, saccades (eye movements), pupil size, and blinks per second.

Fixations per second when a person is viewing a stimuli can indicate how much attention the consumer is paying to, for example, a sample advertisement. In product and package design, eye tracking can test what the consumer is paying visual attention to and gives an idea of the consumer's emotional arousal from pupil dilation. In studies of active shoppers, eye tracking can record where the consumers look in a shopping aisle, on a shelf, or when examining individual products. This information can be used to create a map of where consumers look. Combining eye tracking with shelf plans (planograms) can yield useful insights into how consumers visually search a shelf to find and select products. Such studies can provide a wealth of practical information about the impact of different shelf configurations on product search and selection.

Applying these measures to marketing problems

We borrow an example from Trabulsi, Garcia-Garcia, and Smith, who describe a situation where a marketer tested an advertisement using traditional marketing research methods but found that it was unlikely to be effective.[14] The basic approach still seemed promising, and so the marketer re-created the advertisement but in a more effective manner, with the goal of discovering exactly (to the second) what was failing. Measuring consumer reactions to an advertisement by using EEG, the marketers could precisely find out which seconds of the advertisement were strong and which weak in terms of consumer attention, memory, and emotional reaction. The marketer could also see which elements of the advertisement were especially interesting and/ or confusing by tracking at which seconds when watching the advertisement high demands were being placed on the consumers' cognitive capacities.

Other important measures related to neuro-marketing

This book is not designed to be a specialist neuro-marketing publication, so we have focused on a few important technologies. Within this field, however, there are other techniques used, often simultaneously, with those just described. We might want to know how the consumer's body is reacting. Is the individual excited? Preparing for action? Bored?

Electromyography (EMG) measures facial micro-muscle movements below the level of observable expressions that are involuntarily associated with emotional reactions, such as the "frown" and "smile" muscles.

Electrodermal activity (EDA) is electrical current passing through the skin. It is a function of the amount of perspiration on the skin. Perspiration conducts electricity and is a sign of emotional arousal, which is measured by galvanic skin response (GSR) and skin conductance response (SCR).

Heart rate can slow down when attention increases and speed up with emotional arousal. Respiration measures record how deeply and quickly a person breathes to determine arousal.

Response latencies (time delays) measure how fast we respond to choice and judgment tasks. Quicker action is usually assumed to show a stronger mental association between concepts in long-term memory. Two words or images are presented in rapid succession. When the second item appears, a choice or judgment has to be made as rapidly as possible. The three main types of behavioral response testing are semantic priming, affective priming, and the Implicit Association Test (IAT).

Why use neuro-marketing techniques?

Brand-equity measures often capture the progress of a brand's marketplace performance, but neuro-marketing measures have potential to tell us more about the consumers' experiences at a detailed level. We can also hope to better understand non-conscious consumer reactions, which consumers cannot tell us about in surveys even if they wish to do so.

Where these are likely to be especially useful is where the upfront costs are modest compared to the ongoing marketing costs. Here even a modest increase in understanding can mean large benefits from the more efficiently deployed ongoing costs. A case in point may be advertising where typically media buys (such as time on TV) are a large proportion of the costs. (The cost to create a commercial is often modest compared to the cost to air it on network TV.) Anything that even marginally improves the effectiveness of an advertisement can be highly worthwhile. (For more on advertising testing, see Section 13.3 on the Gross model.)

Example Heritage Inc. has created a 30-second advertisement that is quite effective; for every dollar spent, there was an expected contribution of $1.50. (This comes from the company's internal assessment of past advertising.)

After studying one of Heritage's advertisements, a neuro-marketing consultancy, Electrode Partners, recommended heavy edits to it. A researcher used a combination of eye-tracking and brain activity measures to assess which sections effectively engaged viewers. By eliminating the sections that were less effective and/or confusing, the ad was shortened. This sacrificed a small amount of effectiveness; each spot would be only 80% as effective as the 30-second advertisement, but the new spots would last only 15 seconds. Media costs for a 30-second spot are twice those for a 15-second spot, so although each spot would have only 80% of the impact, each spot would be half the cost.

Heritage is committed to its media spend, given its agreement with the TV network. Heritage will, therefore, buy twice as many 15-second spots as it would 30-second spots, and the company treats media spend as a fixed cost. The costs of Electrode's study and the costs of making the necessary edits to the advertisement totaled $250,000. In Table 2.9 we can see that the return on investment is quite substantial for the study. (For more on return on investment, see Section 12.2.)

Table 2.9 Return on investment for study (all dollar terms in $000s)

Calculation Objective	Formula	Baseline	After study
Effectiveness of 30-sec./15-sec. spot (A)	Given	100%	80%
Relative # of Spots 30 sec./15 sec. (B)	Given	1	2
Relative Effectiveness (C)	A * B	100%	160%
Expected Lift from 30-sec. Spot (D)	Given	1.5	1.5
Expected Lift from Media Spend (E)	C * D	1.5	2.4
Media Spend (F)	Given	$1,000	$1,000
Contribution from Media Spend (G)	E * F	$1,500	$2,400
Profit from Media Spend (H)	G − F	$500	$1,400
Study and Advertisement Change Costs (I)	Given		$250
Profit Without Study (J)	H	$500	

Calculation Objective	Formula	Baseline	After study
Profit With Study (K)	H – I		$1,150
Profit Change from Study (L)	K – J		$650
ROI of Study (M)	L / I		260%

The study's success was driven by the fact that the study's upfront cost was less than the ongoing benefits gained through more efficient deployment of the media spend. The 15-second advertisements give much more bang for the buck than the 30-second advertisements.

The benefits from small improvements in effectiveness get even greater when the ongoing spending increases relative to the initial costs. Table 2.10 shows the benefits that would have been gained had Heritage been committed to five times more media spend.

Table 2.10 Return on investment for study when media spend is higher (all dollar terms in $000s)

Calculation Objective	Formula	Baseline	After study
Media Spend is 5x Higher (F')	Given	$5,000	$5,000
Contribution from Spots (G')	E * F'	$7,500	$12,000
Profit Without Study (J')	G' – F'	$2,500	
Profit With Study (K')	G' – F' – I		$6,750
Profit Change from Study (L')	K' – J'		$4,250
ROI of Study (M')	L' / I		1,700%

Data sources, complications, and cautions

One of the main limitations of neuro-marketing techniques is that the machinery can be cumbersome and hard or impossible to deploy in everyday situations. While we can ask consumers to participate in these tests, their reactions will, to a certain extent, be influenced by the setting they are in. Participating in an experiment in an fMRI scanner is not (yet) the same as shopping in your local grocery store, even if some of the measuring devices are rapidly becoming smaller and more comfortable. As technology for gathering neuroscience metrics becomes less obtrusive, we might expect some of these problems to be alleviated.

Compared to other marketing metrics, neuro-marketing requires specific expertise and training in the underlying science to interpret the data. Further, although companies are accumulating studies that assess reliability and validity of the technologies and metrics, much remains to be done.

As Varan and his colleagues note, the need to assess the variance and reliability of neuro-metrics within and between firms has become increasingly apparent.[15] There remains considerable variation among suppliers and uncertainty about what differences are due to lack of reliability versus what differences are driven by each firm's unique collection methods.

Our understanding of the brain has increased considerably in recent years, but it still remains limited. Scientists may talk of areas of the brain that are associated with a certain feeling or activity. This does not mean that there is a specific spot in the brain that, if we were to find it, could tell exactly a person's brand preference. Neither can we hope to understand a consumer's precise willingness to pay for any good. Neuro-marketing techniques may be useful in understanding how consumers are likely to behave and so may help at an early stage of the marketing process. Table 2.11 provides a summary of neuro-marketing measures.

Further reading

Banaji, Mahzarin R., and Anthony G. Greenwald. (2013). *Blindspot: Hidden Biases of Good People*, Delacorte Press.

Hendrickson, Kirk, and Kusum L. Ailawadi. (2014). "Six Lessons for In-Store Marketing from Six Years of Mobile Eye-Tracking Research," in Dhruv Grewal, Anne L. Roggeveen, Jens NordfÄlt (Eds.), *Shopper Marketing and the Role of In-Store Marketing* (pp. 57–74), Emerald Group Publishing Limited.

Knutson, Rick B., G. E. Wimmer, D. Prelec, and G. Loewenstein. (2007). "Neural Predictors of Purchases," *Neuron*, 53(1), 147–156.

McClure, Samuel M., Jian Li, Damon Tomlin, Kim S. Cypert, Latané M. Montague, and P. Read Montague. (2004). "Neural Correlates of Behavioral Preference for Culturally Familiar Drinks," *Neuron*, 44(2), 379–387.

Teixeira, Thales, Michel Wedel, and Rik Pieters. (2012). "Emotion-Induced Engagement in Internet Video Advertisements," *Journal of Marketing Research*, 49, 144–159.

Trabulsi, Julia, Manuel Garcia-Garcia, and Michael E. Smith. (2015). "Consumer Neuroscience: A Method for Optimizing Marketing Communication," *Journal of Cultural Marketing Strategy*, 1(1), 80–89.

Varan, Duane, Annie Lang, Patrick Barwise, Rene Weber, and Steven Bellman. (2015). "How Reliable Are Neuromarketers' Measures of Advertising Effectiveness: Data from Ongoing Research Holds No Common Truth Among Vendors," *Journal of Advertising Research*, 55(2), 176–191.

Venkatraman, Vinod, Angelika Dimoka, Paul A. Pavlou, Khoi Vo, William Hampton, Bryan Bollinger, Hal E. Hershfield, Masakazu Ishihara, and Russell S. Winer. (2015). "Predicting Advertising Success Beyond Traditional Measures: New Insights from Neurophysiological Methods and Market Response Modeling," *Journal of Marketing Research*, 52(4), 436–452.

Willke, Joe, and Blake Burrus. (2013). "Making Advertising More of a Science Than an Art," *What's Next*, 1(2).

Table 2.11 Summary of neuro-metrics

Technology	Metric/measure	Measurement unit	Technological specifications	Targeted processes	Potential marketing uses
Electroencephalography (EEG)	Voltage fluctuations of thousands of neurons per millisecond at a spatial resolution of up to a single centimeter.	Hertz (frequency) and micro-voltage (amplitude) together define characteristic wave forms.	Surface electrodes arranged in headgear (cap, helmet, etc.) are painless and relatively comfortable. Costs associated with EEGs can range from $500 (single scan) to more than $10,000 for the setup of an entire EEG hardware and software set.	Well suited to explore general cognitive decision making, initial responses, problem solving, etc., due to the high temporal resolution of the datasets acquired.	**Branding:** Identify brain-wave patterns that emerge when presented with words or images that are strongly associated in memory. **Advertising:** Measure of attention, changes in brain-wave patterns.
Functional Magnetic Resonance Imaging (fMRI)	Blood-oxygen-level-dependent (BOLD) brain tracking resolves activity to the micrometer scale per second.	Voxel (3D-pixel and volume) intensity is color coded. Red normally depicts high brain activity and blue lower brain activity.	Two magnetic fields stabilize and excite brain nuclei and measure the resulting changes via magnetic coils. fMRIs range from $500 to $800 for a single scan and from $1 million to $3 million for an entire setup.	Can pinpoint brain regions corresponding with behavior. Best for attempting to find brain regions responsible for sustained behaviors such as food or drink seeking and judgment.	**Branding:** Identify brain regions that attract greater blood flow when strong associations are triggered.

Facial Action Coding System (FACS)	User classifies movements, features into action units (AUs). Relative intensities used to indirectly assess mood or intentions.	No standard unit. Employs more than 50 facial AU characterizations along with another 50 general head and specific subfacial movements.	Users are trained to accurately identify the (50+) various facial characterizations. Automating AU classification can be done via facial recognition software.	Well suited to identify a person's underlying mood or intentions, which may not otherwise be explicitly expressed.	**Product testing:** Analyze customer reactions to proposed product features. **Advertising testing:** Choose between ad versions or determine why ad campaigns failed. **Brand emotions:** Measures responses to brand.
Eye Tracking	Video recordings track pupil via (near) infrared light. Additional hardware can track gaze when moving.	Fixations per second, saccade linear mapping, blinks per second, and voxels (for attentiveness heat maps).	Small, high-resolution video cameras placed near the eyes use small non-invasive light to track the view. In parallel other cameras capture the scene. Hardware and software packages vary greatly and can cost anywhere from hundreds to tens of thousands of dollars.	Useful for investigating the visual system, particularly the length and order in which a subject views various aspects of a scene.	**Product and package design:** Test attention/arousal. **Advertising:** Measure the number of fixations per second (fps) when viewing an ad. **Shopper marketing:** Measure where consumers look in aisle, on shelf, or on product.

Margins and profits

3

Key concepts covered in this chapter:

- Margins

- Selling prices and channel margins

- Average price per unit and price per statistical unit

- Variable costs and fixed costs

- Marketing spending—total, fixed, and variable

- Break-even analysis and contribution analysis

- Target volume

Introduction

Peter Drucker has written that the purpose of a business is to create a customer. As marketers, we agree. But we also recognize that a business can't survive unless it makes a margin as well as a customer. At one level, margins are simply the difference between a product's price and its cost. This calculation becomes more complicated, however, when multiple variations of a product are sold at multiple prices, through multiple channels, incurring different costs along the way. For example, a *Business Week* article noted that less "than two-thirds of GM's sales are retail. The rest go to rental-car agencies or to company employees and their families—sales that provide lower gross margins."[1] Although it is still the case that a business can't survive unless it earns a positive margin, it can be a challenge to determine precisely what margin the firm actually does earn.

In the first section of this chapter, we explain the basic computation of unit and percentage margins, and we introduce the practice of calculating margins as a percentage of selling price.

Next, we show how to "chain" this calculation through two or more levels in a distribution channel and how to calculate end-user purchase price on the basis of a marketer's selling price. We explain how to combine sales through different channels to calculate average margins and how to compare the economics of different distribution channels.

In the third section, we discuss the use of "statistical" and standard units in tracking price changes over time.

In the fourth section, we turn our attention to measuring product costs, with particular emphasis on the distinction between fixed and variable costs. The margin between a product's unit price and its variable cost per unit represents a key calculation. It tells us how much the sale of each unit of that product will contribute to covering a firm's fixed costs. "Contribution margin" on sales is one of the most useful marketing concepts. It requires, however, that we separate fixed from variable costs, which can be challenging.

Frequently, marketers must take "as a given" which of their firm's operating and production costs are fixed and which are variable. They are likely, however, to be responsible for making these fixed versus variable distinctions for marketing costs. That is the subject of the fifth section of this chapter.

In the sixth section, we discuss the use of fixed- and variable-cost estimates in calculating the break-even levels of sales and contribution. Finally, we extend our calculation of break-even points, showing how to identify sales and profit targets that are mutually consistent.

	Metric	*Construction*	*Considerations*	*Purpose*
3.1	Unit Margin	Unit price less the unit cost.	What are the standard units in the industry? May not reflect contribution margin if some fixed costs are allocated.	Determine value of incremental sales. Guide pricing and promotion.
3.1	Margin (%)	Unit margin as a percentage of unit price.	May not reflect contribution margin if some fixed costs are allocated.	Compare margins across different products/sizes/ forms of product. Determine value of incremental sales. Guide pricing and promotion decisions.

	Metric	Construction	Considerations	Purpose
3.2	Channel Margins	Channel profits as percentage of channel selling price.	Distinguish margin on sales (usual) from markup on cost (also encountered).	Evaluate channel value added in context of selling price. Calculate effect of price changes at one level of channel on prices and margins at other levels in the same channel (supply chain).
3.3	Average Price per Unit	Can be calculated as total revenue divided by total unit sales.	Some units may have greater relevance from producers' perspective than consumers' (for example, ounces of shampoo versus bottles). Changes may not be result of pricing decisions.	Understand how average prices are affected by shifts in pricing and product mix.
3.3	Price per Statistical Unit	SKU prices weighted by relevant percentage of each SKU in a statistical unit.	Percentage SKU mix should correspond over medium term to actual mix of sales.	Isolate effect of price changes from mix changes by standardizing the SKU mix of a standard unit.
3.4	Variable and Fixed Costs	Divide costs into two categories: those that vary with volume (variable) and those that do not (fixed).	Variable costs may include production, marketing, and selling expenses. Some variable costs depend on units sold; others depend on revenue.	Understand how costs are affected by changes in sales volume.
3.5	Marketing Spending	Analyze costs that comprise marketing spending.	Can be divided into fixed and variable marketing costs.	Understand how marketing spending changes with sales.

	Metric	Construction	Considerations	Purpose
3.6	Contribution per Unit	Unit price less unit variable cost.	Ensure that marketing variable costs have not already been deducted from price.	Understand profit impact of changes in volume. Calculate break-even level of sales.
3.6	Contribution Margin (%)	Contribution per unit divided by unit price.	Ensure that variable costs are consistently based on units or revenue, as appropriate.	Same as above but applies to dollar sales.
3.6	Break-Even Sales Level	For unit break-even, divide fixed costs by contribution per unit. For revenue break-even, divide fixed costs by contribution margin (%).	Variable- and fixed-cost estimates may be valid only over certain ranges of sales and production.	Rough indicator of project attractiveness and ability to earn profit.
3.7	Target Volume	Adjust break-even calculation to include profit target.	Variable marketing costs must be reflected in contribution margins. Sales increases often require increased investment or working capital.	Ensure that unit sales objectives will enable firm to achieve financial hurdle rates for profit, ROS, or ROI.
3.7	Target Revenues	Convert target volume to target revenues by using average prices per unit. Alternatively, combine cost and target data with knowledge of contribution margins.	Same as above.	Same as above, applied to revenue objectives.

3.1 Margins

Margin (on sales) is the difference between selling price and cost. This difference is typically expressed either as a percentage of selling price or on a per-unit basis.

$$\text{Unit Margin (\$)} = \text{Selling Price per Unit (\$)} - \text{Cost per Unit (\$)}$$

$$\text{Margin (\%)} = \frac{\text{Unit Margin (\$)}}{\text{Selling Price per Unit (\$)}}$$

Managers need to know margins for almost all marketing decisions. Margins represent a key factor in pricing, return on marketing spending, earnings forecasts, and analyses of customer profitability.

Purpose: to determine the value of incremental sales and to guide pricing and promotion decisions.

Margin on sales is a key factor behind many of the most fundamental business considerations, including budgets and forecasts. All managers should—and generally do—know their approximate business margins. Managers differ widely, however, in the assumptions they use in calculating margins and in the ways they analyze and communicate these important figures.

Percentage margins and unit margins: A fundamental variation in the way people talk about margins lies in the difference between percentage margins and unit margins on sales. The difference is easy to reconcile, and managers should be able to switch back and forth between the two.

What is a unit?

Every business has its own notion of a "unit," ranging from a ton of margarine to 64 ounces of cola to a bucket of plaster. Many industries work with multiple units and calculate margin accordingly. The cigarette industry, for example, sells "sticks," "packs," "cartons," and master cases (which hold 10,000 individual cigarettes). Banks calculate margin on the basis of accounts, customers, loans, transactions, households, and branch offices. Marketers must be prepared to shift between such varying perspectives with little effort because decisions can be grounded in any of these perspectives.

Construction

$$\text{Unit Margin (\$)} = \text{Selling Price per Unit (\$)} - \text{Cost per Unit (\$)}$$

$$\text{Margin (\%)} = \frac{\text{Unit Margin (\$)}}{\text{Selling Price per Unit (\$)}}$$

Percentage margins can also be calculated using total sales revenue and total costs.

$$\text{Margin (\%)} = \frac{[\text{Total Sales Revenue (\$)} - \text{Total Cost (\$)}]}{\text{Total Sales Revenue (\$)}}$$

When working with either percentage or unit margins, marketers can perform a simple check by verifying that the individual parts sum to the total.

To verify a Unit Margin (\$): Selling Price per Unit = Unit Margin + Cost per Unit

To verify a Margin (%): Cost as % of Sales = 100% − Margin %

Example A company markets sailcloth by the lineal yard. Its cost basis and selling price for standard cloth are as follows:

Unit Selling Price (Selling Price per Unit) = \$24 per Lineal Yard

Unit Cost (Cost per Unit) = \$18 per Lineal Yard

To calculate unit margin, we subtract the cost from the selling price:

Unit Margin = \$24 per Yard − \$18 per Yard

= \$6 per Yard

To calculate the percentage margin, we divide the unit margin by the selling price:

$$\text{Margin (\%)} = \frac{(\$24 - \$18) \text{ per Yard}}{\$24}$$

$$= \frac{\$6}{\$24} = 25\%$$

Let's verify that our calculations are correct:

Unit Selling Price = Unit Margin + Unit Cost

\$24 per Yard = \$6 per Yard + \$18 per Yard   **correct**

A similar check can be made on our calculations of percentage margin:

100% − Margin on Sales (%) = Cost as % of Selling Price

$$100\% - 25\% = \frac{\$18}{\$24}$$

75% = 75%   **correct**

When considering multiple products with different revenues and costs, we can calculate overall margin (%) on either of two bases:

- Total revenue and total costs for all products
- The dollar-weighted average of the percentage margins of the different products

Example The sailcloth company produces a new line of deluxe cloth, which sells for $64 per lineal yard and costs $32 per yard to produce. The margin on this item is 50%.

$$\text{Unit Margin (\$)} = \$64 \text{ per Yard} - \$32 \text{ per Yard}$$

$$= \$32 \text{ per Yard}$$

$$\text{Margin (\%)} = \frac{(\$64 - \$32)}{\$64}$$

$$= \frac{\$32}{\$64}$$

$$= 50\%$$

Because the company now sells two different products, its average margin can only be calculated when we know the volume of each type of goods sold. It would not be accurate to take a simple average of the 25% margin on standard cloth and the 50% margin on deluxe cloth unless the company sells the same dollar volume of both products.

If, one day, the company sells 20 yards of standard cloth and 2 yards of deluxe cloth, we can calculate its margins for that day as follows (see also Table 3.1):

$$\text{Total Sales} = 20 \text{ Yards at \$24, and 2 Yards at \$64}$$

$$= \$608$$

$$\text{Total Costs} = 20 \text{ Yards at \$18, and 2 Yards at \$32}$$

$$= \$424$$

$$\text{Margin (\$)} = \$184$$

$$\text{Margin (\%)} = \frac{\text{Margin (\$184)}}{\text{Total Sales (\$608)}}$$

$$= 30\%$$

Because dollar sales differ between the two products, the company's margin of 30% is not a simple average of the margins of those products.

Table 3.1 Sales, costs, and margins

	Standard	Deluxe	Total
Sales in Yards	20	2	22
Selling Price per Yard	$24.00	$64.00	
Total Sales ($)	$480.00	$128.00	$608.00
Cost per Yard	$18.00	$32.00	
Total Costs ($)	$360.00	$64.00	$424.00
Total Dollar Margin ($)	$120.00	$64.00	$184.00
Unit Margin	$6.00	$32.00	$8.36
Margin (%)	25%	50%	30%

Data sources, complications, and cautions

After you determine which units to use, you need two inputs to determine margins: *unit costs* and *unit selling prices.*

Selling prices can be defined before or after various "charges" are taken
Rebates, customer discounts, brokers' fees, and commissions can be reported to management either as costs or as deductions from the selling price. Furthermore, external reporting can vary from management reporting because accounting standards might dictate a treatment that differs from internal practices. Reported margins can vary widely, depending on the calculation technique used. This can result in deep organizational confusion on a question as fundamental as what the price of a product actually is.

Please see Section 9.4 on price waterfalls for cautions on deducting certain discounts and allowances in calculating "net prices." Often, there is considerable latitude on whether certain items are subtracted from list price to calculate a net price or are added to costs. One example is the retail practice of providing gift certificates to customers who purchase certain amounts of goods. It is not easy to account for these in a way that avoids confusion among prices, marketing costs, and margins. In this context, two points are relevant: (1) Certain items can be treated either as deductions from prices or as increments to cost but not both. (2) The treatment of such an item will not affect the unit margin but will affect the percentage margin.

Margin as a percentage of costs
Some industries, particularly retail, calculate margin as a percentage of costs, not of selling prices. Using this technique in the previous example, the percentage margin on a yard of standard sailcloth would be reckoned as the $6.00 unit margin divided by the $18.00 unit cost, or 33%. This can lead to confusion. Marketers must become

familiar with the practices in their industry and stand ready to shift between them as needed.

Markup or margin?

Although some people use the terms *margin* and *markup* interchangeably, doing so is not appropriate. The term *markup* commonly refers to the practice of adding a percentage to costs in order to calculate selling prices.

To get a better idea of the relationship between margin and markup, let's calculate a few. For example, a 50% markup on a variable cost of $10 would be $5, yielding a retail price of $15. By contrast, the margin on an item that sells at a retail price of $15 and that carries a variable cost of $10 would be $5/$15, or 33.3%. Table 3.2 shows some common margin/markup relationships.

Table 3.2 Relationship between margins and markups

Price	Cost	Margin	Markup
$10	$9.00	10%	11%
$10	$7.50	25%	33%
$10	$6.67	33.3%	50%
$10	$5.00	50%	100%
$10	$4.00	60%	150%
$10	$3.33	66.7%	200%
$10	$2.50	75%	300%

One of the peculiarities that can occur in retail is that prices are "marked up" as a percentage of a store's purchase price (its variable cost for an item) but "marked down" during sales events as a percentage of retail price. Most customers understand that a 50% "sale" means that retail prices have been marked down by 50%.

Example An apparel retailer buys t-shirts for $10 and sells them at a 50% markup. As noted previously, a 50% markup on a variable cost of $10 yields a retail price of $15. Unfortunately, the goods don't sell, and the store owner wants to sell them at cost to clear shelf space. He carelessly asks a sales assistant to mark the goods down by 50%. This 50% markdown, however, reduces the retail price to $7.50. Thus, a 50% markup followed by a 50% markdown results in a loss of $2.50 on each unit sold.

It is easy to see how confusion can occur. We generally prefer to use the term *margin* to refer to margin on sales. We recommend, however, that all managers clarify with their colleagues what is meant by this important term.

Example A wireless provider sells a handset for $100. The handset costs $50 to manufacture and includes a $20 mail-in rebate. The provider's internal reports add this rebate to the cost of goods sold. Its margin calculations therefore run as follows:

$$\text{Unit Margin (\$)} = \text{Selling Price} - \text{Cost of Goods Sold and Rebate}$$

$$= \$100 - (\$50 + \$20) = \$30$$

$$\text{Margin (\%)} = \frac{\$30}{\$100} = 30\%$$

The relevant accounting standards mandate, however, that external reports deduct rebates from sales revenue (see Table 3.3). Under this construction, the company's margin calculations run differently and yield a different percentage margin:

$$\text{Unit Margin (\$)} = \text{Selling Price, Net of Rebate} - \text{Cost of Goods Sold}$$

$$= (\$100 - \$20) - \$50 = \$30$$

$$\text{Margin (\%)} = \frac{\$30}{(\$100 - \$20)}$$

$$= \frac{\$30}{\$80} = 37.5\%$$

Table 3.3 Internal and external reporting may vary

	Internal reporting	External reporting
Dollars Received from Customer	$100	$100
Rebate	—	$20
Sales	$100	$80
Manufacturing Cost	$50	$50
Rebate	$20	—
Cost of Goods Sold	$70	$50
Unit Margin ($)	$30	$30
Margin (%)	30.0%	37.5%

In this example, managers add the rebate to cost of goods sold for the sake of internal reports. In contrast, accounting regulations require that the rebate be deducted from sales for the purpose of external reports. This means that the percentage margin varies between the internal and external reports. This can cause considerable confusion within the company when quoting a percentage margin.

As a general principle, internal margins can follow formats mandated for external reporting in order to limit confusion. There may be good reasons to depart from financial reporting standards for internal management-focused reports. However, these departures should be documented internally to enable reconciliation while preserving confidential company information.

Various costs may or may not be included

The inclusion or exclusion of costs generally depends on the intended purpose of the relevant margin calculations. We'll return to this issue several times. At one extreme, if all costs are included, then margin and net profit will be equivalent. On the other hand, a marketer may choose to work with "contribution margin" (deducting only variable costs), "operating margin," or "margin before marketing." By using certain metrics, marketers can distinguish fixed from variable costs and can isolate particular costs of an operation or of a department from the overall business.

Related metrics and concepts

> **Gross Margin:** The difference between revenue and cost before accounting for certain other costs. Generally, it is calculated as the selling price of an item, less the cost of goods sold (essentially production or acquisition costs). Gross margin can be expressed as a percentage or in total dollar terms. If the latter, it can be reported on a per-unit basis or on a per-period basis for a company.

3.2 Prices and channel margins

> Channel margins can be expressed on a per-unit basis or as a percentage of selling price. In "chaining" the margins of sequential distribution channels, the selling price of one channel member becomes the "cost" of the channel member for which it serves as a supplier.
>
> $$\text{Supplier Selling Price (\$)} = \text{Customer Selling Price (\$)} - \text{Customer Margin (\$)}$$
>
> $$\text{Customer Selling Price (\$)} = \frac{\text{Supplier Selling Price (\$)}}{[1 - \text{Customer Margin (\%)}]}$$
>
> When there are several levels in a distribution chain—including a manufacturer, distributor, and retailer, for example—one must not simply add all channel margins as reported in order to calculate "total" channel margin. Instead, use the selling prices at the beginning and end of the distribution chain (that is, at the levels of the manufacturer and the retailer) to calculate total channel margin. Marketers should be able to work forward from their own selling price to the consumer's purchase price and should understand channel margins at each step.

Purpose: to calculate selling prices at each level in the distribution channel.

Marketing often involves selling through a series of "value-added" resellers. Sometimes, a product changes form through this progression. At other times, its price is simply "marked up" along its journey through the distribution channel (see Figure 3.1).

Figure 3.1 Example of a distribution channel

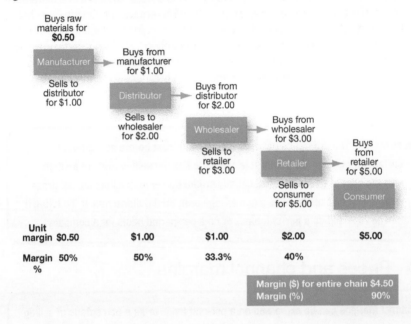

In some industries, such as imported beer, there may be as many as four or five channel members that sequentially apply their own margins before a product reaches the consumer. In such cases, it is particularly important to understand channel margins and pricing practices in order to evaluate the effects of price changes.

Remember: Selling Price = Cost + Margin

Construction

First, decide whether you want to work "backward," from customer selling prices to supplier selling prices, or "forward." We provide two equations to use in working backward, one for dollar margins and the other for percentage margins:

Supplier Selling Price ($) = Customer Selling Price ($) − Customer Margin ($)

Supplier Selling Price ($) = Customer Selling Price ($) * [1 − Customer Margin (%)]

Example Aaron owns a small furniture store. He buys BookCo brand bookcases from a local distributor for $200 per unit. Aaron is considering buying directly from BookCo, and he wants to calculate what he would pay if he received the same price that BookCo charges his distributor. Aaron knows that the distributor's percentage margin is 30%.

The manufacturer supplies the distributor. That is, in this link of the chain, the manufacturer is the supplier, and the distributor is the customer. Thus, because we know the customer's percentage margin, in order to calculate the manufacturer's price to Aaron's distributor, we can use the second of the two previous equations:

$$\text{Supplier Selling Price (\$)} = \text{Customer Selling Price (\$)}$$
$$* [1 - \text{Customer Margin (\%)}]$$
$$= \$200 * 70\% = \$140$$

Aaron's distributor buys each bookcase for $140 and sells it for $200, earning a margin of $60 (30%).

Although the previous example may be the most intuitive version of this formula, by rearranging the equation, we can also work forward in the chain, from supplier prices to customer selling prices. In a forward-looking construction, we can solve for the customer selling price—that is, the price charged to the next level of the chain, moving toward the end consumer.[2]

$$\text{Customer Selling Price (\$)} = \frac{\text{Supplier Selling Price (\$)}}{[1 - \text{Customer Margin (\%)}]}$$

$$\text{Customer Selling Price (\$)} = \text{Supplier Selling Price (\$)} + \text{Customer Margin (\$)}$$

Example Clyde's Concrete sells 100 cubic yards of concrete for $300 to a road construction contractor. The contractor wants to include this in her bill of materials, to be charged to a local government (see Figure 3.2). Further, she wants to earn a 25% margin. What is the contractor's selling price for the concrete?

Figure 3.2 Customer relationships

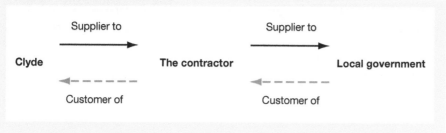

This question focuses on the link between Clyde's Concrete (supplier) and the contractor (customer). We know the supplier's selling price is $300, and the customer's intended margin is 25%. With this information, we can use the first of the two previous equations.

$$\text{Customer Selling Price} = \frac{\text{Supplier Selling Price}}{(1 - \text{Customer Margin \%})}$$

$$= \frac{\$300}{(1 - 25\%)}$$

$$= \frac{\$300}{75\%} = \$400$$

To verify our calculations, we can determine the contractor's percentage margin, based on a selling price of $400 and a cost of $300.

$$\text{Customer Margin} = \frac{(\text{Customer Selling Price} - \text{Supplier Selling Price})}{\text{Customer Selling Price}}$$

$$= \frac{(\$400 - \$300)}{\$400}$$

$$= \frac{\$100}{\$400} = 25\%$$

First Channel Member's Selling Price

Equipped with these equations and with knowledge of all the margins in a chain of distribution, we can work all the way back to the selling price of the first channel member in the chain.

First Channel Member's Selling Price ($) = Last Channel Member's Selling Price ($) * [1 − Last Channel Margin (%)] * [1 − Next-to-last Channel Margin (%)] * [1 − Next-to-next-to-last Channel Margin (%)] . . . and so on

Example The following margins are received at various steps along the chain of distribution for a jar of pasta sauce that sells for a retail price of $5.00 (see Table 3.4).

What does it cost the manufacturer to produce a jar of pasta sauce? The retail selling price ($5.00), multiplied by 1 less the retailer margin, will yield the wholesaler

Table 3.4 Example: pasta sauce distribution margins

Distribution Stage	Margin
Manufacturer	50%
Distributor	50%
Wholesaler	33%
Retailer	40%

selling price. The wholesaler selling price can also be viewed as the cost to the retailer. The *cost* to the wholesaler (distributor selling price) can be found by multiplying the wholesaler selling price by 1 less the wholesaler margin, and so forth. Alternatively, one might follow the next procedure, using a channel member's percentage margin to calculate its dollar margin, and then subtracting that figure from the channel member's selling price to obtain its cost (see Table 3.5).

Table 3.5 Cost (purchase price) of retailer

Stage	Margin %	$
Cost to Consumer		$5.00
Retailer Margin	40%	$2.00
Cost to Retailer		$3.00
Wholesaler Margin	33%	$1.00
Cost to Wholesaler		$2.00
Distributor Margin	50%	$1.00
Cost to Distributor		$1.00
Manufacturer Margin	50%	$0.50
Manufacturer's Cost		$0.50

Thus, a jar of pasta that sells for $5.00 at retail actually costs the manufacturer 50 cents to make.

The margins taken at multiple levels of a distribution process can have a dramatic effect on the price paid by consumers. To work backward in analyzing these, many people find it easier to convert markups to margins. Working forward does not require this conversion.

Example To show that margins and markups are two sides of the same coin, let's demonstrate that we can obtain the same sequence of prices by using the markup method here. Let's look at how the pasta sauce is marked up to arrive at a final consumer price of $5.00.

As noted previously, the manufacturer's cost is $0.50. The manufacturer's percentage markup is 100%. Thus, we can calculate its dollar markup as $0.50 ∗ 100% = $0.50. Adding the manufacturer's markup to its cost, we arrive at its selling price: $0.50 (cost) + $0.50 (markup) = $1.00. The manufacturer sells the sauce to a distributor for $1.00. The distributor applies a markup of 100%, taking the price to $2.00, and sells the sauce to a wholesaler. The wholesaler applies a markup of 50% and sells the sauce to a retailer for $3.00. Finally, the retailer applies a markup of 66.7% and sells the pasta sauce to a consumer for $5.00. In Table 3.6, we track these markups to show the pasta sauce's journey from a manufacturer's cost of $0.50 to a retail price (consumer's cost) of $5.00.

Table 3.6 Markups along the distribution channel

Stage	Markup %	$	Margin
Manufacturer's Cost		$0.50	
Manufacturer Markup	100%	$0.50	50%
Cost to Distributor		$1.00	
Distributor Markup	100%	$1.00	50%
Cost to Wholesaler		$2.00	
Wholesaler Markup	50%	$1.00	33.3%
Cost to Retailer		$3.00	
Retailer Markup	67%	$2.00	40%
Cost to Consumer		$5.00	

Data sources, complications, and cautions

The information needed to calculate channel margins is the same as for basic margins. Complications arise, however, because of the layers involved. In this structure, the selling price for one layer in the chain becomes the cost to the next layer. This is clearly visible in consumer goods industries, where there are often multiple levels of distribution between the manufacturer and the consumer, and each channel member requires its own margin.

Cost and selling price depend on location within the chain. One must always ask, "Whose cost is this?" and "Who sells at this price?" The process of "chaining" a sequence of margins is not difficult. One need only clarify who sells to whom. In tracking this, it can help first to draw a horizontal line and label all the channel members along the chain, with the manufacturer at the far left and the retailer on the right. For example, if a beer exporter in Germany sells to an importer in the United States, and that importer sells to a distributor in Virginia, who sells the beer to a retailer, then four distinct selling prices and three channel margins will intervene between the exporter and retail store customer. In this scenario, the exporter is the first supplier. The importer is the first customer. To avoid confusion, we recommend mapping out the channel and calculating margins, purchase prices, and selling prices at each level.

Throughout this section, we've assumed that all margins are "gross margins," calculated as selling price minus cost of goods sold. Of course, channel members will incur other costs in the process of "adding value." If a wholesaler pays his salespeople a commission on sales, for example, that would be a cost of doing business. But it would not be a part of the cost of goods sold, and so it is not factored into gross margin.

Related metrics and concepts

Hybrid (mixed) channel margins

> **Hybrid Channel:** The use of multiple distribution systems to reach the same market. A company might approach consumers through stores, the internet, and telemarketing, for example. Margins often differ among such channels. Hybrid channels may also be known as mixed channels.

Increasingly, businesses "go to market" in more than one way. An insurance company, for example, might sell policies through independent agents, toll-free telephone lines, and the internet. Multiple channels often generate different channel margins and cause a supplier to incur different support costs. As business migrates from one channel to another, marketers must adjust pricing and support in economically sensible ways. To make appropriate decisions, they must recognize the more profitable channels in their mix and develop programs and strategies to fit these.

When selling through multiple channels with different margins, it is important to perform analyses on the basis of *weighted* average channel margins, as opposed to a simple average. Using a simple average can lead to confusion and poor decision making.

As an example of the variations that can occur, let's suppose that a company sells ten units of its product through six channels. It sells five units through one channel at a 20% margin, and one unit through each of the other five channels at a 50% margin. Calculating its average margin on a weighted basis, we arrive at the following figure:

$$\text{Percentage Margin (\%)} = \frac{[(5 * 20\%) + (5 * 50\%)]}{10} = 35\%$$

By contrast, if we calculate the average margin among this firm's six channels on a simple basis, we arrive at a very different figure:

$$\text{Percentage Margin (\%)} = \frac{[(1 * 20\%) + (5 * 50\%)]}{6} = 45\%$$

This difference in margin could significantly blur management decision making.

Average margin

When assessing margin in dollar terms, use percentage of unit sales.

Average Margin (\$) = [Percentage of Unit Sales through Channel 1 (%) * Margin Earned in Channel 1 (\$)] + [Percentage of Unit Sales through Channel 2 (%) * Margin Earned in Channel 2 (\$)] + Continued to Last Channel

When assessing margin in percentage terms, use percentage of dollar sales.

Average Margin (%) = [Percentage of Dollar Sales through Channel 1 (%) * Margin Earned in Channel 1 (%)] + [Percentage of Dollar Sales through Channel 2 (%) * Margin Earned in Channel 2 (%)] + Continued to Last Channel

Example Gael's Glass sells through three channels: phone, online, and store. These channels generate the following margins: 50%, 40%, and 30%, respectively. When Gael's wife asks what his average margin is, he initially calculates a simple margin and says it's 40%. Gael's wife investigates further, however, and learns that her husband answered too quickly. Gael's company sells a total of ten units. It sells one unit by phone at a 50% margin, four units online at a 40% margin, and five units in the store at a 30% margin. To determine the company's average margin among these channels, the margin in each must be weighted by its relative sales volume. On this basis, Gael's wife calculates the weighted average margin as follows:

Average Channel Margin = (Percentage of Unit Sales by Phone * Phone Channel Margin) + (Percentage of Unit Sales Online * Online Channel Margin) + (Percentage of Unit Sales through Store * Store Channel Margin)

= (1/10 * 50%) + (4/10 * 40%) + (5/10 * 30%)

= 5% + 16% + 15%

Average Channel Margin = 36%

Example Sadetta, Inc. has two channels—online and retail—which generate the following results: One customer orders online, paying $10 for one unit of goods that costs the company $5. This generates a 50% margin for Sadetta. A second customer shops at the store, buying two units of product for $12 each. Each costs $9. Thus, Sadetta earns a 25% margin on these sales. Summarizing:

Online Margin (1) = 50%. Selling Price (1) = $10. Supplier Selling Price (1) = $5.

Store Margin (2) = 25%. Selling Price (2) = $12. Supplier Selling Price (2) = $9.

In this scenario, the relative weightings are easy to establish. In unit terms, Sadetta sells a total of three units: one unit (33.3%) online and two (66.6%) in the store. In dollar terms, Sadetta generates a total of $34 in sales: $10 (29.4%) online and $24 (70.6%) in the store.

Thus, Sadetta's average unit margin ($) can be calculated as follows: The online channel generates a $5 margin, and the store generates a $3 margin. The relative weightings are online 33.3% and store 66.6%.

Average Unit Margin ($) = [Percentage Unit Sales Online (%) * Unit Margin Online ($)]
+ [Percentage Unit Sales in Store (%) * Unit Margin in Store ($)]

= 33.3% * $5.00 + 66.6% * $3.00

= $1.67 + $2.00

= $3.67

Sadetta's average margin (%) can be calculated as follows: The online channel generates a 50% margin, while the store generates a 25% margin. The relative weightings are online 29.4% and store 70.6%.

Average Margin (%) = [Percentage Dollar Sales Online (%) * Margin Online (%)]
+ [Percentage Dollar Sales in Store (%) * Margin in Store (%)]

= 29.4% * 50% + 70.6% * 25%

= 14.70% + 17.65%

= 32.35%

Average margins can also be calculated directly from company totals. Sadetta generated a total gross margin of $11 by selling three units of product. Its average unit margin was thus $11/3, or $3.67. Similarly, we can derive Sadetta's average percentage margin by dividing its total margin by its total revenue. This yields a result that matches our weighted previous calculations: $11/$34 = 32.35%.

The same weighting process is needed to calculate average selling prices.

Average Selling Price ($) = [Percentage Unit Sales through Channel 1 (%)
* Selling Price in Channel 1 ($)] + [Percentage
Unit Sales through Channel 2 (%) * Selling Price
in Channel 2 ($)] + Continued to [Percentage Unit
Sales through the Last Channel (%)
* Last Channel's Selling Price ($)]

Example Continuing the previous example, we can see how Sadetta, Inc. calculates its average selling price.

Sadetta's online customer pays $10 per item. Its store customer pays $12 per item. Weighting each channel by unit sales, we can derive Sadetta's average selling price as follows:

Average Selling Price ($) = [Percentage Unit Sales Online (%) * Selling Price
Online ($)] + [Percentage Unit Sales in Store (%) *
Selling Price in Store ($)]

= 33.3% * $10 + 66.7% * $12

= $3.33 + $8

= $11.33

The calculation of average supplier selling price is conceptually similar.

Average Supplier Selling Price ($) = [Percentage Unit Sales through Channel
1 (%) * Supplier Selling Price in Channel
1 ($)] + [Percentage Unit Sales through
Channel 2 (%) * Supplier Selling Price in
Channel 2 ($)] + Continued to [Percentage
Unit Sales through the Last Channel (%)
* Last Channel Supplier's Selling Price ($)]

Example Now, let's consider how Sadetta, Inc. calculates its average supplier selling price.

Sadetta's online merchandise cost the company $5 per unit. Its in-store merchandise cost $9 per unit. Thus:

Average Supplier Selling Price ($) = [Percentage Unit Sales Online (%)
* Supplier Selling Price Online ($)] +
[Percentage Unit Sales through Store (%)
* Supplier Selling Price in Store ($)]

$$= 33.3\% * \$5 + 66.7\% * \$9$$

$$= \$1.67 + \$6 = \$7.67$$

With all these pieces of the puzzle, we now have much greater insight into Sadetta, Inc.'s business (see Table 3.7).

Table 3.7 Sadetta's channel measures

	Online	In store	Average/total
Selling Price (SP)	$10.00	$12.00	
Supplier Selling Price (SSP)	$5.00	$9.00	
Unit Margin ($)	$5.00	$3.00	
Margin (%)	50%	25%	
Units Sold	1	2	3
% Unit Sales	33.3%	66.7%	
Dollar Sales	$10.00	$24.00	$34.00
% Dollar Sales	29.4%	70.6%	
Total Margin	$5.00	$6.00	$11.00
Average Unit Margin ($)			$3.67
Average Margin (%)			32.4%
Average Selling Price			$11.33
Average Supplier Selling Price			$7.67

3.3 Average price per unit and price per statistical unit

Average prices represent, quite simply, total sales revenue divided by total units sold. Many products, however, are sold in multiple variants, such as bottle sizes. In such cases, managers face a challenge: They must determine "comparable" units.

Average prices can be calculated by weighting different unit selling prices by the percentage of unit sales (mix) for each product variant. If we use a standard, rather than an actual, mix of sizes and product varieties, the result is price per statistical unit. Statistical units are also known as equivalent units.

$$\text{Average Price per Unit } (\$) = \frac{\text{Revenue } (\$)}{\text{Unit Sold } (\#)}$$

or

$$= [\text{Price of SKU 1}(\$) * \text{SKU 1 Percentage of Sales } (\%)]$$
$$+ [\text{Price of SKU 2}(\$) * \text{SKU 2 Percentage of Sales } (\%)]$$

$$\text{Price per Statistical Unit } (\$) = \text{Total Price of a Bundle of SKUs Comprising a Statistical Unit } (\$)$$

$$\text{Unit Price per Statistical Unit } (\$) = \frac{\text{Price per Statistical Unit } (\$)}{\text{Total Units in the Bundle of SKUs Comprising That Statistical Unit } (\#)}$$

Average price per unit and prices per statistical unit are needed by marketers who sell the same product in different packages, sizes, forms, or configurations at a variety of different prices. As in analyses of different channels, these product and price variations must be reflected accurately in overall average prices. If they are not, marketers may lose sight of what is happening to prices and why. If the price of each product variant remained unchanged, for example, but the mix of volume sold shifted, then the average price per unit would change, but the price per statistical unit would not. Both of these metrics have value in identifying market movements.

Purpose: to calculate meaningful average selling prices within a product line that includes items of different prices.

Many brands or product lines include multiple models, versions, flavors, colors, sizes, or—more generally—stock keeping units (SKUs). Brita water filters, for example, are sold in a number of SKUs. They are sold in single-filter packs, double-filter packs, and special banded packs that may be restricted to club stores. They are sold on a stand-alone basis and in combination with pitchers. These various packages and product forms may be known as SKUs, models, items, and so on.

Stock Keeping Unit (SKU): A term used by retailers to identify individual items that are carried, or "stocked," within an assortment. This is the most detailed level at which the inventory and sales of individual products are recorded.

Marketers often want to know both their own average prices and those of retailers. By reckoning in terms of SKUs, they can calculate an average price per unit at any level in the distribution chain. Two of the most useful of these averages are

- A unit price average that includes all sales of all SKUs, expressed as an average price per defined unit. In the water filter industry, for example, these might include such figures as $2.23/filter, $0.03/filtered ounce, and so on.

- A price per statistical unit that consists of a fixed bundle (number) of individual SKUs. This bundle is often constructed to reflect the actual mix of sales of the various SKUs.

The average price per unit changes when there is a shift in the percentage of sales represented by SKUs with different unit prices. It also changes when the prices of the individual SKUs are modified. This contrasts with price per statistical unit, which, by definition, has a fixed proportion of each SKU. Consequently, a price per statistical unit changes only when there is a change in the price of one or more of the SKUs included in it.

The information gleaned from a price per statistical unit can be helpful in considering price movements within a market. Price per statistical unit, in combination with unit price averages, provides insight into the degree to which the average prices in a market are changing as a result of shifts in "mix"—proportions of sales generated by differently priced SKUs—versus price changes for individual items. Alterations in mix—such as a relative increase in the sale of larger versus smaller ice cream tubs at retail grocers, for example—affect average unit price but not price per statistical unit. Pricing changes in the SKUs that make up a statistical unit, however, lead to a change in the price of that statistical unit.

Construction

As with other marketing averages, average price per unit can be calculated either from company totals or from the prices and shares of individual SKUs.

$$\text{Average Price per Unit (\$)} = \frac{\text{Revenue (\$)}}{\text{Unit Sales (\#)}}$$

or

$$= [\text{Unit Price of SKU 1(\$)} * \text{SKU 1 Percentage of Sales (\%)}] + [\text{Unit Price of SKU 2(\$)} * \text{SKU 2 Percentage of Sales (\%)}] + \text{and so forth}$$

The average price per unit depends on both unit prices and unit sales of individual SKUs. The average price per unit can be driven upward by a rise in unit prices, or by an increase in the unit shares of higher-priced SKUs, or by a combination of the two.

An "average" price metric that is not sensitive to changes in SKU shares is the price per statistical unit.

Price per statistical unit

Procter & Gamble and other companies face a challenge in monitoring prices for a wide variety of product sizes, package types, and product formulations. Many consumer brands have multiple SKUs, and each SKU may have a different price. In these situations, how do marketers determine a brand's overall price level in order to compare it to competitive offerings or to track whether prices are rising or falling? One solution is to use the "statistical unit," also known as the "statistical case" or—in volumetric or weight measures—the statistical liter or statistical ton. A statistical case of 288 ounces of liquid detergent, for example, might be defined as comprising

Four 4-oz bottles = 16 oz

Twelve 12-oz bottles = 144 oz

Two 32-oz bottles = 64 oz

One 64-oz bottle = 64 oz

Note that the contents of this statistical case were carefully chosen so that it contains the same number of ounces as a standard case of 24 12-ounce bottles. In this way, the statistical case is comparable in size to a standard case. The advantage of a statistical case is that its contents can approximate the mix of SKUs the company actually sells.

Whereas a statistical case of liquid detergent will be filled with whole bottles, in other instances a statistical unit might contain fractions of certain packaging sizes in order for its total contents to match a required volumetric or weight total.

Statistical units are composed of fixed proportions of different SKUs. These fixed proportions ensure that changes in the prices of the statistical unit reflect only changes in the *prices* of the SKUs that comprise it.

The price of a statistical unit can be expressed either as a total price for the bundle of SKUs comprising it or in terms of that total price divided by the total volume of its contents. The former might be called the "price per statistical unit"; the latter, the "unit price per statistical unit."

Example Carl's Coffee Creamer (CCC) is sold in three sizes: a 1-liter economy size, a 0.5-liter "fridge-friendly" package, and a 0.05-liter single serving. Carl defines a 12-liter statistical case of CCC as

2 units of the economy size = 2 liters (2 * 1.0 liter)

19 units of the fridge-friendly package = 9.5 liters (19 * 0.5 liter)

10 single servings = 0.5 liter (10 * .05)

Prices for each size and the calculation of total price for the statistical unit are shown in Table 3.8.

Table 3.8 Statistical unit price

SKU Names	Size	Price of item	Number in statistical case	Liters in statistical case	Total price
Economy	1 liter	$8.00	2	2.0	$16.00
Fridge-Friendly	0.5 liter	$6.00	19	9.5	$114.00
Single Serving	0.05 liter	$1.00	10	0.5	$10.00
Total				12	$140.00

Thus, the total price of the 12-liter statistical case of CCC is $140. The per-liter price within the statistical case is $11.67.

Note that the $140 price of the statistical case is higher than the $96 price of a case of 12 economy packs. This higher price reflects the fact that smaller packages of CCC command a higher price per liter. If the proportions of the SKUs in the statistical case exactly match the actual proportions sold, then the per-liter price of the statistical case will match the per-liter price of the actual liters sold.

Example Carl sells 10,000 1-liter economy packs of CCC, 80,000 fridge-friendly 0.5-liter packs, and 40,000 single servings. What is his average price per liter?

$$\text{Average Price per Unit (\$)} = \frac{\text{Revenue (\$)}}{\text{Unit Sales (\#)}}$$

$$= \frac{(\$8 * 10k + \$6 * 80k + \$1 * 40k)}{(1 * 10k + 0.5 * 80k + 0.05 * 40k)}$$

$$= \frac{\$600k}{52k} = \$11.54$$

Note that Carl's average price per liter, at $11.54, is less than the per-liter price in his statistical case. The reason is straightforward: Whereas fridge-friendly packs outnumber economy packs by almost ten to one in the statistical case, the actual sales ratio of these SKUs was only eight to one. Similarly, whereas the ratio of single-serving items to economy items in the statistical case is five to one, their actual sales ratio was only four to one. Carl's company sold a smaller percentage of the higher (per liter) priced items than was represented in its statistical case. Consequently, its actual average price per liter was less than the per-liter price within its statistical unit.

Table 3.9 illustrates the calculation of the average price per unit as the weighted average of the unit prices and unit shares of the three SKUs of Carl's Coffee Creamer. Unit prices and unit (per-liter) shares are provided.

Table 3.9 Weighted unit price

SKU Name	Size	Price	SKUs sold	Units sold (Liters)	Unit price (per Liter)	Unit share
Economy	1 liter	$8	10k	10k	$8	19.23%
Fridge-Friendly	0.5 liter	$6	80k	40k	$12	76.92%
Single Serving	0.05 liter	$1	40k	2k	$20	3.85%
Total			130k	52k		100%

On this basis, the average price per unit ($) = ($8 * 0.1923) + ($12 * 0.7692) + ($20 * 0.0385) = $11.54.

Data sources, complications, and cautions

With complex and changing product lines, and with different selling prices charged by different retailers, marketers need to understand a number of methodologies for calculating average prices. Merely determining how many units of a product are sold, and at what price, throughout the market is a major challenge. As a standard method of tracking prices, marketers use statistical units, which are based on constant proportions of sales of different SKUs in a product line.

Typically, the proportions of SKUs in a statistical unit correspond—at least approximately—to historical market sales. Sales patterns can change, however. In consequence, these proportions need to be monitored carefully in evolving markets and changing product lines.

Calculating a meaningful average price is complicated by the need to differentiate between changes in sales mix and changes in the prices of statistical units. In some industries, it is difficult to construct appropriate units for analyzing price and sales data. In the chemical industry, for example, an herbicide might be sold in a variety of different sizes, applicators, and concentration levels. When we factor in the complexity of different prices and different assortments offered by competing retail outlets, calculating and tracking average prices becomes a non-trivial exercise.

Similar challenges arise in estimating inflation. Economists calculate inflation by using a basket of goods. Their estimates might vary considerably, depending on the goods included. It is also difficult to capture quality improvements in inflation figures. Is a 2015 car, for example, truly comparable to a car built 30 years earlier?

In evaluating price increases, marketers are advised to bear in mind that a consumer who shops for large quantities at discount stores may view such increases very differently from a retiree who buys small quantities at local stores. Establishing a "standard" basket for such different consumers requires astute judgment. In seeking to summarize the aggregate of such price increases throughout an economy, economists may view inflation as, in effect, a statistical unit price measure for that economy.

3.4 Variable costs and fixed costs

Variable costs can be aggregated into a total or expressed on a per-unit basis. Fixed costs, by definition, do not change with the number of units sold or produced. Variable costs are assumed to be relatively constant on a per-unit basis. Total variable costs increase directly and predictably with unit sales volume. Fixed costs, on the other hand, do not change as a direct result of short-term unit sales increases or decreases.

$$\text{Total Costs (\$)} = \text{Fixed Costs (\$)} + \text{Total Variable Costs (\$)}$$

$$\text{Total Variable Costs (\$)} = \text{Unit Volume (\#)} * \text{Variable Cost per Unit (\$)}$$

Marketers need to have an idea of how costs divide between variable and fixed. This distinction is crucial in forecasting the earnings generated by various changes in unit sales and thus the financial impact of proposed marketing campaigns. It is also fundamental to an understanding of price and volume trade-offs.

Purpose: to understand how costs change with volume.

At first glance, variable versus fixed costs appears to be an easy subject to master. If a marketing campaign will generate 10,000 units of additional sales, we need only know how much it will cost to supply that additional volume.

The problem, of course, is that no one really knows how changes in quantity will affect a firm's total costs—in part because the workings of a firm can be complex. Companies simply can't afford to employ armies of accountants to answer every possible expense question precisely. Indeed, some questions can't really be answered precisely. Instead, we often use a simple model of cost behavior that is good enough for most purposes. Models of cost behavior usually have to strike compromises between the complexity and expense of achieving precision and ease of implementation and administration.

Construction

The standard linear equation, $Y = mX + b$, helps explain the relationship between total costs and unit volume. In this application, Y will represent a company's total cost, m will be its variable cost per unit, X will represent the quantity of products sold (or produced), and b will represent the fixed cost (see Figure 3.3).

Figure 3.3 Fixed and variable costs

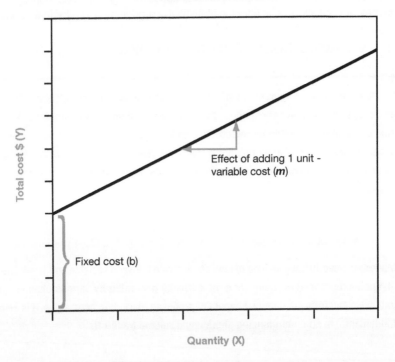

Fixed and variable costs

Total Cost ($) = Variable Cost per Unit ($) * Quantity (#) + Fixed Cost ($)

On this basis, to determine a company's total cost for any given quantity of prod-ucts, we need only multiply its variable cost per unit by that quantity and add its fixed cost.

To communicate fully the implications of fixed costs and variable costs, it may help to separate this graph into two parts (see Figure 3.4).

By definition, fixed costs remain the same, regardless of volume. Consequently, they are represented by a horizontal line across the graph in Figure 3.4. Fixed costs do not increase vertically—that is, they do not add to the total cost—as quantity rises.

The result of multiplying variable cost per unit by quantity is often called the *total variable cost*. Variable costs differ from fixed costs in that, when there is no pro-duction, their total is zero. Their total increases in a steadily rising line, however, as quantity increases.

We can represent this model of cost behavior in a simple equation:

Total Cost ($) = Total Variable Cost ($) + Fixed Cost ($)

Figure 3.4 Total cost consists of fixed and variable costs

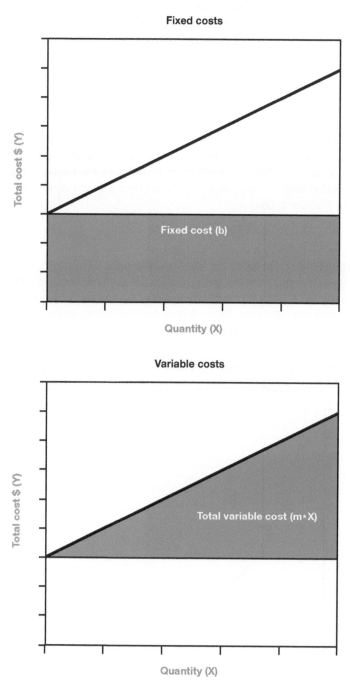

Fixed costs

Total cost $ (Y)

Fixed cost (b)

Quantity (X)

Variable costs

Total cost $ (Y)

Total variable cost (m*X)

Quantity (X)

To use this model, of course, we must place each of a firm's costs into one or the other of these two categories. If an expense does not change with volume (rent, for example), then it is part of fixed costs and will remain the same, regardless of how many units the firm produces or sells. If a cost *does* change with volume (sales commissions, for example), then it is a variable cost.

Total Variable Costs ($) = Unit Volume (#) * Variable Cost per Unit ($)

Total cost per unit

It is possible to express the total cost for a given quantity on a per-unit basis. The result might be called total cost per unit, unit total cost, average cost, full cost, or even fully loaded cost. For our simple linear cost model, the total cost per unit can be calculated in either of two ways. The most obvious would be to divide the total cost by the number of units.

$$\text{Total Cost per Unit (\$)} = \frac{\text{Total Cost (\$)}}{\text{Quantity (\#)}}$$

This can be plotted graphically, and it tells an interesting tale (see Figure 3.5). As the quantity rises, the total cost per unit (average cost per unit) declines. The shape of this curve will vary among firms with different cost structures, but wherever there are both fixed and variable costs, the total cost per unit will decline as fixed costs are spread across an increasing quantity of units.

Figure 3.5 Total cost per unit falls with volume (typical assumptions)

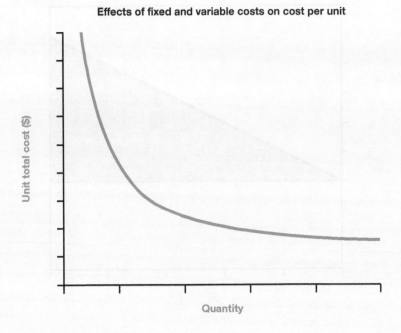

Effects of fixed and variable costs on cost per unit

Quantity

The apportionment of fixed costs across units produced leads us to another common formula for the total cost per unit:

Total Cost per Unit (\$) = Variable Cost per Unit (\$) + [Fixed Cost (\$)/Quantity (#)]

As the quantity increases—that is, as fixed costs are spread over an increasing number of units—the total cost per unit declines in a non-linear way.[3]

Example As a company's unit sales increase, its fixed costs hold steady at \$500. The variable cost per unit remains constant at \$10 per unit. Total variable costs increase with each unit sold. The total cost per unit (also known as average total cost) decreases as incremental units are sold and as fixed costs are spread across this rising quantity. Eventually, as more and more units are produced and sold, the company's total cost per unit approaches its variable cost per unit (see Table 3.10).

Table 3.10 Fixed and variable costs at increasing volume levels

Units Sold	1	10	100	1,000
Fixed Costs	\$500	\$500	\$500	\$500
Total Variable Costs	\$10	\$100	\$1,000	\$10,000
Total Costs	\$510	\$600	\$1,500	\$10,500
Total Cost per Unit	\$510.00	\$60.00	\$15.00	\$10.50
Variable Cost per Unit	\$10	\$10	\$10	\$10

In summary, the simplest model of cost behavior is to assume total costs increase linearly with quantity supplied. Total costs are composed of fixed and variable costs. Total cost per unit decreases in a non-linear way with rising quantity supplied.

Data sources, complications, and cautions

Total cost is typically assumed to be a linear function of quantity supplied. That is, the graph of total cost versus quantity will be a straight line. Because some costs are fixed, total cost starts at a level above zero, even when no units are produced. This is because fixed costs include expenses such as factory rent and salaries for full-time employees, which must be paid regardless of whether any goods are produced and sold. Total variable costs, by contrast, rise and fall with quantity. Within our model, however, variable cost *per unit* is assumed to hold constant—at \$10 per unit for example—regardless of whether 1 unit or 1,000 units are produced. This is a useful model. In using it, however, marketers must recognize that it fails to account for certain complexities.

The linear cost model does not fit every situation

Quantity discounts, expectations of future process improvements, and capacity limitations, among other factors, introduce dynamics that limit the usefulness of the fundamental linear cost equation.

$$\text{Total Cost} = \text{Fixed Cost} + \text{Variable Cost per Unit} * \text{Quantity}$$

Even the notion that quantity determines the total cost can be questioned. Although firms pay for *inputs*, such as raw materials and labor, marketers want to know the cost of the firm's *outputs*—that is, finished goods sold. This distinction is clear in theory. In practice, however, it can be difficult to uncover the precise relationship between a quantity of outputs and the total cost of the wide array of inputs that go into it.

The classification of costs as fixed or variable depends on context

Even though the linear model may not work in all situations, it does provide a reasonable approximation for cost behavior in many contexts. Some marketers have trouble, however, with the fact that certain costs can be considered fixed in some contexts and variable in others. In general, for shorter time frames and modest changes in quantity, many costs are fixed. For longer time frames and larger changes in quantity, most costs are variable. Let's consider rent, for example. Small changes in quantity do not require a change in workspace or business location. In such cases, rent should be regarded as a fixed cost. A major change in quantity, however, would require more or less workspace. Rent, therefore, would become variable over that range of quantity.

Don't confuse total cost per unit with variable cost per unit

In our linear cost equation, the variable cost per unit is the amount by which total costs increase if the firm increases its quantity by one unit. This number should not be confused with the total cost per unit, calculated as

$$\text{Total Cost per Unit} = \text{Variable Cost per Unit} + (\text{Fixed Cost}/\text{Quantity})$$

If a firm has fixed costs, then its total cost per unit will always be greater than the variable cost per unit. Total cost per unit represents the firm's average cost per unit at the current quantity—and *only* at the current quantity. Do not make the mistake of thinking of total cost per unit as a figure that applies to changing quantities. Total cost per unit only applies at the volume at which it was calculated.

A related misunderstanding may arise at times from the fact that total cost per unit generally decreases with rising quantity. Some marketers use this fact to argue for aggressively increasing quantity in order to "bring our costs down" and improve profitability. Total cost, by contrast with total cost *per unit*, almost always increases with quantity. Only with certain quantity discounts or rebates that "kick in" when target volumes are reached can total cost decrease as volume increases.

3.5 Marketing spending—total, fixed, and variable

To predict how selling costs change with sales, a firm must distinguish between fixed selling costs and variable selling costs.

Total Selling (Marketing) Costs ($) = Total Fixed Selling Costs ($)

+ Total Variable Selling Costs ($)

Total Variable Selling Costs ($) = Revenue ($) * Variable Selling Cost (%)

Recognizing the difference between fixed and variable selling costs can help firms account for the relative risks associated with alternative sales strategies. In general, strategies that incur variable selling costs are less risky because variable selling costs will remain lower in the event that sales fail to meet expectations.

Purpose: to forecast marketing spending and assess budgeting risk.

Marketing spending: Total expenditure on marketing activities. This typically includes advertising and non-price promotion. It sometimes includes sales force spending and may also include price promotions.

Marketing costs are often a major part of a firm's overall discretionary expenditures. As such, they are important determinants of short-term profits. Of course, marketing and selling budgets can also be viewed as investments in acquiring and maintaining customers. From either perspective, however, it is useful to distinguish between fixed marketing costs and variable marketing costs. That is, managers must recognize which marketing costs will hold steady and which will change with sales. Generally, this classification requires a line-item-by-line-item review of the entire marketing budget.

In prior sections, we have viewed total variable costs as expenses that vary with unit sales volume. With respect to selling costs, we need a slightly different conception. Rather than varying with unit sales, total variable selling costs are more likely to vary directly with the monetary value of the units sold—that is, with revenue. Thus, it is more likely that variable selling costs will be expressed as a percentage of revenue rather than as a certain monetary amount per unit.

The classification of selling costs as fixed or variable depends on an organization's structure and on the specific decisions of management. A number of items, however, typically fall into one category or the other—with the proviso that their status as fixed or variable can be time specific. In the long run, all costs eventually become variable.

Over typical planning periods of a quarter or a year, fixed marketing costs might include

- Sales force salaries and support

- Major advertising campaigns, including production costs

- Marketing staff

- Sales promotion material, such as point-of-purchase sales aids, coupon production, and distribution costs

- Cooperative advertising allowances based on prior-period sales

Variable marketing costs might include

- Sales commissions paid to sales force, brokers, or manufacturer representatives

- Sales bonuses contingent on reaching sales goals

- Off-invoice and performance allowances to trade, which are tied to current volume

- Early payment terms (if included in sales promotion budgets)

- Coupon face-value payments and rebates, including processing fees

- Bill-backs for local campaigns conducted by retailers but reimbursed by national brand and cooperative advertising allowances, based on current-period sales

Marketers often don't consider their budgets in fixed and variable terms, but they can derive at least two benefits by doing so.

First, if marketing spending is in fact variable, then budgeting in this way is more accurate. Some marketers budget a *fixed* amount and then face an end-of-period discrepancy, or "variance," if sales miss their declared targets. By contrast, a flexible budget—that is, one that takes account of its genuinely variable components—will reflect actual results, regardless of where sales end up.

Second, the short-term risks associated with fixed marketing costs are greater than those associated with variable marketing costs. If marketers expect revenues to be sensitive to factors outside their control—such as competitive actions or production shortages—they can reduce risk by including more variable and less fixed spending in their budgets.

A classic decision that hinges on fixed marketing costs versus variable marketing costs is the choice between engaging third-party contract sales representatives versus an in-house sales force. Hiring a salaried—or predominantly salaried—sales force entails more risk than the alternative because salaries must be paid even if the firm fails to achieve its revenue targets. By contrast, when a firm uses third-party brokers to sell its goods on commission, its selling costs decline when sales targets are not met.

Construction

$$\text{Total Selling (Marketing) Costs (\$)} = \text{Total Fixed Selling Costs (\$)}$$
$$+ \text{Total Variable Selling Costs (\$)}$$

$$\text{Total Variable Selling Costs (\$)} = \text{Revenue (\$)} * \text{Variable Selling Cost (\%)}$$

Commissioned sales costs

Sales commissions represent one example of selling costs that vary in proportion to revenue. Consequently, any sales commissions should be included in variable selling costs.

Example Henry's Catsup spends $10 million a year to maintain a sales force that calls on grocery chains and wholesalers. A broker offers to perform the same selling tasks for a 5% commission.

At $100 million in revenue,

$$\text{Total Variable Selling Cost} = \$100 \text{ million} * 5\% = \$5 \text{ million}$$

At $200 million in revenue,

$$\text{Total Variable Selling Cost} = \$200 \text{ million} * 5\% = \$10 \text{ million}$$

At $300 million in revenue,

$$\text{Total Variable Selling Cost} = \$300 \text{ million} * 5\% = \$15 \text{ million}$$

If revenues run less than $200 million, the broker will cost less than the in-house sales force. At $200 million in revenue, the broker will cost the same as the sales force. At revenue levels greater than $200 million, the broker will cost more.

Of course, the transition from a salaried sales staff to a broker may itself cause a change in revenues. Calculating the revenue level at which selling costs are equal is only a starting point for analysis. But it is an important first step in understanding the trade-offs.

There are many types of variable selling costs. For example, selling costs could be based upon a complicated formula specified in a firm's contracts with its brokers and dealers. Selling costs might include incentives to local dealers that are tied to the achievement of specific sales targets. They might include promises to reimburse retailers for spending on cooperative advertising. By contrast, payments to a web-site for a fixed number of impressions or click-throughs, in a contract that calls for specific dollar compensation, would more likely be classified as fixed costs. On the other hand, payments for conversions (sales) would be classified as variable marketing costs.

Example A small manufacturer of a regional food delicacy must select a budget for a television advertising campaign that it plans to launch. Under one plan, it might pay to create a commercial and air it in a certain number of time slots. Its spending level would thus be fixed. It would be selected ahead of time and would not vary with the results of the campaign.

Under an alternative plan, the company could produce the advertisement—still a fixed cost—but ask retailers to air it in their local markets and pay the required media fees to television stations as part of a cooperative advertising arrangement. In return for paying the media fees, local stores would receive a discount (a bill-back) on every unit of the company's product that they sell.

Under the latter plan, the product discount would be a variable cost, as its total amount would depend on the number of units sold. By undertaking such a cooperative advertising campaign, the manufacturer would make its marketing budget a mix of fixed and variable costs. Is such cooperative advertising a good idea? To decide this, the company must determine its expected sales under both arrangements, as well as the consequent economics and its tolerance for risk.

Data sources, complications, and cautions

Fixed costs are often easier to measure than variable costs. Typically, fixed costs might be assembled from payroll records, lease documents, or financial records. For variable costs, it is necessary to measure the rate at which they increase as a function of activity level. Although variable selling costs often represent a predefined percentage of revenue, they may alternatively vary with the number of *units* sold (as in a dollar-per-case discount). An additional complication arises if some variable selling costs apply to only a portion of total sales. This can happen, for example, when some dealers qualify for cash discounts or full-truckload rates and some do not.

In a further complication, some expenses may appear to be fixed when they are actually stepped. That is, they are fixed to a point, but they trigger further expenditures beyond that point. For example, a firm may contract with an advertising agency for up to three campaigns per year. If it decides to buy more than three campaigns, it would incur an incremental cost. Typically, stepped costs can be treated as fixed—provided that the boundaries of analysis are well understood.

Stepped payments can be difficult to model. Rebates for customers whose purchases exceed a certain level and bonuses for salespeople who exceed quota can be challenging functions to describe. Creativity is important in designing marketing discounts. But this creativity can be difficult to reflect in a framework of fixed and variable costs.

In developing their marketing budgets, firms must decide which costs to expense in the current period and which to amortize over several periods. The latter course is appropriate for expenditures that are correctly viewed as investments. One example of such an investment would be a special allowance for financing receivables from new distributors. Rather than add such an allowance to the current period's budget, it would be better to view it as a marketing item that increases the firm's investment in working capital. By contrast, advertising that is projected to generate long-term impact may be loosely called an investment, but it would often be treated as a marketing expense. Although there may be a valid theoretical case for amortizing advertising, that discussion is beyond the scope of this book.

Related metrics and concepts

Levels of marketing spending are often used to compare companies and to demonstrate how heavily they "invest" in this area. For this purpose, marketing spending is generally viewed as a percentage of sales.

> **Marketing as a percentage of sales:** The level of marketing spending as a fraction of sales. This figure provides an indication of how heavily a company is marketing. The appropriate level for this figure varies among products, strategies, and markets.

$$\text{Marketing as a Percentage of Sales (\%)} = \frac{\text{Marketing Spending (\$)}}{\text{Revenue (\$)}}$$

Variants on this metric are used to examine components of marketing in comparison with sales. Examples include trade promotion as a percentage of sales or sales force as a percentage of sales. One particularly common example is advertising as a percentage of sales.

> **Advertising as a percentage of sales:** Advertising expenditures as a fraction of sales. Generally, this is a subset of marketing as a percentage of sales.

Before using such metrics, marketers are advised to determine whether certain marketing costs have already been subtracted in the calculation of sales revenue. Trade allowances, for example, are often deducted from "gross sales" to calculate "net sales."

> **Slotting allowances:** A particular form of selling costs encountered when new items are introduced to retailers or distributors. Essentially, such an allowance represents a charge made by retailers for making a "slot" available for a new item in their stores and warehouses. This charge may take the form of a one-time cash payment, free goods, or a special discount. The exact terms of the slotting allowance determine whether it constitutes a fixed or a variable selling cost or a mix of the two.

3.6   Break-even analysis and contribution analysis

The break-even level represents the sales amount—in either unit or revenue terms—
that is required to cover total costs (both fixed and variable). Profit at break-even is
zero. Break-even is possible only if a firm's prices are higher than its variable costs
per unit. If so, then each unit of product sold will generate some contribution toward
covering fixed costs. The difference between price per unit and variable cost per unit
is defined as contribution per unit.

$$\text{Contribution per Unit (\$)} = \text{Selling Price per Unit (\$)} - \text{Variable Cost per Unit (\$)}^4$$

$$\text{Contribution Margin (\%)} = \frac{\text{Contribution per Unit (\$)}}{\text{Selling Price per Unit (\$)}}$$

$$\text{Break-Even Volume (\#)} = \frac{\text{Fixed Costs (\$)}}{\text{Contribution per Unit (\$)}}$$

$$\text{Break-Even Revenue (\$)} = \text{Break-Even Volume (Units) (\#)} * \text{Price per Unit (\$)}$$

or

$$= \frac{\text{Fixed Costs (\$)}}{\text{Contribution Margin (\%)}}$$

Break-even analysis is the Swiss Army knife of marketing economics. It is useful in a
variety of situations and is often used to evaluate the likely profitability of marketing
actions that affect fixed costs, prices, or variable costs per unit. Break-even is often
derived in a "back-of-the-envelope" calculation that determines whether a more
detailed analysis is warranted.

*Purpose: to provide a rough indicator of the earnings
impact of a marketing activity.*

The break-even point for any business activity is defined as the level of sales at
which neither a profit nor a loss is made on that activity—that is, where Total
Revenues = Total Costs. Provided that a company sells its goods at a price per
unit that is greater than its variable cost per unit, the sale of each unit will make a
contribution toward covering some portion of fixed costs. That contribution can be
calculated as the difference between price per unit (revenue) and variable cost per
unit. On this basis, break-even constitutes the minimum level of sales at which total
contribution fully covers fixed costs.

Construction

To determine the break-even point for a business program, one must first calculate the fixed costs of engaging in that program. For this purpose, managers do not need to estimate projected volumes. Fixed costs are constant, regardless of activity level. Managers do, however, need to calculate the difference between revenue per unit and variable costs per unit. This difference represents contribution per unit ($). Contribution rates can also be expressed as a percentage of selling price.

Example Apprentice Mousetraps wants to know how many units of its Magic Mouse Trapper it must sell to break even. The product sells for $20. It costs $5 per unit to make. The company's fixed costs are $30,000. Break-even will be reached when total contribution equals fixed costs.

$$\text{Break-Even Volume} = \frac{\text{Fixed Costs}}{\text{Contribution per Unit}}$$

$$\text{Contribution per Unit} = \text{Sale Price per Unit} - \text{Variable Cost per Unit}$$

$$= \$20 - \$5 = \$15$$

$$\text{Break-Even Volume} = \frac{\$30,000}{\$15} = 2,000 \text{ mousetraps}$$

This dynamic can be summarized in a graph that shows fixed costs, variable costs, total costs, and total revenue (see Figure 3.6). Below the break-even point, total costs exceed total revenue, creating a loss. Above the break-even point, a company generates profits.

> **Break-even:** Break-even occurs when the total contribution equals the fixed costs. Profits and losses at this point equal zero.

One of the key building blocks of break-even analysis is the concept of contribution. Contribution represents the portion of sales revenue that is not consumed by variable costs and so contributes to the coverage of fixed costs.

$$\text{Contribution per Unit (\$)} = \text{Selling Price per Unit (\$)} - \text{Variable Cost per Unit (\$)}$$

Contribution can also be expressed in percentage terms, quantifying the fraction of the sales price that contributes to covering fixed costs. This percentage is often called the *contribution margin*.

$$\text{Contribution Margin (\%)} = \frac{\text{Contribution per Unit (\$)}}{\text{Selling Price per Unit (\$)}}$$

Figure 3.6 At break-even, total costs = total revenues

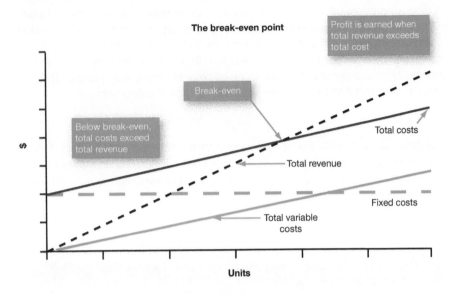

Formulas for total contribution include the following:

$$\text{Total Contribution (\$)} = \text{Units Sold (\#)} * \text{Contribution per Unit (\$)}$$

$$\text{Total Contribution (\$)} = \text{Total Revenues (\$)} - \text{Total Variable Costs (\$)}$$

As previously noted,

$$\text{Total Variable Costs} = \text{Variable Costs per Unit} * \text{Units Sold}$$

$$\text{Total Revenues} = \text{Selling Price per Unit} * \text{Units Sold}$$

> **Break-even volume: The number of units that must be sold to cover fixed costs.**

$$\text{Break-Even Volume (\#)} = \frac{\text{Fixed Costs (\$)}}{\text{Contribution per Unit (\$)}}$$

Break-even will occur when an enterprise sells enough units to cover its fixed costs. If the fixed costs are \$10 and the contribution per unit is \$2, then a firm must sell five units to break even.

> **Break-even revenue: The level of dollar sales required to break even.**

$$\text{Break-Even Revenue (\$)} = \text{Break-Even Volume (Units) (\#)} * \text{Price per Unit (\$)}$$

This formula is the simple conversion of volume in units to the revenues generated by that volume.

Example Apprentice Mousetraps wants to know how many dollars' worth of its Deluxe Mighty Mouse Trapper it must sell to break even. The product sells for $40 per unit. It costs $10 per unit to make. The company's fixed costs are $30,000.

With fixed costs of $30,000, and a contribution per unit of $30, Apprentice must sell $30,000/$30 = 1,000 deluxe mousetraps to break even. At $40 per trap, this corresponds to revenues of 1,000 * $40 = $40,000.

$$\text{Break-Even Revenue (\$)} = \text{Break-Even Volume (\#)} * \text{Price per Unit (\$)}$$

$$= 1,000 * \$40 = \$40,000$$

Break-even in dollar terms can also be calculated by dividing fixed costs by the fraction of the selling price that represents contribution.

$$\text{Break-Even Revenue} = \frac{\text{Fixed Costs}}{(\text{Selling Price} - \text{Variable Costs})/\text{Selling Price}}$$

$$= \frac{\$30,000}{(\$40 - \$10)/\$40}$$

$$= \frac{\$30,000}{75\%} = \$40,000$$

Break-even on incremental investment

Break-even on incremental investment is a common form of break-even analysis. It examines the additional investment needed to pursue a marketing plan, and it calculates the additional sales required to cover that expenditure. Any costs or revenues that would have occurred, regardless of the investment decision, are excluded from this analysis.

Example John's Clothing Store employs three salespeople. It generates annual sales of $1 million and an average contribution margin of 30%. Rent is $50,000. Each salesperson costs $50,000 per year in salary and benefits. How much would sales have to increase for John to break-even on hiring an additional salesperson?

If the additional "investment" in a salesperson is $50,000, then break-even on the new hire will be reached when sales increase by $50,000/30%, or $166,666.67.

Data sources, complications, and cautions

To calculate a break-even sales level, one must know the revenues per unit, the variable costs per unit, and the fixed costs. To establish these figures, one must classify all costs as either fixed (those that do not change with volume) or variable (those that increase linearly with volume).

The time scale of the analysis can influence this classification. Indeed, one's managerial intent can be reflected in the classification. (Will the company fire employees and sublet factory space if sales turn down?) As a general rule, all costs become variable in the long term. Firms generally view rent, for example, as a fixed cost. But in the long term, even rent becomes variable as a company may move into larger quarters when sales grow beyond a certain point.

Before agonizing over these judgments, managers are urged to remember that the most useful application of the break-even exercise is to make a rough judgment about whether more detailed analyses are likely to be worth the effort. The break-even calculation enables managers to judge various options and proposals quickly. It is not, however, a substitute for more detailed analyses, including projections of target profits (Section 3.7), risk, and the time value of money (Sections 5.3 and 12.4).

Related metrics and concepts

Payback period: The period of time required to recoup the funds expended in an investment. The payback period is the time required for an investment to reach break-even (see previous sections).

3.7   Profit-based sales targets

In launching a program, managers often start with an idea of the dollar profit they desire and ask what sales levels will be required to reach it. Target volume (#) is the unit sales quantity required to meet an earnings goal. Target revenue ($) is the corresponding figure for dollar sales. Both of these metrics can be viewed as extensions of break-even analysis.

$$\text{Target Volume (\#)} = \frac{[\text{Fixed Costs (\$)} + \text{Target Profits (\$)}]}{\text{Contribution per Unit (\$)}}$$

$$\text{Target Revenue (\$)} = \text{Target Volume (\#)} * \text{Selling Price per Unit (\$)}$$

or

$$= \frac{[\text{Fixed Costs (\$)} + \text{Target Profits (\$)}]}{\text{Contribution Margin (\%)}}$$

> Increasingly, marketers are expected to generate volumes that meet the target profits of their firm. This often requires them to revise sales targets as prices and costs change.

Purpose: to ensure that marketing and sales objectives mesh with profit targets.

In the previous section, we explored the concept of break-even, the point at which a company sells enough to cover its fixed costs. In target volume and target revenue calculations, managers take the next step: They determine the level of unit sales or revenues needed not only to cover a firm's costs but also to attain its profit targets.

Construction

> **Target volume:** The volume of sales necessary to generate the profits specified in a company's plans.

The formula for target volume will be familiar to those who have performed break-even analysis. The only change is to add the required profit target to the fixed costs. From another perspective, the break-even volume equation can be viewed as a special case of the general target volume calculation—one in which the profit target is zero, and a company seeks only to cover its fixed costs. In target volume calculations, the company broadens this objective to solve for a desired profit.

$$\text{Target Volume (\#)} = \frac{\text{Fixed Costs (\$)} + \text{Target Profits (\$)}}{\text{Contribution per Unit (\$)}}$$

Example Mohan, an artist, wants to know how many caricatures he must sell to realize a yearly profit objective of $30,000. Each caricature sells for $20 and costs $5 in materials to make. The fixed costs for Mohan's studio are $30,000 per year:

$$\text{Target Volume} = \frac{\text{Fixed Costs} + \text{Target Profits}}{\text{Sales Price} - \text{Variable Costs}}$$

$$= \frac{\$30,000 + \$30,000}{\$20 - \$5}$$

$$= 4,000 \text{ caricatures per year}$$

It is quite simple to convert unit target volume to target revenues. One need only multiply the volume figure by an item's price per unit. Continuing the example of Mohan's studio,

$$\text{Target Revenue (\$)} = \text{Target Volume (\#)} * \text{Selling Price (\$)}$$

$$= 4{,}000 * \$20 = \$80{,}000$$

Alternatively, we can use a second formula:

$$\text{Target Revenue} = \frac{\text{Fixed Costs (\$)} + \text{Target Profits (\$)}}{\text{Contribution Margin (\%)}}$$

$$= \frac{\$30{,}000 + \$30{,}000}{\$15/\$20}$$

$$= \frac{\$60{,}000}{0.75} = \$80{,}000$$

Data sources, complications, and cautions

The information needed to perform a target volume calculation is essentially the same as that required for break-even analysis: fixed costs, selling price, and variable costs. Of course, before determining target volume, one must also set a profit target.

The major assumption here is the same as in break-even analysis: Costs are linear with respect to unit volume over the range explored in the calculation.

Related metrics and concepts

Target volumes not based on target profit: In this section, we have assumed that a firm starts with a profit target and seeks to determine the volume required to meet it. In certain instances, however, a firm might set a volume target for reasons other than short-term profit. For example, firms sometimes adopt top-line growth as a goal. Please do not confuse this use of target volume with the profit-based target volumes calculated in this section.

Returns and targets: Companies often set hurdle rates for return on sales and return on investment and require that projections achieve these before any plan can be approved. Given these targets, we can calculate the sales volume required for the necessary return. (See Section 12.2 for more details.)

Example Niesha runs business development at Gird, a company that has established a return on sales target of 15%. That is, Gird requires that all programs generate profits equivalent to 15% of sales revenues. Niesha is evaluating a program that will add $1,000,000 to fixed costs. Under this program, each unit of product will be sold for $100 and will generate a contribution margin of 25%. To reach break-even on this program, Gird must sell $1,000,000/$25 = 40,000 units of product. How much must Gird sell to reach its target return on sales (ROS) of 15%?

To determine the revenue level required to achieve a 15% ROS, Niesha can use either a spreadsheet model and trial and error or the following formula:

$$\text{Target Revenue} = \frac{\text{Fixed Costs (\$)}}{\text{Contribution Margin (\%)} - \text{Target ROS (\%)}}$$

$$= \frac{\$1,000,000}{0.25 - 0.15}$$

$$= \frac{\$1,000,000}{0.1} = \$10,000,000$$

Thus, Gird will achieve its 15% ROS target if it generates $10,000,000 in sales. At a selling price of $100 per unit, this is equivalent to unit sales of 100,000.

Product and portfolio management

4

Key concepts covered in this chapter:

- Trial, repeat, penetration, and volume projections

- Growth: percentage and CAGR

- Cannibalization rate and fair share draw rate

- Brand equity metrics

- Conjoint utilities and consumer preference

- Segmentation and conjoint utilities

- Conjoint utilities and volume projection

Introduction

Effective marketing comes from customer knowledge and an understanding of how a product fits customers' needs. In this chapter, we describe metrics used in product strategy and planning. These metrics address the following questions: What volumes can marketers expect from a new product? How will sales of existing products be affected by the launch of a new offering? Is brand equity increasing or decreasing? What do customers really want, and what are they willing to sacrifice to obtain it?

We start with a section on trial and repeat rates, explaining how these metrics are determined and how they're used to generate sales forecasts for new products. Because forecasts involve growth projections, we then discuss the difference between year-on-year growth and compound annual growth rates (CAGR). Because growth of one product sometimes comes at the expense of an existing product line, it is important to understand cannibalization metrics, which reflect the impact of new products on a portfolio of existing products.

Next, we cover selected metrics associated with brand equity—a central focus of marketing. Indeed, many of the metrics throughout this book can be useful in evaluating brand equity. Certain metrics, however, have been developed specifically to measure the "health" of brands. This chapter discusses them.

Although branding strategy is a major aspect of a product offering, there are others, and managers must be prepared to make trade-offs among them, informed by a sense of the "worth" of various features. Conjoint analysis helps identify customers' valuation of specific product attributes. Increasingly, this technique is used to improve products and to help marketers evaluate and segment new or rapidly growing markets. In the final sections of this chapter, we discuss conjoint analysis from multiple perspectives.

	Metric	Construction	Considerations	Purpose
4.1	Trial	First-time users as a percentage of the target population.	Distinguish "ever-tried" from "new" triers in current period.	Measure whether sales eventually rely less on trial and more on repeat purchasers.
4.1	Repeat Volume	Repeat buyers, multiplied by the number of products they buy in each purchase, multiplied by the number of times they purchase per period.	Depending on when trial was achieved, not all triers will have an equal opportunity to make repeat purchases.	Measure the stability of a brand franchise.
4.1	Penetration	Users in the previous period, multiplied by repeat rate for the current period, plus new triers in the current period.	The length of the period affects norms—that is, more customers buy in a year than in a month.	Measure the population buying in the current period.
4.1	Volume Projections	Combine trial volume and repeat volume.	Adjust trial and repeat rates for time frame. Not all triers will have time or opportunity to repeat.	Plan production and inventories for both trade sales and consumer off-take.

Metric	Construction	Considerations	Purpose
4.2 Year-on-Year Growth	Percentage change from one year to the next.	Distinguish unit and dollar growth rates.	Plan production and budgeting.
4.2 Compound Annual Growth Rate (CAGR)	Ending value divided by starting value to the power of 1/N, in which N is the number of periods.	May not reflect individual year-on-year growth rates.	Average growth rates over long periods.
4.3 Cannibalization Rate	Percentage of new product sales taken from existing product line.	Market expansion effects should also be considered.	Account for the fact that new products often reduce the sales of existing products.
4.3 Fair Share Draw	Assumption that new entrants in a market capture sales from established competitors in proportion to established market shares.	May not be a reasonable assumption if there are significant differences among competing brands.	Generate an estimate of sales and shares after entry of new competitor.
4.4 Brand Equity Metrics	Numerous measures, such as Conjoint Utility Attributed to Brand.	Metrics tracking essence of brand may not track health and value.	Monitor health of a brand. Diagnose weaknesses, as needed.
4.5 Conjoint Utilities	Regression coefficients for attribute levels derived from conjoint analysis.	May be function of number, level, and type of attributes in study.	Indicate the relative values that customers place on attributes of which product offerings are composed.

Metric	Construction	Considerations	Purpose
4.6 Segment Utilities	Clustering of individuals into market segments on the basis of sum-of-squares distance between regression coefficients drawn from conjoint analysis.	May be function of number, level, and type of attributes in conjoint study. Assumes homogeneity within segments.	Use customer valuations of product attributes to help define market segments.
4.7 Conjoint Utilities and Volume Projection	Used within conjoint simulator to estimate volume.	Assumes awareness and distribution levels are known or can be estimated.	Forecast sales for alternative products, designs, prices, and branding strategies.

4.1 Trial, repeat, penetration, and volume projections

Test markets and volume projections enable marketers to forecast sales by sampling customer intentions through surveys and market studies. By estimating how many customers will try a new product and how often they'll make repeat purchases, marketers can establish the basis for such projections.

First-Time Triers in Period t (#) = Total Population (#) * Trial Rate (%)

Penetration t (#) = [Penetration in $t - 1$ (#) * Repeat Rate Period t (%)] + First-Time Triers in Period t (#)

Projection of Sales t (#) = Penetration t (#) * Average Frequency of Purchase (#) * Average Units per Purchase (#)

Projections from customer surveys are especially useful in the early stages of product development and in setting the timing for product launch. Through such projections, customer response can be estimated without the expense of a full product launch.

Purpose: to understand volume projections.

When projecting sales for relatively new products, marketers typically use a system of trial and repeat calculations to anticipate sales in future periods. This works on the principle that everyone buying the product will either be a new customer (a "trier") or a repeat customer. By adding new and repeat customers in any period, we can establish the penetration of a product in the marketplace.

It is challenging, however, to project sales to a large population on the basis of simulated test markets or even full-fledged regional rollouts. Marketers have developed various solutions to increase the speed and reduce the cost of test marketing, such as stocking a store with products (or mockups of new products) or giving customers money to buy the products of their choice. These simulate real shopping conditions but require specific models to estimate full-market volume on the basis of test results. To illustrate the conceptual underpinnings of this process, we offer a general model for making volume projections on the basis of test market results.

Construction

The penetration of a product in a future period can be estimated on the basis of population size, trial rates, and repeat rates.

> **Trial rate (%):** The percentage of a defined population that purchases or uses a product for the first time in a given period.

Example A cable TV company keeps careful records of the names and addresses of its customers. The firm's vice president of marketing notes that 150 households made first-time use of his company's services in March 2019. The company has access to 30,000 households. To calculate the trial rate for March, we can divide 150 by 30,000, yielding 0.5%.

> **First-time triers in period t (#):** The number of customers who purchase or use a product or brand for the first time in a given period.

$$\text{Penetration } t \text{ (#)} = [\text{Penetration in } t - 1 \text{ (#)} * \text{Repeat Rate Period } t \text{ (%)}] + \text{First-Time Triers in Period } t \text{ (#)}$$

Example A cable TV company started selling a monthly sports package in January. The company typically has an 80% repeat rate and anticipates that this will continue for the new offering. The company sold 10,000 sports packages in January. In February, it expects to add 3,000 customers for the package. On this basis, we can calculate expected penetration for the sports package in February.

$$\text{Penetration in February} = (\text{Penetration January} * \text{Repeat Rate})$$
$$+ \text{First-Time Triers in February}$$

$$= (10,000 * 80\%) + 3,000 = 11,000$$

Later that year, in September, the company has 20,000 subscribers. Its repeat rate remains 80%. The company had 18,000 subscribers in August. Management wants to know how many new customers the firm added for its sports package in September:

$$\text{First-Time Triers} = \text{Penetration} - \text{Repeat Customers}$$
$$= 20,000 - (18,000 * 80\%) = 5,600$$

From penetration, it is a short step to projections of sales.

$$\text{Projection of Sales (\#)} = \text{Penetration (\#)} * \text{Frequency of Purchase (\#)}$$
$$* \text{Units per Purchase (\#)}$$

Simulated test market results and volume projections

Trial volume

Trial rates are often estimated on the basis of surveys of potential customers. Typically, these surveys ask respondents whether they will "definitely" or "probably" buy a product. As these are the strongest of several possible responses to questions of purchase intentions, they are sometimes referred to as the "top two boxes." The less favorable responses in a standard five-choice survey include "may or may not buy," "probably won't buy," and "definitely won't buy." (Refer to Section 2.7 for more on intention to purchase.)

Because not all respondents follow through on their declared purchase intentions, firms often make adjustments to the percentages in the top two boxes in developing sales projections. For example, some marketers estimate that 80% of respondents who say they'll "definitely buy" and 30% of those who say that they'll "probably buy" will in fact purchase a product when given the opportunity.[1] (The adjustment for customers following through is used in the following model.) Although some respondents in the bottom three boxes might buy a product, their number is assumed to be insignificant. By reducing the score for the top two boxes, marketers derive a more realistic estimate of the number of potential customers who will try a product, given the right circumstances. Those circumstances are often shaped by product awareness and availability.

Awareness

Sales projection models include an adjustment for lack of awareness of a product within the target market (see Figure 4.1). Lack of awareness reduces the trial rate because it excludes some potential customers who might try the product but don't know about it. By contrast, if awareness is 100%, then all potential customers know about the product, and no potential sales are lost due to lack of awareness.

Figure 4.1 Schematic of simulated test market volume projection

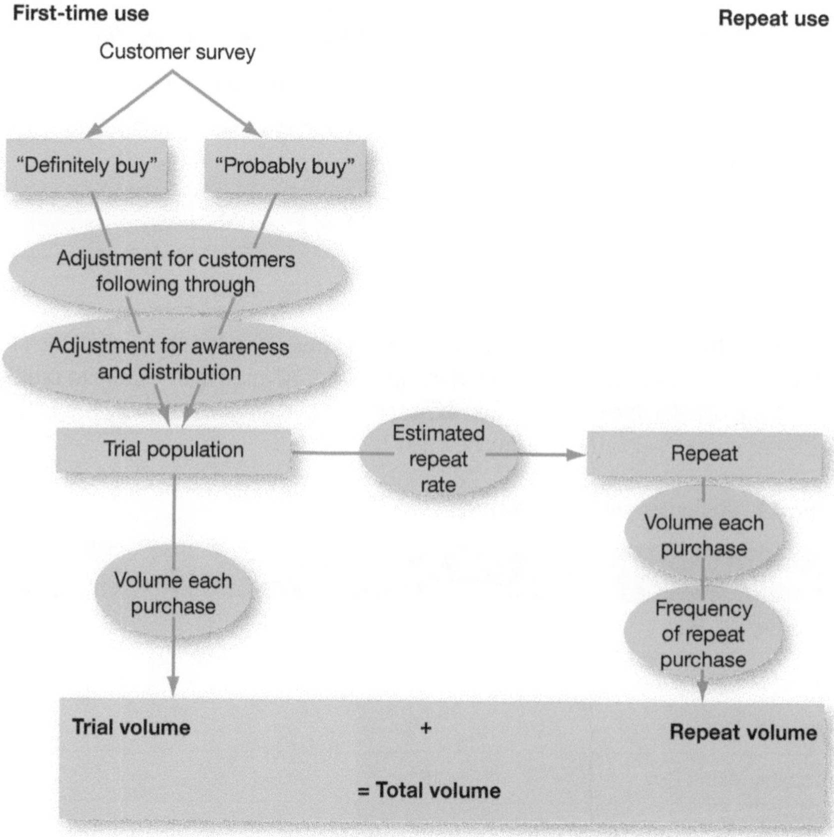

First-time use   **Repeat use**

Customer survey

"Definitely buy"   "Probably buy"

Adjustment for customers following through

Adjustment for awareness and distribution

Trial population → Estimated repeat rate → Repeat

Volume each purchase

Volume each purchase

Frequency of repeat purchase

Trial volume   +   **Repeat volume**

= Total volume

Distribution

Another adjustment to test market trial rates is usually applied: accounting for the estimated availability of the new product. Even survey respondents who say they'll "definitely" try a product are unlikely to do so if they can't find it easily. In making this adjustment, companies typically use an estimated distribution, a percentage of total stores that will stock the new product, such as ACV % distribution. (See Section 7.1 for further detail.)

$$\text{Adjusted Trial Rate (\%)} = \text{Trial Rate (\%)} * \text{Awareness (\%)} * \text{ACV (\%)}$$

After making these modifications, marketers can calculate the number of customers who are expected to try the product, simply by applying the adjusted trial rate to the target population.

$$\text{Trial Population (\#)} = \text{Target Population (\#)} * \text{Adjusted Trial Rate (\%)}$$

Estimated in this way, trial population (#) is identical to penetration (#) in the trial period.

To forecast trial volume, multiply trial population by the projected average number of units of a product that will be bought in each trial purchase. This is often assumed to be one unit because most people will experiment with a single unit of a new product before buying larger quantities.

$$\text{Trial Volume (\#)} = \text{Trial Population (\#)} * \text{Units per Purchase (\#)}$$

Combining all these calculations, the entire formula for trial volume is

$$\text{Trial Volume (\#)} = \text{Target Population (\#)} * [(80\% * \text{Definitely Buy (\#)})$$
$$+ (30\% * \text{Probably Buy (\#)}) * \text{Awareness (\%)} * \text{ACV (\%)}]$$
$$* \text{Units per Purchase (\#)}$$

Example The marketing team of an office supply manufacturer has a great idea for a new product: a safety stapler. To sell the idea internally, the team wants to project the volume of sales the company can expect over the stapler's first year. The team's customer survey yields the results shown in Table 4.1.

Table 4.1 Customer survey responses

Response	Percentage of customers responding
Definitely Will Buy	20%
Probably Will Buy	50%
May/May Not Buy	15%
Probably Won't Buy	10%
Definitely Won't Buy	5%
Total	100%

On this basis, the company estimates a trial rate for the new stapler by applying the industry-standard expectation that 80% of "definites" and 30% of "probables" will in fact buy the product if given the opportunity.

$$\text{Trial Rate} = 80\% \text{ of "Definites"} + 30\% \text{ of "Probables"}$$

$$= (80\% * 20\%) + (30\% * 50\%)$$

$$= 31\%$$

Thus, 31% of the population is expected to try the product if they are aware of it and if it is available in stores. The company has a strong advertising presence and a solid distribution network. Consequently, its marketers believe they can obtain an ACV of approximately 60% for the stapler and that they can generate awareness at a similar level. On this basis, they project an adjusted trial rate of 11.16% of the population:

$$\text{Adjusted Trial Rate} = \text{Trial Rate} * \text{Awareness} * \text{ACV}$$

$$= 31\% * 60\% * 60\% = 11.16\%$$

The target population comprises 20 million people. The trial population can be calculated by multiplying this figure by the adjusted trial rate.

$$\text{Trial Population} = \text{Target Population} * \text{Adjusted Trial Rate}$$

$$= 20 \text{ million} * 11.16\% = 2.232 \text{ million}$$

Assuming that each person buys one unit when trying the product, the trial volume will total 2.232 million units.

We can also calculate the trial volume by using the full formula:

$$\text{Trial Volume} = \text{Target Population}$$
$$* [((80\% * \text{Definites}) + (30\% * \text{Probables})) * \text{Awareness} * \text{ACV}]$$
$$* \text{Units per Purchase}$$

$$= 20m * [((80\% * 20\%) + (30\% * 50\%)) * 60\% * 60\%] * 1$$

$$= 2.232 \text{ million}$$

Repeat volume

The second part of projected volume concerns the fraction of people who try a product and then repeat their purchase decision. The model for this dynamic uses a single estimated repeat rate to yield the number of customers who are expected to purchase again after their initial trial. In reality, initial repeat rates are often lower than subsequent repeat rates. For example, it is not uncommon for 50% of trial purchasers to make a first repeat purchase but for 80% of those who purchase a second time to go on to purchase a third time.

$$\text{Repeat Buyers (\#)} = \text{Trial Population (\#)} * \text{Repeat Rate (\%)}$$

To calculate the repeat volume, the repeat buyers figure can then be multiplied by an expected volume per purchase among repeat customers and by the number of times these customers are expected to repeat their purchases within the period under consideration.

$$\text{Repeat Volume (\#)} = \text{Repeat Buyers (\#)} * \text{Repeat Unit Volume per Customer (\#)} * \text{Repeat Occasions (\#)}$$

This calculation yields the total volume that a new product is expected to generate among repeat customers over a specified introductory period. The full formula can be written as

$$\text{Repeat Volume (\#)} = [\text{Trial Population (\#)} * \text{Repeat Rate (\%)}] \\ * \text{Repeat Unit Volume per Customer (\#)} \\ * \text{Repeat Occasions (\#)}$$

Example Continuing the previous office supplies example, the safety stapler has a trial population of 2.232 million. Marketers expect the product to be of sufficient quality to generate a 10% repeat rate in its first year. This will yield 223,200 repeat buyers:

$$\text{Repeat Buyers} = \text{Trial Population} * \text{Repeat Rate}$$

$$= 2.232 \text{ million} * 10\%$$

$$= 223,200$$

On average, the company expects each repeat buyer to purchase on four occasions during the first year. On average, each purchase is expected to comprise two units.

$$\text{Repeat Volume} = \text{Repeat Buyers} * \text{Repeat Unit Volume per Customer} \\ * \text{Repeat Occasions}$$

$$= 223,200 * 2 * 4$$

$$= 1,785,600 \text{ units}$$

This can be represented in the full formula:

$$\text{Repeat Volume (\#)} = [\text{Repeat Rate (\%)} * \text{Trial Population (\#)}] \\ * \text{Repeat Volume per Customer (\#)} \\ * \text{Repeat Occasions (\#)}$$

$$= (10\% * 2,232,000) * 2 * 4$$

$$= 1,785,600 \text{ units}$$

Total volume

Total volume is the sum of trial volume and repeat volume, as all volume must be sold to either new customers or returning customers.

$$\text{Total Volume (\#)} = \text{Trial Volume (\#)} + \text{Repeat Volume (\#)}$$

To capture total volume in its fully detailed form, we need only combine the previous formulas.

$$
\begin{aligned}
\text{Total Volume (\#)} = &[\text{Target Population} * ((0.8 * \text{Definitely Buy} + 0.3 \\
&* \text{Probably Buy}) \\
&* \text{Awareness} * \text{ACV}) * \text{Units per Trial Purchase}] \\
&+ [(\text{Trial Population} * \text{Repeat Rate}) \\
&* \text{Repeat Volume per Customer} * \text{Repeat Occasions}]
\end{aligned}
$$

Example Total volume in year 1 for the stapler is the sum of trial volume and repeat volume.

$$
\begin{aligned}
\text{Total Volume} &= \text{Trial Volume} + \text{Repeat Volume} \\
&= 2{,}232{,}000 + 1{,}785{,}600 \\
&= 4{,}017{,}600 \text{ Units}
\end{aligned}
$$

A full calculation of this figure and a template for a spreadsheet calculation are presented in Table 4.2.

Table 4.2 Volume projection spreadsheet

Preliminary Data	Source	
Definitely Will Buy	Customer survey	20%
Probably Will Buy	Customer survey	50%
Likely Buyers		
Likely Buyers from Definites	= Definitely Buy * 80%	16%
Likely Buyers from Probables	= Probably Buy * 30%	15%
Trial Rate (%)	Total of Likely Buyers	31%
Marketing Adjustments		
Awareness	Estimated from Marketing Plan	60%
ACV	Estimated from Marketing Plan	60%
Adjusted Trial Rate (%)	= Trial Rate * Awareness * ACV	11.2%
Target Population (#) (thousands)	Marketing Plan Data	20,000
Trial Population (#) (thousands)	= Target Population * Adjusted Trial Rate	2,232

Table 4.2 *Continued*

Preliminary Data	Source	
Unit Volume Purchased per Trial (#)	Estimated from Marketing Plan	1
Trial Volume (#) (Thousands)	**= Trial Population * Volume per Trier**	**2,232**
Repeat Rate (%)	Estimated from Marketing Plan	10%
Repeat Buyers (#)	= Repeat Rate * Trial Population	223,200
Avg. Volume per Repeat Purchase (#)	Estimated from Marketing Plan	2
Repeat Purchase Frequency ** (#)	Estimated from Marketing Plan	4
Repeat Volume (#) (Thousands)	**= Repeat Buyers * Repeat Volume per Purchase * Repeat Purchase**	**1,786**
Total Volume (#) (Thousands)		**4,018**

**Note: The average frequency of repeat purchases per repeat purchaser should be adjusted to reflect the time available for first-time triers to repeat, the purchase cycle (frequency) for the category, and availability. For example, if trial rates are constant over the year, the number of repeat purchases would be about 50% of what it would have been if all had tried on day 1 of the period.

Data sources, complications, and cautions

Sales projections based on test markets will always require the inclusion of key assumptions. In setting these assumptions, marketers face tempting opportunities to make the assumptions fit the desired outcome. Marketers must guard against that temptation and perform sensitivity analysis to establish a range of predictions.

Relatively simple metrics such as trial and repeat rates can be difficult to capture in practice. Although strides have been made in gaining customer data—through customer loyalty cards, for example—it is often difficult to determine whether customers are new or repeat buyers.

When considering awareness and distribution, keep in mind that assumptions concerning the level of public awareness to be generated by launch advertising are fraught with uncertainty. Marketers are advised to think about what sort of awareness the product needs and what complementary promotions can aid the launch.

Trial and repeat rates are both important. Some products generate strong results in the trial stage but fail to maintain ongoing sales. Consider the following example.

Example Let's compare the safety stapler with a new product, such as an enhanced envelope sealer. The envelope sealer generates less marketing buzz than the stapler but enjoys a greater repeat rate. To predict results for the envelope sealer, we have adapted the data from the safety stapler by reducing the top two box responses by half (reflecting the lower initial enthusiasm) and raising the repeat rate from 10% to 33% (showing stronger product response after use).

At the six-month mark, sales results for the safety stapler are superior to those for the envelope sealer. After one year, sales results for the two products are equal. On a three-year time scale, however, the envelope sealer—with its loyal base of customers—emerges as the clear winner in sales volume (see Figure 4.2).

The data for the graph are derived as shown in Table 4.3.

Figure 4.2 Time horizon influences perceived results

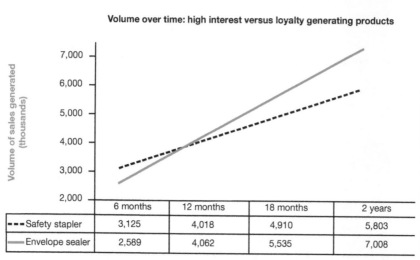

Volume over time: high interest versus loyalty generating products

	6 months	12 months	18 months	2 years
---Safety stapler	3,125	4,018	4,910	5,803
—Envelope sealer	2,589	4,062	5,535	7,008

Time from product launch

Table 4.3 High initial interest or long-term loyalty—results over time

Preliminary Data	Source	6 months		12 months		18 months		2 years	
		Prod A	Prod B	Prod A	Prod B	Prod A	Prod B	Prod A	Prod B
Definitely Will Buy	Customer Survey	20%	10%	20%	10%	20%	10%	20%	10%
Probably Will Buy	Customer Survey	50%	25%	50%	25%	50%	25%	50%	25%
Likely Buyers									
Likely Buyers from Definites	= Definitely Buy * 80%	16%	8%	16%	8%	16%	8%	16%	8%
Likely Buyers from Probables	= Probably Buy * 30%	15%	8%	15%	8%	15%	8%	15%	8%
Trial Rate	Total of Likely Buyers	31%	16%	31%	16%	31%	16%	31%	16%
Marketing Adjustments									
Awareness	Estimated from Marketing Plan	60%	60%	60%	60%	60%	60%	60%	60%
ACV	Estimated from Marketing Plan	60%	60%	60%	60%	60%	60%	60%	60%
Adjusted Trial Rate	= Trial Rate * Awareness * ACV	11.2%	5.6%	11.2%	5.6%	11.2%	5.6%	11.2%	5.6%
Target Population (Thousands) Marketing Plan Data		20,000	20,000	20,000	20,000	20,000	20,000	20,000	20,000

Trial Population (Thousands)	= Target Population * Adjusted Trial Rate	2,232	1,116	2,232	1,116	2,232	1,116	2,232	1,116
Unit Volume Purchased at Trial	Estimated from Marketing Plan	1	1	1	1	1	1	1	1
Trial Volume (Thousands)	= Trial Population * Volume Bought	2,232	1,116	2,232	1,116	2,232	1,116	2,232	1,116
Repeat Rate	Estimated from Marketing Plan	10%	33%	10%	33%	10%	33%	10%	33%
Repeat Buyers (Thousands)	= Repeat Rate * Trial Population	223.20	368.28	223.20	368.28	223.20	368.28	223.20	368.28
Repeat Purchase Unit Volume	Estimated from Marketing Plan	2	2	2	2	2	2	2	2
Number of Repeat Purchases	Estimated from Marketing Plan	2	2	4	4	6	6	8	8
Repeat Volume (Thousands)	= Repeat Buyers * Repeat Volume * Number of Repeat Purchases	893	1,473	1,786	2,946	2,678	4,419	3,571	5,892
Total Volume (Thousands)		3,125	2,589	4,018	4,062	4,910	5,535	5,803	7,008

Repeating and trying

Some models assume that customers, after they stop repeating purchases, are lost and do not return. However, customers may be acquired, lost, reacquired, and lost again. In general, the trial-repeat model is best suited to projecting sales over the first few periods. Other means of predicting volume include share of requirements and penetration metrics (refer to Sections 2.4 and 2.5). Those approaches may be preferable for products that lack reliable repeat rates.

	Market size	Penetration share	Share of requirements	Usage index	Market share	Units sold
New Product	1,000,000	5%	80%	1.2	4.8%	48,000
Source	Estimated	Estimated	Estimated	Estimated	Penetration Share ★ Share of Requirements ★ Usage Index	Share ★ Market Size

Related metrics and concepts

Ever-tried: This is slightly different from trial in that here it measures the percentage of the target population that has "ever" (in any previous period) purchased or consumed the product under study. Ever-tried is a cumulative measure and can never add up to more than 100%. Trial, by contrast, is an incremental measure. It indicates the percentage of the population that tries the product for the first time in a given period. Even here, however, there is potential for confusion. If a customer stops buying a product but tries it again six months later, some marketers will categorize that individual as a returning purchaser, and others will categorize that individual as a new customer. By the latter definition, if individuals can "try" a product more than once, then the sum of all "triers" could equal more than the total population. To avoid confusion, when reviewing a set of data, it's best to clarify the definitions behind it.

Variations on trial: Certain scenarios reduce the barriers to trial but entail a lower commitment by the customer than a standard purchase.

- **Forced Trial:** No other similar product is available. For example, many people who prefer Pepsi-Cola have "tried" Coca-Cola in restaurants that only serve the latter and vice versa.

- **Discounted Trial:** Consumers buy a new product but at a substantially reduced price.

Forced and discounted trials are usually associated with lower repeat rates than trials made through volitional purchase.

Evoked set: The set of brands that consumers name in response to questions about which brands they consider (or might consider) when making a purchase in a specific category. The Evoked Set for breakfast cereals, for example, is often quite large, while for coffee it may be smaller.

Number of new products: The number of products introduced for the first time in a specific time period.

Revenue from new products: Usually expressed as the percentage of sales generated by products introduced in the current period or, at times, in the most recent three to five periods.

Margin on new products: The dollar or percentage profit margin on new products. This can be measured separately but does not differ mathematically from margin calculations.

Company profit from new products: The percentage of company profits derived from new products. In working with this figure, it is important to understand how "new product" is defined.

Target market fit: Of customers purchasing a product, target market fit represents the percentage who belong in the demographic, psychographic, or other descriptor set for that item. Target market fit is useful in evaluating marketing strategies. If a large percentage of customers for a product belongs to groups that have not previously been targeted, marketers may reconsider their targets—and their allocation of marketing spending.

4.2 Growth: percentage and CAGR

There are two common measures of growth. Year-on-year percentage growth uses the prior year as a base for expressing percentage change from one year to the next. Over longer periods of time, Compound Annual Growth Rate (CAGR) is a generally accepted metric for average growth rates.

$$\text{Year-on-Year Growth (\%)} = \frac{\text{Value (\$, \#, \%)}\ t - \text{Value (\$, \#, \%)}\ t-1}{\text{Value (\$, \#, \%)}\ t-1}$$

Compound Annual Growth Rate, or CAGR (%) = {[Ending Value (\$, #, %)/Starting Value (\$, #, %)] ^ [1/Number of Years (#)]} − 1

Same Stores Growth is a metric that calculates growth only on the basis of stores that were fully established in both the prior and current periods.

Purpose: *to measure growth.*

Growth is the aim of virtually all businesses. Indeed, perceptions of the success or failure of many enterprises are based on assessments of their growth. Measures of year-on-year growth, however, are complicated by two factors:

- **Changes over time in the base from which growth is measured:** Such changes might include increases in the number of stores, markets, or salespeople generating sales. This issue is addressed by using "same store" measures (or corollary measures for markets, sales personnel, and so on).

- **Compounding of growth over multiple periods:** For example, if a company achieves 30% growth in one year, but its results remain unchanged over the two subsequent years, this would not be the same as 10% growth in each of three years. CAGR is a metric that addresses this issue.

Construction

Percentage growth is the central plank of year-on-year analysis. It addresses the question: What has the company achieved this year, compared to last year? Dividing the results for the current period by the results for the prior period will yield a comparative figure. Subtracting one from the other will highlight the increase or decrease between periods. When evaluating comparatives, one might say that results in Year 2 were, for example, 110% of those in Year 1. To convert this figure to a growth rate, one need only subtract 100%.

The periods considered are often years, but any time frame can be chosen.

$$\text{Year-on-Year Growth (\%)} = \frac{\text{Value (\$, \#, \%)}\ t - \text{Value (\$, \#, \%)}\ t - 1}{\text{Value (\$, \#, \%)}\ t - 1}$$

Example Ed's is a small deli that has had great success in its second year of operation. Revenues in Year 2 are $570,000, compared with $380,000 in Year 1. Ed calculates his second-year sales results to be 150% of first-year revenues, indicating a growth rate of 50%.

$$\text{Year-on-Year Sales Growth} = \frac{\$570,000 - \$380,000}{\$380,000} = 50\%$$

Same stores growth: This metric is at the heart of retail analysis. It enables marketers to analyze results from stores that have been in operation for the entire period under consideration. The logic is to eliminate the stores that have not been open for the full period to ensure comparability. Thus, this metric sheds light on the effectiveness with which equivalent resources were used in the period under study versus the prior period. In retail, modest same stores

> growth and high general growth rates would indicate a rapidly expanding
> organization, in which growth is driven by investment. When both same stores
> growth and general growth are strong, a company can be viewed as effectively
> using its existing base of stores.

Example A small retail chain in Bavaria posts impressive percentage growth figures, moving from €58 million to €107 million in sales (84% growth) from one year to the next. Despite this dynamic growth, however, analysts cast doubt on the firm's business model, warning that its Same Stores Growth measure suggests that its concept is failing (see Table 4.4).

Table 4.4 Revenue of a Bavarian chain store

Store	Opened	Revenue first year (millions)	Revenue second year (millions)
A	Year 1	€10	€9
B	Year 1	€19	€20
C	Year 1	€20	€15
D	Year 1	€9	€11
E	Year 2	n/a	€52
		€58	€107

Same Stores Growth excludes stores that were not open at the beginning of the first year under consideration. For simplicity, we assume that stores in this example were opened on the first day of Years 1 and 2, as appropriate. On this basis, same stores revenue in Year 2 would be €55 million—that is, the €107 million total for the year less the €52 million generated by the newly opened Store E. This adjusted figure can be entered into the Same Stores Growth formula:

$$\text{Same Stores Growth} = \frac{(\text{Stores A–D Sales Year 2}) - (\text{Stores A–D Sales Year 1})}{\text{Stores A–D Sales Year 1}}$$

$$= \frac{€55m - €58m}{€58} = -5\%$$

As demonstrated by its negative Same Stores Growth figure, sales growth at this firm has been fueled entirely by a major investment in a new store. This raises serious doubts about its existing store concept. It also leads to a question: Did the new store "cannibalize" existing store sales? (See the next section for cannibalization metrics.)

Compounding growth, value at future period: By compounding, managers adjust growth figures to account for the iterative effect of improvement. For example, 10% growth in each of two successive years would not be the same as a total of 20% growth over the two-year period. The reason: Growth in the second year is built upon the elevated base achieved in the first. Thus, if sales run $100,000 in Year 0 and rise by 10% in Year 1, then Year 1 sales come to $110,000. If sales rise by a further 10% in Year 2, however, then Year 2 sales do not total $120,000. Rather, they total $110,000 + (10% * $110,000) = $121,000.

The compounding effect can be easily modeled in spreadsheet packages, which enable you to work through the compounding calculations one year at a time. To calculate a value in Year 1, multiply the corresponding Year 0 value by one plus the growth rate. Then use the value in Year 1 as a new base and multiply it by one plus the growth rate to determine the corresponding value for Year 2. Repeat this process through the required number of years.

Example Over a three-year period, $100, compounded at a 10% growth rate, yields $133.10.

Year 0 to Year 1 $100 + 10% Growth (that is, $10) = $110

Year 1 to Year 2 $110 + 10% Growth (that is, $11) = $121

Year 2 to Year 3 $121 + 10% Growth (that is, $12.10) = $133.10

There is a mathematical formula that generates this effect. It multiplies the value at the beginning—that is, in Year 0—by one plus the growth rate to the power of the number of years over which that growth rate applies.

$$\text{Value in Future Period (\$, \#, \%)} = \text{Current Value (\$, \#, \%)} * [(1 + \text{CAGR (\%)}) \wedge \text{Number of Periods (\#)}]$$

Example Using the formula, we can calculate the impact of 10% annual growth over a period of three years. The value in Year 0 is $100. The number of years is 3. The growth rate is 10%.

$$\text{Value in Future Period} = \text{Value in Year 0} * (1 + \text{Growth Rate}) \wedge \text{Number of Years}$$

$$= \$100 * (100\% + 10\%) \wedge 3$$

$$= \$100 * 133.1\% = \$133.10$$

> Compound annual growth rate (CAGR): A constant year-on-year growth rate
> applied over a period of time. Given starting and ending values and the length
> of the period involved, it can be calculated as follows:
>
> $$\text{CAGR (\%)} = \{[\text{Ending Value (\$, \#)}/\text{Starting Value (\$, \#)}]$$
> $$\wedge \; 1/\text{Number of Periods (\#)}\} - 1$$

Example Let's assume we have the results of the compounding growth observed in the previous example, but we don't know what the growth rate was. We know that the starting value was $100, the ending value was $133.10, and the number of years was 3. We can simply enter these numbers into the CAGR formula to derive the CAGR.

$$\text{CAGR} = [(\text{Ending Value/Starting Value}) \wedge (1/\text{Number of Years})] - 1$$

$$= [(\$133.10/\$100) \wedge 1/3] - 1$$

$$= [1.331(\text{The Increase}) \wedge 1/3(\text{Cube Root})] - 1 = 1.1 - 1 = 10\%$$

Thus, we determine that the growth rate was 10%.

Data sources, complications, and cautions

Percentage growth is a useful measure as part of a package of metrics. It can be deceiving, however, if not adjusted for the addition of such factors as stores, sales-people, or products or for expansion into new markets. "Same store" sales and similar adjustments for other factors tell us how effectively a company uses comparable resources. These adjustments, however, are limited by their deliberate omission of factors that weren't in operation for the full period under study. Adjusted figures must be reviewed in tandem with measures of total growth.

Be careful about the difference between percentage changes and changes in percentage points. Consider a firm that grew 10% last year. This year, a marketer might say that the rate of growth increased by 10%. This means that the growth was 10% more than last year, so 10% * (1 + 10%) means growth was 11%. If growth increased by 10 *percentage points*, growth would now be 20%. It had increased from 10% and added 10 more percentage points. This is dramatically different.

You may also hear about basis points, a related term. *Basis points* are simply percentage points divided by 100, so 50 basis points equal 0.5%. Basis points are often used in finance because fractional percentage point differences can make very significant differences in outcomes, and it is easier to speak of basis points than fractions of a percentage point.

Life cycle: Marketers view products as passing through four stages of development:

- **Introductory:** Small markets not yet growing fast
- **Growth:** Larger markets with faster growth rates
- **Mature:** Largest markets but little or no growth
- **Decline:** Variable size markets with negative growth rates

This is a rough classification. No generally accepted rules exist for making these classifications.

4.3 Cannibalization rates and fair share draw

Cannibalization is the reduction in sales (units or dollars) of a firm's existing products due to the introduction of a new product. The cannibalization rate is generally calculated as the percentage of a new product's sales that represents a loss of sales (attributable to the introduction of the new entrant) of a specific existing product or products.

$$\text{Cannibalization Rate (\%)} = \frac{\text{Sales Lost from Existing Products (\#, \$)}}{\text{Sales of New Product (\#, \$)}}$$

Cannibalization rates represent an important factor in the assessment of new product strategies.

Fair share draw constitutes an assumption or expectation that a new product will capture sales (in unit or dollar terms) from existing products in proportion to the market shares of those existing products.

Cannibalization is a familiar business dynamic. A company with a successful product that has strong market share faces two conflicting ideas. The first is that it wants to maximize profits on its existing product line, concentrating on the current strengths that promise success in the short term. The second idea is that this company—or its competitors—may identify opportunities for new products that better fit the needs of certain segments. If the company introduces a new product in this field, however, it may "cannibalize" the sales of its existing products. That is, it may weaken the sales of its proven, already successful product line. If the company declines to introduce the new product, however, it leaves itself vulnerable to competitors launching such a product and thereby capturing sales and market share from the company. Often, when new segments are emerging and there are advantages to being early to market, the key factor becomes timing. If a company launches its new product too early, it may lose too much income on its existing line; if it launches too late, it may miss the new opportunity altogether.

> **Cannibalization:** A market phenomenon in which sales of one product are achieved at the expense of some of a firm's other products.

The cannibalization rate is the percentage of sales of a new product that comes from a specific set of existing products.

$$\text{Cannibalization Rate (\%)} = \frac{\text{Sales Lost from Existing Products (\#, \$)}}{\text{Sales of New Product (\#, \$)}}$$

Example A company has a single product that sold 10 units in the previous period. The company plans to introduce a new product that will sell 5 units with a cannibalization rate of 40%. Thus, 40% of the sales of the new product (40% $\star$ 5 units = 2 units) comes at the expense of the old product. Therefore, after cannibalization, the company can expect to sell 8 units of the old product and 5 of the new product, or 13 units in total.

Any company considering introducing a new product should confront the potential for cannibalization. A firm would do well to ensure that the amount of cannibalization is estimated beforehand to provide an idea of how the product line's contribution as a whole will change. If performed properly, this analysis will tell a company whether overall profits can be expected to increase or decrease with the introduction of the new product line.

Example Lois sells umbrellas on a small beach, where she is the only provider. Her financials for last month were as follows:

Umbrella Sales Price:	$20
Variable Cost per Umbrella:	$10
Umbrella Contribution per Unit:	$10
Total Unit Sales per Month:	100
Total Monthly Contribution:	**$1,000**

Next month, Lois plans to introduce a bigger, lighter-weight umbrella called the "Big Block." Projected financials for the Big Block are as follows:

Big Block Sales Price:	$30
Variable Cost per Big Block:	$15
Big Block Contribution per Unit:	$15
Total Unit Sales per Month (Big Block):	50
Total Monthly Contribution (Big Block):	**$750**

If there is no cannibalization, Lois thus expects her total monthly contribution will be $1,000 + $750 = $1,750. Upon reflection, however, Lois thinks that the unit cannibalization rate for Big Block will be 60%. Her projected financials after accounting for cannibalization are therefore as follows:

Big Block Unit Sales:	50
Cannibalization Rate:	60%
Regular Umbrella Sales Lost:	50 * 60% = 30
New Regular Umbrella Sales:	100 − 30 = 70
New Total Contribution (Regular):	70 Units * $10 Contribution per Unit = $700
Big Block Total Contribution:	50 Units * $15 Contribution per Unit = $750
Lois's Total Monthly Contribution:	**$1,450**

Under these projections, total umbrella sales will increase from 100 to 120, and total contribution will increase from $1,000 to $1,450. Lois will replace 30 regular sales with 30 Big Block sales and gain an extra $5 unit contribution on each. She will also sell 20 more umbrellas than she sold last month and gain $15 unit contribution on each.

In this scenario, Lois is in the enviable position of being able to cannibalize a lower-margin product with a higher-margin one. Sometimes, however, new products carry unit contributions lower than those of existing products. In such instances, cannibalization reduces overall profits for the firm.

An alternative way to account for cannibalization is to use a weighted contribution margin. In the previous example, the weighted contribution margin would be the unit margin Lois receives for Big Block after accounting for cannibalization. Because each Big Block contributes $15 directly and cannibalizes the $10 contribution generated by regular umbrellas at a 60% rate, Big Block's weighted contribution margin is $15 − (0.6 * $10), or $9 per unit. Because Lois expects to sell 50 Big Blocks, her total contribution is projected to increase by 50 * $9, or $450. This is consistent with our previous calculations.

If the introduction of Big Block requires some fixed marketing expenditure, then the $9 weighted margin can be used to find the break-even number of Big Block sales required to justify that expenditure. For example, if the launch of Big Block requires $360 in one-time marketing costs, then Lois needs to sell $360/$9, or 40 Big Blocks to break even on that expenditure.

If a new product has a margin lower than that of the existing product that it cannibalizes, and if its cannibalization rate is high enough, then its weighted contribution margin might be negative. In that case, company earnings will decrease with each unit of the new product sold.

Cannibalization refers to a dynamic in which one product of a firm takes share from one or more other products of *the same firm*. When a product takes sales from a competitor's product, that is not cannibalization, although managers sometimes incorrectly state that their new products are "cannibalizing" sales of a competitor's goods. You can only cannibalize your own sales; taking sales from rivals is not considered cannibalization.

Though it is not cannibalization, the impact of a new product on the sales of competing goods is an important consideration in a product launch. One simple assumption about how the introduction of a new product might affect the sales of existing products is called fair share draw.

> **Fair share draw: The assumption that a new product will capture sales (in unit or dollar terms) from existing products in direct proportion to the market shares held by those existing products.**

Example Three rivals compete in the youth fashion market in a small town. Their sales and market shares for last year appear in the following table:

Firm	Sales	Share
Threadbare	$500,000	50%
Too Cool for School	$300,000	30%
Tommy Hitchhiker	$200,000	20%
Total	$1,000,000	100%

A new entrant is expected to enter the market in the coming year and to generate $300,000 in sales. Two-thirds of those sales are expected to come at the expense of the three established competitors. Under an assumption of fair share draw, how much will each firm sell next year?

If the new firm takes two-thirds of its sales from existing competitors, then this "capture" of sales will total (2/3) * $300,000, or $200,000. Under fair share draw, the breakdown of that $200,000 will be proportional to the shares of the current competitors. Thus, 50% of the $200,000 will come from Threadbare, 30% from Too Cool, and 20% from

Tommy. The following table shows the projected sales and market shares next year of the four competitors under the fair share draw assumption:

Firm	Sales	Share
Threadbare	$400,000	36.36%
Too Cool for School	$240,000	21.82%
Tommy Hitchhiker	$160,000	14.55%
New Entrant	$300,000	27.27%
Total	$1,100,000	100%

Notice that the new entrant expands the market by $100,000, an amount equal to the sales of the new entrant that *do not* come at the expense of existing competitors. Notice also that under fair share draw, the relative shares of the existing competitors remain unchanged. For example, Threadbare's share, relative to the total of the original three competitors, is 36.36/(36.36 + 21.82 + 14.55), or 50%—equal to its share before the entry of the new competitor.

The opposite of cannibalization is incremental sales. This is when the introduction of a new product may boost sales for a complementary product—one that naturally goes with the product.

Data sources, complications, and cautions

As noted previously, with cannibalization, one of a firm's products takes sales from one or more of *that* firm's other products. Sales taken from the products of competitors are not "cannibalized" sales, although some managers label them as such.

Cannibalization rates depend on how the features, pricing, promotion, and distribution of the new product compare to those of a firm's existing products. The greater the similarity of their respective marketing strategies, the higher the cannibalization rate is likely to be.

Although cannibalization is always an issue when a firm launches a new product that competes with its established line, this dynamic is particularly damaging to the firm's profitability when a low-margin entrant captures sales from the firm's higher-margin offerings. In such cases, the new product's weighted contribution margin can be negative. Even when cannibalization rates are significant, however, and even if the net effect on the bottom line is negative, it may be wise for a firm to proceed with a new product if management believes that the original line is losing its competitive strength. The following example is illustrative.

Example A producer of powdered-milk formula has an opportunity to introduce a new, improved formula. The new formula has certain attributes not found in the firm's existing products. Due to higher costs, however, it will carry a contribution margin of only $8, compared with the $10 margin of the established formula. Analysis suggests that the unit cannibalization rate of the new formula will be 90% in its initial year. If the firm expects to sell 300 units of the new formula in its first year, should it proceed with the introduction?

Analysis shows that the new formula will generate $8 * 300, or $2,400 in direct contribution. Cannibalization, however, will reduce contribution from the established line by $10 * 0.9 * 300, or $2,700. Thus, the company's overall contribution will decline by $300 with the introduction of the new formula. (Note also that the weighted unit margin for the new product is −$1.) This simple analysis suggests that the new formula should not be introduced.

The following table, however, contains the results of a more detailed four-year analysis. Reflected in this table are management's beliefs that without the new formula, sales of the regular formula will decline to 700 units in Year 4. In addition, unit sales of the new formula are expected to increase to 600 in Year 4, while cannibalization rates decline to 60%.

	Year 1	Year 2	Year 3	Year 4	Total
Unit Sales of Regular Formula *Without* New Product Launch	1,000	900	800	700	3,400
		—		—	
Unit Sales of New Formula	300	400	500	600	1,800
Cannibalization Rate	90%	80%	70%	60%	—
Unit Sales of Regular Formula *With* New Product Launch	730	580	450	340	2,100

Without the new formula, total four-year contribution is projected as $10 * 3,400 = $34,000. With the new formula, total contribution is projected as ($8 * 1,800) + ($10 * 2,100) = $35,400. Although forecast contribution is lower in Year 1 with the new formula than without it, total four-year contribution is projected to be higher with the new product due to increases in new-formula sales and decreases in the cannibalization rate.

4.4 Brand equity metrics

Brand equity is strategically crucial but famously difficult to quantify. Many experts have developed tools to analyze this asset, but there's no universally accepted way

▶

▶

to measure it. In this section, we consider the following techniques to gain insight in this area:

Brand Equity Ten (Aaker)

BrandAsset® Valuator (BAV Group/VSLY&R)

Brand Finance

BrandZ (Millward Brown)

Brand Valuation Model (Interbrand)

Purpose: to measure the value of a brand.

A brand encompasses the name, logo, image, and perceptions that identify a product, service, or provider in the minds of customers. It takes shape in advertising, packaging, and other marketing communications and becomes a focus of the relationship with consumers. In time, a brand comes to embody a promise about the goods it identifies—a promise about quality, performance, or other dimensions of value that can influence consumers' choices among competing products. When consumers trust a brand and find it relevant, they may select the offerings associated with that brand over those of competitors, even at a premium price. Often people refer to *brand equity* as the incremental unit sales and/or price a product commands. Be careful not to confuse a brand's equity with only the premium price that it can command in a market. It should be noted that a complete measure of brand equity should also include the additional volume that is generated because of the product's name. Some firms elect to capture most of this value in price, such as for luxury goods, and sometimes in volume, such as for discounters. Most of the time, it is some of both.

When a brand's promise extends beyond a particular product, its owner may leverage it to enter new markets. This is another component of the brand's equity. As when measuring brand equity in its traditional market, the brand's equity in the new market is the incremental volume and/or price the product is able to attain in this new market attributable to the brand itself. As such, a brand can hold tremendous value.

Brand equity can be remarkably difficult to measure. At a corporate level, when one company buys another, analysts might apportion some of the excess of the purchase price over the value of recorded assets purchased to shed light on the value of the brands acquired. Beyond the value of its assets on the firm's balance sheet, a company's brands typically constitute important, unrecorded, intangible assets. Of course, a company's brands are rarely the only unrecorded items acquired in such a transaction. The excess of purchase price over recorded value frequently encompasses intellectual property, distribution systems, customer lists, and other intangibles in addition to brand. Firm valuations (sales or share prices) are also subject to economic cycles, investor "exuberance," and other influences that are difficult to separate from the intrinsic value. One often wants to consider the discounted cash flow from the incremental volume and price into current dollars. This requires forecasting sales and the influence of the brand into the future, which adds another degree of complexity to this measure.

From a consumer's perspective, the value of a brand might be the amount she would be willing to pay for merchandise that carries the brand's name, over and above the price she'd pay for identical unbranded goods.[2] Marketers strive to estimate this premium in order to gain insight into brand equity. Here again, however, they encounter daunting complexities, as individuals vary not only in their awareness of different brands but in the criteria by which they judge them, the evaluations they make, and the degree to which those opinions guide their purchase behavior. In a similar vein, the value of the brand might be the increased propensity to buy the product because it carries the brand name. This heterogeneity across the population reflects that the brand's value to one individual might be very different from another's. For example, the Starbucks brand might be very appealing to an individual, and it might make the person more likely to buy coffee at a Starbucks and willing to pay extra for it because it is Starbucks coffee. For another individual who may not like the taste of Starbucks coffee or the atmosphere of Starbucks shops, the value of the Starbucks brand might be zero and perhaps even negative.

Theoretically, a marketer might aggregate these preferences across an entire population to estimate the total premium its members would pay for goods of a certain brand. Even that, however, wouldn't fully capture brand equity. Kusum Ailawadi and her colleagues contend that the equity of a brand is better captured by its overall revenue premium (relative to generic goods) than by its price per unit alone. The revenue figure incorporates both price and quantity and so reflects a jump from one demand curve to another rather than a movement along a single curve.[3]

A successful brand shifts the demand curve for its goods or services outward; that is, it not only enables a provider to charge a higher price (P' rather than P, as shown in Figure 4.3), but it also sells an increased quantity (Q' rather than Q). Thus, brand equity in this example can be viewed as the difference between the revenue with the brand (P' * Q') and the revenue without the brand (P * Q)—depicted as the shaded area in Figure 4.3. (Of course, this example focuses on revenue, when, in fact, it is profit or present value of profits that matters more. But, given that the increase in price associated with the brand comes with no incremental variable costs, this lift represents profits as well.)

Figure 4.3 Brand equity: outward shift of demand curve

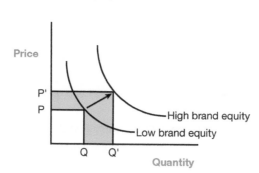

In practice, of course, it's difficult to measure a demand curve, and few marketers do so. Because brands are crucial assets, however, both marketers and academic researchers have devised means to contemplate their value. David Aaker, for example, tracks ten attributes of a brand to assess its strength, VSLY&R, a marketing consultancy, has developed a tool called the BrandAsset® Valuator, which measures a brand's power on the basis of differentiation, relevance, esteem, and knowledge. An even more theoretical conceptualization of brand equity is the difference of the firm value with and without the brand. If you find it difficult to imagine a firm without its brand, then you can appreciate how difficult it is to quantify brand equity. Interbrand, a brand strategy agency, draws upon its own model to separate tangible product value from intangible brand value and uses the latter to rank the top 100 global brands each year. Finally, conjoint analysis can shed light on a brand's value because it enables marketers to measure the impact of that brand on customer preference, treating it as one among many attributes that consumers trade off in making purchase decisions (see Section 4.5).

Construction

The International Organization for Standardization (ISO) has standards for brand valuation (10668) and brand evaluation (20671). (*Valuation* is usually used to refer to supplying dollar values, whereas *evaluation* is a wider term related to general brand health.) MASB sees ISO 20671, which was adopted in 2018, as a crucial step in helping accountable marketers build and manage their brands. A key requirement of the recent ISO standard is that there be a regular brand evaluation. Marketers should actively manage and monitor brands, which are a key asset for many firms.

Brand Equity Ten (Aaker)

David Aaker, a marketing professor and brand consultant, highlights ten attributes of a brand that can be used to assess its strength: differentiation, satisfaction or loyalty, perceived quality, leadership or popularity, perceived value, brand personality, organizational associations, brand awareness, market share, and market price and distribution coverage. Aaker doesn't weight the attributes or combine them in an overall score, as he believes any weighting would be arbitrary and would vary among brands and categories. Rather, he recommends tracking each attribute separately.

BrandAsset Valuator (BAV Group/VSLY&R)

BrandAsset® Valuator is a tool for diagnosing the power and value of a brand by surveying consumers' perspectives along four dimensions:

- **Differentiation:** The defining characteristics of the brand and its distinctiveness relative to competitors
- **Relevance:** The appropriateness and connection of the brand to a given consumer
- **Esteem:** Consumers' respect for and attraction to the brand
- **Knowledge:** Consumers' awareness of the brand and understanding of what it represents

BAV Group/VSLY&R maintains that these criteria reveal important factors behind brand strength and market dynamics. For example, although powerful brands score high on all four dimensions, growing brands may earn higher grades for differentiation and relevance than for knowledge and esteem. Fading brands often show the reverse pattern, as they're widely known and respected but may be declining toward commoditization or irrelevance (see Figure 4.4).

Figure 4.4 BAV Group/VSLY&R BrandAsset® Valuator patterns of brand equity

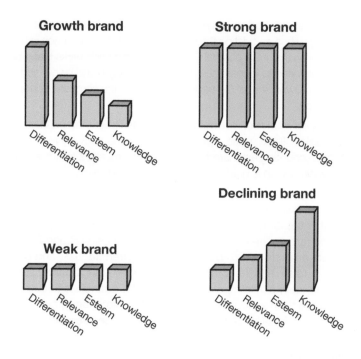

The BrandAsset® Valuator is a proprietary tool, but the concepts behind it have broad appeal. Many marketers apply these concepts by conducting independent research and exercising judgment about their own brands relative to the competition. Leon Ramsellar of Philips Consumer Electronics, for example, has reported using four key measures in evaluating brand equity and offers sample questions for assessing them:[4]

- **Uniqueness:** Does this product offer something new to me?
- **Relevance:** Is this product relevant for me?
- **Attractiveness:** Do I want this product?
- **Credibility:** Do I believe in the product?

Clearly, Ramsellar's list is not the same as the BrandAsset® Valuator, but the similarity of the first two factors is hard to miss.

Brand Finance

Founded in 1996, Brand Finance is an independent intangible asset valuation consultancy based in the UK with offices in more than 20 countries. It focuses on valuation of a firm's intangible assets.

The Brand Finance methodology specifies three alternative brand valuation approaches: the market, cost, and income approaches.

The basis for its calculation is centered around a concept of "Royalty Relief"—that is, how much a company would have to pay for the use of the brand name if it belonged to someone else.

- **Royalty Relief methodology:** Brand Finance uses a Royalty Relief methodology when calculating the value of a brand. This approach is based on the assumption that if the company did not own the trademarks that it benefits from, it would need to license them from a third-party brand owner and pay a licensing fee. Ownership of the trademarks relieves the company from paying this royalty fee.

- **Royalty Relief valuation formula:** The Royalty Relief method involves estimating likely future sales, applying an appropriate royalty rate to them, and then discounting estimated future, post-tax royalties to arrive at a net present value, which is held to represent the brand value.

- **Brand ratings:** In determining the appropriate royalty rate, Brand Finance establishes a range of comparable royalty rates and determines the point within the range where the brand under review falls by reference to a brand rating. The brand rating is calculated using Brand Finance's BrandBeta analysis, which benchmarks the strength, risk, and potential of a brand, relative to its competitors, on a scale ranging from AAA to D. It is conceptually similar to a credit rating. The data used to calculate the ratings come from various sources, including Bloomberg, annual reports, client-commissioned research, and Brand Finance internal research.

BrandZ (Millward Brown)

BrandZ, which is Millward Brown's brand equity database, holds data from more than 2 million consumers and professionals across 50 markets and compares more than 165,000 brands (www.brandz.com/about-us). The database is used to estimate brand valuations, and each year since 2006, it has been used to generate a list of the top 100 global brands.

The objective of the BrandZ methodology is to peel away all financial components of brand value to determine how much brand alone contributes to brand value. BrandZ conducts worldwide, ongoing, in-depth quantitative consumer research and builds up a global picture of brands on category-by-category and country-by-country bases. BrandZ uses the following pillars to anchor its brand valuation:

- **Meaningful:** In any category, meaningful brands appeal more, generate greater "love," and meet the individual's expectations and needs.

- **Different:** Different brands are unique in a positive way and "set the trends," staying ahead of the curve for the benefit of the consumer.
- **Salient:** Salient brands come spontaneously to mind as brands of choice for key needs.

BrandZ uses the following valuation process:

1. *Calculate financial value:*
  Part A

- Determine total corporate earnings from the corporation's entire portfolio of brands.
- Analyze financial information from annual reports and other sources, such as Kantar Worldpanel and Kantar Retail. This analysis yields a metric called Attribution Rate.
- Multiply Corporate Earnings by Attribution Rate to arrive at Branded Earnings, the amount of Corporate Earnings attributed to a particular brand. If the Attribution Rate of a brand is 50%, for example, then half the Corporate Earnings are identified as coming from that brand.

  Part B

- Determine future earnings and attribute an earnings multiple to the company. Information supplied by Bloomberg data is used to calculate the Brand Multiple. BrandZ multiplies Branded Earnings by Brand Multiple to arrive at Financial Value.

2. *Calculate brand contribution:*

- To arrive at Brand Value, peel away a few more layers, such as other factors that influence the value of the branded business (for example, price, convenience, availability, and distribution).
- Because a brand exists in the mind of the consumer, assess the brand's uniqueness and its ability to stand out from the crowd, generate desire, and cultivate loyalty. This unique role played by brand is called Brand Contribution.

3. *Calculate brand value:*

- Multiply Financial Value by Brand Contribution, which is expressed as a percentage of Financial Value. The result is Brand Value. Brand Value is the dollar amount a brand contributes to the overall value of a corporation. Isolating and measuring this intangible asset reveals an additional source of shareholder value that otherwise would not exist.

Brand Valuation Model (Interbrand)
Interbrand, a division of Omnicom, is a brand consultancy headquartered in New York City (see www.interbrand.com).

Interbrand publishes the Best Global Brands report on an annual basis. The report identifies the world's 100 most valuable brands. To develop the report, Interbrand examines three key aspects that contribute to a brand's value:

- The financial performance of the branded products or service
- The role the brand plays in influencing consumer choice
- The strength the brand has to command a premium price or secure earnings for the company

Interbrand has refined its brand valuation into a five-step Economic Value Added methodology. Through a similar methodology, Interbrand releases an annual ranking of the best global brands in its Best Global Brands report, which evaluates each brand's financial performance, role, and strength. To qualify, brands must have a presence on at least three major continents and must have broad geographic coverage in growing and emerging markets. Thirty percent of revenues must come from outside the home country, and no more than 50% of revenues should come from any one continent. Economic profit must be expected to be positive over the longer term, delivering a return above the brand's cost of capital. *The brand must have a public profile and awareness across the major economies of the world.*

The brand valuation methodology involves three key metrics:

- **Financial Analysis:** This metric measures the overall financial return to an organization's investors, or its "economic profit." Economic profit is the after-tax operating profit of the brand minus a charge for the capital used to generate the brand's revenue and margins.

- **Role of Brand:** Role of Brand measures the portion of the purchase decision attributable to the brand, as opposed to other factors (for example, purchase drivers like price, convenience, or product features). Role of Brand Index (RBI) quantifies this as a percentage. RBI determinations for Best Global Brands derive, depending on the brand, from one of three methods: primary research, a review of historical roles of brands for companies in that industry, or expert panel assessment.

- **Brand Strength:** Brand Strength measures the ability of the brand to create loyalty and, therefore, sustainable demand and profit into the future. Brand Strength analysis is based on an evaluation across several factors that Interbrand believes make a strong brand; factors are weighted and add up to 100. These factors include leadership (25), stability (15), market (10), geographic spread (25), trend (10), support (10), and protection (5). Performance on these factors is judged relative to other brands in the industry and relative to other world-class brands. The Brand Strength analysis delivers a snapshot of the strengths and weaknesses of the brand and is used to generate a road map of activity to enhance the strength and value of the brand in the future.

Conjoint analysis

Marketers use conjoint analysis to measure consumers' preference for various attributes of a product, service, or provider, such as features, design, price, or location (see Section 4.5). By including brand and price as two of the attributes under consideration, they can gain insight into consumers' valuation of a brand—that is, their willingness to pay a premium for it.

Data sources, complications, and cautions

The methods described previously represent experts' best attempts to place a value on a complex and intangible entity. Almost all of the metrics in this book are relevant to brand equity along one dimension or another.

Related metrics and concepts

Brand strategy is a broad field and includes several concepts that at first may appear to be measurable. Strictly speaking, however, brand strategy is not a metric.

> **Brand identity:** This is the marketer's vision of an ideal brand—the company's goal for perception of that brand by its target market. All physical, emotional, visual, and verbal messages should be directed toward realization of that goal, including name, logo, signature, and other marketing communications. Brand Identity, however, is not stated in quantifiable terms.
>
> **Brand position and brand image:** These metrics refer to consumers' actual perceptions of a brand, often relative to its competition. Brand Position is frequently measured along product dimensions that can be mapped in multidimensional space. If measured consistently over time, these dimensions may be viewed as metrics—as coordinates on a perceptual map. (See Section 2.7 for a discussion of attitude, usage measures, and the hierarchy of effects.)
>
> **Product differentiation:** This is one of the most frequently used terms in marketing, but it has no universally agreed-upon definition. More than mere "difference," it generally refers to distinctive attributes of a product that generate increased customer preference or demand. These are often difficult to view quantitatively because they may be actual or perceived—as well as non-monotonic. In other words, although certain attributes such as price can be quantified and may follow a linear preference model (that is, either more or less is always better), others can't be analyzed numerically or may fall into a sweet spot, outside of which neither more nor less would be preferred (the spiciness of a food, for example). For all these reasons, Product Differentiation is hard to analyze as a metric and has been criticized as a "meaningless term."[5]

4.5 Conjoint utilities and consumer preference

Conjoint analysis is a form of data collection and analysis that measures relative customer preferences for a level of an attribute. Conjoint analysis has had several different names over the years. Trade-off analysis and choice modeling are extensions of the original conjoint methodology. We refer to "conjoint" to describe this entire class of analysis.

Conjoint utilities or weights measure consumer preference for an attribute level and then—by combining the valuations of multiple attributes—measure preference for an overall choice. Measures are generally made on an individual basis, although this analysis can also be performed at the segment level. In recent years, another variant of Bayesian choice modeling or Bayesian discrete choice modeling has been used to similarly measure the relative attribute-level weights leading to option or brand choice. In the frozen pizza market, for example, conjoint utilities can be used to determine how much a customer values superior taste (one attribute) versus paying extra for premium cheese (a second attribute).

Conjoint utilities can also play a role in analyzing compensatory decisions—that is, where weaknesses in some attributes can be made up, or compensated for, in other attributes. A weakness in a non-compensatory factor cannot be overcome by other strengths.

Conjoint analysis can be useful in determining what customers want and—when price is included as an attribute—is sometimes used for what they'll pay for it. In launching new products, marketers find such analyses useful for achieving a deeper understanding of the values that customers place on various product attributes. Throughout product management, conjoint utilities can help marketers focus their efforts on the attributes of greatest importance to customers.

Purpose: to understand the relative preferences of consumers for product attributes.

Conjoint analysis is a method used to estimate customers' preferences, based on how customers weight the attributes on which a choice is made. The premise of conjoint analysis is that a customer's preference between product options can be broken into a set of attributes that are weighted to form an overall evaluation. Rather than ask people directly what they want and why, in conjoint analysis, marketers ask people about their overall preferences for a set of choices described on their attributes and then decompose those into the component dimensions and weights underlying them. A model can be developed to compare sets of attributes to determine which represents the most appealing bundle of attributes for customers.

Conjoint analysis is a technique commonly used to assess the attributes of a product or service that are important to targeted customers and to assist in the following:

- Product design
- Advertising copy
- Pricing
- Segmentation
- Forecasting

Construction

> **Conjoint analysis/Choice modeling: A method of estimating customers' preference by assessing the overall preferences or choices customers assign to alternative options.**

An individual's preference or choice can be expressed as the total of his or her baseline preferences for any option, plus the partworths (relative values) for that choice expressed by the individual.

In a linear form, this can be represented by the following formula:

Conjoint Preference Linear Form (I) = [Partworth of Attribute1 to Individual (I) * Attribute Level (1)] + [Partworth of Attribute2 to Individual (I) * Attribute Level (2)] + [Partworth of Attribute3 to Individual (I) * Attribute Level (3)] and so on

Example Two attributes of a smartphone, its price and its size, are ranked through conjoint analysis, yielding the results shown in Table 4.5.

Table 4.5 Conjoint analysis: price and size of a smartphone

Attribute	Level	Partworth
Price	$500	0.9
Price	$600	0.1
Price	$700	**−1**
Size	Small	0.7
Size	Medium	−0.1
Size	Large	−0.6

A small smartphone for $500 has a partworth to customers of 1.6 (derived as 0.9 + 0.7). This is the highest result observed in this exercise. A small but expensive ($700) phone is rated as −0.3 (that is, −1 + 0.7). The desirability of this small smartphone is offset by its price. A large, expensive smartphone is least desirable to customers, generating a partworth of −1.6 (that is, −1 + −0.6).

On this basis, we determine that the customer whose views are analyzed here would prefer a medium-size phone at $600 (utility = 0) to a small phone at $700 (utility = −0.3). Such information would be informative to decisions concerning the trade-offs between product design and price.

This analysis also demonstrates that, within the ranges examined, price is more important than size from the perspective of this consumer. Price generates a range of effects from 0.9 to −1 (that is, a total spread of 1.9), while the effects generated by the most and least desirable sizes span a range only from 0.7 to −0.6 (total spread = 1.3).

Ideally, if the partworths are measured correctly, by assessing the partworth of a feature relative to the corresponding partworth for price, it would be possible to measure a willingness to pay (WTP) for a feature or level of a feature.[6]

Compensatory versus non-compensatory consumer decisions

A compensatory decision process is one in which a customer evaluates choices with the perspective that strengths along one or more dimensions can compensate for weaknesses along others.

In a non-compensatory decision process, by contrast, if certain attributes of a product are weak, no compensation is possible, even if the product possesses strengths along other dimensions. In the previous smartphone example, for instance, some customers may feel that if a phone were greater than a certain size, no price would make it attractive.

In another example, most people choose a grocery store on the basis of proximity. Any store within a certain radius of home or work may be considered. Beyond that distance, however, all stores will be excluded from consideration, and there is nothing a store can do to overcome this. Even if it posts extraordinarily low prices, offers a stunningly wide assortment, creates great displays, and stocks the freshest foods, for example, a store will not entice consumers to travel 400 miles to buy groceries.

Although this example is extreme to the point of absurdity, it illustrates an important point: When consumers make a choice on a non-compensatory basis, marketers need to define the dimensions along which certain attributes *must* be delivered simply to qualify for consideration of their overall offering.

One form of non-compensatory decision making is elimination by aspect. In this approach, consumers look at an entire set of choices and then eliminate those that do not meet their expectations in the order of the importance of the attributes. In the selection of a grocery store, for example, this process might run as follows:

● Which stores are within 5 miles of my home?
● Which ones are open after 8 p.m.?

- Which carry the spicy mustard that I like?
- Which carry fresh flowers?

The process continues until only one choice is left.

In the ideal situation, in analyzing customers' decision processes, marketers would have access to information on an individual level, revealing

- Whether the decision for each customer is compensatory or not
- The priority order of the attributes
- The "cut-off" levels for each attribute
- The relative importance weight of each attribute if the decision follows a compensatory process

More frequently, however, marketers have access only to past behavior in making inferences regarding these items.

In the absence of detailed, individual information for customers throughout a market, conjoint analysis provides a means to gain insight into the decision-making processes of a sampling of customers. In conjoint analysis, we generally assume a compensatory process. That is, we assume utilities are additive. Under this assumption, if a choice is weak along one dimension (for example, if a store does not carry spicy mustard), it can compensate for this with strength along another (for example, it does carry fresh-cut flowers)—at least in part. Conjoint analyses can approximate a non-compensatory model by assigning non-linear weighting to an attribute across certain levels of its value. For example, the weightings for distance to a grocery store might run as follows:

Within 1 mile:	0.9
1–5 miles away:	0.8
5–10 miles away:	−0.8
More than 10 miles away:	−0.9

In this example, stores outside a 5-mile radius cannot practically make up the loss of utility they incur as a result of distance. Distance becomes, in effect, a non-compensatory dimension.

By studying customers' decision-making processes, marketers gain insight into the attributes needed to meet consumer expectations. They learn, for example, whether certain attributes are compensatory or non-compensatory. A strong understanding of customers' valuation of different attributes also enables marketers to tailor products and allocate resources effectively.

Several potential complications arise in considering compensatory versus non-compensatory decisions. Customers often don't know whether an attribute is compensatory or not, and they may not be readily able to explain their decisions. Therefore, it is often necessary either to infer a customer's decision-making process or to determine that process through an evaluation of choices, rather than a description of the process.

It is possible, however, to uncover non-compensatory elements through conjoint analysis. Any attribute for which the valuation spread is so high that it cannot practically be made up by other features is, in effect, a non-compensatory attribute.

Example Among grocery stores, Juan prefers the Acme market because it's close to his home, despite the fact that Acme's prices are generally higher than those at the local Shoprite store. A third store, Vernon's, is located in Juan's apartment complex. But Juan avoids it because Vernon's doesn't carry his favorite soda.

From this information, we know that Juan's shopping choice is influenced by at least three factors: price, distance from his home, and whether a store carries his favorite soda. In Juan's decision process, price and distance seem to be compensating factors. He trades price for distance. Whether the soda is stocked seems to be a non-compensatory factor. If a store doesn't carry Juan's favorite soda, it will not win his business, regardless of how well it scores on price and location.

Data sources, complications, and cautions

Prior to conducting a conjoint study, it is necessary to identify the attributes of importance to a customer. Focus groups are commonly used for this purpose. After attributes and levels are determined, a typical approach to conjoint analysis is to use a fractional factorial orthogonal design, which is a partial sample of all possible combinations of attributes. This reduces the total number of choice evaluations required by the respondent. With an orthogonal design, the attributes remain independent of one another, and the test doesn't weigh one attribute disproportionately to another.

There are multiple ways to gather data, but a straightforward approach would be to present respondents with choices and to ask them to rate those choices according to their preferences. Those preferences then become the dependent variable in a regression, in which attribute levels serve as the independent variables, as in the previous equation. Conjoint utilities constitute the weights determined to best capture the preference ratings provided by the respondent.

Often, certain attributes work in tandem to influence customer choice. For example, a fast *and* sleek sports car may provide greater value to a customer than would be suggested by the sum of the fast and sleek attributes. Such relationships between attributes are not captured by a simple conjoint model unless one accounts for interactions.

Ideally, conjoint analysis is performed on an individual level because attributes can be weighted differently across individuals. Marketers can also create a more balanced view by performing analysis across a sample of individuals. It is appropriate to perform the analysis within consumer segments that have similar weights. Conjoint analysis can be viewed as a snapshot in time of a customer's desires. It will not necessarily translate indefinitely into the future.

It is vital to use the correct attributes in any conjoint study. People can only tell you their preferences within the parameters you set. If the correct attributes are not included in a study, while it may be possible to determine the *relative* importance of those attributes that *are* included, and it may technically be possible to form segments on the basis of the resulting data, the analytic results may not be valid for forming *useful* segments. For example, in a conjoint analysis of consumer preferences regarding colors and styles of cars, one may correctly group customers as to their feelings about these attributes. But if consumers really care most about engine size, then those segmentations will be of little value.

4.6   Segmentation using conjoint utilities

Understanding customers' desires is a vital goal of marketing. Segmenting, or clustering similar customers into groups, can help managers recognize useful patterns and identify attractive subsets within a larger market. With that understanding, managers can select target markets, develop appropriate offerings for each, determine the most effective ways to reach the targeted segments, and allocate resources accordingly. Conjoint analysis can be highly useful in this exercise.

Purpose: to identify segments based on conjoint utilities.

As described in the previous section, conjoint analysis is used to determine customers' preferences on the basis of the attribute weightings that they reveal in their decision-making processes. These weights, or utilities, are generally evaluated on an individual level.

Segmentation entails the grouping of customers who demonstrate similar patterns of preference and weighting with regard to certain product attributes, distinct from the patterns exhibited by other groups. Using segmentation, a company can decide which group(s) to target and can determine an approach to appeal to the segment's members. After segments have been formed, a company can set strategy based on their attractiveness (size, growth, purchase rate, diversity) and on the company's capability to serve these segments, relative to competitors.

Construction

To complete a segmentation based on conjoint utilities, one must first determine utility scores at an individual customer level. Next, one must cluster these customers into segments of like-minded individuals. This is generally done through a methodology known as cluster analysis.

Cluster analysis

Cluster analysis is a technique that calculates the distances between customers and forms groups by minimizing the differences within each group and maximizing the differences between groups.

Cluster analysis operates by calculating a "distance" (a sum of squares) between individuals and, in a hierarchical fashion, starts pairing those individuals together. The process of pairing minimizes the "distance" within a group and creates a manageable number of segments within a larger population.

Example The Samson-Finn Company has three customers. In order to help manage its marketing efforts, Samson-Finn wants to organize like-minded customers into segments. Toward that end, it performs a conjoint analysis in which it measures its customers' preferences among products that are either reliable or very reliable and either fast or very fast (see Table 4.6). It then considers the conjoint utilities of each of its customers to see which of them demonstrate similar wants. When clustering on conjoint data, the distances are calculated on the partworths.

Table 4.6 Customer conjoint utilities

	Very reliable	Reliable	Very fast	Fast
Bob	0.4	0.3	0.6	0.2
Erin	0.9	0.1	0.2	0.7
Yogesh	0.3	0.3	0.5	0.2

The analysis looks at the difference between Bob's view and Erin's view on the importance of reliability on their choice. Bob's score is 0.4, and Erin's is 0.9. We can square the difference between these to derive the "distance" between Bob and Erin.

Using this methodology, the distance between each pair of Samson-Finn's customers can be calculated as follows:

Distances	Very reliable	Reliable	Very fast	Fast
Bob and Erin:	$= (0.4 - 0.9)^2$	$+ (0.3 - 0.1)^2$	$+ (0.6 - 0.2)^2$	$+ (0.2 - 0.7)^2$
	$= 0.25$	$+ 0.04$	$+ 0.16$	$+ 0.25$
	$= 0.7$			
Bob and Yogesh:	$= (0.4 - 0.3)^2$	$+ (0.3 - 0.3)^2$	$+ (0.6 - 0.5)^2$	$+ (0.2 - 0.2)^2$
	$= 0.01$	$+ 0.0$	$+ 0.01$	$+ 0.0$
	$= 0.02$			
Erin and Yogesh:	$= (0.9 - 0.3)^2$	$+ (0.1 - 0.3)^2$	$+ (0.2 - 0.5)^2$	$+ (0.7 - 0.2)^2$
	$= 0.36$	$+ 0.04$	$+ 0.09$	$+ 0.25$
	$= 0.74$			

On this basis, Bob and Yogesh appear to be very close to each other because their sum of squares is 0.02. As a result, they should be considered part of the same segment. Conversely, in light of the high sum-of-squares distance established by her preferences, Erin should not be considered a part of the same segment with either Bob or Yogesh.

Of course, most segmentation analyses are performed on large customer bases. This example merely illustrates the process involved in the cluster analysis calculations.

Data sources, complications, and cautions

As noted previously, a customer's utilities may not be stable, and the segment to which a customer belongs can shift over time or across occasions. An individual might belong to one segment for personal air travel, in which price might be a major factor, and another for business travel, in which convenience might become more important. Such a customer's conjoint weights (utilities) would differ depending on the purchase occasion.

Determining the appropriate *number* of segments for an analysis can be somewhat arbitrary. There is no generally accepted statistical means for determining the "correct" number of segments. Ideally, marketers look for a segment structure that fulfills the following qualifications:

- Each segment constitutes a homogeneous group, within which there is relatively little variance between attribute utilities of different individuals.

- Groupings are heterogeneous across segments; that is, there is a wide variance of attribute utilities *between* segments.

4.7   Conjoint utilities and volume projection

The conjoint utilities of products and services are sometimes used to forecast the market share that each will achieve and the volume that each will sell. Marketers project market share for a given product or service on the basis of the proportion of individuals who select it from a relevant choice set, as well as its overall utility. This, of course, assumes that the attributes included in the conjoint study are the ones on which customers make their decisions. Omitting important attributes that vary across the choices in the marketplace will lead to incorrect forecasts of market share.

Purpose: to use conjoint analysis to project the market share and the sales volume that will be achieved by a product or service.

Conjoint analysis is used to measure the utilities for a product. The combination of these utilities, generally additive, represents a scoring of sorts for the expected popularity of that product. These scores can be used to rank products. However, further information is needed to estimate market share. One can anticipate that the top-ranked product in a selection set will have a greater probability of being chosen by an individual than products ranked lower for that individual. (This is one method to estimate market share.) Adding the number of customers who rank the brand first should allow the calculation of customer share.

Data sources, complications, and cautions

To complete a sales volume projection, it is necessary to conduct a full conjoint analysis. This analysis must include all the important features according to which consumers make their choice. Defining the "market" is clearly crucial to a meaningful result.

To define a market, it is important to identify all the choices in that market. Calculating the percentage of "first choice" selections for each alternative merely provides a "share of preferences." To extend this to market share, one must estimate (1) the volume of sales per customer, (2) the level of distribution or availability for each choice, and (3) the percentage of customers who will defer their purchase until they can find their first choice.

The greatest potential error in this process would be to exclude meaningful attributes from the conjoint analysis.

Network effects can also distort a conjoint analysis. In some instances, customers do not make purchase decisions purely on the basis of a product's attributes but are also affected by its level of acceptance in the marketplace. Such network effects, and the importance of harnessing or overcoming them, are especially evident during shifts in technology industries.

Further reading

Aaker, D. A. (1991). *Managing Brand Equity: Capitalizing on the Value of a Brand Name*, Free Press.

Aaker, D. A. (1996). *Building Strong Brands*, Free Press.

Aaker, D. A., and J. M. Carman. (1982). "Are You Overadvertising?" *Journal of Advertising Research,* 22(4), 57–70.

Aaker, D. A., and K. L. Keller. (1990). "Consumer Evaluations of Brand Extensions," *Journal of Marketing,* 54(1), 27–41.

Ailawadi, Kusum, and Kevin Keller. (2004). "Understanding Retail Branding: Conceptual Insights and Research Priorities," *Journal of Retailing,* 80(4), 331–342.

Ailawadi, Kusum, Donald Lehman, and Scott Neslin. (2003). "Revenue Premium as an Outcome Measure of Brand Equity," *Journal of Marketing,* 67(4), 1–17.

Bruno, Hernan A., Unmish Parthasarathi, and Nisha Singh, eds. (2005). "The Changing Face of Measurement Tools Across the Product Lifecycle," *Does Marketing Measure Up? Performance Metrics: Practices and Impact,* Marketing Science Institute, No. 05-301.

Rangan, V. Kasturi, and Marie Bell. (1995). *Nestle Refrigerated Foods: Contadina Pasta & Pizza (A).* Harvard Business School.

Customer profitability

5

Key concepts covered in this chapter:

- Customers, recency, and retention

- Customer profit

- Customer lifetime value

- Acquisition versus retention spending

- Prospect value versus customer value

Introduction

Chapter 2, "Share of hearts, minds, and markets," presents metrics designed to measure how well a firm is doing with its customers on the whole. To this point in the book, we have discussed metrics that provide summaries of firm performance with respect to customers for entire markets or market segments. In this chapter, we cover metrics that measure the performance of individual customer relationships. We start with metrics designed to simply count how many customers the firm serves. As this chapter illustrates, it is far easier to count the number of units sold than to count the number of people or businesses buying those units.

Section 5.2 introduces the concept of customer profit. Just as some brands are more profitable than others, so too are some customer relationships. Whereas customer profit is a metric that summarizes the past financial performance of a customer relationship, customer lifetime value looks forward in an attempt to value existing customer relationships.

Section 5.3 discusses how to calculate and interpret customer lifetime value. One of the most important uses of customer lifetime value is to inform prospecting decisions. Section 5.4 explains how this can be accomplished and draws the careful distinction between prospect and customer value.

Section 5.5 discusses Average Acquisition Cost and Average Retention Cost—two metrics firms track in order to monitor the performance of two important kinds of marketing spending: spending designed to acquire new customers and spending designed to retain and profit from existing customers.

	Metric	Construction	Considerations	Purpose
5.1	Customers	The number of people (or businesses) who bought from the firm during a specified time period.	Avoid double counting people who bought more than one product. Carefully define customer as individual/household/screen name/division who bought/ordered/registered.	Measure how well the firm is attracting and retaining customers.
5.1	Recency	The length of time since a customer's last purchase.	In non-contractual situations, the firm will want to track the recency of its customers.	Track changes in number of active customers.
5.1	Retention Rate	The ratio of customers retained to the number at risk.	Not to be confused with growth (decline) in customer counts. Retention refers only to existing customers in contractual situations.	Track changes in the ability of the firm to retain customers.
5.2	Customer Profit	The difference between the revenues earned from and the costs associated with the customer relationship during a specified period.	Requires assigning revenues and costs to individual customers.	Identify which customers are profitable and which are not as a precursor to differential treatment designed to improve firm profitability.

	Metric	Construction	Considerations	Purpose
5.3	Customer Lifetime Value	The present value of the future cash flows attributed to the customer relationship.	Requires a projection of future cash flows from a customer relationship. This is easier to do in a contractual situation. Formulations of CLV differ with respect to the treatment of the initial margin.	Customer relationship management decisions should be made with the objective of improving CLV. Acquisition budgeting should be based on CLV.
5.4	Prospect Lifetime Value	The response rate times the sum of the initial margin and the CLV of the acquired customer minus the cost of the prospecting effort.	There are a variety of equivalent ways to do the calculations necessary to see whether a prospecting effort is worthwhile.	Guide the firm's prospecting decisions. Prospecting is beneficial only if the expected prospect lifetime value is positive.
5.5	Average Acquisition Cost	The ratio of acquisition spending to the number of new customers acquired.	It is often difficult to isolate acquisition spending from total marketing spending.	Track the cost of acquiring new customers and to compare that cost to the value of the newly acquired customers.
5.5	Average Retention Cost	The ratio of retention spending to the number of customers retained.	It is often difficult to isolate retention spending from total marketing spending. The average retention cost number is not very useful in making retention budgeting decisions.	Monitor retention spending on a per-customer basis.

5.1 Customers, recency, and retention

These three metrics are used to count customers and track customer activity, regardless of the number of transactions (or dollar value of those transactions) made by each customer. Here "customer" is a general term referring to individuals, households, accounts, or other firms who buy from the firm.

- **Customer Count:** The number of customers of a firm for a specified time period.

- **Recency:** The length of time since a customer's last purchase. A six-month customer is someone who purchased from the firm at least once within the last six months.

- **Retention Rate:** The ratio of the number of retained customers to the number at risk.

In contractual situations, it makes sense to talk about the number of customers currently under contract and the percentage retained when the contract period runs out.

In non-contractual situations (such as catalog sales), it makes less sense to talk about the *current* number of customers; instead, it is appropriate to count the number of customers of a specified recency.

Purpose: to monitor firm performance in attracting and retaining customers.

Only recently have most marketers worried about developing metrics that focus on individual customers. In order to begin to think about managing individual customer relationships, a firm must first be able to count its customers. Although consistency in counting customers is probably more important than formulating a precise definition, a definition is needed nonetheless. In particular, we think the definition of and the counting of customers are different in contractual versus non-contractual situations.

Construction

Counting customers

In contractual situations, it should be fairly easy to count how many customers are currently under contract at any point in time. For instance, Bell Canada, a Canadian communications firm, reported 9.61 million direct customers (subscribers) in 2018 for its wireless service.[1]

One complication in counting customers in contractual situations is the handling of contracts that cover two or more individuals. Does a family plan that includes five phones on one bill count as one or five? Does a business-to-business contract with one base fee and charges for each of 1,000 phones in use count as 1 or 1,000 customers? Does the answer to the previous question depend on whether the individual users pay the wireless company, pay their company, or pay nothing? In situations such as these, the firm must select some standard definition of a customer (such as policyholder or member) and implement it consistently.

A second complication of counting customers in contractual situations is the treatment of customers with multiple contracts with a single firm. USAA, a global insurance and diversified financial services association, provides insurance and financial services to the U.S. military community and their families. Each customer is considered a member and has a unique membership number. This allows USAA to know exactly how many members it has at any time—nearly 13 million at the end of 2018—most of whom avail themselves of a variety of member services.

For other financial services companies, however, counts are often listed separately for each line of business. State Farm Insurance, for example, as of December 2019, listed a total of 82.9 million policies and accounts, giving a breakdown among auto, fire, life, and so on.[2] The 82.9 million figure is a count of policies and not customers. Presumably because some customers use State Farm for auto, fire, and life insurance, they get double and even triple counted in the 82.9 million number. Because State Farm knows the names and addresses of all its policyholders, it seems feasible that it could count how many individual customers it serves. The fact that State Farm counts policies and not customers suggests an emphasis on selling policies rather than managing customer relationships.

Finally, we offer an example of a natural gas company that went out of its way to double count customers—defining a customer to be "a consumer of natural gas distributed in any one billing period at one location through one meter. An entity using gas at separate locations is considered a separate customer at each location."[3] For this natural gas company, customers were synonymous with meters. This is probably a great way to view things if your job is to install and service meters. It is not such a great way to view things if your job is to market natural gas.

In non-contractual situations, the ability of a firm to count customers depends on whether individual customers are identifiable. If customers are not identifiable, firms can only count visits or transactions. Because Wal-Mart does not identify its shoppers, its customer counts are nothing more than the number of transactions that go through the cash registers in a day, week, or year. These "traffic" counts are akin to turnstile numbers at sporting events and visits to a website. In one sense, they count people, but when summed over several periods, they no longer measure separate individuals. So whereas home attendance at Atlanta Braves games in 1993 was 3,884,720, the number of people attending one or more Braves games that year was some smaller number.[4]

In non-contractual situations with identifiable customers (direct mail, retailers with frequent shopper cards, warehouse clubs, purchases of rental cars and lodgings that require registration), a complication is that customer purchase activity is sporadic. Whereas *The New York Times* knows exactly how many *current* customers (subscribers) it has, the sporadic buying of retailer L.L.Bean's customers means that it makes no sense to talk about the number of *current* L.L.Bean customers. L.L.Bean will know the number of orders it receives daily, it will know the number of catalogs it mails monthly, but it cannot be expected to know the number of current customers because it is difficult to define a "current" customer.

Firms in non-contractual situations count how many customers have bought within a certain period of time. This is the concept of recency—the length of time since the last purchase. Customers of recency one year or less are customers who have bought within the past year. Firms in non-contractual situations with identifiable customers do count customers of various recencies.

> Recency: The length of time since a customer's last purchase.

For example, eBay reported 183 million active users in the fourth quarter of 2019. Active users were defined as the number of users of the eBay platform who had bid, bought, or listed an item within the previous 12-month period. eBay also indicated that 179 million active users were reported in the same period a year earlier.[5]

Notice that eBay counts "active users" rather than "customers" and uses the concept of recency to track the number of active users across time. The number of active (12-month) users increased from 179 million to 183 million in one year. This tells the firm that the number of active customers increased due in part to customer acquisition. A measure of how well the firm maintained existing customer relationships is the percentage of the 179 million active customers one year earlier who had been active in the previous 12 months. That ratio measure is similar to retention but is better labeled a repeat rate (see Section 2.5).

> Retention: Applies to contractual situations in which customers are either retained or not. Customers either renew their magazine subscriptions or let them run out. Customers maintain a checking account with a bank until they close it out. Renters pay rent until they move out. These are examples of pure customer retention situations where customers are either retained or considered lost for good.

In these situations, firms pay close attention to retention rates.

> Retention rate: The ratio of the number of customers retained to the number at risk.

If 40,000 subscriptions to *Fortune* magazine are set to expire in July and the publisher convinces 26,000 of those customers to renew, we would say that the publisher retained 65% of its subscribers.

The complement of retention is attrition or churn. The attrition or churn rate for the 40,000 *Fortune* subscribers was 35%.

Notice that this definition of retention is a ratio of the number retained to the number at risk (of not being retained). The key feature of this definition is that a customer must be at risk of leaving in order to be counted as a customer successfully retained. This means that new *Fortune* subscribers obtained during July are not part of the equation, nor are the large number of customers whose subscriptions were set to run out in later months.

Finally, we point out that it sometimes makes better sense to measure retention in "customer time" rather than "calendar time." Rather than ask what the firm's retention rate was in 2019, it may be more informative to ask what percentage of customers surviving for three years were retained throughout Year 4.

Data sources, complications, and cautions

The ratio of the total number of customers at the end of the period to the number of customers at the beginning of the period is not a retention rate. Retention during the period does affect this ratio, but customer acquisitions also affect the ratio.

The percentage of customers starting the period who remained customers throughout the period is a lot closer to being a retention rate. This percentage would be a true retention rate if all the customers starting the period were at risk of leaving during the period.

Advice on counting customers[6]

Defining the customer properly is critical

Marketers tend to count "customers" in ways that are easy and consequently get the wrong answers. They tend to gloss over the fundamental and critically important step of *defining the customer*. With the wrong definition, counting doesn't matter.

Banks look at "households" because they are "relationship" obsessed (*relationship* being defined as the number of products sold to customers with a common account address). Banks tend to emphasize the number of products sold—no matter that the household may contain a business owner with nearly all the accounts, a spouse who banks mostly elsewhere, and children who do not bank at all. Household in this situation is meaningless. There are at least three "customers" here: business owner (a great customer), spouse (almost a non-customer), and kids (definitely non-customers).

Retailers count transactions, or "tickets" (cash register receipts), which may cover stuff sold to Mom, Dad, and the kids, along with Aunt Mary and neighbor Sue. Or it may reflect a purchase by a spouse who is buying for his or her partner under specific instructions. In this circumstance, the spouse giving the instructions is the real customer, while the other merely implements the transaction.

Defining the customer is nearly always hard because it requires a clear understanding of both business strategy and buyer behavior.

Not all "customers" are the same

Attracting and retaining "customers" cannot be measured for management action purposes without understanding the differences between customers. Last year, if a major software firm we will call Zapp bought a single copy of a piece of software and another company we will call Tancat bought 100 copies, are these both "customers"? Of course not. Tancat is almost certainly a customer that needs to be retained and possibly expanded into other products. Zapp is probably just evaluating the product in order to stay on top of new software concepts and potentially copy it. One option is to follow up with Zapp about the one-copy purchase to see what is really going on. Zapp could become a great "customer" if we understand what motivated its purchase or if we use that purchase to gain a contact base.

Before you count anything, you have to segment your potential and current product or service users into groups that can be strategically addressed. Some current buyers, such as Zapp, are actually potential buyers in terms of what you should do about them. You must count buyers and prospects who are alike in defined ways.

Where is the "customer"?

Large customers often buy independently from each user location. Is Bank of America the customer, or is each branch office a customer? If Citicorp were to buy centrally, how could you count it as one customer while Bank of America counts as hundreds of customers?

Who is the "customer"?

Defining who is the customer is even trickier. Many "customers" are not those who place the order with your salespeople. The real customer is deep within the bowels of the buyer organization—and it would take a great deal of effort to even identify that person. The account name may be GM, but the real customer may be Burt Cipher, an engineer in some unknown facility. Or the Ford buyer may have consolidated orders from several individuals scattered across the country. In this case, Ford is not the customer for anything but billing purposes. So, what do you count?

Even more common is the multi-headed customer. Buying decisions are made by several people. Different people may be central to a decision at different times or for different products. Big companies have sales teams dedicated to selling into such buying groups. Although they may be counted as a single customer, the dynamics of their buying decision are substantially more complicated than decisions made by a single individual.

Apparel retailers who sell pre-teen clothing have at least two customers: Mom and the pre-teen wearer. Do you count one or both as customers? Marketing might want to treat each as a customer for deciding how to design and place ads. The store might treat them both as a single customer or choose the pre-teen as the target.

The key takeaway is that customer definition for counting depends fundamentally on the purpose of the count. You may have to count the same "customer" in different ways for different purposes. There is no universal customer definition.

5.2 Customer profit

Customer profit (CP) is the profit a firm made from serving a customer or customer group over a specified period of time.

Calculating customer profitability is an important step in understanding which customer relationships are better than others. Often, a firm will find that some customer relationships are unprofitable. The firm may be better off (more profitable) without those customers. At the other end, the firm will identify its most profitable customers and be in a position to take steps to ensure the continuation of these most profitable relationships.

Purpose: to identify the profitability of individual customers.

Companies commonly look at their performance in aggregate. A common phrase is something like: "We had a good year, and the business units delivered $400,000 in profits." When customers are considered, the company is often using an average such as "We made a profit of $2.50 per customer." Although these can be useful metrics, they sometimes disguise an important fact that not all customers are equal and, worse yet, some are unprofitable. Simply put, rather than measure the "average customer," we can learn a lot by finding out what each customer contributes to our bottom line.[7]

Customer profitability: The difference between the revenues earned from and the costs associated with the customer relationship during a specified period.

The overall profitability of a company can be improved by treating dissimilar customers differently.

In essence, think of three different tiers of customer:

- **Top-Tier customers—REWARD:** Your most valuable customers are the ones you most want to retain. They should receive more of your attention than any other group. If you lose these people, your profit suffers the most. Look to reward them in ways other than simply lowering your price. These customers probably value what you do the most and may not be price sensitive.

- **Second-Tier customers—GROW:** The customers in the middle—with middle to low profits associated with them—might be targeted for growth. You might be able to develop these customers into top-tier customers. Look to the share of customer metrics described in Section 5.3 to help figure out which customers have the most growth potential.

- **Third-Tier customers—FIRE:** The company loses money on servicing these people. If you cannot easily promote them to the higher tiers of profitability, you should consider charging them more for the services they currently consume. If you can recognize this group beforehand, it may be best not to acquire these customers in the first place.

A database that can analyze the profitability of customers at an individual level can be a competitive advantage. If you can figure out profitability by customer, you have a chance to defend your best customers and maybe even poach the most profitable consumers from your competitors.

Construction

In theory, this is a trouble-free calculation. Find out the cost to serve each customer and the revenues associated with each customer for a given period. Do the subtraction to get profit for the customer and sort the customers based on profit. Although this is painless in theory, large companies with a multitude of customers will find this a major challenge even with the most sophisticated of databases.

To do the analysis with large databases, it may be necessary to abandon the notion of calculating profit for each individual customer and work with meaningful groups of customers instead.

After you have the sorted list of customer profits (or customer-group profits), the custom is to plot cumulative percentage of total profits versus cumulative percentage of total customers. Given that the customers are sorted from highest profit to lowest profit, the resulting graph usually looks something like the head of a whale.

Profitability will increase sharply and tail off from the very beginning. (Remember that customers have been sorted from most to least profitable.) Whenever there are some negative-profit customers, the graph reaches a peak—above 100%—as profit per customer moves from positive to negative. As we continue through the negative-profit customers, cumulative profits decrease at an ever-increasing rate. The graph always ends at 100% of the customers accounting for 100% of the total profit.

Robert Kaplan (co-developer of Activity-Based Costing and the Balanced Scorecard) likes to refer to these curves as "whale curves."[8] In Kaplan's experience, the whale curve usually reveals that the most profitable 20% of customers can sometimes generate between 150% and 300% of total profits so that the resulting curve resembles a sperm whale rising above the water's surface. See Figure 5.2 for an example of a whale curve.

Example A catalog retailer has grouped customers in ten deciles based on profitability (see Table 5.1 and Figure 5.1). (A decile is a tenth of the population, so 0 to 10% is the most profitable 10% of customers.)

Table 5.1 Customer profitability, ranked by profitability

Customer's decile by profitability	0–10%	10–20%	20–30%	30–40%	40–50%	50–60%	60–70%	70–80%	80–90%	90–100%
Band ($m) Profitability	$100	$50	$25	$10	$5	$3	$2	$0	($8)	($20)
% of Total Profits	60%	30%	15%	6%	3%	2%	1%	0%	–5%	–12%

Here we have a clear illustration that if the company were to stop serving the least profitable 20% of customers, it would be $28 million better off.

Figure 5.1 Customer profitability by decile

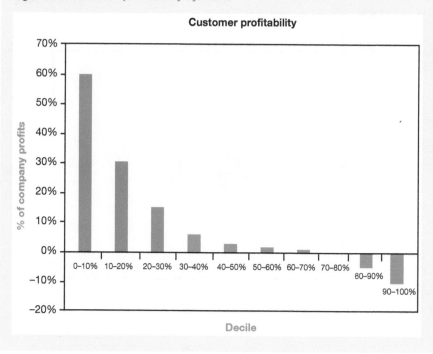

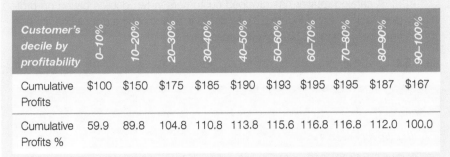

Table 5.2 Cumulative profitability peaks before all customers are served

Customer's decile by profitability	0–10%	10–20%	20–30%	30–40%	40–50%	50–60%	60–70%	70–80%	80–90%	90–100%
Cumulative Profits	$100	$150	$175	$185	$190	$193	$195	$195	$187	$167
Cumulative Profits %	59.9	89.8	104.8	110.8	113.8	115.6	116.8	116.8	112.0	100.0

Table 5.2 presents this same customer information in cumulative form. A plot of cumulative profits across deciles begins to look like a whale with a steeply rising ridge reaching a peak of total profitability above 100% and tapering off thereafter (see Figure 5.2).

Figure 5.2 The whale curve

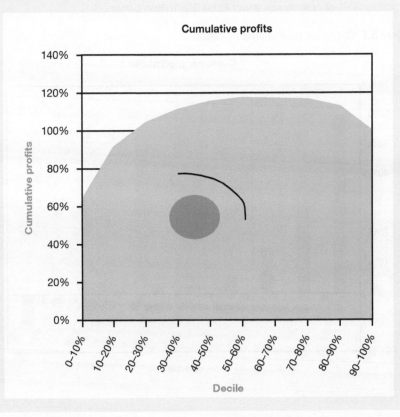

Data sources, complications, and cautions

Measuring customer profitability requires detailed information. Assigning revenues to customers is often the easy part; assigning your costs to customers is much harder. The cost of goods sold obviously gets assigned to the customers based on the goods each customer purchased. Assigning the more indirect costs may require the use of some form of activity-based costing (ABC) system. Finally, there may be some categories of costs that will be impossible to assign to the customer. If so, it is probably best to keep these costs as company costs and be content with the customer profit numbers adding up to something a little different from the total company profit.

When considering the profits from customers, remember that most things change over time. Customers who were profitable last year may not be profitable this year. Because the whale curve reflects past performance, we must be careful when using it to make decisions that shape the future. For example, we may very well want to continue a relationship that was unprofitable in the past if we know things will change for the better in the future. For example, banks typically offer discount packages to students to gain their business. This may well show low or negative customer profits in the short term. The company hopes that future profits will compensate for current losses. Customer lifetime value (addressed in Section 5.3) is a forward-looking metric that attempts to account for the anticipated future profitability of each customer relationship.

When capturing customer information to decide which customers to serve, it is important to consider the legal environment in which the company operates. This can change considerably across countries, where there may be anti-discrimination laws and special situations in some industries. For instance, public utilities are sometimes obligated to serve all customers.

It is also worth remembering that intrusive capturing of customer-specific data can damage customer relationships. Some individuals will be put off by excess data gathering. For a food company, it may help to know which of your customers are on a diet. But the food company's management should think twice before adding this question to the next customer survey.

Sometimes there are sound financial reasons for continuing to serve unprofitable customers. For example, some companies rely on network effects. Take the case of the U.S. Postal Service: Part of its strength is the ability to deliver to the whole country. It may superficially seem profitable to stop deliveries to remote areas. But when that happens, the service becomes less valuable for all customers. In short, sometimes unprofitable customer relationships are necessary for a firm to maintain its profitable ones.

Similarly, companies with high fixed costs that have been assigned to customers during the construction of customer profit must ask whether those costs will go away if they terminate unprofitable customer relationships. If the costs do not go away, ending unprofitable relationships may only serve to make the surviving relationships look even less profitable (after the reallocation of costs) and result in the lowering of company profits. In short, make certain that the negative profit goes away if the relationship is terminated. Certainly the revenue and cost of goods sold will go away, but if some of the other costs do not, the firm could be better off maintaining a negative profit relationship as it contributes to covering fixed cost (refer to Sections 3.4 and 3.6).

Abandoning customers ("firing") is a very sensitive practice, and a business should always consider the public relations consequences of such actions. Similarly, when you get rid of a customer, you cannot expect to attract the customer back very easily if that customer migrates into your profitable segment.

Finally, because the whale curve examines cumulative *percentage* of total profits, the numbers are very sensitive to the dollar amount of total profit. When the total dollar profit is a small number, it is fairly easy for the most profitable customers to represent a huge *percentage* of that small number. So when you hear that 20% of the firm's customers represent 350% of the firm's profit, one of the first things you should consider is the total dollar value of profits. If that total is small, 350% of it can also be a fairly small number of dollars. To cement this idea, ask yourself what the whale curve would look like for a firm with $0 profit.

5.3   Customer lifetime value

Customer lifetime value is the dollar value of a customer relationship based on the present value of the projected future cash flows from the customer relationship.

When margins and retention rates are constant, the following formula can be used to calculate the lifetime value of a customer relationship:

$$\text{Customer Lifetime Value (\$)} = \text{Margin (\$)} * \frac{\text{Retention Rate (\%)}}{1 + \text{Discount Rate (\%)} - \text{Retention Rate (\%)}}$$

Customer lifetime value (CLV) is an important concept in that it encourages firms to shift their focus from quarterly profits to the long-term health of their customer relationships. Customer lifetime value is an important number because it represents an upper limit on spending to acquire new customers.

Purpose: to assess the value of each customer.

As Don Peppers and Martha Rogers are fond of saying, "Some customers are more equal than others."[9] We saw a vivid illustration of this in the last section, when we examined the profitability of individual customer relationships. As we noted, customer profit (CP) is the difference between the revenues and the costs associated with the customer relationship during a specified period. The central difference between CP and CLV is that CP measures the past, and CLV looks forward. As such, CLV can be more useful in shaping managers' decisions but is much more difficult to quantify. Quantifying CP is a matter of carefully reporting and summarizing the results of past activity, whereas quantifying CLV involves forecasting future activity.

> Customer lifetime value (CLV): The present value of the future cash flows attributed to the customer relationship.

We discuss the concept of present value in more detail in Section 12.4. For now, you can think of present value as the discounted sum of future cash flows. We discount (that is, multiply by a carefully selected number less than one) future cash flows before we add them together to account for the fact that there is a time value of money. The time value of money is another way of saying that everyone would prefer to get paid sooner rather than later, and everyone would prefer to pay later rather than sooner. This is true for individuals (the sooner I get paid, the sooner I can pay down my credit card balance and avoid interest charges) as well as for firms. The exact discount factors used depend on the discount rate chosen (10% per year, as an example) and the number of periods until we receive each cash flow. (Dollars received ten years from now must be discounted more than dollars received five years in the future.)

The concept of CLV is nothing more than the concept of present value applied to cash flows attributed to the customer relationship. Because the present value of any stream of future cash flows is designed to measure the single lump sum value today of the future stream of cash flows, CLV represents the single lump sum value today of the customer relationship. Even more simply, CLV is the dollar value of the customer relationship to the firm. One can say that the firm should not be willing to pay more than the CLV to acquire the customer relationship (assuming no further complications like referral values). CLV can also, with assumptions, show an upper limit on the amount the firm would be willing to pay to avoid losing the customer relationship. If we view a customer relationship as an asset of the firm, CLV would present the dollar value of that asset.

Cohort and incubate

One way to project the value of future customer cash flows is to make the heroic assumption that the customers acquired several periods ago are no better or worse (in terms of their CLV) than the ones we currently acquire. We then go back and collect data on a cohort of customers all acquired at about the same time and carefully reconstruct their cash flows over some finite number of periods. The next step is to discount the cash flows for each customer back to the time of acquisition to calculate that customer's sample CLV and then average all of the sample CLVs together to produce an estimate of the CLV of each newly acquired customer. We refer to this method as the "cohort and incubate" approach. Equivalently, one can calculate the present value of the *total* cash flows from the cohort and divide by the number of customers to get the average CLV for the cohort. If the value of customer relationships is stable across time, the average CLV of the cohort sample is an appropriate estimator of the CLV of newly acquired customers.

As an example of this cohort and incubate approach, Berger, Weinberg, and Hanna followed all the customers acquired by a cruise-ship line in 1993. The 6,094 customers in the cohort of 1993 were tracked (incubated) for five years. The total net present value of the cash flows from these customers was $27,916,614. These flows included revenues from the cruises taken (the 6,094 customers took 8,660 cruises over the five-year horizon), variable cost of the cruises, and promotional costs. The total five-year net present value of the cohort expressed on a per-customer basis came out to be $27,916,614/6,094 = $4,581 per customer. This is the average five-year CLV for the cohort.

> *"Prior to this analysis, [cruise-line] management would never spend more than $3,314 to acquire a passenger .... Now, aware of CLV (both the concept and the actual numerical results), an advertisement [that resulted in a cost per acquisition of $3 to $4 thousand] was welcomed—especially because the CLV numbers are conservative (again, as noted, the CLV does not include any residual business after five years.)"*[10]

The cohort and incubate approach works well when customer relationships are stationary—changing slowly over time. When the value of relationships changes slowly, we can use the value of incubated past relationships as predictive of the value of new relationships.

In situations where the value of customer relationships changes more rapidly, firms often use a simple model to forecast the value of those relationships. By a model, we mean some assumptions about how the customer relationship will unfold. If the model is simple enough, it may even be possible to find an equation for the present value of our model of future cash flows. This makes the calculation of CLV even easier because it now requires only the substitution of numbers for our situation into the equation for CLV.

Next, we will explain what is perhaps the simplest model for future customer cash flows and the equation for the present value of those cash flows. Although it's not the only model of future customer cash flows, this one gets used the most.

Construction

The model for customer cash flows treats the firm's customer relationships as something of a leaky bucket. Each period, a fraction (1 minus the retention rate) of the firm's customers leave and are lost for good.

The CLV model has only three parameters:

- Constant margin (contribution after deducting variable costs including retention spending) per period
- Constant retention probability per period
- Discount rate

Furthermore, the model assumes that a customer not retained is lost for good. Finally, the model assumes that the first margin will be received (with probability equal to the retention rate) at the end of the first period.

The one other assumption of the model is that the firm uses an infinite horizon when it calculates the present value of future cash flows. Although no firm actually has an infinite horizon, the consequences of assuming one are discussed in the following section.

Customer lifetime value: The CLV formula[11] multiplies the per-period cash margin (hereafter we will just use the term "margin") by a factor that represents the present value of the expected length of the customer relationship:

$$\text{Customer Lifetime Value (\$)} = \text{Margin (\$)} * \frac{\text{Retention Rate (\%)}}{1 + \text{Discount Rate (\%)} - \text{Retention Rate (\%)}}$$

Under the assumptions of the model, CLV is a multiple of the margin. The multiplicative factor represents the present value of the expected length (number of periods) of the customer relationship. When retention equals 0, the customer will never be retained, and the multiplicative factor is zero. When retention equals 1, the customer is always retained, and the firm receives the margin in perpetuity. The present value of the margin in perpetuity turns out to be Margin/Discount Rate. For retention values in between, the CLV formula tells us the appropriate multiplier.

Example An Internet Service Provider (ISP) charges $19.95 per month. Variable costs are about $1.50 per account per month. With marketing spending of $6 per year, the company's attrition is only 0.5% per month. At a monthly discount rate of 1%, what is the CLV of a customer?

$$\text{Contribution Margin} = (\$19.95 - \$1.50 - \$6/12) = \$17.95$$
$$\text{Retention Rate} = 0.995$$
$$\text{Discount Rate} = 0.01$$

$$\text{Customer Lifetime Value (CLV)} = \text{Margin} * \frac{\text{Retention Rate (\%)}}{1 + \text{Discount Rate (\%)} - \text{Retention Rate (\%)}}$$

$$\text{CLV} = \$17.95 * [0.995/(1 + 0.01 - 0.995)]$$
$$\text{CLV} = [\$17.95] * [66.33]$$
$$\text{CLV} = \$1,191$$

Data sources, complications, and cautions

Some formulas that you will see subtract acquisition costs before reporting CLV. The challenge here is that CLV loses many useful properties. Given that acquisition cost is sunk, CLV no longer shows the value of the customer-relationship asset. Nor can any number that has factored in a sunk cost, such as acquisition cost, inform retention decisions. Nor does a figure that has subtracted acquisition costs provide a yardstick to assess acquisition costs. Given the problems created by the subtraction, we strongly recommend not subtracting acquisition costs before reporting CLV.

The retention rate (and, by extension, the attrition rate) is a driver of customer value. Very small changes can make a major difference to the lifetime value calculated. Accuracy in this parameter is vital to meaningful results.

The retention rate is assumed to be constant across the life of the customer relationship. For products and services that go through a trial, conversion, and loyalty progression, retention rates increase over the lifetime of the relationship. In those situations, the model explained here might be too simple. If a firm in such a situation wants to estimate a sequence of retention rates, a spreadsheet model might be more useful in calculating CLV.

The discount rate is also a sensitive driver of the lifetime value calculation; as with retention, seemingly small changes can make major differences to customer lifetime value. The discount rate should be chosen with care.

The contribution is assumed to be constant across time. If margin is expected to increase over the lifetime of the customer relationship, the simple model will not apply.

Take care not to use this CLV formula for relationships in which customer inactivity does not signal the end of the relationship. In catalog sales, for example, a small percentage of the firm's customers purchase from any given catalog. Don't confuse the percentage of customers active in a given period (relevant for the cataloger) with the retention rates in this model. If customers often return to do business with the firm after a period of inactivity, this CLV formula does not apply.

Customer lifetime value (CLV) with initial margin

One final source of confusion concerns the timing assumptions inherent in the model. The first cash flow accounted for in the model is the margin received at the end of one period with probability equal to the retention rate. Other models also include an initial margin received at the beginning of the period. If a certain receipt of an initial margin is included, the new CLV will equal the old CLV plus the initial margin. Furthermore, if the initial margin is equal to all subsequent margins, there are at least two ways to write formulas for the CLV that include the initial margin:

$$\text{CLV with Initial Margin (\$)} = \text{Margin (\$)} + \text{Margin (\$)} \; \frac{\text{Retention Rate (\%)}}{1 + \text{Discount Rate (\%)} - \text{Retention Rate (\%)}}$$

or

$$= \text{Margin (\$)} * \frac{1 + \text{Discount Rate (\%)}}{1 + \text{Discount Rate (\%)} - \text{Retention Rate (\%)}}$$

The second formula looks just like the original formula with 1 + Discount Rate taking the place of the retention rate in the numerator of the multiplicative factor. Just remember that the new CLV formula and the original CLV formula apply to the same situations and differ only in the treatment of an initial margin. This new CLV formula includes it, whereas the original CLV formula does not.

The infinite horizon assumption

In some industries and companies, it is typical to calculate four- or five-year customer values instead of using the infinite time horizon inherent in the previous formulas. Of course, over shorter periods, customer retention rates are less likely to be affected by major shifts in technology or competitive strategies and are more likely to be captured by historical retention rates. For managers, the question is: Does it make a difference whether I use the infinite time horizon or (for example) the five-year customer value? The answer to this question is yes, sometimes, it can make a difference because the value over five years can be less than 70% of the value over an infinite horizon.

Table 5.3 calculates the percentages of (infinite horizon) CLV accruing in the first five years. If retention rates are higher than 80% and discount rates are lower than 20%, differences in the two approaches will be substantial. Depending on the strategic risks that companies perceive, the additional complexities of using a finite horizon can be informative.

Table 5.3 Finite-horizon CLV as a percentage of infinite-horizon CLV

Percentage of CLV accruing in the first five years						
Discount rates	Retention rates					
	40%	50%	60%	70%	80%	90%
2%	99%	97%	93%	85%	70%	47%
4%	99%	97%	94%	86%	73%	51%
6%	99%	98%	94%	87%	76%	56%
8%	99%	98%	95%	89%	78%	60%
10%	99%	98%	95%	90%	80%	63%
12%	99%	98%	96%	90%	81%	66%
14%	99%	98%	96%	91%	83%	69%
16%	100%	99%	96%	92%	84%	72%
18%	100%	99%	97%	93%	86%	74%
20%	100%	99%	97%	93%	87%	76%

5.4   Prospect lifetime value versus customer value

> Prospect lifetime value is the expected value of a prospect. It is the value expected from the prospect minus the cost of prospecting. The value expected from the prospect is the expected fraction of prospects who will make a purchase times the sum of the average margin the firm makes on the initial purchase and the CLV of the newly acquired customer.
>
> Only if prospect lifetime value is positive should the firm proceed with the planned acquisition spending.

Purpose: to account for the lifetime value of a newly acquired customer (CLV) when making prospecting decisions.

One of the major uses of CLV is to inform prospecting decisions. A prospect is someone whom the firm will spend money on in an attempt to acquire her or him as a customer. The acquisition spending must be compared not just to the contribution from the immediate sales it generates but also to the future cash flows expected from the newly acquired customer relationship (the CLV). Only with a full accounting of the value of the newly acquired customer relationship will the firm be able to make an informed economic prospecting decision.

Construction

The expected prospect lifetime value (PLV) is the value expected from each prospect minus the cost of prospecting. The value expected from each prospect is the acquisition rate (the expected fraction of prospects who will make a purchase and become customers) times the sum of the initial margin the firm makes on the initial purchases and the CLV. The cost is the amount of acquisition spending per prospect. The formula for expected PLV is as follows:

$$\text{Prospect Lifetime Value (\$)} = \text{Acquisition Rate (\%)} * [\text{Initial Margin (\$)}$$
$$+ \text{CLV (\$)}] - \text{Acquisition Spending (\$)}$$

If PLV is positive, the acquisition spending is a wise investment. If PLV is negative, the acquisition spending should not be made.

The PLV number will usually be very small. Although CLV is sometimes in the hundreds of dollars, PLV can come out to be only a few pennies. Just remember that PLV applies to prospects, not to customers. A large number of small but positive-value prospects can add up to a considerable amount of value for a firm.

Example A service company plans to spend $60,000 on an advertisement reaching 75,000 readers. If the service company expects the advertisement to convince 1.2% of the readers to take advantage of a special introductory offer (priced so low that the firm makes only $10 margin on this initial purchase) and the CLV of the acquired customers is $100, is the advertisement economically attractive?

Here acquisition spending is $0.80 per prospect, the expected acquisition rate is 0.012, and the initial margin is $10. The expected PLV of each of the 75,000 prospects is

$$PLV = 0.012 * (\$10 + \$100) - \$0.80$$

$$= \$0.52$$

The expected PLV is $0.52. The total expected value of the prospecting effort will be 75,000 * $0.52 = $39,000. The proposed acquisition spending *is* economically attractive.

If we are uncertain about the 0.012 acquisition rate, we might ask what the acquisition rate from the prospecting campaign must be in order for it to be economically successful. We can get that number by using Excel's Goal Seek function to find the acquisition rate that sets PLV to zero. Or we can use a little algebra and substitute $0 for PLV and solve for the break-even acquisition rate:

$$\text{Break-Even Acquisition Rate} = \frac{\text{Acquisition Spending (\$)}}{\text{Initial Margin (\$)} + \text{CLV (\$)}}$$

$$= \frac{\$0.80}{\$10 + \$100} = 0.007273$$

Therefore, the acquisition rate must exceed 0.7273% in order for the campaign to be successful.

Data sources, complications, and cautions

In addition to the CLV of the newly acquired customers, the firm needs to know the planned amount of acquisition spending (expressed on a per-prospect basis), the expected success rate (the fraction of prospects expected to become customers), and the average margin the firm will receive from the initial purchases of the newly acquired customers. The initial margin number is needed because CLV, as defined in the previous section, accounts for only the future cash flows from the relationship. The initial cash flow is not included in CLV and must be accounted for separately. Note also that the initial margin must account for any first-period retention spending.

Perhaps the biggest challenge in calculating PLV is estimating CLV. The other terms (acquisition spending, acquisition rate, and initial margin) all refer to flows or outcomes in the near future, whereas CLV requires longer-term projections.

Another caution worth mentioning is that the decision to spend money on customer acquisition whenever PLV is positive rests on an assumption that the customers acquired would not have been acquired had the firm not spent the money. In other words, our approach gives the acquisition spending "full credit" for the subsequent customers acquired. If the firm has several simultaneous acquisition efforts, dropping one of them might lead to increased acquisition rates for the others. Situations such as these (where one solicitation cannibalizes another) require a more complicated analysis.

A firm must be careful to search for the most economical way to acquire new customers. If there are alternative prospecting approaches, the firm must be careful not to simply go with the first one that gives a positive projected PLV. Given a limited number of prospects, the approach that gives the highest expected PLV should be used.

Finally, we want to warn you that there are other ways to do the calculations necessary to judge the economic viability of a given prospecting effort. Although these other approaches are equivalent to the one presented here, they differ with respect to what gets included in CLV.

Example A service company plans to spend $60,000 on an advertisement reaching 75,000 readers. If the service company expects the advertisement to convince 1.2% of the readers to take advantage of a special introductory offer (priced so low that the firm makes only $10 margin on this initial purchase) and the CLV of the acquired customers is $100, is the advertisement economically attractive?

If we include the initial margin in CLV, we get

$$\text{"CLV" [with Initial Margin (\$)]} = \text{Initial Margin (\$)} + \text{CLV (\$)}$$

$$= \$10 + \$110 = \$110$$

The expected PLV is now

$$\text{PLV (\$)} = \text{Acquisition Rate (\%)} * \text{"CLV" [with Initial Margin (\$)]}$$

$$- \text{Acquisition Cost (\$)}$$

$$= 0.012 * \$110 - 0.08 = \$0.52$$

This is the same number as before, calculated using a slightly different CLV—one that includes the initial margin.

We illustrate one final way to do the calculations necessary to judge the economics of a prospecting campaign. The expected value of a new customer is $10 now plus $100 from future sales, or $110 in total. The expected cost to acquire a customer is the total cost of the campaign divided by the expected number of new customers. This average acquisition cost is calculated as $60,000/(0.012 * 75,000) = $66.67. The expected value of a new customer (CLV) minus the expected acquisition cost per customer is $110 − $66.67 = $43.33. Because this is positive, the campaign is economically attractive. Some would label this $43.33 number as the CLV of a new customer, although we would not advise this because it creates confusion, as this number is different from those we outline in Section 5.3.

Notice that $43.33 times the 900 expected new customers equals $39,000, the same total net value from the campaign calculated in the original example as the $0.52 PLV times the 75,000 prospects. The two ways to do the calculations—the sum of CLV minus average acquisition costs versus the sum of PLV—are equivalent.

5.5 Acquisition versus retention cost

> A firm's average acquisition cost is the ratio of acquisition spending to the number of customers acquired. The average retention cost is the ratio of retention spending directed toward a group of customers to the number of those customers successfully retained.
>
> $$\text{Average Acquisition Cost (\$)} = \frac{\text{Acquisition Spending (\$)}}{\text{Number of Customers Acquired (\#)}}$$
>
> $$\text{Average Retention Cost (\$)} = \frac{\text{Retention Spending (\$)}}{\text{Number of Customers Retained (\#)}}$$
>
> These two metrics help the firm monitor the effectiveness of two important categories of marketing spending.

Purpose: to determine the firm's cost of acquisition and retention.

Before a firm can optimize its mix of acquisition and retention spending, it must first assess the status quo. At the current spending levels, how much does it cost the firm (on average) to acquire new customers, and how much is it spending (on average) to retain its existing customers? Does it cost five times as much to acquire a new customer as it does to retain an existing one?

Construction

> Average acquisition cost: The average cost to acquire a customer; the total acquisition spending divided by the number of new customers acquired.
>
> $$\text{Average Acquisition Cost (\$)} = \frac{\text{Acquisition Spending (\$)}}{\text{Number of Customers Acquired (\$)}}$$

> Average retention cost: The average cost to retain an existing customer; the total retention spending divided by the number of customers retained.
>
> $$\text{Average Retention Cost (\$)} = \frac{\text{Retention Spending (\$)}}{\text{Number of Customers Retained (\#)}}$$

Example During the past year, a regional pest control service spent $1.4 million and acquired 64,800 new customers. Of the 154,890 customer relationships in existence at the start of the year, only 87,957 remained at the end of the year, despite the $500,000 or so that the company spent during the year in attempts to retain the 154,890 customers. The calculation of average acquisition cost is relatively straightforward. A total acquisition spend of $1.4 million resulted in 64,800 new customers. The average acquisition cost is $1,400/64.8 = $21.60 per customer. The calculation of average retention cost is also straightforward. A total retention spend of $500,000 resulted in 87,957 retained customers. The average yearly retention cost is $500,000 /87,957 = $5.68. Thus, for the pest control firm, it cost about four times as much to acquire a new customer as it did to retain an existing one.

Data sources, complications, and cautions

For any specific period, a firm needs to know the total amount it spent on customer acquisition and the number of new customers that resulted from that spending. With respect to customer retention, the firm needs to measure the total amount spent during the period attempting to retain the customers in existence at the start of the period and the number of existing customers successfully retained at the end of the period. Notice that retention spending directed at customers acquired within the period is not included in this figure. Similarly, the number retained refers only to those retained from the pool of customers in existence at the start of the period. Thus, the average retention cost calculated will be associated with the length of the period in question. If the period is a year, the average retention cost will be a cost per year per customer retained.

The calculation and interpretation of average acquisition cost is much easier than the calculation and interpretation of average retention cost. This is so because it is often possible to isolate acquisition spending and count the number of new customers that resulted from that spending. A simple division results in the average cost to acquire a customer. The reasonable assumption underlying this calculation is that the new customers would not have been acquired had it not been for the acquisition spending.

Things are not nearly so clear when it comes to average retention cost. One source of difficulty is that retention rates (and costs) depend on the period of time under consideration. Yearly retention is different from monthly retention. The cost to retain a customer for a month will be less than the cost to retain a customer for a year. Thus, the definition of average retention cost requires a specification of the time period associated with the retention.

A second source of difficulty stems from the fact that some customers will be retained even if the firm spends nothing on retention. For this reason, it can be a little misleading to call the ratio of retention spending to the number of retained customers the *average retention cost*. One must not jump to the conclusion that retention goes away if the retention spending goes away. Nor should one assume that if the firm increases the retention budget by the average retention cost that it will retain one more customers. The average retention cost number is not very useful in helping make retention budgeting decisions.

One final caution involves the firm's capability to separate spending into acquisition and retention classifications. Clearly there can be spending that works to improve both the acquisition and retention efforts of the firm. General brand advertisements, for example, serve to lower the cost of both acquisition and retention. Rather than attempt to allocate all spending as either acquisition or retention, we suggest that it is perfectly acceptable to maintain a separate category that is neither acquisition nor retention.

Further reading

Bendle, Neil T., and Bagga, C. K. (2017). "The Confusion About CLV in Case-Based Teaching Materials," *Marketing Education Review*, 27(1), 27–38.

Berger, P. D., B. Weinberg, and R. C. Hanna. (2003). "Customer Lifetime Value Determination and Strategic Implications for a Cruise-Ship Line," *Database Marketing and Customer Strategy Management,* 11(1), 40–52.

Blattberg, R. C., and S. J. Hoch. (1990). "Database Models and Managerial Intuition: 50% Model + 50% Manager," *Management Science,* 36(8), 887–899.

Gupta, Sunil, and Donald R. Lehmann. (2003). "Customers as Assets," *Journal of Interactive Marketing*, 17(1), 9–24.

Kaplan, R. S., and V. G. Narayanan. (2001). "Measuring and Managing Customer Profitability," *Journal of Cost Management*, 15(5), 5–15.

Little, J. D. C. (1970). "Models and Managers: The Concept of a Decision Calculus," *Management Science,* 16(8), B-466–B-485.

McGovern, G. J., D. Court, J. A. Quelch, and B. Crawford. (2004). "Bringing Customers into the Boardroom," *Harvard Business Review,* 82(11), 70–80.

Much, J. G., Lee S. Sproull, and Michal Tamuz. (1989). "Learning from Samples of One or Fewer," *Organization Science: A Journal of the Institute of Management Sciences,* 2(1), 1–12.

Peppers, D., and M. Rogers. (1997). *Enterprise One-to-One: Tools for Competing in the Interactive Age*, Currency Doubleday.

Pfeifer, P. E., M. E. Haskins, and R. M. Conroy. (2005). "Customer Lifetime Value, Customer Profitability, and the Treatment of Acquisition Spending," *Journal of Managerial Issues,* 17(1), 11–25.

Sales force management

6

Key concepts covered in this chapter:

- Sales force coverage

- Sales force goals

- Sales force results

- Sales force compensation

- Pipeline analysis

Introduction

This chapter addresses sales force metrics. It lists and defines the most common measures for determining whether sales force effort and coverage of customers and potential customers are adequate. We also discuss pipeline analysis, which is useful in making sales forecasts and in allocating sales force effort to different stages of the selling process. Pipeline metrics are used to monitor the sequence of selling activities, from lead generation, through follow-up, to conversion and sales. The most important of these represents the percentage of initial leads who ultimately buy. Other measures of activity, productivity, efficiency, and cost can be useful at each stage of the selling process.

	Metric	Construction	Considerations	Purpose
6.1	Workload	Hours required to service clients and prospects.	Prospect numbers may be debatable. Time spent trying to convert prospects can vary by territory, salesperson, and potential client.	Assess the number of salespeople required to service a territory and to ensure balanced workloads.
6.1	Sales Potential Forecast	This is the number of prospects and their buying power.	Doesn't assess the likelihood of converting "potential" accounts. Definitions of buying power are more art than science.	Determine sales targets. Can also help identify territories worthy of allocation of limited sales resources.
6.2	Sales Goal	Individual sales projections may be based on a salesperson's share of forecasted sales, on prior-year sales and a share of increased district projections, or on a management-designed weighting system.	Setting individual targets on the basis of prior-year sales can discourage optimal performance, as strong performance in one year leads to more aggressive targets in the next.	Set targets for individual salespeople and for territories.
6.3	Sales Force Effectiveness	Effectiveness metrics analyze sales in the context of various criteria, including calls, contacts, potential accounts, active accounts, buying power of territory, and expenses.	Depends on factors that also affect sales potential and workload.	Assess the performance of a salesperson or team.

Metric		Construction	Considerations	Purpose
6.4	Compensation	Total payments made to a salesperson, typically consisting of base salary, bonus, and/or commission.	Perceived relationship between incentive reward and controllable activities may vary widely among industries and firms.	Motivate maximum sales effort. Enable salespeople and management to track progress toward goals.
6.4	Break-Even Number of Employees	Sales revenue multiplied by margin net of commission divided by cost per staff member.	Margins may vary across products, time, and salespeople. Sales are not independent of the number of salespeople.	Determine the appropriate personnel level for a projected sales volume.
6.5	Sales Funnel, Sales Pipeline	Portrayal of the number of clients and potential clients at various stages of the sales cycle.	Funnel dimensions depend on type of business and definition of potential clients.	Monitor sales effort and project future sales.

6.1   Sales force coverage: territories

Sales force territories are the customer groups or geographic districts for which individual salespeople or sales teams hold responsibility. Territories can be defined on the basis of geography, sales potential, history, types of customers, or a combination of factors. Companies strive to balance their territories in order to reduce costs and increase sales.

Workload (#) = [Current Accounts (#) * Average Time to Service an Active Account (#)] + [Prospects (#) * Time Spent Trying to Convert a Prospect into an Active Account (#)]

Sales Potential ($) = Number of Possible Accounts (#) * Buying Power ($)

Purpose: to create balanced sales territories.

There are a number of ways to analyze territories.[1] Most commonly, territories are compared on the basis of their potential or size. This is an important exercise. If territories differ sharply or slip out of balance, sales personnel may be given too much or too little work. This can lead to under- or over-servicing of customers. Territories can contain multiple salespersons, but the same challenges apply in terms of ensuring that there is appropriate coverage for the territory.

When sales personnel are stretched too thin, the result can be an *under-servicing* of customers. This can cost a firm business because over-taxed salespeople engage in suboptimal levels of activity in a number of areas. They seek out too few leads, identify too few prospects, and spend too little time with current customers. Those customers, in turn, may take their business to alternate providers.

Over-servicing, in contrast, may raise costs and prices and may therefore indirectly reduce sales. Over-servicing in some territories may also lead to under-servicing in others.

Unbalanced territories also raise the problem of unfair distribution of sales potential among members of a sales force. This may result in distorted compensation and lead talented salespeople to leave a company, seeking superior balance and compensation.

Achieving an appropriate balance among territories is an important factor in maintaining satisfaction among customers, salespeople, and the company as a whole.

Construction

In defining or redefining territories, companies strive to

- Balance workloads
- Balance sales potential
- Develop compact territories
- Minimize disruptions during the redesign

These goals can have different effects on different stakeholders, as represented in Table 6.1.[2]

Before designing new territories, a sales force manager should evaluate the workloads of all members of the sales team. The workload for a territory can be calculated as follows:

$$\text{Workload (\#)} = [\text{Current Accounts (\#)} * \text{Average Time to Service an Active Account (\#)}] + [\text{Prospects (\#)} * \text{Time Spent Trying to Convert a Prospect into an Active Account (\#)}]$$

The sales potential in a territory can be determined as follows:

$$\text{Sales Potential (\$)} = \text{Number of Possible Accounts (\#)} * \text{Buying Power (\$)}$$

Table 6.1 Effects of balancing sales territories

		Balance the workload	Balance sales potential	Minimize disruption	Develop compact territories
Customers	Responsiveness	X			X
	Relationships			X	
Salespeople	Earnings opportunities		X		
	Manageable workload	X			X
	Reduced uncertainty			X	
	Control of overnights				X
Firm	Sales results	X	X	X	
	Effort control	X			
	Motivation	X	X	X	X
	Travel cost control				X

Buying power is a dollar figure based on factors such as average income levels, number of businesses in a territory, average sales of those businesses, and population demographics. Buying power indices are generally specific to individual industries.

Example Among the sales prospects in one of its territories, a copier manufacturer has identified six small businesses, eight medium-sized firms, and two large companies. Enterprises of these sizes have historically made annual copier purchases that average $500, $700, and $1,000, respectively. The sales potential for the territory is thus

$$\text{Sales Potential} = (6 * \$500) + (8 * \$700) + (2 * \$1,000) = \$10,600$$

In addition to workload and sales potential, a third key metric is needed to compare territories. This is size or, more specifically, travel time. In this context, travel time is more useful than size because it more accurately represents the factor that size implies—that is, the amount of time needed to reach customers and potential customers. With changes in the way sales are done—most obviously via web-hosted meetings—geographic territorial size constraints are likely to be a less significant consideration for many firms, but workload still matters.

As a manager's goal is to balance workload and potential among sales personnel, it can be beneficial to calculate combined metrics—such as sales potential or travel time—in order to make comparisons between territories.

Example Imagine that a territory from above is 20 km². The sales potential per square kilometer would be $10,600/20 = $530 per square kilometer, which gives an indication of how concentrated the sales potential is.

Data sources, complications, and cautions

Sales potential can be represented in a number of ways. Of these, the most basic is population—the number of potential accounts in a territory. In the copier case cited earlier, this might be the number of offices in a territory.

Estimating the size of a territory might involve simply calculating the geographic area that it covers. When salespeople have to travel to meet a client, average travel time is also important. Depending on the quality of roads, density of traffic, or distance between businesses, one may find that territories of equal area entail very different travel time requirements. Google Maps and similar services can generate helpful estimates.

Redefining territories is a famously difficult process. To perform it well, in addition to the metrics cited earlier, disruption of customer relationships and feelings of ownership among sales personnel must also be considered.

6.2 Sales force objectives: setting goals

Sales goals are generally needed to motivate salespeople. These goals can have negative effects, however, if set too high or low. Means of establishing sales goals include the following:

Sales Goal ($) = Salesperson's Share of Prior-Year Sales in District (%) * Forecasted Sales for District ($)

Sales Goal ($) = Salesperson's Prior-Year Sales ($) + [Forecasted Sales Increase for District ($) * Territory's Share of Sales Potential in District (%)]

Weighted Share of Sales Allotment (%) = {Salesperson's Share of Prior-Year Sales in District (%) * Assigned Weighting (%)} + {Territory's Share of Sales Potential in District (%) * [1 − Assigned Weighting (%)]}

$$\text{Sales Goal (\$)} = \text{Weighted Share of Sales Allotment (\%)} * \text{Forecasted Sales for District (\$)}$$

Many of these approaches involve a combination of historical results and a weighting of sales potential among the territories. This ensures that overall goals will be attained if all salespeople meet their individual goals.

Purpose: to motivate sales personnel and establish benchmarks for evaluating and rewarding their performance.

In setting sales goals, managers strive to motivate their personnel to stretch themselves and generate the most sales possible. But they don't want to set the bar too high. The correct goal levels will motivate all salespeople and reward most of them.

When planning sales goals, certain guidelines are important. Under the SMART (**s**pecific, **m**easurable, **a**ttainable, **r**ealistic, and **t**ime-bound) strategy recommended by Jack D. Wilner, author of *Seven Secrets to Successful Sales Management*,[3] goals should be

- **Specific:** Goals should be specific to a department, a territory, and even a salesperson. They should be clear and applicable to each individual so that salespeople do not have to derive part of their goal.

- **Measurable:** Measurable goals, expressed in concrete numbers such as "dollar sales" or "percentage increase," enable salespeople to set precise targets and track their progress. Vague goals, such as "more" or "increased" sales, are not effective because they make it difficult to measure progress.

- **Attainable:** Attainable goals are in the realm of possibility. They can be visualized and understood by both the manager and the salesperson.

- **Realistic:** Realistic goals are set high enough to motivate but not so high that salespeople give up before they even start. (An alternative version of SMART uses Relevant to emphasis that goals should connect well to the firm's wider objectives.)

- **Time-bound:** Time-bound goals must be met within a precise time frame. This applies pressure to reach them sooner rather than later and defines an endpoint when results will be checked.

Construction

There are numerous ways of allotting a company's forecast across its sales force. These methods are designed to set goals that are fair, achievable, and in line with historic results. Goals are stated in terms of sales totals for individual salespeople. In the following formulas, which encapsulate these methods, a *district* is composed of the individual territories of multiple salespeople.

A sales goal or allocation based on prior-year sales can be calculated as follows:[4]

Sales Goal ($) = Salesperson's Share of Prior-Year Sales in District (%) * Forecasted Sales for District ($)

A sales goal based on prior-year sales *and* the sales potential of a territory can be calculated as follows:

Sales Goal ($) = Salesperson's Prior-Year Sales ($) + [Forecasted Sales Increase for District ($) * Territory's Share of Sales Potential in District (%)]

Sales goals can also be set by using a combined method, in which management assigns weightings to both the prior-year sales of each salesperson and the sales potential of each territory. These weightings are then used to calculate each salesperson's percentage share of the relevant sales forecast, and percentage shares are used to calculate sales goals in dollar terms.

Weighted Share of Sales Allotment (%) = {Salesperson's Share of Prior-Year Sales in District (%) * Assigned Weighting (%)} + {Territory's Share of Sales Potential in District (%) * [1 − Assigned Weighting (%)]}

Sales Goal ($) = Weighted Share of Sales Allotment (%) * Forecasted Sales for District ($)

Example A salesperson achieved prior-year sales of $1,620, which represented 18% of the sales in her district. This salesperson was responsible for a territory that held 12% of the sales potential in the district. If the salesperson's employer mandates a district sales goal of $10,000 for the coming year—representing an overall increase of $1,000 over prior-year results—then the salesperson's individual sales goal can be calculated in several ways that involve different emphasis on historical sales versus sales potential. Here are four examples:

1 Sales Goal Based on Prior-Year Sales = 18% * $10,000 = $1,800
2 Sales Goal Based on Sales Potential = 12% * $10,000 = $1,200
3 Sales Goal Based on Prior-Year Sales + Sales Potential * Increase = $1,620 + (12% * $1,000) = $1,740
4 Weighted Share of Sales Allotment, in Which Prior-Year Sales and Sales Potential Are Weighted (for Example) by a Factor of 50% Each = (18% * 50%) + (12% * 50%) = 15%

Then...

Sales Goal Based on Weighted Share of Sales Allotment = 15% * $10,000 = $1,500

If there is consistency between salespersons and territories between years, you can allocate sales goals based upon a share of the expected sales of the district.

Data sources, complications, and cautions

Sales goals are generally established by using combinations of bottom-up and top-down procedures. Frequently, top management sets objectives at a corporate level, and the sales manager allocates shares of that overall goal among the various members of the sales force.

Top management generally uses multiple metrics to forecast sales, including prior-year sales of the product in question, total prior-year sales in the relevant market, prior-year sales by competitors, and the company's current market share. After the corporate sales forecast is derived, a sales force manager verifies that these targets are reasonable and pushes back where necessary. The manager then allots the projected sales among the sales force in a district, based at least in part on measures of individual performance from the prior year. Of greatest importance in this calculation are each salesperson's historic percentage of sales and the sales potential of his or her territory.

It is important to reevaluate sales goals *during* the year to ensure that actual performance is running reasonably close to projections. If, at this checkpoint, it appears that more than 90% or less than 50% of the sales force is on track to achieve their goals, then it may be advisable to alter the goals. This will prevent salespeople from easing off too early because their goals are in sight or giving up because their goals are unattainable. In setting goals, one possible rule of thumb would be to plan for a success rate of 75%. That would ensure that enough salespeople reach their goals *and* that the goals are sufficiently challenging.

If "rebudgeting" becomes necessary, it is important to ensure that this is properly recorded. Unless care is taken, revised sales goals can slip out of alignment with financial budgets and the expectations of senior management.

6.3   Sales force effectiveness: measuring effort, potential, and results

By analyzing sales force performance, managers can make changes to optimize sales going forward. Toward that end, there are many ways to gauge the performance of individual salespeople and of the sales force as a whole, in addition to total annual sales.

Sales Force Effectiveness Ratios

$$= \frac{\text{Sales (\$)}}{\text{Contacts with Clients (Calls)(\#)}}$$

$$= \frac{\text{Sales (\$)}}{\text{Potential Accounts (\#)}}$$

$$= \frac{\text{Sales (\$)}}{\text{Active Accounts (\#)}}$$

$$= \frac{\text{Sales (\$)}}{\text{Buying Power (\$)}}$$

$$= \frac{\text{Expenses (\$)}}{\text{Sales (\$)}} \qquad \text{(Also Known As Cost of Sales)}$$

Each can also be calculated on a dollar contribution basis.

Purpose: to measure the performance of a sales force and of individual salespeople.

When analyzing the performance of a salesperson, a number of metrics can be compared. These can reveal more about the salesperson than can be gauged by his or her total sales.

Construction

An authoritative source lists the following ratios as useful in assessing the relative effectiveness of sales personnel:[5]

$$\frac{\text{Sales (\$)}}{\text{Contacts with Clients (Calls)(\#)}}$$

$$\frac{\text{Sales (\$)}}{\text{Potential Accounts (\#)}}$$

$$\frac{\text{Sales (\$)}}{\text{Active Accounts (\#)}}$$

$$\frac{\text{Sales (\$)}}{\text{Buying Power (\$)}}$$

These formulas can be useful for comparing salespeople from different territories and for examining trends over time. They can reveal distinctions that can be obscured by total sales results, particularly in districts where territories vary in size, in number of potential accounts, or in buying power.

These ratios provide insight into the factors behind sales performance. If an individual's sales per call ratio is low, for example, it might indicate that the salesperson in question needs training in moving customers toward larger purchases. Or it might indicate a lack of closing skills. If the sales per potential account or sales per buying power metric is low, the salesperson may not be doing enough to seek out new accounts. These metrics reveal much about prospecting and lead generation because they're based on each salesperson's *entire* territory, including potential as well as current customers. The sales per active account metric provides a useful indicator of a salesperson's effectiveness in maximizing the value of existing customers.

Although it is important to make the most of every call, a salesperson will not reach his or her goal in just one call. A certain amount of effort is required to complete sales. This can be represented graphically as shown in Figure 6.1.[6]

Figure 6.1 Sales resulting from calls to customers

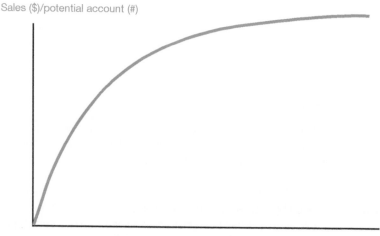

Sales ($)/potential account (#)

Calls (#)/potential account (#)

Although one can increase sales by expending more time and attention on a customer, at a certain point, a salesperson encounters diminishing returns in placing more calls to the same customers. Eventually, the incremental business generated by each call will be worth less than the cost of making the call.

In addition to the formulas described earlier, one other important measure of effectiveness is the ratio of expenses to sales. This cost metric is commonly expressed as a percentage of sales and is calculated as follows:

$$\frac{\text{Expenses (\$)}}{\text{Sales (\$)}}$$

If this ratio is substantially higher for one salesperson than for others, it may indicate that the individual in question has poor control of his or her expenses. Examples of poor expense control could include making unnecessary trips to a client, overproducing product pamphlets, or hosting too many dinners. Alternatively, expenses may represent a high percentage of sales if an individual possesses poor closing skills.

A more challenging set of sales force performance metrics involves customer service. Customer service is difficult to measure because there are no concrete numbers representing it, other than repeat rates or customer complaints. Each of those is telling, but how can a sales manager evaluate the service provided to customers who are not repeating, leaving, or complaining? One possibility is to develop a survey, including an itemized scale to help customers quantify their opinions. After enough of these surveys are completed, managers will be able to calculate average scores for different service metrics. By comparing these with sales figures, managers can correlate sales with customer service and grade salespeople on their performance.

Example To translate customers' opinions into a metric, a company might pose survey questions such as the following:

Please circle the level of service your business received from our sales staff after shipment of the products you ordered:

1	2	3	4	5	6	7	8	9	10
Extremely Poor				Satisfactory				Extremely Good	

Data sources, complications, and cautions

Calculating the effectiveness of a salesperson is not difficult, but it does require keeping track of a few important numbers. Fortunately, these are commonly tracked as part of sophisticated sales management and customer relationship management (CRM) software packages.

The most important statistics are the amount of each sale (in dollars) and the contribution generated by each sale. It may also be important to keep track of which items are sold if a salesperson has been instructed to emphasize a certain product line. Additional useful information would include measures of the number of calls made (including both face-to-face and phone meetings), total accounts active, and total accounts in the territory. Of these, the latter two are needed to calculate the buying power of a territory.

The largest problem in performance review is a tendency to rely on only one or two metrics. This can be dangerous because an individual's performance on any one measure may be anomalous. A salesperson who generates $30,000 per call may be more valuable than one who generates $50,000 per call, for example, if the former generates greater sales per potential account. A salesperson in a small territory may generate low total contribution but high dollar sales per buying power. If this is true, it may be advisable to increase the size of that person's territory. Another salesperson may show a dramatic increase in dollar sales per active account. If achieved simply by eliminating weaker accounts, without generating incremental sales, this would not be grounds for reward. In reviewing sales personnel, managers are advised to evaluate as many performance metrics as possible.

Although the customer service survey described earlier is grounded upon a straightforward concept, managers can find it difficult to gather enough data—or sufficiently representative data—to make it useful. This could be because customers hesitate to fill out the surveys or because they do so only when they encounter a problem. A small sample size or a prevalence of negative responses might distort the results. Even so, some effort to measure customer satisfaction is needed to ensure that salespeople don't emphasize the wrong issues—or neglect issues that have a substantial impact on customers' lifetime value.

6.4 Sales force compensation: salary/reward mix

"The incentive plan needs to align the salesperson's activities with the firm's objectives."[7] Toward that end, an effective plan may be based on the past (growth), the present (comparison with others), or the future (percentage of goal achieved). Key formulas in this area include the following:

$$\text{Compensation (\$)} = \text{Salary (\$)} + \text{Bonus 1 (\$)} + \text{Bonus 2 (\$)}$$

$$\text{Compensation (\$)} = \text{Salary (\$)} + [\text{Sales (\$)} * \text{Commission (\%)}]$$

$$\frac{\text{Break-Even Number}}{\text{of Employees (\#)}} = \frac{(\text{Sales (\$)} * [\text{Margin (\%)} - \text{Commission (\%)}])}{[\text{Salary (\$)} + \text{Expenses (\$)} + \text{Bonus (\$)}]}$$

Purpose: to determine the mix of salary, bonus, and commission that will maximize sales generated by the sales force.

When designing a compensation plan for a sales force, managers face four key considerations: level of pay, mix between salary and incentive, measures of performance, and performance–payout relationships. The level of pay, or compensation, is the amount that a company plans to pay a salesperson over the course of a year. This can be viewed as a range because its total will vary with bonuses or commissions.

The mix between salary and incentive represents a key allocation within total compensation. Salary is a guaranteed sum of money. Incentives can take multiple forms, including bonuses or commissions. In the case of a bonus, a salesperson will receive a lump sum for reaching certain sales targets. With a commission, the incentive is incremental and is earned on each sale. In order to generate incentives, it is important to measure accurately the role a salesperson plays in each sale. The higher the level of causality that can be attributed to a salesperson, the easier it is to use an incentive system.

Various metrics can be used to measure a salesperson's performance. With these, managers can evaluate a salesperson's performance in the context of past, present, or future comparators, as follows:

- **The past:** Measure the salesperson's percentage growth in sales over prior-year results.
- **The present:** Rank salespeople on the basis of current results.
- **The future:** Measure the percentage of individual sales goals achieved by each salesperson.

Sales managers can also select the organizational level on which to focus an incentive plan. The disbursement of incentive rewards can be linked to results at the company, division, or product-line level. In measuring performance and designing compensation plans along all these dimensions, managers seek to align salespeople's incentives with the goals of their firm.

Finally, a time period should be defined for measuring the performance of each salesperson.

Construction

Managers enjoy considerable freedom in designing compensation systems. The key is to start with a forecast for sales and a range within which each salesperson's compensation should reside. After these elements are determined, there are many ways to motivate a salesperson.

In a multi-bonus system, the following formula can represent the compensation structure for a salesperson:

$$\text{Compensation (\$)} = \text{Salary (\$)} + \text{Bonus 1 (\$)} + \text{Bonus 2 (\$)}$$

In this system, bonus 1 might be attained at a level approximately halfway to the individual's sales goal for the year. The second bonus might be awarded when that goal is met.

In a commission system, the following formula would represent compensation for a salesperson:

$$\text{Compensation (\$)} = \text{Salary (\$)} + [\text{Sales (\$)} * \text{Commission (\%)}]$$

Theoretically, in a 100% commission structure, salary might be set as low as $0. Many jurisdictions, however, place limits on such arrangements. Managers must ensure that their chosen compensation structures comply with employment law.

Managers can also combine bonus and commission structures by awarding bonuses on top of commissions at certain sales levels or by increasing the commission rate at certain sales levels.

Example Tina earns a commission of 2% on sales up to $1,000,000 and a 3% commission on sales beyond that point. Her salary is $20,000 per year. If she makes $1,200,000 in sales, her compensation can be calculated as follows:

$$\text{Compensation} = \$20,000 + (0.02) * (\$1,000,000) + (0.03) * (\$200,000)$$

$$= \$46,000$$

After a sales compensation plan has been established, management may want to reevaluate the size of its sales force. Based on forecasts for the coming year, a firm may have room to hire more salespeople, or it may need to reduce the size of the sales force. On the basis of a given value for projected sales, managers can determine the break-even number of employees for a firm as follows:

$$\frac{\text{Break-Even Number}}{\text{of Employees (\#)}} = \frac{\text{Sales (\$)} * [\text{Margin (\%)} - \text{Commission (\%)}]}{[\text{Salary (\$)} + \text{Expenses (\$)} + \text{Bonus (\$)}]}$$

Data sources, complications, and cautions

Measurements commonly used in incentive plans include total sales, total contribution, market share, customer retention, and customer complaints. Because such a plan rewards a salesperson for reaching certain goals, these targets must be defined at the beginning of the year (or other time period). Continual tracking of these metrics will help both the salesperson and the company to plan for year-end compensation.

Timing is an important issue in incentive plans. A firm must collect data in a timely fashion so that both managers and salespeople know where they stand in relation to established goals. The time frame covered by a plan is another important consideration. If a company tries to generate incentives through weekly rewards, its compensation program can become too expensive and time-consuming to maintain. By contrast, if the program covers too long a period, it may slip out of alignment with company forecasts and goals. This could result in a sales force being paid too much or too little. To guard against these pitfalls, managers can develop a program that mixes both short- and long-term incentives. They can link some rewards to a simple, short-term metric, such as calls per week, and others to a more complex, long-term target, such as market share achieved in a year.

A further complication that can arise in incentive programs is the assignment of causality to individual salespeople. This can become a problem in a number of instances, including team collaborations in landing sales. In such a scenario, it can be difficult to determine which team members deserve which rewards. Consequently, managers may find it best to reward all members of the team with equal bonuses for meeting a goal.

A final concern: When an incentive program is implemented, it may reward the "wrong" salespeople. To avoid this, before activating any newly proposed program, sales managers are advised to apply that program to the prior year's results as a test. A "good" plan usually rewards the salespeople whom the manager knows to be the best.

6.5 Sales force tracking: pipeline analysis

> Pipeline analysis is used to track the progress of sales efforts in relation to all current and potential customers in order to forecast short-term sales and to evaluate sales force workload.

Purpose: to forecast upcoming sales and evaluate workload distribution.

A convenient way to forecast sales in the short term and to keep an eye on sales force activity is to create a sales pipeline or sales funnel. Although this concept can be represented graphically, the data behind it are stored electronically in a database or spreadsheet.

The concept of the sales funnel originates in a well-known dynamic: If a sales force approaches a large number of potential customers, only a subset of them will actually make purchases. As salespeople proceed through multiple stages of customer interaction, a number of prospects are winnowed out. At the conclusion of each stage, fewer potential customers remain. By keeping track of the number of potential customers at each stage of the process, a sales force manager can balance the workload within a team and make accurate forecasts of sales.

This analysis is similar to the hierarchy of effects discussed in Section 2.7. Whereas the hierarchy of effects focuses on the impact of advertising or mass media, the sales funnel is used to track individual customers (often by name) and sales force efforts.

Note: In some industries, such as consumer packaged goods, the term *pipeline sales* can refer to sales into a distribution channel. Please do not confuse pipeline sales with a sales pipeline.

Construction

In order to conceptualize a sales funnel or pipeline, it is helpful to draw a diagram showing the stages of the selling process (see Figure 6.2). At any point in the year, it is likely that all stages of the pipeline will include some number of customers. As Figure 6.2

Figure 6.2 Sales force funnel

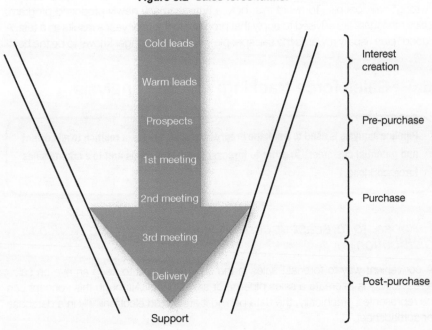

illustrates, although there may be a large number of *potential* customers, those who actually make purchases represent only a percentage of these original leads.

Interest creation

Interest creation entails building awareness of a product through such activities as trade shows, direct mail, and advertising. In the course of interest creation, salespeople can also generate leads. That is, they can identify targets to add to their pool of potential customers. Two main classifications of leads include cold leads and warm leads.

Cold lead: A lead that has not specifically expressed interest. These can be identified through mailing lists, phone books, business listings, and so on.

Warm lead: A lead that is expected to be responsive. These potential customers may have registered through a website or requested product information, for example.

Pre-purchase

The pre-purchase stage involves identifying prospects from among cold and warm leads. Salespeople make this distinction through initial meetings with leads, in which they explain product features and benefits, and cooperate in problem solving with the customer. The desired result of such an early-stage meeting is not a sale but rather the identification of a prospect and the scheduling of another meeting.

Prospect: A potential customer who has been identified as a likely buyer, possessing the ability and willingness to buy.[8]

Purchase

After prospects are identified and agree to additional calls, salespeople engage in second and third meetings with them. It is in these sessions that traditional "selling" takes place. Salespeople engage in persuading, negotiating, and/or bidding. If a purchase is agreed upon, a salesperson can close the deal through a written proposal, contract, or order.

Post-purchase

After a customer has made a purchase, there is still considerable work to be done. This includes delivery of the product or service, installation (if necessary), collection of payments, and possibly training. There is then an ongoing commitment to customer service.

After salespeople visualize the different stages represented in a sales funnel, they can track their customers and accounts more accurately. They can do this electronically by using a database or spreadsheet. If a sales pipeline file is maintained on a shared drive, any member of a sales force will be able to update the relevant data on a regular

Table 6.2 Spreadsheet sales funnel

| Sales-person | Interest creation | | Prospects | Pre-purchase | | Post-purchase | |
	Cold leads	Warm leads		1st/2nd meeting	2nd/3rd meeting	Delivery	Support
Sandy	56	30	19	5	8	7	25
Bob	79	51	33	16	4	14	35

basis. This will also enable a sales manager to view the progress of the team at any point in time. Table 6.2 is an example of a spreadsheet form of a sales funnel.

A manager can use the information stored in such a funnel to prepare for sales in the near future. This is a form of *pipeline analysis*. When a firm faces inventory issues, or when sales goals are being missed, this represents vital information. By applying historical averages, a sales or marketing manager can improve sales forecasts by using the data in a sales funnel. This can be done manually or with specialized software. The underlying assumption behind a sales funnel is that failure at any stage eliminates a prospect from the funnel. The following example illustrates how this bottom-up forecasting could be applied.

Example Using the sales funnel from earlier, Sandy and Bob's manager wants to forecast the number of sales that will require fulfillment in the next five months. Toward that end, she applies certain historical averages:

- 2% of cold calls are converted to sales within five months.
- 14% of warm calls are converted to sales within four months.
- 25% of prospects are converted to sales within three months.
- 36% of customers who agree to a pre-purchase meeting are converted to sales within two months.
- 53% of customers who agree to a purchase meeting are converted to sales within one month.

On this basis:

$$\text{Upcoming Sales} = [(56 + 79) * 2\%] + [(30 + 51) * 14\%] + [(19 + 33) * 25\%] + [(5 + 16) * 36\%)] + [(8 + 4) * 53\%] = 41$$

Note: This example applies to only one product. Often, a firm will need multiple sales funnels for different products or product lines. In addition, a sale may comprise a single item or thousands of items. In the latter case, it would be appropriate to use a metric for "average sale size/customer" in forecasting.

Data sources, complications, and cautions

In order to populate a sales funnel correctly, salespeople must maintain records of all their current and potential customers and the status of each within the purchase process. Each salesperson must also share this information, which can then be aggregated in a comprehensive database of sales force activities. By applying assumptions to these—including assumptions drawn from historical sales results—a firm can project future sales. For example, if 25% of warm leads are generally converted to sales within two months, and 200 warm leads currently appear in a sales funnel, management can estimate that 50 of these will be converted to sales within two months.

At times, the use of a sales funnel leads to the pitfall of over-prospecting. The incremental contribution likely to be generated by a customer should be compared to the probable cost of acquiring that customer, using customer lifetime value metrics as appropriate.

Difficulties in the sales cycle can also arise when a salesperson judges that a potential customer may be a prospect because he or she has the willingness and ability to buy. To solidify this judgment, the salesperson must also confirm that either the customer possesses the *authority* or is likely to obtain approval to buy.

Further reading

Jordan, Jason, and Michelle Vazzana. (2011). *Cracking the Sales Management Code: The Secrets to Measuring and Managing Sales Performance*. McGraw-Hill Education.

Channel management

7

Key concepts covered in this chapter:

- Numeric distribution, ACV distribution, and PCV distribution

- Facings and share of shelf

- Out-of-stock and service levels

- Inventory turns

- Markdowns

- Gross margin return on inventory investment (GMROII)

- Direct product profitability (DPP)

- Online distribution metrics

- Combining search and distribution

- Understanding channel dependencies

Introduction

This chapter discusses measures of the direct effect of push marketing, including increased availability of the brand and products.

If the channel is brick-and-mortar retail, the common measures are Numeric Distribution, ACV, and PCV. These three metrics are measures of the availability enjoyed by the brand or individual products. Numeric Distribution is the simplest. PCV and ACV are based on sales for a given time period, and they capture the end result of many important in-store factors. Inventory Turns, Out-of-Stocks, and Service Levels are three metrics for in-store activity we also discuss in this chapter.

In addition, we present metrics such as GMROII and DPP that retailers use to measure the relative performance of the products carried. These metrics are important to marketers as they can help explain the relative availability of a brand at retail and the sustainability of distribution and retail push efforts.

Given the general trend toward omni-channel marketing, we also include measures of success when the strategy encompasses multiple channels.

	Metric	Construction	Considerations	Purpose
7.1	Numeric Distribution	Percentage of outlets in a defined universe that stock a particular brand or product.	Outlets' size or sales levels are not reflected in this measure. Boundaries by which the distribution universe is defined may be arbitrary.	Assess the degree to which a brand or product is present in its potential channels.
7.1	All Commodity Volume (ACV)	Numeric Distribution, weighted by stocking outlets' shares of sales of all product categories.	Reflects sales of all commodities but may not reflect sales of the relevant product or category.	Assess the degree to which a brand or product has access to retail traffic.
7.1	Product Category Volume (PCV)	Numeric Distribution, weighted by stocking outlets' shares of sales of the relevant product category.	Strong indicator of share potential but may miss opportunities to expand category.	Assess the degree to which a brand or product has access to established outlets for its category.
7.1	Total Distribution	Usually based on ACV or PCV. Sums the relevant measures for each SKU in a brand or product line.	Strong indicator of the distribution of a product *line*, as opposed to an individual SKU.	Assess the extent to which a product line is available.
7.1	Category Performance Ratio	The ratio of a PCV-to-ACV distribution.	Same as for ACV and PCV.	Assess whether a brand's distribution or a particular retailer is performing above or below average for the category.

Metric	Construction	Considerations	Purpose
7.2 Out-of-Stock	Percentage of outlets that "list" or normally stock a product or brand but have none available for sale when measured.	Out-of-stocks can be measured in numeric, ACV, or PCV terms.	Monitor the gaps in availability.
7.2 Inventories	Total amount of product or brand available for sale in a channel.	May be held at different levels and valued in ways that may or may not reflect promotional allowances and discounts.	Calculate ability to meet demand and determine channel investments.
7.3 Markdowns	Percentage discount from the regular selling price and/or percentage of units sold at a discount.	For many products, a certain percentage of markdowns is expected. Too few markdowns may reflect under-ordering. If markdowns are too high, the opposite may be true.	Determine whether channel sales are being made at planned margins.
7.3 Direct Product Profitability (DPP)	The adjusted gross margin of products, less direct product costs.	Cost allocation is often imprecise. Some products may be intended not to generate profit but to drive traffic.	Identify profitable SKUs and realistically calculate their earnings.
7.3 Gross Margin Return on Inventory Investment (GMROII)	Margin divided by the average dollar value of inventory held during a specific period of time.	Allowances and rebates must be considered in margin calculations. For "loss leaders," this measure may be consistently negative and still not present a problem. For most products, negative trends in GMROII are signs of future problems.	Quantify return on working capital invested in inventory.

	Metric	Construction	Considerations	Purpose
7.4	Clicks to Product (#)	Count of clicks to get to a product.	Marketers for a supplier monitor clicks consumer must make to reach their product on, say, Amazon.	Determine how easy it is to get to a product on an online retailer's site.
7.5	% of Organic Sites Stocking the Brand	Number of organic sites on the first search engine results page (SERP) that stock the brand divided by the number of organic sites displayed.	Marketers for suppliers want to know that they are on sites appearing on the first page of organic searches.	Use distributional and search terms to get a better understanding of the market.
7.6	Advocacy	Percentage of reviews that are positive.	Advocacy is exhibited when a consumer positively supports a brand or firm (such as through a review).	Show the value of each channel member.

7.1 Numeric, ACV and PCV distribution, facings/share of shelf

Distribution metrics quantify the availability of products sold through resellers, usually as a percentage of all potential outlets. Often, outlets are weighted by their share of category sales or "all commodity" sales.

$$\text{Numeric Distribution (\%)} = \frac{\text{Number of Outlets Carrying Brand (\#)}}{\text{Total Number of Outlets (\#)}}$$

$$\text{All Commodity Volume (ACV) Distribution (\%)} = \frac{\text{Total Sales of Outlets Carrying Brand (\$)}}{\text{Total Sales of All Outlets (\$)}}$$

$$\text{Product Category Volume (PCV) Distribution}[1] \text{ (\%)} = \frac{\text{Total Category Sales of Outlets Carrying Brand (\$)}}{\text{Total Category Sales of All Outlets (\$)}}$$

$$\text{Category Performance Ratio (\%)} = \frac{\text{PCV (\%)}}{\text{ACV (\%)}}$$

For marketers who sell through resellers, distribution metrics reveal a brand's percentage of market access. Balancing a firm's efforts in "push" (building and maintaining reseller and distributor support) and "pull" (generating customer demand) is an ongoing strategic concern for marketers.

Purpose: to measure a firm's ability to convey a product to its customers.

In broad terms, marketing can be divided into two key challenges:

- The first—and most widely appreciated—is to ensure that consumers or end users want a firm's product. This is generally termed *pull* marketing.
- The second challenge is less broadly recognized but often just as important. *Push* marketing ensures that customers are given opportunities to buy.

Marketers have developed numerous metrics by which to judge the effectiveness of the distribution system that helps create opportunities to buy. The most fundamental of these are measures of product availability.

Availability metrics are used to quantify the number of outlets stocking a product, the fraction of the relevant market served by those outlets, and the percentage of total sales volume in all categories held by the outlets that carry the product.

Construction

There are three popular measures of distribution coverage:

- Numeric Distribution
- All Commodity Volume (ACV)
- Product Category Volume (PCV), also known as weighted distribution

Numeric distribution

This measure is based on the number of outlets that carry a product (that is, outlets that list at least one of the product's stock keeping units, or SKUs). It is defined as the percentage of stores that stock a given brand or SKU, within the universe of stores in the relevant market.

The main use of Numeric Distribution is to understand how many physical locations stock a product or brand. This has implications for delivery systems and for the cost of servicing these outlets.

$$\text{Numeric Distribution (\%)} = \frac{\text{Number of Outlets Carrying Product (\#)}}{\text{Total Number of Outlets in the Market (\#)}}$$

For further information about SKUs, refer to Section 3.3.

Example Alice sells photo albums to gift shops. There are 60 such stores in her area. In order to generate adequate distribution coverage, Alice believes she must reach at least 60% of these stores. In initiating her relationship with each store, however, Alice must provide the store with $4,000 worth of inventory to build a presence. To attain her distribution goal, how much will Alice need to invest in inventory?

To reach her Numeric Distribution target of 60%, Alice must build a presence in 36 stores (that is, 0.60 * 60).

She will therefore have to spend at least $144,000 on inventory (36 stores * $4,000 per store).

All commodity volume

All Commodity Volume (ACV) is a weighted measure of product availability, or distribution, based on total store sales. ACV can be expressed as a dollar value or percentage.

All Commodity Volume (ACV Distribution)(%)

$$= \frac{\text{Total Sales of Stores Carrying Brand (\$)}}{\text{Total Sales of All Stores (\$)}}$$

Example The marketers at Madre's Tortillas want to know the All Commodity Volume of their distribution network (see Table 7.1).

Table 7.1 Distribution for Madre's Tortillas

Outlet	All sales	Tortilla sales	Madre's Tortillas SKUs stocked	Padre's Tortillas SKUs stocked
Store 1	$100,000	$1,000	12 ct, 24 ct	12 ct, 24 ct
Store 2	$75,000	$500	12 ct	24 ct
Store 3	$50,000	$300	12 ct, 24 ct	None
Store 4	$40,000	$400	None	12 ct, 24 ct

Madre's Tortillas are carried by Stores 1–3 but not by Store 4. The ACV of its distribution network is therefore the total sales of Stores 1, 2, and 3, divided by the total sales of all stores. This represents a measure of the sales of all commodities in these stores, not just tortilla sales.

$$\text{Madre's Tortillas ACV (\%)} = \frac{\text{Sales Stores } 1 - 3}{\text{All Store Sales}}$$

$$= \frac{(\$100k + \$75k + \$50k)}{(\$100k + \$75k + \$50k + \$40k)}$$

$$= \frac{\$225k}{\$265k} = 84.9\%$$

The principal benefit of the ACV metric, by comparison with Numeric Distribution, is that it provides a superior measure of customer traffic in the stores that stock a brand. In essence, ACV adjusts Numeric Distribution for the fact that not all retailers generate the same level of sales. For example, in a market composed of two small stores, one superstore, and one kiosk, Numeric Distribution would weight each outlet equally, whereas ACV would place greater emphasis on the value of gaining distribution in the superstore. In calculating ACV when detailed sales data are not available, marketers sometimes use the square footage of stores as an approximation of their total sales volume.

The weakness of ACV is that it does not provide direct information about how well each store merchandises and competes in the relevant product category. A store can do a great deal of general business but sell very little of the product category under consideration.

Product category volume

Product Category Volume (PCV) is a refinement of ACV. In many countries, this metric is known simply as Weighted Distribution. It examines the share of the relevant product category sold by the stores in which a given product has gained distribution. It helps marketers understand whether a given product is gaining distribution in outlets where customers buy products in the category, as opposed to simply high-traffic stores where that product may get lost in the aisles.

Continuing our example of the two small retailers, the kiosk, and the superstore, although ACV may lead the marketer of a chocolate bar to seek distribution in the high-traffic superstore, PCV might reveal that the kiosk, surprisingly, generates the greatest volume in snack sales. In building distribution, the marketer would then be advised to target the kiosk as her highest priority.

> **Product category volume (PCV):** The percentage share, or dollar value, of category sales made by stores that stock at least one SKU of the brand in question, in comparison with all stores in the relevant universe.

$$\text{Product Category Volume (PCV Distribution)(\%)} = \frac{\text{Total Category Sales by Stores Carrying Brand (\$)}}{\text{Total Category Sales of All Stores (\$)}}$$

$$\text{Product Category Volume (PCV Distribution)(\$)} = \frac{\text{Total Category Sales of Stores Carrying Brand (\$)}}{}$$

When detailed sales data are available, PCV can provide a strong indication of the market share within a category to which a given brand has access. If sales data are not available, marketers can calculate an approximate PCV by using square footage devoted to the relevant category as an indication of the importance of that category to a particular outlet or store type.

Example The marketers at Madre's Tortillas want to know how effectively their product is reaching the outlets where customers shop for tortillas. Using data from the previous example, Stores 1, 2, and 3 stock Madre's Tortillas, Store 4 does not. The product category volume of the Madre's Tortillas distribution network can be calculated by dividing total tortilla sales in Stores 1–3 by tortilla sales throughout the market.

$$\text{PCV (\%)} = \frac{\text{Tortilla Sales of Stores Carrying Madre's}}{\text{Tortilla Sales of All Stores}}$$

$$= \frac{\$1,000 + \$500 + \$300}{\$1,000 + \$500 + \$300 + \$400} = 81.8\%$$

> **Total distribution:** The sum of ACV or PCV distribution for all of a brand's SKUs, calculated individually.

In many (perhaps most) product categories, it is important to have more than one SKU available for purchase. Product variants can include flavors, sizes, package types, formulations, and many other variations on the basic product. Measuring ACV% or PCV% distribution for a brand is rarely sufficient as an indicator of the product line's availability. Total Distribution is the sum of the relevant distribution metric across all of a brand's SKUs. For example, consider that Louis's Ice Cocoa Energy Drink (LICED) is offered in four variations: 32 oz chocolate, 32 oz vanilla, 16 oz chocolate, and 16 oz vanilla. The PCV% distribution for these four LICED SKUs is 80%, 70%, 60%, and 40%, respectively. The Total Distribution for LICED is the sum of the SKU distribution or 250%. If the LICED brand PCV distribution is 90%, it would mean that outlets stocking at least one SKU of LICED accounted for 90% of energy drink sales. It would also mean that, on average, stocking outlets would have about 2.8 SKUs on the shelf (250%/90%). Total distribution is a metric that combines breadth of distribution for the brand and depth of distribution for the product line. As brands have proliferated SKUs and variants, it has become more important to track Total Distribution and to compare the Total Distribution for a brand to the same metric for the category. Consider, for example, the number of craft beers now available in your local supermarket or liquor store.

> **Category performance ratio:** The relative performance of a retailer or retailers in a given product category, compared with performance in all product categories.

The category performance ratio compares PCV with ACV and provides insight into whether a brand's distribution network is more or less effective in selling the category of which that brand is a part, compared with its average effectiveness in selling all categories in which members of that network compete.

$$\text{Category Performance Ratio (\%)} = \frac{\text{PCV (\%)}}{\text{ACV (\%)}} \quad \text{Category Performance Ratio (\%)}$$

If a distribution network's category performance ratio is greater than 1, then the outlets comprising that network perform comparatively better in selling the category in question than in selling other categories, relative to the market as a whole.

Example As noted earlier, the PCV of the Madre's Tortillas distribution network is 81.8%. Its ACV is 84.9%. Thus, its category performance ratio is 0.96.

Madre's has succeeded in gaining distribution in the largest stores in its market. Tortilla sales in those stores, however, run slightly below the average of all commodity sales in those stores, relative to the market as a whole. That is, outlets carrying Madre's show a slightly weaker focus on tortillas than the overall universe of stores in this market.

Data sources, complications, and cautions

In many markets, there are data suppliers such as A.C. Nielsen, which specialize in collecting information about distribution. In other markets, firms must generate their own data. Sales force reports and shipment invoices provide a place to start.

For certain merchandise—especially low-volume, high-value items—it is relatively simple to count the limited number of outlets that carry a given product. For higher-volume, lower-cost goods, merely determining the number of outlets that stock an item can be challenging and may require assumptions. Take, for instance, the number of outlets selling a specific soft drink. To arrive at an accurate number, one would have to include vending machines and street vendors as well as traditional grocery stores.

Total outlet sales are often approximated by quantifying selling space (measured in square feet or square meters) and applying this measure to industry averages for sales per area of selling space.

In the absence of specific category sales data, it is often useful to weight ACV to arrive at an approximation of PCV. Marketers may know, for example, that pharmacies, relative to their overall sales, sell proportionally more of a given product than do superstores. In this event, they might increase the weighting of pharmacies relative to superstores in evaluating relevant distribution coverage.

Related metrics and concepts

> **Facing:** A frontal view of a single package of a product on a fully stocked shelf.
>
> **Share of shelf:** A metric that compares the facings of a given brand to the total facing positions available in the category in order to quantify the display prominence of that brand.

$$\text{Share of Shelf (\%)} = \frac{\text{Facings for Brand (\#)}}{\text{Total Facings in the Category (\#)}}$$

Store versus brand measures: Marketers often refer to a grocery chain's ACV. This can be either a dollar number (the chain's total sales of all categories in the relevant geographic market) or a percentage number (its share of dollar sales among the universe of stores). A brand's ACV is simply the sum of the ACVs of the chains and stores that stock that brand. Thus, if a brand is stocked by two chains in a market, and these chains have 40% and 30% ACV, respectively, the ACV of that brand's distribution network is 30% + 40%, or 70%.

Marketers can also refer to a chain's market share in a specific category. This is equivalent to the chain's PCV (%). A brand's PCV, by contrast, represents the sum of the PCVs of the chains that stock that brand.

Inventory: The level of physical stock held, typically measured at different points in a pipeline. A retailer may have inventory on order from suppliers, at warehouses, in transit to stores, in the stores' backrooms, and on the store shelves.

Depth of distribution: The number of SKUs held. Typically, a company will hold a wide range of SKUs—a high depth of distribution—for the products that it is most interested in selling.

Features in store: The percentage of stores offering a promotion in a given time period. This can be weighted by product or by ACV.

ACV on display: Distinctions can be made in all commodity volume metrics to take account of where products are on display. This will reduce the measured distribution of products if they are not in a position to be sold.

ACV on promotion: Marketers may want to measure the ACV of outlets where a given product is on promotion. This is a useful shorthand way of determining a product's reliance on promotion.

7.2 Supply chain metrics

Marketing logistics tracking includes the following metrics:

$$\text{Out-of-Stocks (\%)} = \frac{\text{Outlets Where Brand or Product Is Listed But Unavailable (\#)}}{\text{Total Outlets Where Brand or Product Is Listed (\#)}}$$

▶

▶

$$\text{Service Levels; Percentage on Time Delivery (\%)} = \frac{\text{Deliveries Achieved in Time Frame Promised (\#)}}{\text{All Deliveries Initiated in the Period (\#)}}$$

$$\text{Inventory Turns (I)} = \frac{\text{Product Revenues (\$)}}{\text{Average Inventory (\$)}}$$

Logistics tracking helps ensure that companies are meeting demand efficiently and effectively.

Purpose: to monitor the effectiveness of an organization in managing the distribution and logistics process.

In marketing, logistics is where the rubber meets the road. A lot can be lost at the potential point of purchase if the right goods are not delivered to the appropriate outlets on time and in amounts that correspond to consumer demand. How hard can that be? Well, ensuring that supply meets demand becomes more difficult when

- The company sells more than a few SKUs
- Multiple levels of suppliers, warehouses, and stores are involved in the distribution process
- Product models change frequently
- The channel offers customer-friendly return policies

In this complex field, by monitoring core metrics and comparing them with historical norms and guidelines, marketers can determine how well their distribution channel is functioning as a supply chain for their customers.

By monitoring logistics, managers can investigate questions such as the following: Did we lose sales because the wrong items were shipped to a store that was running a promotion? Are we being forced to pay for the disposal of obsolete goods that stayed too long in warehouses or stores?

Construction

Out-of-Stocks: A metric that quantifies the number of retail outlets where an item is expected to be available for customers but is not. It is often, but not always, expressed as a percentage of stores that list the relevant item.

$$\text{Out-of-Stocks (\%)} = \frac{\text{Outlets Where Brand or Product Is Listed But Unavailable (\#)}}{\text{Total Outlets Where Brand or Product Is Listed (\#)}}$$

Being "listed" by a chain means that a headquarters buyer has "authorized" distribution of a brand, SKU, or product at the store level. For various reasons, being listed does not always ensure presence on the shelf. Local managers may not approve distribution. Alternatively, a product may be distributed but sold out.

Out-of-Stocks is often expressed as a percentage. Marketers must note whether an Out-of-Stock percentage is based on Numeric Distribution, ACV, PCV, or the percentage of distributing stores for a given chain.

The in-stock percentage is the complement of the out-of-stock percentage. A 3% out-of-stock rate would be equivalent to a 97% in-stock rate.

Product category volume (PCV), net out-of-stocks: The PCV of a given product's distribution network, adjusted for out-of-stock situations. A quick way to create this out-of-stocks measure is to multiply PCV by a factor that adjusts it to recognize out-of-stock situations. The adjusting factor is simply 1 minus the out-of-stocks figure.

$$\text{Product Category Volume, Net Out-of-Stocks (\%)} = \text{PCV (\%)} * [1 - \text{Out-of-Stock (\%)}]$$

Alternatively, a longer method is to take the total product category sales of all outlets that have stock and divide this by the total product category sales of all outlets in the relevant retail universe.

Service levels, percentage on-time delivery: There are various service measures in marketing logistics. One particularly common measure is on-time delivery. This metric captures the percentage of customer (or trade) orders that are delivered in accordance with the promised schedule.

$$\text{Service Levels, Percentage On-Time Delivery (\%)} = \frac{\text{Deliveries Achieved in Time Frame Promised (\#)}}{\text{All Deliveries Initiated in the Period (\#)}}$$

Inventories, like Out-of-Stocks and Service Levels, should be tracked at the SKU level. For example, in monitoring inventory, an apparel retailer needs to know not only the brand and design of goods carried but also their size. Simply knowing that there are 30 pairs of suede hiking boots in a store, for example, is not sufficient—particularly if all those boots are the same size and fail to fit most customers.

By tracking inventory, marketers can determine the percentage of goods at each stage of the logistical process—in the warehouse, in transit to stores, or on the retail floor, for example. The significance of this information depends on a firm's resource management strategy. Some firms seek to hold the bulk of their inventory at the warehouse level, for example, particularly if they have an effective transport system to quickly ship goods to stores.

> **Inventory turns:** The number of times that inventory turns over in a year can be calculated on the basis of the revenues associated with a product and the level of inventory held. One need only divide the revenues associated with the product in question by the average level of inventory for that item. As this quotient rises, it indicates that inventory of the item is moving more quickly through the process. Inventory turns can be calculated for companies, brands, or SKUs and at any level in the distribution chain, but they are frequently most relevant for individual trade customers. Important note: In calculating inventory turns, dollar figures for both sales and inventory must be stated either on a cost or wholesale basis, or on a retail or resale basis, but the two bases must not be mixed.

$$\text{Inventory Turns (I)} = \frac{\text{Annual Product Revenues (\$)}}{\text{Average Inventory (\$)}}$$

> **Inventory days:** A metric that also sheds light on the speed with which inventory moves through the sales process. To calculate it, marketers divide the 365 days of the year by the number of inventory turns, yielding the average number of days of inventory carried by a firm. By way of example, if a firm's inventory of a product turned 36.5 times in a year, that firm would, on average, hold 10 days' worth of inventory of the product. High inventory turns—and, by corollary, low inventory days—tend to increase profitability through efficient use of a firm's investment in inventory. But they can also lead to higher out-of-stocks and lost sales.

$$\text{Inventory Days (\#)} = \frac{\text{Days in Year (365)}}{\text{Inventory Turns (I)}}$$

Inventory Days represents the number of days' worth of sales that can be supplied by the inventory present at a given moment. Viewed from a slightly different perspective, this figure advises logistics managers of the time expected to elapse before they suffer a stock-out if replenishment were to stop for some reason, such as a trade war or a problem in the supply chain. To calculate the Inventory Days figure, managers divide product revenue for the year by the value of the inventory days, generating expected annual turns for that inventory level. This can be easily converted into days by using the previous equation.

Example An apparel retailer holds $600,000 worth of socks in inventory January 1 and $800,000 the following December 31. Revenues generated by sock sales totaled $3.5 million during the year.

To estimate average dollar value of inventory during the year, managers might take the average of the beginning and ending numbers: ($600,000 + $800,000)/2 = $700,000 average inventory. On this basis, managers might calculate inventory turns as follows:

$$\text{Inventory Turns} = \frac{\text{Product Revenues}}{\text{Average Inventory}}$$

$$= \frac{\$3,500,000}{\$700,000} = 5$$

This figure can be converted to inventory days in order to measure the average number of days' worth of stock held during the period.

$$\text{Inventory Days} = \frac{\text{Days in Year (365)}}{\text{Inventory Turns}}$$

$$= \frac{365}{5} = 73 \text{ Days' Worth of Inventory}$$

It is worth bearing in mind that stock levels may be atypical around the holiday period. It may be that year-end figures do not accurately represent average inventory levels.

Data sources, complications, and cautions

Although some companies and supply chains maintain sophisticated inventory tracking systems, others must estimate logistical metrics on the basis of less-than-perfect data. Increasingly, manufacturers may also have difficulty purchasing research because retailers that gather such information tend to restrict access or charge high fees for it. Often, the only readily available data may be drawn from incomplete store audits or reports filed by an overloaded sales force. Ideally, marketers would like to have reliable metrics for the following:

- Inventory units and monetary value of each SKU at each level of the distribution chain for each major customer
- Out-of-stocks for each SKU, measured at both the supplier level and the store level
- Percentage of customer orders that were delivered on time and in the correct amount
- Inventory counts in the tracking system that don't match the number in the physical inventory (to facilitate a measure of shrinkage or theft)

When considering the monetary value of inventory, it is important to use comparable figures in all calculations. As an example of the inconsistency and confusion that can arise in this area, a company might value its stock on the retail shelf at the cost to the store, which might include an approximation of all direct costs. Or it might value that stock for some purposes at the retail price. Such figures can be difficult to reconcile with the cost of goods purchased at the warehouse and can also be different from accounting figures adjusted for obsolescence.

When evaluating inventory, managers must also establish a costing system for items that can't be tracked on an individual basis. Such systems include the following:

- **First in, first out (FIFO):** The first unit of inventory received is the first expensed upon sale.

- **Last in, first out (LIFO):** The last unit of inventory received is the first expensed upon sale.

The choice of FIFO or LIFO can have a significant financial impact in inflationary times. At such times, FIFO holds down the cost of goods sold by reporting this figure at the earliest available prices. Simultaneously, it values inventory at its highest possible level—that is, at the most recent prices. The financial impact of LIFO is the reverse.

In some industries, inventory management is a core skill. Examples include the apparel industry, in which retailers must ensure that they are not left with prior seasons' fashions, and the technology industry, in which rapid developments make products hard to sell after only a few months.

In logistical management, firms must beware of creating reward structures that lead to suboptimal outcomes. An inventory manager rewarded solely for minimizing out-of-stocks, for example, would have a clear incentive to overbuy—regardless of inventory holding costs. In this field, managers must ensure that incentive systems are sophisticated enough not to reward undesirable behavior.

Firms must also be realistic about what will be achieved in inventory management. In most organizations, the only way to be completely in stock on every product all the time is to ramp up inventories. This involves huge warehousing costs. It ties up a great deal of the company's capital in buying stocks. And it results in painful obsolescence charges to unload over-purchased items. Good logistics and inventory management entails finding the right trade-off between two conflicting objectives: minimizing both inventory holding costs and sales lost due to out-of-stocks.

Related metrics and concepts

Rain checks and make-goods on promotions: The effect on a store of promotional items being unavailable. In a typical example, a store might track the incidents in which it offers customers a substitute item because it has run out of stock on a promoted item. Rain checks or make-goods might be expressed as a percentage of goods sold or, more specifically, as a percentage of revenues coded to the promotion but generated by sales of items not listed as part of the promotional event.

Mis-shipments: The number of shipments that failed to arrive on time or in the proper quantities.

Deductions: The value of deductions from customer invoices caused by incorrect or incomplete shipments, damaged goods, returns, or other factors. It is often useful to distinguish between the reasons for deductions.

Obsolescence: A vital metric for many retailers, especially those involved in fashion and technology, that is expressed as the monetary value of items that are obsolete or as the percentage of total stock value that comprises obsolete items. If obsolescence is high, then a firm holds a significant amount of inventory that is likely to sell only at a considerable discount.

Shrinkage: Typically a euphemism for theft. It describes a phenomenon in which the value of actual inventory runs lower than recorded inventory, due to an unexplained reduction in the number of units held. This measure is typically calculated as a monetary figure or as a percentage of total stock value.

Pipeline sales: Sales that are required to supply retail and wholesale channels with sufficient inventory to make a product available for sale (refer to Section 6.5).

Consumer off-take: Purchases by consumers from retailers, as opposed to purchases by retailers or wholesalers from their suppliers. When consumer off-take runs higher than manufacturer sales rates, inventories are drawn down.

Diverted merchandise or diverted goods: Products shipped to one customer that are subsequently resold to another customer. For example, if a retail drug chain overbuys vitamins at a promotional price, it may ship some of its excess inventory to a dollar store.

7.3 SKU profitability: markdowns, GMROII, and DPP

Profitability metrics for retail products and categories are generally similar to other measures of profitability, such as unit and percentage margins. Certain refinements have been developed for retailers and distributors, however. Markdowns, for example, are calculated as a ratio of discount to original price charged. Gross Margin Return on Inventory Investment (GMROII) is calculated as margin divided by the cost of

▶

inventory and is expressed as a "rate," or percentage. Direct Product Profitability (DPP) is a metric that adjusts gross margin for other costs, such as storage, handling, and allowances paid by suppliers.

$$\text{Markdown (\%)} = \frac{\text{Reduction in Price of SKU (\$)}}{\text{Initial Price of SKU (\$)}}$$

$$\text{Gross Margin Return on Inventory Investment (\%)} = \frac{\text{Gross Margin on Product Sales in Period (\$)}}{\text{Average Inventory Value at Cost (\$)}}$$

$$\text{Direct Product Profitability (\$)} = \text{Gross Margin (\$)} - \text{Direct Product Costs (\$)}$$

By monitoring markdowns, marketers can gain important insight into SKU profitability. GMROII can be a vital metric in determining whether sales rates justify inventory positions. DPP is a theoretically powerful measure of profit that has fallen out of favor, but it may be revived in other forms (for example, activity-based costing).

Purpose: to assess the effectiveness and profitability of individual product and category sales.

Retailers and distributors have a great deal of choice regarding which products to stock and which to discontinue as they make room for a steady stream of new offerings. By measuring the profitability of individual SKUs, managers develop the insight needed to optimize such product selections. Profitability metrics are also useful in decisions regarding pricing, display, and promotional campaigns.

Figures that affect or reflect retail profitability include markdowns, gross margin return on inventory investment, and direct product profitability. Let's take each one in turn.

Markdowns are not always applied to slow-moving merchandise. Markdowns in excess of budget, however, are almost always regarded as indicators of errors in product assortment, pricing, or promotion. Markdowns are often expressed as a percentage of regular price. As a stand-alone metric, a markdown is difficult to interpret.

Gross margin return on inventory investment (GMROII) applies the concept of return on investment (ROI) to what is often the most crucial element of a retailer's working capital: its inventory.

Direct product profitability (DPP) shares many features with activity-based costing (ABC). Under ABC, a wide range of costs are weighted and allocated to specific products through cost drivers—the factors that cause the costs to be incurred. In measuring DPP, retailers factor such line items as storage, handling, manufacturer's allowances, warranties, and financing plans into calculations of earnings on specific product sales.

Construction

> **Markdown:** A metric that quantifies shop-floor reductions in the price of a SKU. It can be expressed on a per-unit basis or as a total for the SKU. It can also be calculated in dollar terms or as a percentage of the item's initial price.

$$\text{Markdown (\$)} = \text{Initial Price of SKU (\$)} - \text{Actual Sales Price (\$)}$$

$$\text{Markdown (\%)} = \frac{\text{Markdown (\$)}}{\text{Initial Price of SKU (\$)}}$$

> **Gross margin return on inventory investment (GMROII):** A metric that quantifies the profitability of products in relation to the inventory investment required to make them available. It is calculated by dividing the gross margin on product sales by the cost of the relevant inventory.

$$\text{Gross Margin Return on Inventory Investment (\%)} = \frac{\text{Gross Margin on Product Sales in Period (\$)}}{\text{Average Inventory Value at Cost (\$)}}$$

> **Direct product profitability (DPP):** A metric that represents a product's adjusted gross margin, less its direct product costs. Direct product profitability is grounded in a simple concept, but it can be difficult to measure in practice. The calculation of DPP consists of multiple stages. The first stage is to determine the gross margin of the goods in question. This gross margin figure is then modified to take account of other revenues associated with the product, such as promotional rebates from suppliers or payments from financing companies that gain business on its sale. The adjusted gross margin is then reduced by an allocation of direct product costs, described next.

> **Direct product costs:** The costs of bringing a product to customers. They generally include warehouse, distribution, and store costs.

$$\text{Direct Product Costs (\$)} = \text{Warehouse Direct Costs (\$)} + \text{Transportation Direct Costs (\$)} + \text{Store Direct Costs (\$)}$$

As noted earlier, the concept of DPP is quite simple. Difficulties can arise, however, in calculating or estimating the relevant costs. Typically, an elaborate ABC system is needed to generate direct costs for individual SKUs. DPP has fallen somewhat out of favor as a result of these difficulties.

Other metrics have been developed in an effort to obtain a more refined and accurate estimation of the "true" profitability of individual SKUs, factoring in the varying costs of receiving, storing, and selling them. The variations between products in the levels of these costs can be quite significant. In the grocery industry, for example, the cost of warehousing and shelving frozen foods is far greater—per unit or per dollar of sales—than the cost of warehousing and shelving canned goods.

$$\text{Direct Product Profitability (\$)} = \text{Gross Margin (\$)} - \text{Direct Product Costs (\$)}$$

Example The apparel retailer cited earlier wants to probe further into the profitability of its sock line. Toward that end, it assembles the following information. For this retailer, socks generate slotting allowances—in essence, fees paid by the manufacturer to the retailer in compensation for shelf space—in the amount of $50,000 per year. Warehouse costs for the retailer come to $10,000,000 per year. Socks consume 0.5% of warehouse space. Estimated store and distribution costs associated with socks total $80,000.

With this information, the retailer calculates an adjusted gross margin for its sock line.

$$\text{Adjusted Gross Margin} = \text{Gross Margin} + \text{Additional Margin}$$

$$= \$350,000 + \$50,000$$

$$= \$400,000$$

The retailer then calculates direct product costs for its sock line.

$$\text{Direct Product Costs} = \text{Store and Distribution Costs} + \text{Warehouse Costs}$$

$$= \$80,000 + (0.5\% * \$10,000,000)$$

$$= \$80,000 + \$50,000$$

$$= \$130,000$$

On this basis, the retailer calculates the direct product profitability of its sock line.

$$\text{DPP} = \text{Gross Margin} - \text{Direct Product Costs}$$

$$= \$400,000 - \$130,000$$

$$= \$270,000$$

Data sources, complications, and cautions

For GMROII calculations, it is necessary to determine the value of inventory held, at cost. Ideally, this will be an average figure for the period to be considered. The average of inventory held at the beginning and end of the period is often used as a proxy and is generally—but not always—an acceptable approximation. To perform the GMROII calculation, it is necessary to calculate a gross margin figure.

One of the central considerations in evaluating direct product profitability is an organization's ability to capture large amounts of accurate data for analysis. The DPP calculation requires an estimate of the warehousing, distribution, store direct, and other costs attributable to a product. To assemble these data, it may be necessary to gather all distribution costs and apportion them according to the cost drivers identified.

Inventory held, and thus the cost of holding it, can change considerably over time. Although one may usually approximate average inventory over a period by averaging the beginning and ending levels of this line item, this will not always be the case. Seasonal factors may perturb these figures. Also, a firm may hold substantially more—or less—inventory during the course of a year than at its beginning and end. This could have a major impact on any DPP calculation.

DPP also requires a measure of the ancillary revenues tied to product sales.

DPP has great conceptual strength. It tries to account for the wide range of costs that retailers incur in conveying a product to customers and thus to yield a more realistic measure of the profitability of that product. The only significant weakness in this metric is its complexity. Few retailers have been able to implement it. Many firms continue to try to realize its underlying concept, however, through such programs as activity-based costing.

Related metrics and concepts

> **Shopping basket margin: The profit margin on an entire retail transaction, which may include a number of products. This aggregate transaction is termed the "basket" of purchases that a consumer makes.**

One key factor in a firm's profitability is its capability to sell ancillary products in addition to its central offering. In some businesses, more profit can be generated through accessories than through the core product. Beverage and snack sales at movie theaters are a prime example. With this in mind, marketers must understand each product's role within their firm's aggregate offering—be it a vehicle to generate customer traffic, or to increase the size of each customer's basket, or to maximize earnings on that item itself.

7.4   Online distribution metrics

> **Omni-channel retail is a way of describing strategies recognizing that modern consumers access product promotion, information, and purchase opportunities in a wide variety of places both physical and virtual. Marketers want to know whether their products are well represented across the wide range of places consumers might hope to find them. In this section we look at how easy it is to find products and information about them in online environments.**

Purpose: to determine how easy it is to get to find a product on an online site.

Since we wrote the first edition of this book, the idea of omni-channel strategy, specifically for retailers, has become a key component for many marketers. There are several senses in which omni-channel is used. The marketers can be working to create synergies across distributional channels or across promotional channels. Both of these senses of the word can produce valuable insights, emphasizing coordination of strategy to work with the realities of modern marketing. In this section we look at metrics that capture how easy it is for consumers to find products and information about them in an omni-channel environment.

Construction

A couple general terms that are worth discussing:

- **Search engine results page (SERP):** This describes what is shown as a result of an online search. Placement on the first SERP can have very different consequences from later placements, given that many people see only the first page. When consumers are using their mobile devices, they are especially likely to see only the first screen displayed.

- **Above the fold:** This idea comes from newspapers. In the print environment, any story above the fold could be seen when the paper was folded and stacked. In online marketing, *above the fold* refers to anything that is visible on a web page without the need to scroll to it; that is, it is displayed without the need for human intervention, greatly increasing the chance that it will be viewed.

In online stores, there are metrics that capture whether an offering was actually seen. The following are some of them.

> Rank of app in app store (#): A number that captures where a retailer's app appears when displayed in an app store. Generally, placement higher in the rankings is useful in ensuring that the app is visible to more potential customers. Number of downloads (#)—that is, popularity of the app with other consumers—often drives this metric.
>
> Rank of brand/SKU (#): A number that captures where a brand/SKU appears when goods are searched for. Appearing on page 5 of the Amazon listings when a search for your product is made will have very different consequences than appearing on the first page. Clearly, suppliers can work with online retailers to improve their rankings.
>
> Brand on landing page (#): A number that captures whether a brand is featured on an online retailer's landing page.

> Clicks to product (#): A measure of how easy it is to get to a product on an online retailer's site. Marketers consider how many clicks it takes a consumer to reach their product with the understanding that the fewer, the better. Marketers also monitor if there is a "buy" button beside the product. Other considerations include the presence of an Amazon Dash button and the ability to order a product with voice-activated devices.

Data sources, complications, and cautions

Many metrics that consider how easy it is to find a product online vary considerably between products and businesses. In an online store, such as Apple's or Microsoft's, apps for relatively niche retailers are unlikely to appear high on the main listing—not because they aren't good apps but because only a subset of the population actually wants them. Marketers may therefore be more interested in how an app compares in a certain category or against given rivals.

The different ways consumers access information in an omni-channel world mean that one has to dig into what is reported to better understand the implications of metrics. Furthermore, what is below the fold will be different on a mobile device than on a large-screen PC. Given that screen sizes and resolutions differ considerably across devices and even within the same class of device, what is visible will differ considerably. Always clarify how a metric is constructed and what the assumptions are behind the metric, such as assumptions about what will be visible.

7.5 Combining search and distribution

> One of the exciting things about omni-channel retailing is that we can combine distribution and search terms to get a better understanding of the market. A manufacturer will want to know how well a brand (or SKU) is represented online in the results from search engines. To do this, the manufacturer can look at search results and see how many of the high search results are stocking any given product. This gives a better idea of whether the brand is stocked in high-performing online sites. Of course, searching by a specific brand should yield a much higher percentage than searching by product category or another general term.

$$\% \text{ of Organic Sites Stocking the Brand (\%)} = \frac{\text{Number of Original Sites on the First SERP That Stock the Brand (or SKU) (\#)}}{\text{Number of Organic Sites on the First SERP (\#)}}$$

Purpose: to understand online accessibility of products and information about them.

The percentage of organic sites stocking a brand indicates how well represented the brand (or SKU) is among sites that appear on the first page of search engine results. Marketers for the supplier will be interested in ensuring that they are stocked by the internet retailers who are most seen by the public when they search for the product.

Similar metrics can be created for sponsored sites and product listing ads (PLAs).

Construction

Organic search is the result of marketing that does not have a direct cost. Search engine optimization (SEO) is marketing work that helps get a top listing on search results. Retailers that appear high on such search rankings are likely to be popular and probably employ better online marketers. Marketers working for the suppliers will be interested to know that they are well represented on sites that appear on the first page of organic searches.

$$\text{\% of Organic Sites Stocking the Brand (\%)} = \frac{\text{Number of Original Sites on the First SERP That Stock the Brand (or SKU) (\#)}}{\text{Number of Organic Sites on the First SERP (\#)}}$$

Sponsored sites appear in search engine results, such as Google results. These listings result from paid advertising called search engine marketing. Placement on sponsored sites can be influenced by how much is paid. A manufacturer will be interested in knowing whether it is stocked by the retailers that pay for this form of advertising. Presumably these are more aggressive online advertisers.

$$\text{\% of Sponsored Sites Stocking the Brand (\%)} = \frac{\text{Number of Sponsored Sites on the First SERP That Stock the Brand (or SKU) (\#)}}{\text{Number of Sponsored Sites on the First SERP (\#)}}$$

Product listing ads (PLAs) are ads displayed in search results in Google and Bing. Typically, they include a product image, title, price, store name, and link. A similar metric can be constructed for PLAs.

$$\text{\% of PLAs Stocking the Brand (\%)} = \frac{\text{Number of PLAs on the First SERP That Stock the Brand (or SKU)(\#)}}{\text{Number of PLAs on the First SERP (\#)}}$$

Data sources, complications, and cautions

The metrics just discussed simply show whether a product is available on sites that the consumer has easy access to. They do not capture whether any purchases were made.

The search results gained depend on the keywords entered. A firm will be interested in specific keywords, such as 4K TV, and will want to be well represented in such searches. Other keywords will be of much less interest to the manufacturer. Deciding what keywords you care about is a key skill for online marketers.

7.6   Understanding channel dependencies

Relationships between suppliers and retailers can be complex and may require considerable management. The complexity of these relationships is increased in the world of omni-channel marketing, as actions taken by various players at various stages can help deliver results. Retailers can monitor their contributions to the supplier, such as cross-channel returns, advocacy, and cross-channel conversions. Suppliers can assess their contributions through advocacy, own-channel support, and cross-channel support. Both suppliers and retailers typically want to monitor how their partners are doing to encourage optimal results.

Purpose: to show the role of each channel member.

One of the complexities of retail strategy is that retailers and suppliers must work together. Much debate has been conducted about the issue of *showrooming*. This is where physical retailers perform a service to the consumer by displaying a supplier's product, but the consumer then purchases online—either from a different retailer, such as Amazon, or from the physical store's associated online presence, such as Walmart.com. The consumer gains valuable information from the physical store, the supplier benefits as the product is purchased, and the online retailer making the sale also benefits. Unfortunately, the physical retailer does not benefit directly from providing the information to the consumer. The physical retailer will want some way to show the benefit it is providing. If the online retailer is the same company as the physical retailer—such as Target and Target.com—rewarding the physical store can be managed internally by sales attribution. Where the online retailer is different from the physical retailer, the physical retailer will want to show the benefit it is giving to the supplier to, hopefully, extract more favorable terms from the manufacturer or other supplier.

While most attention has been paid to showrooming, a similar issue can occur in the opposite direction: A consumer may research at an online retailer or a supplier website and then purchase from a physical retailer. This is known as *webrooming*. The online presences are providing vital support to the purchase that the physical retailer is not necessarily rewarding the online entity for.

Understanding consumer search versus purchases can allow for better management of this relationship by helping to quantify the benefits provided by the party that does not gain the final sale. The metrics can be useful because the physical retailer wants to know how it is helping the supplier through things such as showrooming. These metrics provide discussion points for negotiations. The supplier may also want to know what retailers are most useful to them.

Similarly, a physical retailer may also want to know what suppliers are most useful to it—by supporting the product being sold by the retailer. In traditional channel settings, this support provided by the supplier would involve cooperative advertising and similar activities. Indeed, thinking more widely, any brand advertising by the supplier, such as advertising by Cadbury, can be seen as a form of support to the retailer that eventually sells the product. Strong brands will be able to make more demands of the retailer because of the support they provide to the final sale. There are a number of ways to promote a brand/SKU online by those not directly involved in the final sale the product, and both retailers and suppliers must work to know what this activity is and its impact. In summary, strong upstream marketer pull efforts can stimulate reseller push downstream.

Construction

Retailers provide a physical presence allowing the retailer to perform services for the customers that virtual venues cannot. The following metrics help show the contribution of a physical retailer to the value delivered to the customer where the physical retailer will not necessarily get credit given that it does not end up making the final sale to the customer.

Cross-channel conversions (#): The number of sales that happen in another channel, such as online, where the customer was served by the physical retailer. This metric captures the contribution to a sale made from showrooming. When it is used to look at sales influenced by online presences that lead to physical retailer sales, it captures the contribution of webrooming to sales. Of course, these estimates of cross-channel conversions are typically difficult to measure with precision.

Cross-channel delivery or returns (#): The number of any given activity (such as a delivery to a store or a return accepted by a store) that is done by a physical retailer and benefits the online retailer. For example, a consumer might buy at IKEA.com and have the product delivered to a local IKEA store for pickup. If IKEA.com gets credit for the sale, IKEA needs a way to compensate the physical store (which may just be notional transfers) to show the full benefit provided by the store. These return figures are considerably more reliable than cross-channel influences on orders and may add insight to the latter.

Cross-channel support ($): A record of the payments made by a supplier for cross-channel conversions, delivery, or returns.

Data sources, complications, and cautions

We have noted that within a single organization—such as Target and Target.com—attribution can give credit to any part of the organization that generates sales (such as by providing a venue for showrooming) but does not finalize the transaction. Determining where to give this credit is not easy in practice and often requires considerable effort on the part of management. Internal credit is a complex political process, and it can get especially contentious when two independent organizations are involved in the discussions.

Further reading

Ailawadi, Kusum L., and Paul W. Farris. (2020). *Getting Multi-Channel Distribution Right*, Wiley.

Ailawadi, Kusum L., and Paul W. Farris. (2017). "Managing Multi-and Omni-Channel Distribution: Metrics and Research Directions," *Journal of Retailing*, 93(1), 120–135.

Wilner, Jack D. (1998). *Seven Secrets to Successful Sales Management*, CRC Press.

Zoltners, Andris A., Prabhakant Sinha, and Greggor A. Zoltners. (2001). *The Complete Guide to Accelerating Sales Force Performance*, AMACON.

Pricing strategy

8

Key concepts covered in this chapter:

- Price premium

- Reservation price

- Percent good value

- Price elasticity of demand

- Optimal prices and linear and constant demand functions

- Own, cross, and residual price elasticity

Introduction

"The cost of . . . lack of sophistication in pricing is growing day by day. Customers and competitors operating globally in a generally more complex marketing environment are making mundane thinking about pricing a serious threat to the firm's financial well being."[1]

A full-fledged evaluation of pricing strategies and tactics is well beyond the scope of this book. However, there are certain key metrics and concepts that are fundamental to the analysis of pricing alternatives, and this chapter addresses them.

First, we describe several of the more common methods of calculating price premiums—also called relative prices.

Next, we discuss the concepts that form the foundation of price–quantity schedules—also known as demand functions or demand curves. These include reservation prices and percent good value.

In the third section, we explain the definition and calculation of price elasticity, a frequently used index of market response to changes in price. This relatively simple ratio of percentage changes in volumes and prices is complicated in practice by variations in measure and interpretation.

For managers, the purpose of understanding price elasticity is to improve pricing. With this in mind, we've devoted a separate section to determining optimal prices for the two main types of demand functions: linear and constant elasticity. The final portion of this chapter addresses the question of whether elasticity has been calculated in a manner that incorporates likely competitive reactions. It explains three types of elasticity: own, cross, and residual price elasticity. Although these may seem at first glance to rest upon subtle or pedantic distinctions, they have major pragmatic implications. The familiar concept of the prisoner's dilemma helps explain their importance.

	Metric	Construction	Considerations	Purpose
8.1	Price Premium	The percentage by which the price of a brand exceeds a benchmark price.	Benchmarks include average price paid, average price charged, average price displayed, and price of a relevant competitor. Prices can be compared at any level in the channel and can be calculated on a gross basis or net of discounts and rebates.	Measure how a brand's price compares to that of its competition.
8.2	Reservation Price	The maximum amount an individual is willing to pay for a product.	Reservation prices are difficult to observe.	Conceptualize a demand curve as the aggregation of reservation prices of potential customers.
8.2	Percent Good Value	The proportion of customers who consider a product to be a good value—that is, to have a selling price below their reservation price.	Percent good value is easier to observe than individual reservation prices.	Conceptualize a demand curve as the relationship between percent good value and price.

	Metric	Construction	Considerations	Purpose
8.3	Price Elasticity of Demand	The responsiveness of demand to a small change in price, expressed as a ratio of percentages.	For linear demand, linear projections based on elasticity are accurate, but elasticity changes with price. For constant elasticity demand, linear projections are approximate, but elasticity is the same for all prices.	Measure the responsiveness of quantity to changes in price. If priced optimally, the margin is the negative inverse of elasticity.
8.4	Optimal Price	For linear demand, optimal price is the average of variable cost and the maximum reservation price. For constant elasticity, optimal price is a known function of variable cost and elasticity. In general, optimal price is the price that maximizes contribution after accounting for how quantity changes with price.	Optimal price formulas are appropriate only if the variable cost per unit is constant, and there are no larger strategic considerations.	Quickly determine the price that maximizes contribution.
8.5	Residual Elasticity	Residual elasticity is "own" elasticity plus the product of competitor reaction elasticity and cross-elasticity.	Rests on an assumption that competitor reaction to a firm's price changes is predictable.	Measure the responsiveness of quantity to changes in price, after accounting for competitor reactions.

8.1 Price premium

Price premium, or relative price, is the percentage by which a product's selling price exceeds (or falls short of) a benchmark price.

$$\text{Price Premium (\%)} = \frac{\text{Brand A Price (\$)} - \text{Benchmark Price (\$)}}{\text{Benchmark Price (\$)}}$$

Marketers need to monitor price premiums as early indicators of competitive pricing strategies. Changes in price premiums can also be signs of product shortages, excess inventories, or other changes in the relationships between supply and demand.

Purpose: to evaluate product pricing in the context of market competition.

Although there are several useful benchmarks with which a manager can compare a brand's price, they all attempt to measure the "average price" in the marketplace. By comparing a brand's price with a market average, managers can gain valuable insight into its strength, especially if they view these findings in the context of volume and market share changes. Indeed, price premium—also known as relative price—is a commonly used metric among marketers and senior managers. Fully 63% of firms report the relative prices of their products to their boards, according to a survey conducted in the United States, United Kingdom, Germany, Japan, and France.[2]

Price premium: The percentage by which the price charged for a specified brand exceeds (or falls short of) a benchmark price established for a similar product or basket of products. Price Premium is also known as Relative Price.

Construction

In calculating a price premium, managers must first specify a benchmark price. Typically, the price of the brand in question will be included in this benchmark, and all prices in the benchmark will be for an equivalent volume of product (for example, price per liter). There are at least four commonly used benchmarks:

- The price of a specified competitor or competitors
- Average price paid (the unit-sales weighted average price in the category)
- Average price displayed (the display weighted average price in the category)
- Average price charged (the simple, unweighted, average price in the category)

Example Ali's company sells "gO2" mineral water in its EU home market at a 12% premium over the price of its main competitor. Ali would like to know whether the same price premium is being maintained in the Turkish market, where gO2 faces quite different competition. He notes that gO2 mineral water sells in Turkey for 2 (new) lira per liter, while its main competitor, Essence, sells for 1.9 lira per liter.

$$\text{Price Premium} = \frac{(2.0 \text{ YTL} - 1.9 \text{ YTL})}{1.9 \text{ YTL}}$$

$$= \frac{0.1 \text{ YTL}}{1.9 \text{ YTL}} = 5.3\% \text{ Premium versus Essence}$$

When assessing a brand's price premium among multiple competitors, managers can use as their benchmark the average price of a selected group of those competitors.

Note that the market average price paid includes the brand under consideration. Note also that changes in unit shares affect the average price paid. If a low-price brand steals shares from a higher-priced rival, the average price paid declines. This causes a firm's price premium (calculated using the average price paid as a benchmark) to rise, even if its absolute price did not change. Similarly, if a brand is priced at a premium, that premium declines as it gains share. The reason: A market share gain by a premium-priced brand causes the overall average price paid in its market to rise. This, in turn, reduces the price differential between that brand and the market average.

Example Ali wants to compare his brand's price to the Average Price Paid for similar products in the market. He notes that gO2 sells for 2.0 lira per liter and has 20% of the unit sales in the market. Its up-market competitor, Panache, sells for 2.1 lira and enjoys 10% unit market share. Essence sells for 1.9 lira and has 20% share. Finally, the budget brand Besik sells for 1.2 lira and commands 50% of the market.

Ali calculates the weighted Average Price Paid as follows:

$$(20\% * 2) + (10\% * 2.1) + (20\% * 1.9) + (50\% * 1.2) = 1.59 \text{ lira}$$

$$
\begin{aligned}
\text{Price Premium (\%)} &= \frac{(2.00 - 1.59)}{1.59} \\
&= \frac{0.41}{1.59} \\
&= 25.8\%
\end{aligned}
$$

To calculate the price premium using the average price paid benchmark, managers can also divide a brand's share of the market in value terms by its share in volume terms. If value and volume market shares are equal, there is no premium. If value share is greater than volume share, then there is a positive price premium.

$$\text{Price Premium (\%)} = \frac{\text{Revenue Market Share (\%)}}{\text{Unit Market Share (\%)}} - 1$$

Calculation of the average price paid requires knowledge of the sales or shares of each competitor. A much simpler benchmark is the average price charged.

Average price charged: The simple unweighted average price of the brands in the category. This benchmark requires knowledge only of prices. As a consequence, the price premium calculated using this benchmark is not affected by changes in unit shares. For this reason, this benchmark serves a slightly different purpose: It captures the way a brand's price compares to prices set by its competitors, without regard to customers' reactions to those prices. It also treats all competitors equally in the calculation of the benchmark price. Large and small competitors are weighted equally when calculating average price charged.

Example Using the previous data, Ali calculates Average Price Charged in the mineral water category as $(2 + 2.1 + 1.9 + 1.2)/4 = 1.8$ lira.

Using the average price charged as his benchmark, he calculates gO2's price premium as

$$\text{Price Premium (\%)} = \frac{(2.0 - 1.8)}{1.8}$$

$$= \frac{0.2}{1.8}$$

$$= 11.1\% \text{ Premium}$$

Average price displayed: A benchmark conceptually situated between average price paid and average price charged. Marketing managers who seek a benchmark that captures differences in the scale and strength of brands' distribution might weight each brand's price in proportion to a numerical measure of distribution. Typical measures of distribution strength include numeric distribution, ACV (%), and PCV (%).

Example Ali calculates Average Price Displayed by using numeric distribution.

Ali's brand, gO2, is priced at 2 lira and is distributed in 500 of the 1,000 stores that carry bottled water. Panache is priced at 2.1 lira and stocked by 200 stores. Essence is priced at 1.9 lira and sold through 400 stores. Besik carries a price of 1.2 lira and has a presence in 900 stores.

Ali calculates relative weighting on the basis of numeric distribution. The total number of stores is 1,000. The weightings are, therefore, for gO2, 500/1,000 = 50%; for Panache, 200/1,000 = 20%; for Essence, 400/1,000 = 40%; and for Besik, 900/1,000 = 90%. As the weightings thus total 200%, in calculating average price displayed, the sum of the weighted prices must be divided by that figure, as follows:

$$\text{Average Price Displayed} = \frac{[(2 * 50\%) + (2.1 * 20\%) + (1.9 * 40\%) + (1.2 * 90\%)]}{200\%}$$

$$= 1.63 \text{ lira}$$

$$\text{Price Premium (\%)} = \frac{(2.00 - 1.63)}{1.63}$$

$$= \frac{0.37}{1.63}$$

$$= 22.7\% \text{ Premium}$$

Data sources, complications, and cautions

Several practical aspects of calculating price premiums deserve mention. Managers may find it easier to select a few leading competitors and focus their analysis and comparison on them. Often, it is difficult to obtain reliable data on smaller competitors.

Managers must exercise care when interpreting price premiums. Different benchmarks measure different types of premiums and must be interpreted accordingly.

Can a price premium be negative?

Yes. Although generally expressed in terms that imply only positive values, a price premium can be negative. If one brand doesn't command a positive premium, a competitor will. Consequently, except in the unlikely event that all prices are exactly equal, managers may want to speak in terms of *positive* premiums. When a given brand's price is at the low end of the market, managers may want to say that the competition holds a price premium of a certain value.

Should we use retail, manufacturer, or distributor pricing?

Each of these types of pricing is useful in understanding the market dynamics at its level. When products have different channel margins, their price premiums differ, depending on the channel under consideration. When stating a price premium, managers are advised to specify the level to which it applies.

Prices at each level can be calculated on a gross basis or net of discounts, rebates, and coupons.

Especially when dealing with distributors or retailers, there are likely to be substantial differences between manufacturer selling prices (retail purchase prices), depending on whether they are adjusted for discounts and allowances.

Related metrics and concepts

> **Theoretical price premium: The price difference that would make potential customers indifferent between two competing products. It represents a different use of the term price premium that is growing in popularity. The theoretical price premium can also be discovered through a conjoint analysis using brand as an attribute. The theoretical price premium is the point at which consumers would be indifferent between a branded item and an unbranded item or between two different brands. We have termed this a "theoretical" price premium because there is no guarantee that the price premiums observed in the market will take this value. (Refer to Section 4.5 for an explanation of conjoint analysis.)**

8.2 Reservation price and percent good value

> The reservation price is the value a customer places on a product. It constitutes an individual's maximum willingness to pay. Indeed "willingness to pay" is often used as a synonym for reservation price. Percent good value represents the proportion of customers who believe a product is a "good value" at a specific price.
>
> These are useful metrics in marketers' evaluation of pricing and customer value.

Purpose: to understand the willingness of customers to pay for a product.

Reservation prices provide a basis for estimating products' demand functions in situations where other data are not available. They also offer marketers insight into pricing latitude. When it is not possible or convenient to ask customers about their reservation prices, percent good value can provide a substitute for that metric.

Construction

> Reservation price: The price above which a customer will not buy a product. Also known as the maximum willingness to pay.
>
> Percent good value: The proportion of customers who perceive a product to represent a good value—that is, to carry a selling price at or below their reservation price.

By way of example, suppose that a market consists of 11 individuals with reservation prices for a given product of $30, $40, $50, $60, $70, $80, $90, $100, $110, $120, and $130. The manufacturer of that product seeks to decide on its price. Clearly, it might do better to offer more than a single price. For now, however, let's assume that tailored prices are impractical. The variable cost to produce the product is $60 per unit.

With these reservation prices, the manufacturer might expect to sell 11 units at $30 or less, 10 units at a price greater than $30 but less than or equal to $40, and so on. It would make no sales at a unit price greater than $130. (For convenience, we have assumed that people buy at their reservation price. This assumption is consistent with a reservation price being the *maximum* an individual is willing to pay.)

Table 8.1 shows this price–quantity relationship, together with the contribution to the firm at each possible price.

Table 8.1 Price–quantity relationship

Price	% Good value	Quantity	Total contribution
$20	100.00%	11	–$440
$30	100.00%	11	–$330
$40	90.91%	10	–$200
$50	81.82%	9	–$90
$60	72.73%	8	$0
$70	63.64%	7	$70
$80	54.55%	6	$120
$90	45.45%	5	$150
$100	36.36%	4	$160
$110	27.27%	3	$150
$120	18.18%	2	$120
$130	9.09%	1	$70
$140	0.00%	0	$0
$150	0.00%	0	$0
Variable cost is $60 per unit.			

A table of quantities expected at each of several prices is often called a *demand schedule* (or *curve*). This example shows that one way to conceptualize a demand curve is as the accumulation of individual reservation prices. Although it would clearly be difficult in practice to measure individual reservation prices, the point here is simply to illustrate the use of reservation prices in pricing decisions. In this example, the optimal price—that is, the price that maximizes total contribution—is $100. At $100, the manufacturer expects to sell four units. Its contribution margin is $40, yielding a total contribution of $160.

This example also illustrates the concept of consumer surplus. Consumer surplus: A term that is frequently used by economists and is the difference between the price that consumers pay and the price that they are willing to pay. At $100, the manufacturer sells three items at a price point below customers' reservation prices. The consumer with the reservation price of $110 enjoys a surplus of $10. The consumer with the reservation price of $120 receives a surplus of $20. Finally, the consumer with the highest reservation price, $130, receives a surplus of $30. From the manufacturer's perspective, the total consumer surplus—$60— represents an opportunity for increased contribution if it can find a way to capture this unclaimed value.

Data sources, complications, and cautions

Finding reservation prices is no easy matter. Two techniques are frequently used to gain insight into this metric:

- **Second-price auctions:** In a second-price auction, the highest bidder wins but pays only the second-highest bid amount. Auction theory suggests that when bidding on items of known value in such auctions, individuals have an incentive to bid their reservation prices. Certain survey techniques have been designed to mimic this process. In one of these, customers are asked to name their prices for an item, with the understanding that these prices will then be subjected to a lottery. If the price drawn in the lottery is less than the price named, the respondent gains an opportunity to purchase the item in question at the drawn price.

- **Conjoint analysis:** In this analytical technique, marketers gain insight into customer perceptions regarding the value of any set of attributes through the trade-offs they are willing to make.

Such tests can, however, be difficult to construct and impractical in many circumstances. Consequently, as a fallback technique, marketers can measure percent good value. Rather than seek to learn each customer's reservation price, they may find it easier to test a few candidate prices by asking customers whether they consider an item a "good value" at each of those prices.

Linear demand

The price–quantity schedule formed by an accumulation of reservation prices can take a variety of shapes. When the distribution of reservation prices is uniform—that is, when reservation prices are equally spaced, as in our example—the demand schedule is linear (see Figure 8.1). That is, each increment in price reduces quantity by an equal amount. As the linear function is by far the most commonly used representation of demand, we provide a description of this function as it relates to the distribution of underlying reservation prices.

It takes only two points to determine a straight line. Likewise, it takes only two parameters to write an equation for that line. Generally, that equation is written as $Y = mX + b$, in which m is the slope of the line and b is its Y-intercept.

A line, however, can also be defined in terms of the two points where it crosses the axes. In the case of linear demand, these crossing points (intercepts) have useful managerial interpretations.

The quantity-axis intercept can be viewed as a representation of the maximum willing to buy (MWB). This is the total number of potential customers for a product. A firm can serve all these customers only at a price of zero. Assuming that each potential customer buys one unit, MWB is the quantity sold when the price is zero.

Figure 8.1 Maximum willing to buy and maximum reservation price

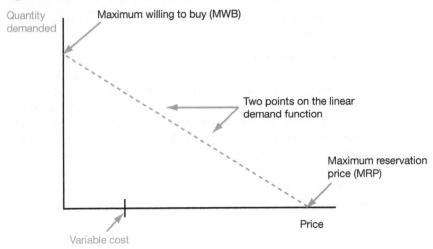

The price-axis intercept can be viewed as the maximum reservation price (MRP). The MRP is a number slightly greater than the highest reservation price among all those willing to buy. If a firm prices its product at or above MRP, no one will buy.

> Maximum reservation price (MRP): **The lowest price at which quantity demanded equals zero.**
>
> Maximum willing to buy (MWB): **The quantity that customers will "buy" when the price of a product is zero. This is an artificial concept used to anchor a linear demand function.**

In a linear demand curve defined by MWB and MRP, the equation for quantity (Q) as a function of price (P) can be written as follows:

$$Q = (MWB) * \left[1 - \frac{P}{MRP} \right]$$

Example Erin knows that the demand for her soft drink is a simple linear function of price. She can sell 10 units at a price of zero. When the price hits $5 per unit, demand falls to zero. How many units will Erin sell if the price is $3 (see Figure 8.2)?

Figure 8.2 Simple linear demand (price–quantity) function

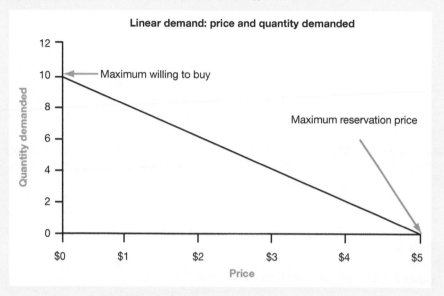

Linear demand: price and quantity demanded

For Erin's soft drink, the MRP is $5, and the MWB is 10 units. At a price of $3, Erin will sell 10 * (1 − $3/$5), or 4 units.

When demand is linear, any two points on the price–quantity demand function can be used to determine MRP and MWB. If P_1 and Q_1 represent the first price–quantity point on the line, and P_2 and Q_2 represent the second, the following two equations can be used to calculate MWB and MRP:

$$MWB = Q_1 - \left(\frac{Q_2 - Q_1}{P_2 - P_1}\right) * P_1$$

$$MRP = P_1 - \left(\frac{P_2 - P_1}{Q_2 - Q_1}\right) * Q_1$$

Example Early in this chapter, we met a firm that sells five units at a price of $90 and three units at a price of $110. If demand is linear, what are MWB and MRP?

$$MWB = 5 - (-2/\$20) * \$90$$
$$= 5 + 9$$
$$= 14$$
$$MRP = \$90 - (\$20/-2) * 5$$
$$= \$90 + \$50$$
$$= \$140$$

The equation for quantity as a function of price is thus:

$$Q = 14 * \left(1 - \frac{P}{\$140}\right)$$

The market in this example, as you may recall, comprises 11 potential buyers with reservation prices of $30, $40,…, $120, $130. At a price of $130, the firm sells one unit. If we set price equal to $130 in the previous equation, our calculation does indeed result in a quantity of one. For this to hold true, the MRP must be a number slightly higher than $130.

A linear demand function often yields a reasonable approximation of actual demand only over a limited range of prices. In our 11-person market, for example, demand is linear only for prices between $30 and $130. To write the equation of the linear function that describes demand between $30 and $130, however, we must use an MWB of 14 and an MRP of $140. When we use this linear equation, we must remember that it reflects actual demand only for prices between $30 and $130, as illustrated in Figure 8.3.

Figure 8.3 Example of linear demand function

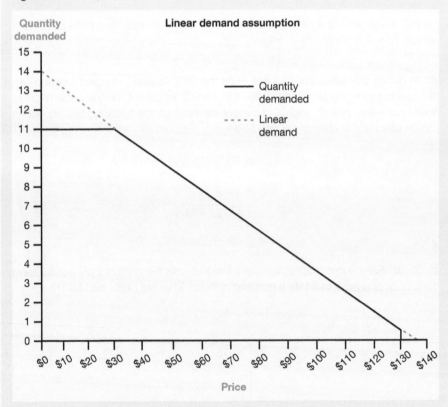

8.3   Price elasticity of demand

> Price elasticity measures the responsiveness of quantity demanded to a small change in price.
>
> $$\text{Price Elasticity (I)} = \frac{\text{Change in Quantity (\%)}}{\text{Change in Price (\%)}}$$
>
> Price elasticity can be a valuable tool, enabling marketers to set an optimal price.

Purpose: to understand market responsiveness to changes in price.

Price elasticity is the most commonly employed measure of market responsiveness to changes in price. Many marketers, however, use this term without a clear understanding of what it entails. This section helps clarify some of the potentially dangerous details associated with estimates of price elasticity. This is challenging material but is well worth the effort. A strong command of price elasticity can help managers set optimal prices.

> Price elasticity: The responsiveness of demand to a small change in price, expressed as a ratio of percentages. If price elasticity is estimated at −1.5, for example, then we expect the percentage change in quantity to be approximately 1.5 times the percentage change in price. The fact that this number is negative indicates that when price rises, the quantity demanded is expected to decline and vice versa.

Construction

If we raise the price of a product, do we expect demand to hold steady or crash through the floor? In markets that are unresponsive to price changes, we say demand is inelastic. If minor price changes have a major impact on demand, we say demand is elastic. Most of us have no trouble understanding elasticity at a qualitative level. The challenges come when we quantify this important concept.

Challenge 1: We need to agree on the sign.
The first challenge in elasticity is to agree on its sign. Elasticity is the ratio of the percentage change in quantity demanded to the percentage change in price for a small change in price. If an increase in price leads to a decrease in quantity, this ratio will be negative. Consequently, by this definition, elasticity will almost always be a negative number.

Many people, however, simply assume that quantity goes down as price goes up and jump immediately to the question of "by how much." For such people, price elasticity answers that question and is a positive number. In their eyes, if elasticity is 2, then a small percentage increase in price will yield twice that percentage decrease in quantity.

In this book, under that scenario, we would say price elasticity is −2.

Challenge 2: When demand is linear, elasticity changes with price.
For a linear demand function, the slope is constant, but elasticity is not. The reason: Elasticity is not the same as slope. Slope is the change in quantity for a small change in price. Elasticity, by contrast, is the *percentage* change in quantity for a small *percentage* change in price.

Example Consider three points on a linear demand curve: ($8, 100 units), ($9, 80 units), and ($10, 60 units) (see Figure 8.4). Each dollar change in price yields a 20-unit change in quantity. The slope of this curve is a constant −20 units per dollar.

As price rises from $8 to $9 (a 12.5% increase), quantity declines from 100 to 80 (a 20% decrease). The ratio of these percentages is 20%/12.5%, or −1.6. Similarly, as price rises from $8 to $10 (a 25% increase), quantity declines from 100 to 60 (a 40% decrease). Once again, the ratio (40%/25%) is −1.6. It appears that the ratio of percentage change in quantity to percentage change in price is −1.6, regardless of the size of the change made in the $8 price.

Figure 8.4 Linear demand function

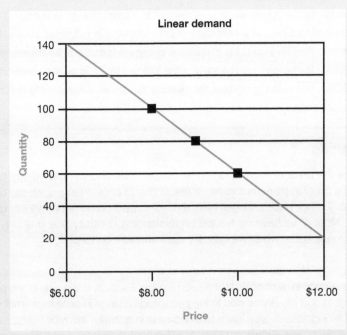

Consider, however, what happens when price rises from $9 to $10 (an 11.11% increase). Quantity declines from 80 to 60 (a 25% decrease). The ratio of these figures, 25%/11.11%, is now −2.25. A price decline from $9 to $8 also yields an elasticity ratio of −2.25. It appears that this ratio is −2.25 at a price of $9, regardless of the direction of any change in price.

As an exercise, verify that the ratio of percentage change in quantity to percentage change in price at the price of $10 is −3.33 for every conceivable price change.

For a linear demand curve, elasticity changes with price. As price increases, elasticity gains in magnitude. Thus, for a linear demand curve, the absolute unit change in quantity for an absolute dollar change in price (slope) is constant, and the percentage change in quantity for a percentage change in price (elasticity) is not. Demand becomes more elastic—that is, elasticity becomes more negative—as price increases.

For a linear demand curve, the elasticity of demand can be calculated in at least three ways:

$$\text{Elasticity } (P_1) = \frac{\dfrac{Q_2 - Q_1}{Q_1}}{\dfrac{P_2 - P_1}{P_1}}$$

$$= \frac{Q_2 - Q_1}{P_2 - P_1} * \left(\frac{P_1}{Q_1}\right)$$

$$= \text{Slope} * \left(\frac{P_1}{Q_1}\right)$$

To emphasize the idea that elasticity changes with price on a linear demand curve, we write Elasticity (P), reflecting the fact that elasticity is a function of price. We also use the term *point elasticity* to cement the idea that a given elasticity applies only to a single point on the linear demand curve.

Equivalently, because the slope of a linear demand curve represents the change in quantity for a given change in price, price elasticity for a linear demand curve is equal to the slope, multiplied by the price, divided by the quantity. This is captured in the third equation here.

Example Revisiting the demand function from earlier, we see that the slope of the curve reflects a 20-unit decline in demand for each dollar increase in price. That is, slope equals −20.

The slope formula for elasticity can be used to verify our earlier calculations. Calculate price/quantity at each point on the curve and multiply this by the slope to yield the price elasticity at that point (see Table 8.2).

For example, at a price of $8, quantity sold is 100 units. Thus:

$$\text{Elasticity (\$8)} = -20 * (8/100)$$
$$= -1.6$$

Table 8.2 Elasticities at a point calculated from the slope of a function

Price	Quantity demanded	Price–quantity	Slope	Price elasticity at point
$8.00	100	0.08	(20.00)	(1.60)
$9.00	80	0.11	(20.00)	(2.25)
$10.00	60	0.17	(20.00)	(3.33)

In a linear demand function, point elasticities can be used to predict the percentage change in quantity to be expected for any percentage change in price.

Example Xavi manages the marketing of a toothpaste brand. He knows the brand follows a linear demand function. At the current price of $3.00 per unit, his firm currently sells 60,000 units with an elasticity of −2.5. A proposal is floated to raise the price to $3.18 per unit in order to standardize margins across brands. At $3.18, how many units would be sold?

The proposed change to $3.18 represents a 6% increase over the current $3 price. Because elasticity is −2.5, such an increase can be expected to generate a decrease in unit sales of 2.5 * 6 = 15%. A 15% reduction in current sales of 60,000 units would yield a new quantity of 0.85 * 60,000 = 51,000.

Constant elasticity: demand curve with a constantly changing slope

A second common form of function used to estimate demand entails constant elasticity.[3] This form is responsible for the term *demand curve* because it is, indeed, curved. In contrast with the linear demand function, the conditions in this scenario are reversed: Elasticity is constant, and the slope changes at every point.

The assumption underlying a constant elasticity demand curve is that a small percentage change in price causes the same percentage change in quantity, regardless of the value of the initial price. That is, the rate of change in quantity versus price, expressed as a ratio of percentages, is equal to a constant throughout the curve. That constant is the elasticity.

In mathematical terms, in a constant elasticity demand function, slope multiplied by price divided by quantity is equal to a constant (the elasticity) for all points along the curve (see Figure 8.5). The constant elasticity function can also be expressed in an equation that is easily calculated in spreadsheets:

$$Q(P) = A * P^{ELAS}$$

In this equation, ELAS is the price elasticity of demand. It is usually a negative number. A is a scaling factor. It can be viewed as the quantity that would be sold at a price of $1 (assuming that $1 is a reasonable price for the product under consideration).

Figure 8.5 Constant elasticity function

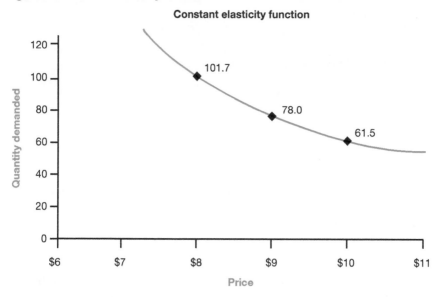

Example Plot a demand curve with a constant elasticity of −2.25 and a scaling factor of 10,943.1. For every point on this curve, a small percentage increase in price yields a percentage decrease in quantity that is 2.25 times as great. This 2.25 ratio holds, however, only for the very smallest percentage changes in price. This is because the slope changes at every point. The use of the 2.25 ratio to project the results of a finite percentage increase in price is always approximate.

The curve traced in this example should look like the constant elasticity curve in Figure 8.5. More exact figures for demand at prices $8, $9, and $10 would be 101.669, 78.000, and 61.538 units.

In a way, constant elasticity is analogous to the continuous compounding of interest. In a constant elasticity function, every small percentage increase in price generates the same percentage decrease in quantity. These percentage decreases compound at a constant rate, leading to an overall percentage decrease that does not precisely equal the continuous rate. For this reason, given any two points on a constant elasticity demand curve, we can no longer calculate elasticity using finite differences as we could when demand was linear. Instead, we must use a more complicated formula grounded in natural logarithms:

$$\text{ELAS} = \frac{\ln(Q_2/Q_1)}{\ln(P_2/P_1)}$$

Example Taking any two points from the previous constant elasticity demand curve, we can verify that elasticity is −2.25.

At \$8, for example, the quantity is 101.669. Call the points P_1 and Q_1.
At \$9, the quantity is 78.000. Call the points P_2 and Q_2.
Inserting these points into our formula, we determine that

$$\text{ELAS} = \frac{\ln(78.000/101.669)}{\ln(9/8)}$$

$$= \frac{-0.265}{0.118}$$

$$= -2.25$$

If we had set P_2 equal to \$8, and P_1 equal to \$9, we would have arrived at the same figure for elasticity. In fact, regardless of which two points we select on this constant elasticity curve, and regardless of the order in which we consider them, elasticity will always be −2.25.

In summary, elasticity is the standard measure of market responsiveness to changes in price. In general, it is the "percentage slope" of the demand function (curve), obtained by multiplying the slope of the curve for a given price by the ratio of price to quantity.

$$\text{Elasticity }(P) = \text{Slope} * \left(\frac{P}{Q}\right)$$

Elasticity can also be viewed as the percentage change in quantity for a small percentage change in price.

In a linear demand function, the slope is constant, but elasticity changes with price. In this scenario, marketers can use elasticity estimates to calculate the result of an anticipated price change in either direction, but they must use the elasticity that is appropriate for their initial price point. The reason: In a linear demand function, elasticity varies across price points, but projections based on these elasticities are accurate.

In a constant elasticity demand function, elasticity is the same at all price points, but projections based on these elasticities will be approximate. Assuming that they are estimated with precision, using the constant elasticity demand function itself to make sales projections on the basis of price changes will be more accurate.

Data sources, complications, and cautions

Price elasticity is generally estimated on the basis of available data. These data can be drawn from actual sales and price changes observed in the market, conjoint studies of customer intentions, consumer surveys about reservation prices or percent good value, or test-market results. In deriving elasticity, price–quantity functions can be sketched on paper, estimated from regressions in the form of linear or constant elasticity equations, or estimated through more complex expressions that include other variables in the marketing mix, such as advertising or product quality.

To confirm the validity and usefulness of these procedures, marketers must thoroughly understand the implications of the resulting elasticity estimate for customer behavior. Through this understanding, marketers can determine whether their estimate makes sense or requires further validation. That done, the next step is to use it to decide on pricing.

8.4   Optimal prices and linear and constant demand functions

The optimal price is the most profitable price for any product. In a linear demand function, the optimal price is halfway between the maximum reservation price and the variable cost of the product.

$$\text{Optimal Price for a Linear Demand Function (\$)} = \frac{\text{Maximum Reservation Price (\$) + Variable Cost (\$)}}{2}$$

Generally, the gross margin on a product at its optimal price is the negative inverse of its price elasticity.

$$\text{Gross Margin at Optimal Price (\%)} = \frac{-1}{\text{Elasticity (l)}}$$

Although it can be difficult to apply, this relationship offers a powerful insight: In a constant elasticity demand function, optimal margin follows directly from elasticity. This greatly simplifies the determination of the optimal price for a product of known variable cost.

Purpose: to determine the price that yields the greatest possible contribution.

Although *optimal price* can be defined in a number of ways, a good starting point is the price that generates the greatest contribution by a product after deducting its variable cost—that is, the most profitable price for the product.

If managers set price too low, they forgo revenue from customers who would willingly have paid more. In addition, a low price can lead customers to value a product less than they otherwise might. That is, it causes them to lower their reservation prices.

By contrast, if managers set price too high, they risk losing contributions from people who could have been served profitably.

Construction

For linear demand, the optimal price is the midpoint between the maximum reservation price and the variable cost of the product.

In linear demand functions, the price that maximizes total contribution for a product is always precisely halfway between the maximum reservation price (MRP) and the variable cost to produce that product. Mathematically, if P* represents the optimal price of a product, MRP is the X-intercept of its linear demand function, and VC is its variable cost per unit:

$$P^* = (MRP + VC)/2$$

Example Jaime's business sells goods that cost $1 to produce. Demand is linear. If his goods are priced at $5, Jaime believes he won't sell anything. For every dollar decrease in price, Jaime believes he will sell one additional unit.

Given that the variable cost is $1, the maximum reservation price is $5, and the demand function is linear, Jaime can anticipate that he'll achieve maximum contribution at a price midway point between VC and MRP. That is, the optimal price is ($5 + $1)/2 = $3 (see Figure 8.6).[4]

In a linear demand function, managers don't need to know the quantity of a product demanded in order to determine its optimal price. For those who seek to examine Jaime's contribution figures, Table 8.3 provides the details.

Figure 8.6 Optimal price midway between variable cost and MRP

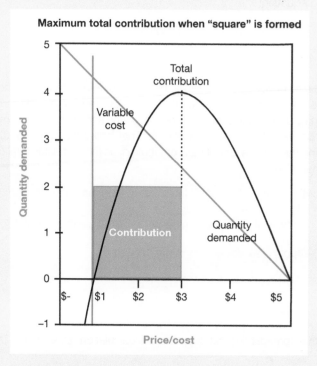

Table 8.3 Optimal price = ½ (MRP + variable cost)

Price	Quantity demanded	Variable cost per unit	Contribution per unit	Total contribution
$0	5	$1	−$1	−$5
$1	4	$1	$0	$0
$2	3	$1	$1	$3
$3	**2**	**$1**	**$2**	**$4**
$4	1	$1	$3	$3
$5	0	$1	$4	$0

The previous optimal price formula does not reveal the quantity sold at a given price or the resulting contribution. To determine optimal contribution, managers can use the following equation:

$$\text{Contribution*} = (\text{MWB/MRP}) * (P^* - VC)^2$$

Example Jaime develops a new, similar product. Its demand follows a linear function in which the maximum willing to buy (MWB) is 200 and the maximum reservation price (MRP) is $10. Variable cost is $1 per unit. Jaime knows that his optimal price will be midway between MRP and variable cost. That is, it will be ($1 + $10)/2 = $5.50 per unit. Using the formula for optimal contribution, Jaime calculates total contribution at the optimal price:

Contribution at Optimal Price for a Linear Demand Function ($)

$$= [\text{MWB (\#)/MRP (\$)}] * [\text{Price (\$)} - \text{Variable Costs (\$)}]\wedge 2$$

$$= (200/10) * (\$5.50 - \$1) \wedge 2$$

$$= 20 * \$4.5 \wedge 2$$

$$= \$405$$

Jaime builds a spreadsheet that supports this calculation, as shown in Table 8.4.

Table 8.4 Contribution maximized at the optimal price

Price	Variable costs	Quantity demanded	Contribution per unit	Total contribution
$6	$1	80	$5.00	$400
$5.50	$1	90	$4.50	$405
$5	$1	100	$4.00	$400
$4	$1	120	$3.00	$360
$3	$1	140	$2.00	$280
$2	$1	160	$1.00	$160
$1	$1	180	$0.00	$0

This relationship holds across all linear demand functions, regardless of slope. For such functions, it is therefore possible to calculate the optimal price for a product on the basis of only two inputs: variable cost per unit and maximum reservation price.

Example Brands A, B, and C each have a variable cost of $2 per unit and follow linear demand functions, as shown in Table 8.5.

Table 8.5 The optimal price formula applies to all linear demand functions

Price	Demand Brand A	Demand Brand B	Demand Brand C
$2	12	20	16
$3	10	18	15
$4	8	16	14
$5	6	14	13
$6	4	12	12
$7	2	10	11
$8	0	8	10
$9	0	6	9
$10	0	4	8
$11	0	2	7
$12	0	0	6

On the basis of these inputs, we can determine the maximum reservation price—that is, the lowest price at which demand is zero. For Brand C, for example, we know that demand follows a linear function in which quantity declines by one unit for each dollar increase in price. If six units are demanded at $12, then $18 will be the lowest price at which no one will buy a single unit. This is the maximum reservation price. We can make similar determinations for Brands A and B (see Table 8.6).

Table 8.6 In linear demand functions, the determination of optimal price requires only two inputs

	Brand A	Brand B	Brand C
Maximum Reservation Price	$8	$12	$18
Variable Costs	$2	$2	$2
Optimal Price	$5	$7	$10

To verify that the optimal prices so determined will generate the maximum attainable contribution, see Table 8.7.

Table 8.7 Verifying the optimal prices for linear demand functions

Price	Variable costs	Unit contri- bution = P – VC	Demand Brand A (Given)	Total contri- bution Brand A	Demand Brand B (Given)	Total contri- bution Brand B	Demand Brand C (Given)	Total contri- bution Brand C
P	VC	UC	Q	Q*UC	Q	Q*UC	Q	Q*UC
$2	$2	$0	12	$0	20	$0	16	$0
$3	$2	$1	10	$10	18	$18	15	$15
$4	$2	$2	8	$16	16	$32	14	$28
$5	$2	$3	**6**	**$18**	14	$42	13	$39
$6	$2	$4	4	$16	12	$48	12	$48
$7	$2	$5	2	$10	**10**	**$50**	11	$55
$8	$2	$6	0	$0	8	$48	10	$60
$9	$2	$7	0	$0	6	$42	9	$63
$10	$2	$8	0	$0	4	$32	**8**	**$64**
$11	$2	$9	0	$0	2	$18	7	$63
$12	$2	$10	0	$0	0	$0	6	$60

Because slope doesn't influence optimal price, all demand functions with the same maximum reservation price and variable cost yield the same optimal price.

Example A manufacturer of chair cushions operates in three different markets—urban, suburban, and rural—that vary greatly in size. Demand is far higher in the city than in the suburbs or in the country. Variable cost, however, is the same in all markets, at $4 per unit. The maximum reservation price, at $20 per unit, is also the same in all markets. Regardless of market size, the optimal price is therefore $12 per unit in all three markets (see Figure 8.7 and Table 8.8).

The optimal price of $12 is verified with the calculations in Table 8.9.

Figure 8.7 Linear demand functions with the same MWP and variable cost

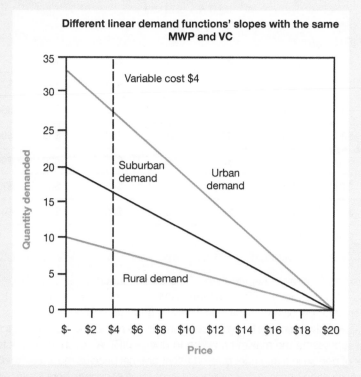

Different linear demand functions' slopes with the same MWP and VC

Table 8.8 The slope doesn't influence the optimal price

Maximum Willingness to Pay	$20
Variable Cost	$4
Optimal Price	$12

Table 8.9 Linear demand functions with different slopes

Price	Contri-bution per unit	Suburban demand	Rural demand	Urban demand	Suburban contri-bution	Rural contri-bution	Urban contri-bution
$0	–$4	$20	$10	$30	–$80	–$40	–$120
$2	–$2	$18	$9	$27	–$36	–$18	–$54
$4	$0	$16	$8	$24	$0	$0	$0

Price	Contribution per unit	Suburban demand	Rural demand	Urban demand	Suburban contribution	Rural contribution	Urban contribution
$6	$2	$14	$7	$21	$28	$14	$42
$8	$4	$12	$6	$18	$48	$24	$72
$10	$6	$10	$5	$15	$60	$30	$90
$12	**$8**	**$8**	**$4**	**$12**	**$64**	**$32**	**$96**
$14	$10	$6	$3	$9	$60	$30	$90
$16	$12	$4	$2	$6	$48	$24	$72
$18	$14	$2	$1	$3	$28	$14	$42
$20	$16	—	—	—	—	—	—

In this example, it might help to think of the urban, suburban, and rural markets as groups of people with identical, uniform distributions of reservation prices. In each, the reservation prices are uniform between $0 and the maximum willingness to pay (MWP). The only difference between segments is the number of people in each. That number represents the maximum willing to buy (MWB). As might be expected, the *number* of people in a segment doesn't affect optimal price as much as the *distribution* of reservation prices in that segment. As all three segments here show the same distribution of reservation prices, they all carry the same optimal price.

Another useful exercise is to consider what would happen if the manufacturer in this example were able to increase everyone's reservation price by $1. This would raise the optimal price by half that amount, or $0.50. Likewise, the optimal price would rise by half the amount of any increase in variable cost.

Optimal price in general

When demand is linear, we have an easy-to-use formula for optimal price. Regardless of the shape of the demand function, there is a simple relationship between gross margin and elasticity at the optimal price.

> **Optimal price relative to gross margin:** The price at which a product's gross margin is equal to the negative of the reciprocal of its elasticity of demand.[5]

$$\text{Gross Margin at Optimal Price (\%)} = \frac{-1}{\text{Elasticity at Optimal Price}}$$

A relationship such as this, which holds at the optimal price, is called an *optimality condition*. If elasticity is constant, then we can easily use this optimality condition to determine the optimal price. We simply find the negative of the reciprocal of the constant elasticity. The result will be the optimal gross margin. If variable costs are known and constant, then we need only determine the price that corresponds to the calculated optimal margin.

Example The manager of a stall selling replica sporting goods knows that the demand for jerseys has a constant price elasticity of −4. To price optimally, she sets her gross margin equal to the negative of the reciprocal of the elasticity of demand. (Some economists refer to the price–cost margin as the Lerner Index.)

$$\text{Gross Margin at Optimal Price} = \frac{-1}{-4}$$

$$= 25\%$$

If the variable cost of each jersey is $5, the optimal price will be $5/(1 − 0.25) = $6.67.

The optimal margins for several price elasticities are listed in Table 8.10.

Table 8.10 Optimal margins for sample elasticities

Price elasticity	Gross margin
−1.5	67%
−2	50%
−3	33%
−4	25%

Thus, if a firm's gross margin is 50%, its price will be optimal only if its elasticity at that price is −2. By contrast, if the firm's elasticity is −3 at its current price, then its pricing will be optimal only if it yields a gross margin of 33%.

This relationship between gross margin and price elasticity at the optimal price is one of the principal reasons that marketers take such a keen interest in the price elasticity of demand. Price elasticities can be difficult to measure, but margins generally are not. Marketers might now ask whether their current margins are consistent with estimates of price elasticity. In the next section, we will explore this issue in greater detail.

For now, if elasticity changes with price, marketers can use this optimality condition to solve for the optimal price. This condition applies to linear demand functions as well. Because the optimal price formula for linear demand is relatively simple, however, marketers rarely use the general optimality condition in this instance.

Data sources, complications, and cautions

The shortcuts for determining optimal prices from linear and constant elasticity demand functions rest on an assumption that variable costs hold constant over the range of volumes considered. If this assumption is not valid, marketers will likely find that a spreadsheet model offers the easiest way to determine optimal price.

We have explored these relationships in detail because they offer useful perspectives on the relationship between margins and the price elasticity of demand. In day-to-day management, margins constitute a starting point for many analyses, including those of price. One example of this dynamic would be cost-plus pricing.

Cost-plus pricing has received bad press in the marketing literature. It is portrayed not only as internally oriented but as naive, in that it may sacrifice profits. However, cost-plus pricing can be viewed as an attempt to maintain margins. If managers select the correct margin—one that relates to the price elasticity of demand—then pricing to maintain it may in fact be optimal if demand has constant elasticity. Thus, cost-plus pricing can be more customer oriented than is widely perceived.

Related metrics and concepts

Price tailoring (A.K.A. Price discrimination)

Marketers have invented a variety of price discrimination tools, including coupons, rebates, and discounts. All these tools are designed to exploit variations in price sensitivity among customers. Whenever customers have different sensitivities to price, or different costs to serve, an astute marketer can find an opportunity to claim incremental value through price tailoring.

Example The demand for a particular brand of sunglasses is composed of two segments: style-focused consumers who are less sensitive to price (more inelastic) and value-focused consumers who are more sensitive to price (more elastic) (see Figure 8.8). The style-focused group has a maximum reservation price of $30 and a maximum willing to buy of 10 units. The value-focused group has a maximum reservation price of $10 and a maximum willing to buy of 40 units.

Figure 8.8 Two segments form demand

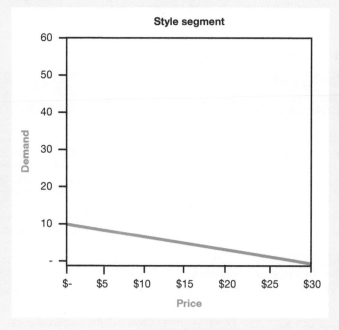

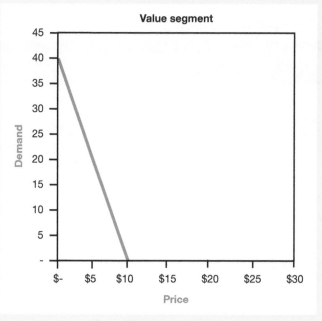

Alternative A: One price for both segments

Suppose the sunglasses manufacturer plans to offer one price to both segments. Table 8.11 shows the contributions of several candidate prices. The optimal single price (to the nearest cent) is $6.77, generating a total contribution of $98.56.

Table 8.11 Two segments: one price for both segments

Single price	Value quantity demanded	Style quantity demanded	Total demand	Total contribution
$5	20	8.33	28.33	$85.00
$6	16	8.00	24.00	$96.00
$6.77	**12.92**	**7.74**	**20.66**	**$98.56**
$7	12	7.67	19.67	$98.33
$8	8	7.33	15.33	$92.00

Alternative B: Price per segment

If the manufacturer can find a way to charge each segment its own optimal price, it will increase total contribution. In Table 8.12, we show the optimal prices, quantities, and contributions attainable if each segment pays a distinct optimal price.

Table 8.12 Two segments: price tailoring

	MRP	Variable costs	Optimal price	Quantity	Revenue	Contribution
Style	$30	$2	$16	4.67	$74.67	$65.33
Value	$10	$2	$6	16	$96.00	$64.00
Total				20.67	$170.67	**$129.33**

These optimal prices were calculated as the midpoints between maximum reservation price (MRP) and variable cost (VC). Optimal contributions were calculated with the formula

$$\text{Contribution}^* = (MWB/MRP) * (P^* - VC)^2$$

In the style-focused segment, for example, this yields

$$\text{Contribution}^* = (10/30) * (\$16 - \$2)^2$$

$$= 1/3 * 14^2 = \$65.33$$

Thus, through price tailoring, the sunglasses manufacturer can increase total contribution from $98.56 to $129.33 while holding quantity constant.

Where variable costs differ between segments, as in an airline's costs of service in business class versus economy class, the fundamental calculations are the same. To determine optimal prices, marketers need only change the variable cost per unit in each segment to correspond to actual costs.

Caution: regulation

In most industrial economies, governments have passed regulations concerning price discrimination. In the United States, the most important of these is the Robinson–Patman Act. According to Supreme Court interpretations of this statute (as of late 2019), Robinson–Patman forbids price discrimination *to the extent that it threatens to injure competition*.[6] Price discrimination to consumers is generally considered legal, except when implemented on the basis of race, religion, nationality, or gender. The act contemplates two main types of injury:

- **Primary line competitive injury:** Price discrimination might be used as a predatory tactic. That is, a firm might set prices below cost for certain customers in order to harm competition at the supplier level. Antitrust authorities apply this standard to predatory pricing claims under the Sherman Act and the Federal Trade Commission Act in order to evaluate allegations of price discrimination.

- **Secondary line competitive injury:** A seller that charges different prices to competing buyers of the same commodity or that discriminates in providing "allowances"—such as compensation for advertising or other services—may be violating the Robinson–Patman Act. Such discrimination can impair competition by awarding favored customers an edge that has nothing to do with superior efficiency.

In the United States, price discrimination is often lawful, particularly if it reflects different costs of dealing with diverse buyers or if it results from a seller's attempts to meet a competitor's prices or services.[7] The situation isn't always perfectly clear as relevant laws can differ between states, and in some states the courts have yet to rule on pertinent cases. Clearly, this is not intended to be a legal opinion, however. Legal advice should be sought for a company's individual circumstances.

8.5   Own, cross, and residual price elasticity

> The concept of residual price elasticity introduces competitive dynamics into the pricing process. It incorporates competitor reactions and cross elasticity. This, in turn, helps explain why prices in daily life are rarely set at the optimal level suggested by a simpler view of elasticity. Marketers consciously or unconsciously factor competitive dynamics into their pricing decisions.

▶

> Residual Price Elasticity (I) = Own Price Elasticity (I) + Competitor Reaction Elasticity (I) $*$ Cross Elasticity (I)
>
> **The greater the competitive reaction anticipated, the more residual price elasticity differs from a company's own price elasticity.**

Purpose: to account for both customers' price elasticity and potential competitive reactions when planning price changes.

Often, in daily life, price elasticity doesn't quite correspond to the relationships discussed in the prior section. Managers may find, for example, that their estimates of this key metric are not equal to the negative of the reciprocal of their margins. Does this mean they're setting prices that are not optimal? Perhaps.

It is more likely, however, that they're including competitive factors in their pricing decisions. Rather than use elasticity as estimated from current market conditions, marketers may estimate—or intuit—what elasticity *will be* after competitors respond to a proposed change in price. This introduces a new concept, *residual price elasticity*, which is customers' elasticity of demand in response to a change in price *after* accounting for any increase or decrease in competitors' prices that may be triggered by the initial change.

Residual price elasticity is a combination of three factors:

- **Own price elasticity:** The change in units sold due to the reaction of a firm's *customers* to its changes in price.

- **Competitor reaction elasticity:** The reaction of *competitors* to a firm's price changes.

- **Cross elasticity:** The reaction of a firm's customers to price changes by its competitors.

These factors and their interactions are illustrated in Figure 8.9.

> Own price elasticity: **How customers in the market react to price changes.**
>
> Competitive reaction elasticity: **How competitors respond to a company's price changes.**
>
> Cross elasticity: **How customers respond to the price changes of competitors.**

Figure 8.9 Residual price elasticity

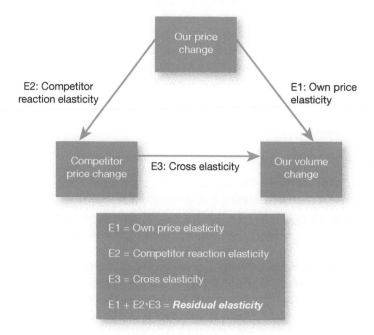

The distinction between own and residual price elasticity is not made clear in the literature. Some measures of price elasticity, for example, incorporate past competitive reactions and thus are more indicative of residual price elasticity. Others principally reflect own price elasticity and require further analysis to determine where sales and income will ultimately settle. The following sequence of actions and reactions is illustrative:

1 A firm changes price and observes the resulting change in sales. As an alternative, it may track another measure correlated with sales, such as share of choice or preference.

2 Competitors observe the firm's change in price and its increase in sales and/ or their own decrease in sales.

3 Competitors decide whether and by how much to change their own prices. The market impact of these changes depends on (1) the direction and degree of the changes and (2) the degree of cross elasticity (that is, the sensitivity of the initial firm's sales quantity to changes in competitors' prices). Thus, after tracking the response to its own price change, the initial firm may observe a further shift in sales as competitors' price changes take effect in the market.

Due to this dynamic, if a firm measures price elasticity only through customer response to its initial actions, it will miss an important potential factor: competitive reactions and their effects on sales. Only monopolists can make pricing decisions without regard to competitive response. Other firms may neglect or decline to consider competitive reactions, dismissing such analyses as speculation. But this generates a risk of shortsightedness and can lead to dangerous surprises. Still other firms may embrace game theory and seek a Nash equilibrium to anticipate where prices will ultimately settle. (In this context, the Nash equilibrium would be the point at which none of the competitors in a market has a profit-related incentive to change prices.)

Although a detailed exploration of competitive dynamics is beyond the scope of this book, we offer a simple framework for residual price elasticity next.

Construction

To calculate residual price elasticity, three inputs are needed:

- **Own price elasticity:** The change in a firm's unit sales, resulting from its initial price change, assuming that competitors' prices remain unchanged.

- **Competitor reaction elasticity:** The extent and direction of the price changes that are likely to be made by competitors in response to a firm's initial price change. If competitor reaction elasticity is 0.5, for example, then as a firm reduces its prices by a small percentage, competitors can be expected to reduce their own prices by half that percentage. If competitor reaction elasticity is −0.5, then as a firm reduces its prices by a small percentage, competitors will *increase* their prices by half that percentage. This is a less common scenario, but it is possible.

- **Cross elasticity with regard to competitor price changes:** The percentage and direction of the change in the initial firm's sales that will result from a small percentage change in competitors' prices. If cross elasticity is 0.25, then a small percentage increase in competitors' prices will result in an increase of one-fourth that percentage in the initial firm's sales. Note that the sign of cross elasticity is generally the reverse of the sign of own price elasticity. When competitors' prices rise, a firm's sales usually increase and vice versa.

$$\text{Residual Price Elasticity (I)} = \text{Own Price Elasticity (I)} + \text{Competitor Reaction Elasticity (I)} * \text{Cross Elasticity (I)}$$

The percentage change in a firm's sales can be approximated by multiplying its own price change by its residual price elasticity:

$$\text{Change in Sales from Residual Elasticity (\%)} = \text{Own Price Change (\%)} * \text{Residual Price Elasticity (I)}$$

Forecasts of any change in sales to be generated by a price change thus should take into account the subsequent competitive price reactions that can be reasonably expected, as well as the second-order effects of those reactions on the sales of the firm making the initial change. The net effect of adjusting for such reactions might be to amplify, diminish, or even reverse the direction of the change in sales that was expected from the initial price change.

Example A company decides to reduce price by 10% (price change $= -10\%$). It has estimated its own price elasticity to be -2. Ignoring competitive response, the company would expect a 10% price reduction to yield an approximately 20% increase in sales ($-2 * -10\%$). (Note: As observed in our earlier discussion of elasticity, projections based on point elasticity are accurate only for linear demand functions. Because this example does not specify the shape of the demand function, the projected 20% increase in sales is an approximation.)

The company estimates competitor reaction elasticity to be 1. That is, in response to the firm's action, competitors are expected to shift pricing in the same direction and by an equal percentage.

$$\text{Residual Elasticity} = \text{Own Price Elasticity} + \text{Competitor Reaction Elasticity}$$
$$* \text{ Cross Elasticity}$$
$$= -2 + 1 * 0.7$$
$$= -2 + 0.7$$
$$= -1.3$$

$$\text{Sales Increase} \approx \text{Change in Price} * \text{Residual Elasticity}$$
$$= -10\% * -1.3$$
$$= 13\% \text{ Increase in Sales}$$

The company estimates cross elasticity to be 0.7. That is, a small percentage change in competitors' prices will result in a change in the firm's own sales of 0.7%. On this basis competitor reactions and cross elasticity are expected to reduce the firm's initially projected sales increase from 20% to 13%.

Data sources, complications, and cautions

Accounting for potential competitive reactions is important, but there may be simpler and more reliable methods of managing price strategy in a contested market. Game theory and price leadership principles offer some guidance.

It is important for managers to distinguish between price elasticity measures that are inherently unable to account for competitive reactions and those that may already incorporate some competitive dynamics. For example, in "laboratory" investigations of price sensitivity—such as surveys, simulated test markets, and conjoint analyses—consumers may be presented with hypothetical pricing scenarios. These can measure both own price elasticity and the cross elasticities that result from specific combinations of prices. But an effective test is difficult to achieve.

Econometric analysis of historical data—evaluation of the sales and prices of firms in a market over longer periods of time (that is, annual or quarterly data)—may be better able to incorporate competitive changes and cross elasticities. To the extent that a firm has changed price somewhat randomly in the past, and to the extent that competitors have reacted, the estimates of elasticity that are generated by such analyses will measure residual elasticity. Still, the challenges and complexities involved in measuring price elasticity from historical data are daunting.

By contrast, short-term test market experiments are unlikely to yield good estimates of residual price elasticity. Over short periods, competitors might not learn of price changes or have time to react. Consequently, elasticity estimates based on test markets are much closer to own price elasticity.

Less obvious, perhaps, are econometric analyses based on transactional data, such as scanner sales and short-term price promotions. In these studies, prices decline for a short time, rise again for a longer period, decline briefly, rise again, and so forth. Even if competitors conduct their own price promotions during the study period, estimates of price elasticity derived in this way are likely to be affected by two factors. First, competitors' reactions likely will not be factored into an elasticity estimate because the competitors won't have had time to react to the initial firm's pricing moves. That is, their actions will have been largely motivated by their own plans. Second, to the extent that consumers stock up during price deals, any estimates of price elasticity will be higher than would be observed over the course of long-term price changes.

Prisoner's dilemma pricing

Prisoner's dilemma pricing describes a situation in which the pursuit of self-interest by all parties leads to suboptimal outcomes for all. This phenomenon can lead to stability at prices above the expected optimal price. In many ways, these higher-than-optimal prices have the appearance of cartel pricing. But they can be achieved without explicit collusion, provided that all parties understand the dynamics, as well as their competitors' motivations and economics.

The prisoner's dilemma phenomenon derives its name from a story illustrating the concept. Two members of a criminal gang are arrested and imprisoned. Each prisoner is placed in solitary confinement, and the two have no means of speaking to each other. Because the police don't have enough evidence to convict the pair on the principal charge, they plan to sentence both to a year in prison on a lesser charge. First, however, they try to get one or both to confess. Simultaneously, they offer each prisoner a Faustian bargain. If the prisoner testifies against his partner, he will go free, and the partner will be sentenced to three years in prison on the main charge. But there's a catch: If *both* prisoners testify against each other, *both* will be sentenced to two years in jail.[8] On this basis, each prisoner reasons that he'll do best by testifying against his partner, regardless of what the partner does.

For a summary of the choices and outcomes in this dilemma, please see Figure 8.10, which is drawn in the first person from the perspective of one of the prisoners. First-person outcomes are listed in blue. Partner outcomes are italicized.

Figure 8.10 Prisoner's dilemma payoff grid

	I testify	I refuse to testify
My partner refuses to testify	3 years / I go free	1 year / 1 year
My partner testifies	2 years / 2 years	My partner goes free / 3 years

Continuing the first-person perspective, each prisoner reasons as follows: *If my partner testifies, I'll be sentenced to two years in prison if I testify as well or three years if I don't. On the other hand, if my partner refuses to testify, I'll go free if I testify, but I'll serve one year in prison if I don't. In either case, I do better if I testify. But this raises a dilemma. If I follow this logic and testify—and my partner does the same—we end up in the lower-left cell of the table, both serving two years in prison.*

Figure 8.11 uses arrows to track these preferences: a black arrow for the first-person narrator in this reasoning and a blue arrow for his partner.

Figure 8.11 Payoff matrix with arrows representing preferences for prisoners

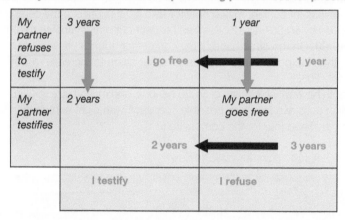

	I testify	I refuse
My partner refuses to testify	3 years / I go free	1 year / 1 year
My partner testifies	2 years / 2 years	My partner goes free / 3 years

The dilemma, of course, is that it seems perfectly logical to follow the arrows and testify. But when both prisoners do so, they both end up worse off than they would have if they'd both refused. That is, when both testify, both are sentenced to two years in prison. When they both refuse, they both shorten that term to a single year.

Admittedly, it takes a good deal of time to grasp the mechanics of the prisoner's dilemma—and far longer to appreciate its implications. But the story serves as a powerful metaphor, encapsulating a wide range of situations in which acting in one's own best interest leads to outcomes in which everyone is worse off.

In pricing, there are many situations in which a firm and its competitors face a prisoner's dilemma. Often, one firm perceives that it could increase profits by reducing prices, regardless of competitors' pricing policies. Simultaneously, its competitors perceive the same forces at work. That is, they too could earn more by cutting prices, regardless of the initial firm's actions. If *both* the initial firm and its competitors reduce prices, however—that is, if all parties follow their own unilateral best interests—they will, in many situations, all end up worse off. The industry challenge in these situations is to keep prices high despite the fact that each firm will benefit by lowering them.

Given a choice between high and low prices, a firm faces a prisoner's dilemma pricing situation when the following conditions apply:

- Its contribution is greater at the low price when selling against both high and low competitor prices.

- Competitors' contributions are greater at their low price when selling against both the high and low prices of the initial firm.

- For both the initial firm and its competitors, contribution is lower if all parties set their price low than it would have been if all parties had priced high.

Example As shown in Table 8.13, my firm faces one main competitor. Currently my price is $2.90, my competitor's price is $2.80, and I hold a 40% share of a market that totals 20 million units. If I reduce my price to $2.60, I expect my share will rise to 55%—unless, of course, my competitor also cuts its price. If my competitor also reduces price by $0.30—to $2.50—then I expect our market shares to remain constant at 40/60. On the other hand, if my competitor cuts its price but I hold steady at $2.90, then I expect my competitor's market share to increase to 80%, leaving me with only 20%.

If we both have variable costs of $1.20 per unit, and market size remains constant at 20 million units, we face four possible scenarios with eight contribution figures—four for my firm and four for the competition.

Table 8.13 Scenario planning payoff table

Pricing scenario	My price	My volume (m)	My sales ($m)	My variable costs ($m)	My contribution ($m)
My Firm High, Competition High	$2.90	8	$23.2	$9.6	$13.6
My Firm High, Competition Low	$2.90	4	$11.6	$4.8	$6.8

My Firm Low, Competition Low	$2.60	8	$20.8	$9.6	$11.2
My Firm Low, Competition High	$2.60	11	$28.6	$13.2	$15.4
My Firm High, Competition High	$2.80	12	$33.6	$14.4	$19.2
My Firm High, Competition Low	$2.50	16	$40.0	$19.2	$20.8
My Firm Low, Competition Low	$2.50	12	$30.0	$14.4	$15.6
My Firm Low, Competition High	$2.80	9	$25.2	$10.8	$14.4

Is this a prisoner's dilemma situation?

Figure 8.12 shows the four contribution possibilities for both my firm and my competitor.

Figure 8.12 Payoff matrix with expected values (values in the millions of dollars)

	My price = $2.60 Low	My price = $2.90 High
Their price = $2.80 High	$14.4 / $15.4	$19.2 / $13.6
Their price = $2.50 Low	$15.6 / $11.2	$20.8 / $6.8

Let's check to see whether the conditions for the prisoner's dilemma are met:

1 My contribution is higher at the low price for both high and low competitor prices ($15.4m > $13.6m, and $11.2m > $6.8m). No matter what my competitor does, I make more money at the low price.

2 My competitor's contribution is higher at the low price, regardless of my price ($15.6m > $14.4m, and $20.8m > $19.2m). The competitor, too, is better off at the low price, regardless of my price.

3 For both my firm and my competitor, however, contribution is lower if we both price low than it would be if we both price high ($15.6m < $19.2m, and $11.2m < $13.6m).

The conditions for the prisoner's dilemma are met (see Figure 8.13).

Figure 8.13 Payoff matrix with expected values and preference arrows (contribution values in the millions of dollars)

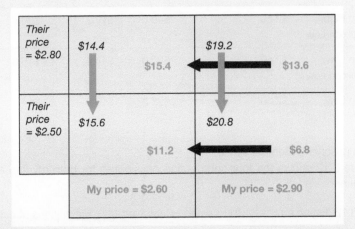

The implication for my firm is clear: Although it is tempting to lower my price, seeking increased share and a $15.4 million contribution, I must recognize that my competitor faces the same incentives. It, too, has an incentive to cut price, grab share, and increase its contribution. But if my competitor lowers its price, I'll probably lower mine. If I lower my price, my competitor will probably lower its price. If we both reduce our prices, I'll earn only $11.2m in contribution—a sharp decline from the $13.6m I make now.

To determine whether you face a prisoner's dilemma situation, project the dollar contributions for both your firm and your competition at four combinations of high and low prices. Projections may require assumptions about your competitors' economics. These, in turn, will require care. If competitors' economics differ greatly from your projections, they may not face the decisions or motivations ascribed to them in your model. In addition, there are a number of reasons the logic of the prisoner's dilemma won't always hold, even if all assumptions are correct.

Below are a selection of reasons why the prisoner's dilemma won't hold:

- **Other criteria in decision making besides contribution:** In our example, we used contribution as the objective for both firms. Market share, however, may have importance to one or more firms, above and beyond its immediate, direct effect on contribution. Whatever a firm's objective may be, if it is quantifiable, we can place it in our table to better understand the competitive situation.

- **Legal issues:** Certain activities designed to discourage competition and maintain high prices are illegal. Our purpose here is to help managers understand the economic trade-offs involved in competitive pricing. Managers should be aware of their legal environment and behave accordingly.

- **Multiple competitors:** Pricing becomes more complicated when there are multiple competitors. The test for a multi-party prisoner's dilemma is the logical extension of the test described earlier. A major difference, however, arises in practice. As a general principle, the greater the number of independent competitors, the more difficult it is to keep prices high.

- **Single versus repeated play:** In our original story, two prisoners decide whether to testify in a single investigation. In game theory terms, they play the game a single time. Experiments have shown that in a single play of a prisoner's dilemma, the likely outcome is that both prisoners will testify. If the game is played repeatedly, however, it is more likely that both prisoners will refuse to testify. Because pricing decisions are made repeatedly, this evidence suggests that high prices are a more likely outcome. Most businesses eventually learn to live with their competition.

- **More than two possible prices:** We have examined a situation in which each player considers two prices. In reality, there may be a wide range of prices under consideration. In such situations, we might extend our analysis to more boxes. Once again, we might add arrows to track preferences. Using these more complex views, one sometimes finds areas within the table in which a prisoner's dilemma applies (usually at the higher prices), and others where it does not (usually at the lower prices). One might also find that the arrows lead to a particular cell in the middle of the table called the equilibrium. A prisoner's dilemma situation generally applies for prices higher than the set of equilibrium prices.

Applying the lessons of the prisoner's dilemma, we see that optimal price calculations based on own price elasticity may lead us to act in our own unilateral best interest. By contrast, when we factor residual price elasticity into our calculations, competitive response becomes a key element of our pricing strategy. As the prisoner's dilemma shows, over the long term, a firm is not always best served by acting in its apparent unilateral best interest.

Further reading

Dolan, Robert J., and Hermann Simon. (1996). *Power Pricing: How Managing Price Transforms the Bottom Line*, Free Press.
Roegner, E. V., M. V. Marn, and C. C. Zawada. (2005). "Pricing," *Marketing Management,* 14(1), 23–28.

Promotion

9

Introduction

Price promotions can be divided into two broad categories:

- Temporary price reductions
- Permanent features of pricing systems[1]

With both of these types of price promotions, firms seek to change the behavior of consumers and trade customers in ways that increase sales and profits over time, although a promotion's short-term effect on profits will often be negative. There are multiple routes to sales and profit growth, and there are many potential reasons for offering price promotions. Such programs might be aimed at affecting the behavior of end users (consumers), trade customers (distributors or retailers), competitors, or even a firm's own salespeople. Although the goal of a promotion is often to increase sales, these programs can also affect costs. Examples of specific, short-term promotional objectives include the following:

- To stimulate trial and acquire new customers
- To appeal to new or different segments that are more price sensitive than a firm's traditional customers
- To increase the purchase rates of existing customers or to increase loyalty
- To gain new trade accounts (that is, distribution)

- To introduce new SKUs to the trade
- To increase shelf space
- To blunt competitors' efforts by encouraging the firm's customers to "load up" on inventory
- To smooth production in seasonal categories by inducing customers to order earlier (or later) than they ordinarily would

The metrics for many of these interim objectives, including trial rate and percentage of new product sales, are covered elsewhere. In this chapter, we focus on metrics for monitoring the acceptance of price promotions and their effects on sales and profits.

The most powerful framework for evaluating temporary price promotions is to partition sales into two categories: baseline and incremental. Baseline sales are those that a firm would have expected to achieve if no promotion had been run. Incremental sales represent the "lift" in sales resulting from a price promotion. By separating baseline sales from incremental lift, managers can evaluate whether the sales increase generated by a temporary price reduction compensates for the concomitant decrease in prices and margins. Similar techniques are used in determining the profitability of coupons and rebates.

Although the short-term effect of a price promotion is almost invariably measured by its increase in sales, over longer periods, management becomes concerned about the percentage of sales on deal and the percentage of time during which a product is on deal. In some industries, list price has become such a fiction that it is used only as a benchmark for discussing discounts.

Average deal depth and the price waterfall help capture the depth of price cuts and explain how one arrives at a product's net price (pocket price) after accounting for all discounts. There are often major differences between the discounts offered to trade customers and the extent to which those discounts are accepted. There may also be a difference between the discounts received by the trade and those that the trade shares with its customers. The pass-through percentage and price waterfall are analytic structures designed to capture those dynamics and thus to measure the impact of a firm's promotions.

	Metric	Construction	Considerations	Purpose
9.1	Baseline Sales	Intercept in regression of sales as function of marketing variables. Baseline sales equal total sales less incremental sales generated by a marketing program or programs.	Marketing activities also contribute to baseline.	Determine the extent to which current sales are independent of specific marketing efforts.

	Metric	Construction	Considerations	Purpose
9.1	Incremental Sales, or Promotional Lift	Total sales less baseline sales. Regression coefficient to marketing variables cited above.	Need to consider competitive actions.	Determine short-term effects of marketing effort.
9.2	Redemption Rates	Coupons redeemed divided by coupons distributed.	Will differ significantly by mode of coupon distribution.	Get a rough measure of coupon "lift" after adjusting for sales that would have been made without coupons.
9.2	Costs for Coupons and Rebates	Coupon face amount plus redemption charges multiplied by the number of coupons redeemed.	Does not consider margins that would have been generated by those willing to buy product without coupon.	Budget for coupon expense.
9.2	Percentage Sales with Coupon	Sales via coupon divided by total sales.	Doesn't factor in magnitude of discount offered by specific coupons.	Measure brand dependence on promotional efforts.
9.3	Percent Sales on Deal	Sales with temporary discounts as a percentage of total sales.	Does not make distinction for depth of discounts offered.	Measure brand dependence on promotional efforts.
9.3	Pass-Through	Promotional discounts provided by the trade to consumers divided by discounts provided to the trade by the manufacturer.	Can reflect power in the channel or deliberate management or segmentation.	Measure the extent to which a manufacturer's promotions generate promotional activity further along the distribution channel.

Metric	Construction	Considerations	Purpose
9.4 Price Waterfall	Actual average price per unit divided by list price per unit. Can also be calculated by working backward from list price, taking account of potential discounts, weighted by the frequency with which each is exercised.	Some discounts may be offered at an absolute level, not on a per-item basis.	Indicate the price actually paid for a product and the sequence of channel factors affecting that price.

9.1 Baseline sales, incremental sales, and promotional lift

Estimates of baseline sales establish a benchmark for evaluating the incremental sales generated by specific marketing activities. This baseline also helps isolate incremental sales from the effects of other influences, such as seasonality or competitive promotions. The following equations can be applied for defined periods of time and for the specific element of the marketing mix that is used to generate incremental sales.

$$\text{Total Sales (\$, \#)} = \text{Baseline Sales (\$, \#)} + \text{Incremental Sales from Marketing (\$, \#)}$$

$$\text{Incremental Sales from Marketing (\$, \#)} = \text{Incremental Sales from Advertising (\$, \#)} + \text{Incremental Sales from Trade Promotion (\$, \#)} + \text{Incremental Sales from Consumer Promotion (\$, \#)} + \text{Incremental Sales from Other (\$, \#)}$$

$$\text{Lift (from Promotion) (\%)} = \frac{\text{Incremental Sales (\$, \#)}}{\text{Baseline Sales (\$, \#)}}$$

$$\text{Cost of Incremental Sales (\$)} = \frac{\text{Marketing Spending (\$)}}{\text{Incremental Sales (\$, \#)}}$$

The justification of marketing spending almost always involves estimating the incremental effects of the program under evaluation. However, because some marketing costs are often assumed to be fixed (for example, marketing staff and sales force salaries), one rarely sees incremental sales attributed to these elements of the mix.

Purpose: to select a baseline of sales against which the incremental sales and profits generated by marketing activity can be assessed.

A common problem in marketing is estimating the sales "lift" attributable to a specific campaign or set of marketing activities. Evaluating lift entails making a comparison with baseline sales, the level of sales that would have been achieved without the program under evaluation. Ideally, experiments or control groups would be used to establish baselines. If it were quick, easy, and inexpensive to conduct such experiments, this approach would dominate. In lieu of using such control groups, marketers often use historical sales adjusted for expected growth, taking care to control for seasonal influences. Regression models that attempt to control for the influence of these other changes are often used to improve estimates of baseline sales. Ideally, both controllable and uncontrollable factors, such as competitive spending, should be included in baseline sales regression models. When regression is used, the intercept is often considered to be the baseline.

Construction

In theory, determining incremental sales is as simple as subtracting baseline sales from total sales. Challenges arise, however, in determining baseline sales.

Baseline sales: Expected sales results, excluding the marketing programs under evaluation.

When reviewing historical data, total sales are known. The analyst's task then is to separate these into baseline sales and incremental sales, which is typically done with regression analysis. The process can also involve test market results and other market research data.

Total Sales ($, #) = Baseline Sales ($, #) + Incremental Sales ($, #)

Analysts also commonly separate incremental sales into portions attributable to the various marketing activities used to generate them.

Incremental Sales ($, #) = Incremental Sales from Advertising ($, #)
+ Incremental Sales from Trade Promotion ($, #)
+ Incremental Sales from Consumer Promotion
($, #) + Incremental Sales from Other ($, #)

Baseline sales are generally estimated through analyses of historical data. Firms often develop sophisticated models for this purpose, including variables to adjust for market growth, competitive activity, and seasonality, for example. That done, a firm can use its model to make forward-looking projections of baseline sales and use those projections to estimate incremental sales.

Incremental sales can be calculated as total sales less baseline sales for any period of time (for example, a year, a quarter, or the term of a promotion). The lift achieved by a marketing program measures incremental sales as a percentage of baseline sales. The cost of incremental sales can be expressed as a cost per incremental sales dollar or a cost per incremental sales unit (for example, cost per incremental case).

$$\text{Incremental Sales (\$, \#)} = \text{Total Sales (\$, \#)} - \text{Baseline Sales (\$, \#)}$$

$$\text{Lift (\%)} = \frac{\text{Incremental Sales (\$, \#)}}{\text{Baseline Sales (\$, \#)}}$$

$$\text{Cost of Incremental Sales (\$)} = \frac{\text{Marketing Spending (\$)}}{\text{Incremental Sales (\$, \#)}}$$

Example A retailer expects to sell $24,000 worth of light bulbs in a typical month without advertising. In May, while running a newspaper ad campaign that cost $1,500, the store sells $30,000 worth of light bulbs. It engages in no other promotions or non-recurring events during the month. Its owner calculates incremental sales generated by the ad campaign as follows:

$$\text{Incremental Sales (\$)} = \text{Total Sales (\$)} - \text{Baseline Sales (\$)}$$

$$= \$30,000 - \$24,000 = \$6,000$$

The store owner estimates incremental sales to be $6,000. This represents a lift (%) of 25%, calculated as follows:

$$\text{Lift (\%)} = \frac{\text{Incremental Sales (\$)}}{\text{Baseline Sales (\$)}}$$

$$= \frac{\$6,000}{\$24,000} = 25\%$$

The cost of incremental sales is $0.25, calculated as follows:

$$\text{Cost of Incremental Sales (\$)} = \frac{\text{Marketing Spending (\$)}}{\text{Incremental Sales (\$)}}$$

$$= \frac{\$1,500}{\$6,000} = 0.25$$

Total sales can be analyzed or projected as a function of baseline sales and lift. When estimating combined marketing mix effects, one must be sure to determine whether lift is estimated through a multiplicative equation or through an additive equation. Additive equations combine marketing mix effects as follows:

Total Sales ($, #) = Baseline Sales + [Baseline Sales ($, #) * Lift (%) from Advertising] + [Baseline Sales ($, #) * Lift (%) from Trade Promotion] + [Baseline Sales ($, #) * Lift (%) from Consumer Promotion] + [Baseline Sales ($, #) * Lift (%) from Other]

This additive approach is consistent with the conception of total incremental sales as a sum of the incremental sales generated by various elements of the marketing mix. It is equivalent to a statement that

Total Sales ($, #) = Baseline Sales + Incremental Sales from Advertising + Incremental Sales from Trade Promotion + Incremental Sales from Consumer Promotion + Incremental Sales from Other

Multiplicative equations, by contrast, combine marketing mix effects by using a multiplication procedure, as follows:

Total Sales ($, #) = Baseline Sales ($, #) * (1 + Lift (%) from Advertising) * (1 + Lift (%) from Trade Promotion) * (1 + Lift (%) from Consumer Promotion) * (1 + Lift (%) from Other)

When using multiplicative equations, it makes little sense to talk about the incremental sales from a single mix element. In practice, however, one may encounter statements that attempt to do exactly that.

Example Company A collects data from past promotions and estimates the lift it achieves through different elements of the marketing mix. One researcher believes that an additive model would best capture these effects. A second researcher believes that a multiplicative model might better reveal the ways in which multiple elements of the mix combine to increase sales. The product manager for the item under study receives the two estimates shown in Table 9.1.

Table 9.1 Expected returns to marketing spending

Spending	Additive			Multiplicative		
	Adver-tising lift	Trade promo-tion lift	Consumer promotion lift	Adver-tising lift	Trade promo-tion lift	Consumer promotion lift
$0	0%	0%	0%	1	1	1
$100k	5.5%	10%	16.5%	1.05	1.1	1.15
$200k	12%	24%	36%	1.1	1.2	1.3

Fortunately, both models estimate baseline sales to be $900,000. The product manager wants to evaluate the following spending plan: advertising ($100,000), trade promotion ($0), and consumer promotion ($200,000). He projects sales using each method as follows:

Additive:

$$\text{Projected Sales (\$)} = \$900,000 + [\$900,000 * 5.5\%] + [\$900,000 * 0]$$
$$+ [\$900,000 * 36\%]$$
$$= \$900,000 + \$49,500 + \$0 + \$324,000$$
$$= \$1,273,500$$

Multiplicative:

$$\text{Projected Sales} = \text{Baseline} * \text{Advertising Lift} * \text{Trade Promotion Lift}$$
$$* \text{Consumer Promotion Lift}$$
$$= \$900,000 * 1.05 * 1 * 1.3$$
$$= \$1,228,500$$

Note: Because these models are constructed differently, they will inevitably yield different results at most levels. The multiplicative method accounts for a specific form of interactions between marketing variables. The additive method, in its current form, does not account for interactions.

When historic sales have been separated into baseline and incremental components, it is relatively simple to determine whether a given promotion was profitable *during the period under study*. Looking forward, the profitability[2] of a proposed marketing activity can be assessed by comparing projected levels of profitability with and without the program:

$$\text{Profitability of a Promotion (\$)} = \text{Profits Achieved with Promotion (\$)}$$
$$- \text{Estimated Profits Without Promotion}$$
$$\text{(that is, Baseline) (\$)}$$

Example Fred, the VP of Marketing, and Jeanne, the VP of Finance, receive estimates that sales will total 30,000 units after special displays have been erected. Because the proposed promotion involves a considerable investment ($100,000), the CEO asks for an estimate of the incremental profit associated with the displays. Because this program involves no change in price, contribution per unit during the promotion is expected to be the same as at other times: $12.00 per unit. Thus, total contribution during the promotion is expected to be 30,000 * $12 = $360,000. Subtracting the incremental fixed cost of specialized displays, profits for the period are projected to be $360,000 − $100,000 = $260,000.

Fred estimates that baseline sales total 15,000 units. On this basis, he calculates that contribution without the promotion would be $12 * 15,000 = $180,000. Thus, he projects that the special displays can be expected to generate incremental profit of $360,000 − $180,000 − $100,000 = $80,000.

Jeanne argues that she would expect sales of 25,000 units without the promotion, generating baseline contribution of $12 * 25,000 = $300,000. Consequently, if the promotion is implemented, she anticipates an incremental *decline* in profits from $300,000 to $260,000. In her view, the promotion's lift would not be sufficient to cover its incremental fixed costs. Under this promotion, Jeanne believes that the firm would be spending $100,000 to generate incremental contribution of only $60,000 (that is, 5,000 units * $12 contribution per unit).

The baseline sales estimate is a crucial factor here.

Example A luggage manufacturer faces a difficult decision regarding whether to launch a new promotion. The firm's data show a major increase in product sales in November and December, but its managers are unsure whether this is a permanent trend of higher sales or merely a blip—a successful period that can't be expected to continue (see Figure 9.1).

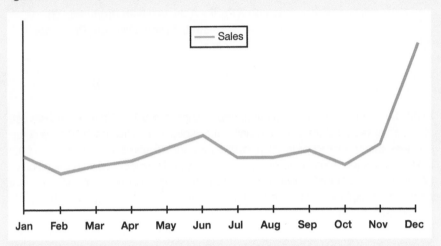

Figure 9.1 Monthly sales patterns

The firm's VP of Marketing strongly supports the proposed promotion. He argues that the increased volume can't be expected to continue and that the firm's historic baseline (26,028 units) should be used as the level of sales that can be anticipated without the promotion. In addition, the VP of Marketing argues that only the variable cost of each sale should be considered. "After all, the fixed costs will be with us whatever we do," he says. On this basis, the relevant cost per unit subject to analysis would be $25.76.

The CEO hires a consultant who has a very different opinion. In the consultant's view, the November–December sales increase was more than a blip. The market has grown, she says, and the strength of the firm's brand has grown with it. Consequently, a more appropriate estimate of baseline sales would be 48,960 units. The consultant also points out that in the long term, no costs are fixed. Therefore, for purposes of analysis, fixed costs should be allocated to the cost of the product because the product must ultimately generate a return after expenses such as factory rent are paid. On this basis, the full cost of each unit, $34.70, should be used as the cost of incremental sales (see Table 9.2).

Table 9.2 Baseline matters when considering profitability

	Consultant		VP of Marketing	
	Promotion	Baseline	Promotion	Baseline
Price	$41.60	$48.00	$41.60	$48.00
Cost	$34.70	$34.70	$25.76	$25.76
Margin	$6.90	$13.30	$15.84	$22.24

Sales	75,174	48,960	75,174	26,028
Profit	$518,701	$651,168	$1,190,756	$578,863
Profitability of Promotion	−$132,467		$611,893	

The VP of Marketing and the consultant make very different projections of the profit-ability of the promotion. Once again, the choice of the baseline matters. Also, we can see that establishing a shared understanding of costs and margins can be critical.

Data sources, complications, and cautions

Finding a baseline estimate of what a company can be expected to sell, "all things being equal," is a complex and inexact process. Essentially, the baseline is the level of sales that can be expected without significant marketing activities. When certain marketing activities, such as price promotions, have been employed for several peri-ods, it can be especially difficult to separate "incremental" and "baseline" sales.

In many companies, it is common to measure sales performance against historic data. In effect, this sets historic sales as the baseline level for analysis of the impact of marketing spending. For example, retailers can evaluate their performance on the basis of same store sales (to remove differences caused by the addition or removal of outlets). Further, they can compare each current period to the same period in the prior year in order to avoid seasonality biases and to ensure that they measure periods of special activity (such as sales events) against times of similar activity.

It is also common practice to adjust the profitability of promotions for longer-term effects. These effects can include a decline in sales levels in periods immediately fol-lowing a promotion, as well as higher or lower sales in related product categories that are associated with a promotion. Adjustments can be negative or positive. Additional long-term effects—such as obtaining trial by new consumers, gaining distribution with trade customers, and increased consumption rates—are discussed briefly in the chapter introduction.

Long-term effects of promotions

Over time, the effects of promotions may be to "ratchet" sales up or down (see Figures 9.2 and 9.3). Under one scenario, in response to one firm's promotions, competitors may also increase their promotional activity, and consumers and trade customers in the field may learn to wait for deals, increasing sales for no one (see the prisoner's dilemma in Section 8.5).

Figure 9.2 Downward spiral: promotional effectiveness

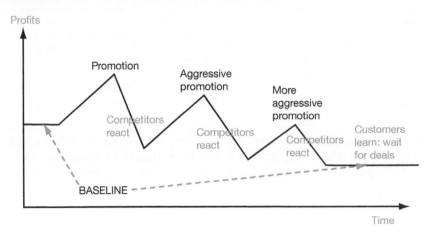

Under a different, more heartening scenario, promotions can generate trial for new products, build trade distribution, and encourage loyalty, thus raising the long-term level of baseline sales.

Figure 9.3 Successful promotion with long-term benefits

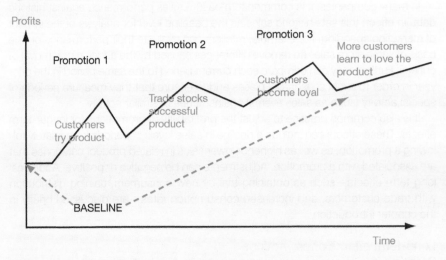

9.2 Redemption rates, costs for coupons and rebates, and percentage sales with coupon

> The redemption rate is the percentage of distributed coupons or rebates that are used (redeemed) by consumers.
>
> $$\text{Coupon Redemption Rate (\%)} = \frac{\text{Coupons Redeemed (\#)}}{\text{Coupons Distributed (\#)}}$$
>
> $$\text{Cost per Redemption (\$)} = \text{Coupon Face Amount (\$)} + \text{Redemption Charges (\$)}$$
>
> $$\text{Total Coupon Cost (\$)} = \text{Cost per Redemption (\$)} * \text{Coupons Redeemed (\#)} + \text{Coupon Printing and Distribution Cost (\$)}$$
>
> $$\text{Percentage Sales with Coupon (\%)} = \frac{\text{Sales with Coupon (\$)}}{\text{Sales (\$)}}$$
>
> The redemption rate is an important metric for marketers assessing the effectiveness of their coupon distribution strategy. It helps determine whether coupons are reaching the customers who are motivated to use them. Similar metrics apply to mail-in rebates.
>
> Cost per redemption measures variable costs per coupon redeemed. Coupon distribution costs are usually viewed as fixed costs.

Purpose: to track and evaluate coupon usage.

Some people hate coupons, some like them, and some say they hate coupons but really like them. Businesses often say they hate coupons but continue to use them. Coupons and rebates are used to introduce new products, to generate trial of existing products by new customers, and to "load" consumers' pantries and encourage long-term consumption.

Almost all of the interim objectives discussed in the introduction to this chapter can apply to coupons and rebates. Coupons can be used to offer lower prices to more price-sensitive consumers. Coupons also serve as a form of advertising, so they are dual-purpose marketing vehicles. Coupon clippers will see a brand name and pay closer attention to it—considering whether they desire the product—than would an average consumer exposed to an advertisement without a compelling offer. Finally, both rebates and coupons can serve as focus points for retailer promotions. To generate traffic, retailers can double or even triple coupon amounts—generally up to a declared limit. Retailers also often advertise prices "after rebates" in order to promote sales and perceptions of value.

Construction

$$\text{Coupon Redemption Rate (\%)} = \frac{\text{Coupons Redeemed (\#)}}{\text{Coupons Distributed (\#)}}$$

$$\text{Cost per Redemption (\$)} = \text{Coupon Face Amount (\$)} + \text{Redemption Charges (\$)}$$

> **Total coupon cost: A measure of distribution, printing,[3] and redemption costs to estimate the total cost of a coupon promotion.**

$$\text{Total Coupon Cost (\$)} = \text{Coupons Redeemed (\#)} * \text{Cost per Redemption (\$)}$$
$$+ \text{Coupon Printing and Distribution Cost (\$)}$$

$$\text{Total Cost per Redemption (\$)} = \frac{\text{Total Coupon Cost (\$)}}{\text{Coupons Redeemed (\#)}}$$

$$\text{Percentage Sales with Coupon (\%)} = \frac{\text{Sales with Coupon (\$, \#)}}{\text{Sales (\$, \#)}}$$

To determine the profitability of coupons and rebates, managers require approaches similar to those used in estimating baseline and incremental sales, as discussed in the previous section of this chapter. By themselves, redemption rates are not a good measure of success. Under certain circumstances, even low redemption rates can be profitable. Under other circumstances, by contrast, high redemption rates can be quite damaging.

Example Yvette is the manager of analysis for a small regional consumer packaged goods firm. Her product has a dominant share of the retail distribution in a narrow geographic area. Her firm decides to launch a coupon campaign, and Yvette is charged with reporting on the program's success. Her assistant looks at the figures and realizes that of the 100,000 coupons distributed in the local paper, 5,000 were used to buy product. The assistant is excited when he calculates that this represents a 5% redemption rate—a much higher figure than the company has ever previously seen.

Yvette, however, is more cautious in judging the promotion a success. She checks the sales of the relevant product and learns that they increased by only 100 units during the promotion period. Yvette concludes that the vast majority of coupon use was by customers who would have bought the product anyway. For most customers, the sole impact of the coupon was to reduce the price of the product below the level they would have willingly paid. Until she conducts a full profitability analysis, evaluating the profit generated by the 100 incremental sales and comparing this to coupon costs and the value lost on most coupon sales, Yvette can't be sure that the program made an overall loss. But she feels certain that she should curtail the celebrations.

Data sources, complications, and cautions

To calculate coupon redemption rates, managers must know the number of coupons placed in circulation (distributed) as well as the number redeemed. Companies generally engage distribution services or media companies to place coupons in circulation. Redemption numbers are usually derived from the invoices presented by coupon clearinghouses.

Related metrics and concepts

Mail-in rebates

A rebate, in effect, is a form of coupon that is popular for big-ticket items. Its usage dynamics are straightforward: Customers pay the full price for a product, enabling retailers to meet a specific price point. The customer then exercises the rebate and receives back a specified dollar amount.

By using rebates, marketers gain information about customers, which can be useful in remarketing and product control. Mail-in rebates also reduce the effective price of an item for customers who are sufficiently price-conscious to take advantage of them. Others pay full price. The "non-redemption rates" for rebates are sometimes called "breakage."

> **Breakage: The number of rebates not redeemed by customers. The breakage rate is the percentage of rebates not redeemed.**

Example A cell phone company sold 40,000 handsets in one month. On each purchase, the customer was offered a $30 rebate. Customers successfully claimed 30,000 rebates.

In volume terms, the rebate redemption rate can be calculated by dividing the number of rebates successfully claimed (30,000) by the number offered (40,000):

$$\text{Redemption Rate (in volume terms)} = \frac{30,000}{40,000} = 75\%$$

Managers often balk at the cost of distributing coupons. Because promotions rely on adequate distribution, however, it is inadvisable to create arbitrary cutoffs for distribution costs. The total cost of incremental sales generated would represent a better metric to evaluate coupon efficiency—and thus to determine the point at which diminishing returns make further coupon distribution unattractive.

In evaluating a coupon or rebate program, companies should also consider the overall level of benefit provided to consumers. Retailers commonly increase the value of coupons, offering customers a discount of double or even triple the coupons' face value. This enables retailers to identify price-sensitive customers and offer them additional savings. Of course, by multiplying the savings afforded consumers, the practice of doubling or tripling coupons undoubtedly raises some redemption rates.

9.3 Promotions and pass-through

Of the promotional value provided by a manufacturer to its retailers and distributors, the pass-through percentage represents the portion that ultimately reaches the consumer.

$$\text{Percentage Sales on Deal (\%)} = \frac{\text{Sales with Any Temporary Discount (\$, \#)}}{\text{Total Sales (\$, \#)}}$$

$$\text{Pass-Through (\%)} = \frac{\text{Value of Temporary Promotional Discounts Provided to Consumers by the Trade (\$)}}{\text{Value of Temporary Discounts Provided to Trade by Manufacturer (\$)}}$$

Manufacturers offer many discounts to their distributors and retailers (often called "the trade"), with the objective of encouraging them to offer their own promotions, in turn, to their customers. If trade customers or consumers do not find promotions attractive, this will be indicated by a decline in percentage sales on deal. Likewise, low pass-through percentages can indicate that too many deals—or the wrong kinds of deals—are being offered.

Purpose: to measure whether trade promotions are generating consumer promotions.

Pass-through: The percentage of the value of manufacturer promotions paid to distributors and retailers that is reflected in discounts provided by the trade to their own customers.

"Middlemen" are a part of the channel structure in many industries. Companies may face one, two, three, or even four levels of resellers before their product reaches the ultimate consumer. For example, a beer manufacturer may sell to an exporter, who sells to an importer, who sells to a local distributor, who sells to a retail store. If each channel adds its own margin, without regard for how others are pricing, the resulting price can be higher than a marketer would like. This sequential application of individual margins has been referred to as "double marginalization."[4]

Construction

$$\text{Percentage Sales on Deal (\%)} = \frac{\text{Sales with Any Temporary Discount (\#, \$)}}{\text{Total Sales (\#, \$)}}$$

Promotional discount represents the total value of promotional discounts given throughout the sales channel.

$$\text{Promotional Discount (\$)} = \text{Sales with Any Temporary Discount (\$)} \\ * \text{Average Depth of Discount as Percent of List (\%)}$$

$$\text{Depth of Discount as Percent of List (\%)} = \frac{\text{Unit Discount (\$)}}{\text{Unit List Price (\$)}}$$

Pass-through is calculated as the value of discounts given by the trade to their customers, divided by the value of temporary discounts provided by a manufacturer to the trade.

$$\text{Pass-Through (\%)} = \frac{\text{Promotional Discounts Provided by the Trade to Consumers (\$)}}{\text{Discounts Provided to the Trade by Manufacturer (\$)}}$$

Data sources, complications, and cautions

Manufacturers often compete with one another for the attention of retailers, distributors, and other resellers. Toward that end, they build special displays for their products, change assortments to include new offerings, and seek to elicit increasing attention from resellers' sales personnel. Significantly, in their effort to increase channel "push," manufacturers also offer discounts and allowances to the trade. It is important to understand the rates and amounts of discounts provided to the trade, as well as the proportions of those discounts that are passed along to the resellers' customers. At times, when resellers' margins are thin, manufacturers' discounts are designed to enhance them. Market leaders often worry that trade margins are too thin to support push efforts. Other manufacturers may be concerned that retail margins are too high, and that too few of their discounts are being passed along. The metrics discussed in this chapter should be interpreted with these thoughts in mind.

Resellers may decide that optimizing an entire product line is more important than maximizing profits on any given product. If a reseller stocks multiple competing lines, it can be difficult to find an overall solution that suits both that reseller and its suppliers. Manufacturers strive to motivate resellers to market their goods aggressively and to grow their shared sales through such programs as incentives for "exclusivity" or rebates based on increasing shares of category sales or on year-to-year growth in sales.

Resellers learn to adapt their buying and selling practices to take advantage of manufacturer pricing incentives. In this area, marketers must pay special attention to the law of unforeseen consequences. For example, resellers have been known to

- Buy larger quantities of a product than they can sell—or want to sell—in order to qualify for volume discounts. The excess goods are then sold (diverted) to other retailers, stored for future sales, or even destroyed or returned to the manufacturer for "credit."

- Time their purchases at the ends of accounting periods in order to qualify for rebates and allowances. This results in "lumpy" sales patterns for manufacturers, making forecasting difficult, increasing problems with out-of-date products and returns, and raising production costs.

In some instances, a particularly powerful channel "captain" can impose pricing discipline on an entire channel. In most cases, however, each "link" in the distribution chain can coordinate only its own pricing. A manufacturer, for example, may work out appropriate pricing incentives for wholesalers, and the wholesalers in turn may develop their own pricing incentives for retailers.

In many countries and industries, it is illegal for suppliers to dictate the selling prices of resellers. Manufacturers can't dictate wholesaler selling prices, and wholesalers can't dictate retail prices. Consequently, members of the channel seek indirect methods of influencing resellers' prices.

9.4 Price waterfall

The price waterfall is a way of describing the progression of prices from published list price to the final price paid by a customer. Each drop in price represents a drop in the "water level." For example:

$100
List Price
    Dealer Discount
        $90
        Cash Discount
            $85
            Annual Rebate
                $82
                Co-op Advertising
                    Net Price $80

$$\text{Price Waterfall (\%)} = \frac{\text{Net Price per Unit (\$)}}{\text{List Price per Unit (\$)}}$$

In this structure, the average price paid by customers depends on the list price of a product, the sizes of discounts given, and the proportion of customers taking advantage of those discounts.

By analyzing the price waterfall, marketers can determine where product value is being lost. This can be especially important in businesses that allow the sales channel to reduce prices in order to secure customers. The price waterfall can help focus attention on deciding whether these discounts make sense for the business.

Purpose: to assess the actual price paid for a product in comparison with the list price.

In pricing, the bad news is that marketers can find it difficult to determine the right list price for a product. The good news is that few customers will actually pay that price anyway. Indeed, a product's net price—the price actually paid by customers—often falls between 53% and 94% of its base price.[5]

Net price: The actual price paid for a product by customers after all discounts and allowances have been factored in. Also called the pocket price.

List price: The price of a good or service before discounts and allowances are considered.

Invoice price: The price specified on the invoice for a product. This price is typically stated net of some discounts and allowances, such as dealer, competitive, and order size discounts, but does not reflect other discounts and allowances, such as those for special terms and cooperative advertising. The invoice price is therefore typically less than the list price but greater than the net price.

Price waterfall: The reduction of the price actually paid by customers for a product as discounts and allowances are given at various stages of the sales process. Because few customers take advantage of all discounts, in analyzing a product's price waterfall, marketers must consider not only the amount of each discount but also the percentage of sales to which it applies.

As customers vary in their use of discounts, net price can fall into a wide range relative to list price.

Construction

To assess a product's price waterfall, one must plot the price a customer will pay at each stage of the waterfall, specifying potential discounts and allowances in the sequence in which those are usually taken or applied. For example, broker commissions are generally applied *after* trade discounts.

> **Net price:** The actual average price paid for a product at a given stage in its distribution channel, which can be calculated as its list price less discounts offered, with each discount multiplied by the probability that it will be applied. When all discounts are considered, this calculation yields the product's net price.

Net Price (\$) = List Price (\$) – [Discount A (\$) * Proportion of Purchases on Which Discount A Is Taken (%)] – [Discount B (\$) * Proportion of Purchases on Which Discount B Is Taken (%)] and so on

$$\text{Price Waterfall Effect (\%)} = \frac{\text{Net Price per Unit (\$)}}{\text{List Price per Unit (\$)}}$$

Example Hakan manages his own firm. In selling his product, Hakan grants two discounts or allowances. The first of these is a 12% discount on orders of more than 100 units. This is given on 50% of the firm's business and appears on its invoicing system. Hakan also gives an allowance of 5% for cooperative advertising. This is not shown on the invoicing system. It is completed in separate procedures that involve customers submitting advertisements for approval. Upon investigation, Hakan finds that 80% of customers take advantage of this advertising allowance.

The invoice price of the firm's product can be calculated as the list price (50 dinar per unit), less the 12% order size discount, multiplied by the chance of that discount being given (50%).

Invoice Price = List Price – [Discount * Proportion of Purchases on Which Discount Is Taken]

= 50 dinar – [(50 * 12%) * 50%]

= 50 dinar – 3 dinar = 47 dinar

The net price further reduces the invoice price by the average amount of the cooperative advertising allowance granted, as follows:

Net Price = List Price – [Discount * Proportion of Purchases on Which Discount Is Taken] – [Advertising Allowance * Proportion of Purchases on Which Ad Allowance Is Taken] = 50 dinar – [(50 * 12%) * 50%] – [(50 * 5%) * 80%] = 50 – 3 – 2 = 45 dinar

To find the effect of the price waterfall, divide the net price by the list price.

$$\text{Price Waterfall (\%)} = \frac{45}{50} = 90\%$$

Data sources, complications, and cautions

To analyze the impact of discounts, allowances, and the overall price waterfall effect, marketers require full information about sales, in both revenue and unit volume terms, at an individual product level, including not only discounts and allowances that are formally recorded in the billing system but also those granted that do not appear on invoices.

The major challenge in establishing the price waterfall is securing product-specific data at all of these various levels in the sales process. In all but the smallest businesses, this is likely to be quite difficult, particularly because many discounts are granted on an off-invoice basis, so they might not be recorded at a product level in a firm's financial system. Further complicating matters, not all discounts are based on list price. Cash discounts, for example, are usually based on net invoice price.

Where discounts are known in theory, but the financial system doesn't fully record their details, the problem is determining how to calculate the price waterfall. Toward that end, marketers need not only the amount of each discount but also the percentage of unit sales for which customers take advantage of that discount.

The typical business offers a number of discounts from list prices. Most of these serve the function of encouraging particular customer behaviors. For example, trade discounts can encourage distributors and resellers to buy in full truckloads, pay invoices promptly, and place orders during promotional periods or in a manner that smooths production. Over time, these discounts tend to multiply as manufacturers find it easier to raise list price and add another discount than to eliminate discounts altogether.

Problems with discounts include the following:

- Because it's difficult to record discounts on a per-item basis, firms often record them in aggregate. On this basis, marketers may see the total discounts provided but might have difficulty allocating them to specific products. Some discounts are offered on the total size of a purchase, exacerbating this problem. This increases the challenge of assessing product profitability.

- Once given, discounts tend to be sticky: It is hard to take them away from customers. Consequently, inertia often leaves special discounts in place long after the competitive pressures that prompted them are removed.

- To the extent that discounts are not recorded on invoices, management often loses track of them in decision making.

As the Professional Pricing Society advises, when considering the price of a product: Look past the invoice price.

Related metrics and concepts

Deductions: Some "discounts" are actually deductions applied by a customer to an invoice, adjusting for goods damaged in shipment, incorrect deliveries, late deliveries, or in some cases, for products that did not sell as well as hoped. Deductions might not be recorded in a way that can be analyzed, and they often are the subject of disputes.

Everyday low prices (EDLP): EDLP refers to a strategy of offering the same pricing level from period to period. For retailers, there is a distinction between buying at EDLP and selling at EDLP. For example, some suppliers offer constant selling prices to retailers but negotiate periods during which a product will be offered on deal with display and other retail promotions. Rather than grant temporary price discounts to retailers, suppliers often finance these programs through "market development funds."

HI-LO (High-Low): This pricing strategy constitutes the opposite of EDLP. In HI-LO pricing, retailers and manufacturers offer a series of "deals" or "specials"— times during which prices are temporarily decreased. One purpose of HI-LO pricing and other temporary discounts is to realize price discrimination in the economic—not the legal—sense of the term.

Price discrimination and tailoring

When firms face distinct and separable market segments with different willingness to pay (price elasticities), charging a single price means that the firm will leave money on the table—that is, fail to capture the full consumer value.

There are three conditions for price tailoring to be profitable:

- Segments must have different elasticities (willingness to pay), and/or marketers must have different costs of serving the segments (say shipping expenses), and the incremental volume must be sufficiently large to compensate for the reduction in margin.
- Segments must be separable. That is, charging different prices does not just result in transfer between segments (for example, your father cannot buy your dinner and apply the senior citizen discount).
- The incremental profit from price tailoring exceeds the costs of implementing multiple prices for the same product or service.

Price tailoring is clearly a euphemism for price discrimination. However, the latter term is loaded with legal implications, and marketers understandably use it with caution.

When facing a total demand curve composed of identifiable segments with different demand slopes, a marketer can use optimal pricing for each segment recognized, as opposed to using the same price based upon aggregate demand. This is usually done based on three factors:

- **Time:** For example, subways or movie theaters charging a higher price during rush or peak hour or products that are launched at a high price in the beginning to earn extra profits from less price sensitive early adopters
- **Geography:** For example, international market divisions with different prices in different regions for DVDs or other products
- **Tolerable discrimination:** Identifying acceptable forms of segmentation, such as discriminating between students or senior citizens and the general public

Price differences cause gray markets; goods are imported from low-price markets to high-price markets. Gray markets are common for some fashion goods and pharmaceuticals.

Caution: regulations

Most countries have regulations that apply to price discrimination. As a marketer, you should understand these regulations. In the United States, the most important regulation is the Robinson–Patman Act, which is mainly intended to control price differences that might injure competition.[6] We encourage you to visit the Federal Trade Commission's website (www.ftc.gov) for more information.

Further reading

Abraham, M. M., and L. M. Lodish. (1990). "Getting the Most Out of Advertising and Promotion," *Harvard Business Review*, 68(3), 50–51, 53, 56.

Ailawadi, K., P. Farris, and E. Shames. (1999). "Trade Promotion: Essential to Selling Through Resellers," *Sloan Management Review*, 41(1), 83–92.

Christen, M., S. Gupta, J. C. Porter, R. Staelin, and D. R. Wittink. (1997). "Using Market-Level Data to Understand Promotion Effects in a Nonlinear Model," *Journal of Marketing Research*, 34(3), 322–334.

Roegner, E. V., M. V. Marn, and C. C. Zawada. (2005). "Pricing," *Marketing Management,* 14(1), 23–28.

Advertising and sponsorship metrics

10

Key concepts covered in this chapter:

- Advertising: impressions, gross rating points, and opportunities-to-see

- Cost per thousand impressions (CPM) rates

- Reach/net reach and frequency

- Frequency response functions

- Effective reach and effective frequency

- Share of voice

- Advertising elasticity of demand

- Return on advertising spend (ROAS)

- Equivalent media value from sponsorship

- Sponsorship ROI

Introduction

Advertising is the cornerstone of many marketing strategies. The positioning and communications conveyed by advertising often set the tone and timing for many other sales and promotion efforts. While advertising can be the defining element of the marketing mix, it can also be expensive and is notoriously difficult to evaluate. It is not easy to track the incremental sales associated with advertising decisions. For many marketers, media metrics are particularly confusing. A command of the vocabulary involved in this field is needed to work with media planners, buyers, and agencies. A strong understanding of media metrics can help marketers ensure that advertising budgets are spent efficiently and directed toward specific aims.

In this chapter, we discuss media metrics that reveal how many people may be exposed to an advertising campaign, how often those people have opportunities to see the ads, and the cost of each potential impression. Toward that end, we introduce the vocabulary of advertising metrics, including such terms as *impressions*, *exposures*, *OTS*, *rating points*, *GRPs*, *net reach*, *effective frequency*, *CPMs*, and *ROAS*.

This chapter also discusses sponsorship metrics as sponsorship often has similar aims to advertising and can also be fiendishly hard to measure through to a final objective. The metrics covered here include Equivalent Media Value, and Sponsorship ROI.

	Metric	Construction	Considerations	Purpose
10.1	Impressions	An impression is generated each time an advertisement is viewed. The number of impressions achieved is a function of an ad's reach (the number of people seeing it) multiplied by its frequency (the number of times they see it).	As a metric, impressions do not account for quality of viewings. A glimpse will have less effect than a detailed study. Impressions are also called exposures and opportunities-to-see (OTS).	Understand how many times an advertisement is viewed.
10.1	Gross Rating Points (GRPs)	Impressions divided by the number of people in the audience for an advertisement.	Impressions expressed in relation to population. GRPs are cumulative across media vehicles, making it possible to achieve GRPs of more than 100%. Target Rating Points (TRPs) are measured in relation to defined target populations.	Measure impressions in relation to the number of people in the audience for an advertising campaign.

	Metric	Construction	Considerations	Purpose
10.2	Cost per Thousand Impressions (CPM)	Cost of advertising divided by the number of impressions generated (in thousands).	CPM is a measure of cost per thousand advertising impressions. Working with cost per thousands of impressions is easier than working with cost per single impression.	Measure the cost-effectiveness of the generation of impressions.
10.3	Net Reach	The number of people who are exposed to an advertisement.	Equivalent to reach. Measures unique viewers of an advertisement. Often best mapped on a Venn diagram.	Measure the breadth of an advertisement's spread across a population.
10.3	Average Frequency	The average number of times that an individual is exposed to an advertisement, given that he or she is indeed exposed to the ad.	Frequency is measured only among people who have been exposed to the advertisement under study.	Measure how often an advertisement is exposed to a given population.
10.4	Frequency Response Functions	Linear: All advertising impressions have equal impact. Threshold: A certain number of impressions are needed before an advertising message will sink in. Learning curve: An advertisement has little impact at first but gains force with repetition and then tails off as saturation is achieved.	Linear model is often unrealistic, especially for complex products. Threshold model is often used, as it is simple and intuitive. Learning curve models are often hypothesized, but they are difficult to test for accuracy. Simpler models often work as well.	Model the response of an audience to additional exposures of an advertisement.

▶

	Metric	Construction	Considerations	Purpose
10.5	Effective Reach	Reach achieved among individuals who are exposed to an advertisement with a frequency greater than or equal to the effective frequency.	The effective frequency rate constitutes a crucial assumption in the calculation of this metric.	Measure the portion of an audience that is exposed to an advertisement enough times to be influenced.
10.5	Effective Frequency	The number of times an individual must see an advertisement in order to respond at the desired or target level.	As a rule of thumb in planning, marketers often use an effective frequency of 3. To the extent that it promises to have a significant impact on campaign results, this assumption should be tested.	Determine optimal exposure levels for an advertisement or a campaign, trading the risk of over-spending against the risk of failing to achieve the desired impact.
10.6	Share of Voice	Quantifies the advertising "presence" of a brand, campaign, or firm in relation to total advertising in a market.	Market definition is central to meaningful results. Impressions or ratings represent a conceptually strong basis for share of voice calculations. Often, however, such data are unavailable. Consequently, marketers use spending, an input, as a proxy for output.	To evaluate the relative strength of an advertising program within its market.
10.7	Advertising Elasticity of Demand	Change in advertising spend and change in demand.	Represents the responsiveness of sales to advertising.	Estimate the optimal level of advertising spend.
10.8	Return on Advertising Spend (ROAS)	Incremental revenue generated by an advertising campaign divided by the cost of advertising.	Be careful: This is not the same as ROI. The return is revenue, not profit.	Describe incremental revenue generated per ad campaign dollar.

	Metric	Construction	Considerations	Purpose
10.9	Equivalent Media Value from Sponsorship	Impressions created and the value of each impression.	Equivalent Media Value directly compares the visibility gained from sponsorship to the value of impressions generated.	Estimate what equivalent impressions from advertising would have cost.
10.10	Sponsorship ROI	Compares the return (the incremental profit from the sponsorship) with the costs of the sponsorship.	ROI can be used in a casual way. Sponsorship ROI is often any positive outcome, but that can be confusing.	Consider the cost of a sponsorship relative to the profit generated.

10.1 Advertising: impressions, exposures, opportunities-to-see (OTS), gross rating points (GRPs), and target rating points (TRPs)

Advertising impressions, exposures, and opportunities-to-see (OTS) all refer to the same metric: an estimate of the audience for a media "insertion" (one ad) or campaign.

Impressions = OTS = Exposures. In this chapter, we use all these terms. It is important to distinguish between "reach" (number of unique individuals exposed to certain advertising) and "frequency" (the average number of times each such individual is exposed).

Rating point = Reach of a media vehicle as a percentage of a defined population. (For example, a television show with a rating of 2 reaches 2% of the population.)

Gross rating points (GRPs) = Total ratings achieved by multiple media vehicles expressed in rating points. (For example, advertisements on five television shows with an average rating of 30% would achieve 150 GRPs.)

GRPs are impressions expressed as a percentage of a defined population and often total more than 100%. This metric refers to the defined population reached rather than an absolute number of people. Whereas GRPs are used with a broader

▶

audience, the term target rating points (TRPs) denotes a narrower definition of the target audience. For example, TRPs might consider a specific segment such as youths aged 15 to 19, whereas GRPs might be based on the total TV viewing population.

Purpose: to measure the audience for an advertisement.

Impressions, exposures, and opportunities-to-see (OTS) are the "atoms" of media planning. Every advertisement released into the world has a fixed number of planned exposures, depending on the number of individuals in its audience. For example, an advertisement that appears on a billboard on the Champs-Élysées in central Paris will have an estimated number of impressions, based on the flow of traffic from visitors and locals. An advertisement is said to *reach* a certain number of people on a number of occasions or to provide a certain number of *impressions* or *opportunities-to-see*. These impressions or opportunities-to-see are a function of the number of people reached and the number of times each such person has an opportunity to see the advertisement.

Methodologies for estimating opportunities-to-see vary by type of media. In magazines, for example, opportunities-to-see do not equal circulation because each copy of the magazine may be read by more than one person. In broadcast media, it is assumed that the quantified audience comprises those individuals available to hear or see an advertisement. In print and outdoor media, an opportunity-to-see might range from a brief glance to a careful consideration. To illustrate this range, imagine that you're walking down a busy street. How many billboard advertisements catch your eye? You may not realize it, but you're contributing to the impressions of several advertisements, regardless of whether you ignore them or study them with great interest.

When a campaign involves several types of media, marketers may need to adjust their measures of opportunities-to-see in order to maintain consistency and allow for comparability among the different media.

Gross rating points (GRPs) are related to impressions and opportunities-to-see. They quantify impressions as a percentage of the population reached rather than in absolute numbers of people reached. Target rating points (TRPs) express the same concept but with regard to a more narrowly defined target audience.

Construction

Impressions, opportunities-to-see (OTS), and exposures: The number of times a specific advertisement is available to be seen or otherwise exposed to media audiences. This is an estimate of the audience for a media "insertion" (one ad) or campaign. *Impressions = OTS = Exposures.*

Impressions

The process of estimating reach and frequency begins with data that sum all of the impressions from different advertisements to arrive at total "gross" impressions.

$$\text{Impressions (\#)} = \text{Reach (\#)} * \text{Average Frequency (\#)}$$

The same formula can be rearranged as follows to convey the average number of times that an audience was given the opportunity to see an advertisement:

$$\text{Average Frequency (\#)} = \frac{\text{Impressions (\#)}}{\text{Reach (\#)}}$$

Average frequency is defined as the average number of impressions per individual "reached" by an advertisement or campaign.

Similarly, the reach of an advertisement—that is, the number of people with an opportunity to see the ad—can be calculated as follows:

$$\text{Reach (\#)} = \frac{\text{Impressions (\#)}}{\text{Average Frequency (\#)}}$$

Although reach can thus be quantified as the number of individuals exposed to an advertisement or campaign, it can also be calculated as a percentage of the population. In this text, we distinguish between the two conceptualizations of this metric as reach (#) and reach (%).

The reach of a specific media vehicle, which may deliver an advertisement, is often expressed in rating points. Rating points are calculated as individuals reached by that vehicle, divided by the total number of individuals in a defined population and expressed in "points" that represent the resulting percentage. Thus, a television program with a rating of 2 would reach 2% of the population.

The rating points of all the media vehicles that deliver an advertisement or campaign can be summed, yielding a measure of the aggregate reach of the campaign, known as gross rating points (GRPs).

Gross rating points (GRPs): The sum of all rating points delivered by the media vehicles carrying an advertisement or campaign.

Example A campaign that delivers 150 GRPs might expose 30% of the population to an advertisement at an average frequency of 5 impressions per individual (150 = 30 * 5). If 15 separate insertions of the advertisement were used, a few individuals might be exposed as many as 15 times, and many more of the 30% reached would only have 1 or 2 opportunities-to-see.

$$\text{Gross Rating Points (GRPs) (\%)} = \text{Reach (\%)} * \text{Average Frequency (\#)}$$

$$\text{Gross Rating Points (GRPs) (\%)} = \frac{\text{Impressions (\#)}}{\text{Defined Population (\#)}}$$

> **Target rating points (TRPs):** The gross rating points delivered by a media vehicle to a specific target audience.

Example A firm places 10 advertising insertions in a market with a population of 5 people. The resulting impressions are outlined in the following table, in which 1 represents an opportunity-to-see, and 0 signifies that an individual did not have an opportunity to see a particular insertion.

In this campaign, the impressions across the entire population total 22.

Insertion	Individual A	B	C	D	E	Impressions	Rating points (Impressions/ Population)
1	1	1	0	0	1	3	60
2	1	1	0	0	1	3	60
3	1	1	0	1	0	3	60
4	1	1	0	1	0	3	60
5	1	1	0	1	0	3	60
6	1	0	0	1	0	2	40
7	1	0	0	1	0	2	40
8	1	0	0	0	0	1	20
9	1	0	0	0	0	1	20
10	1	0	0	0	0	1	20
Totals	**10**	**5**	**0**	**5**	**2**	**22**	**440**

As insertion 1 generates impressions on three of the five members of the population, so it reaches 60% of that population and gets 60 rating points. As insertion 6 generates impressions on two of the five members of the population, so it reaches 40% of the population and gets 40 rating points. GRPs for the campaign can be calculated by adding the rating points of each insertion.

$$\text{Gross Rating Points (GRPs)} = \text{Rating Points of Insertion 1} + \text{Rating Points of Insertion 2} + \text{etc.}$$

$$= 440$$

Alternatively, GRPs can be calculated by dividing total impressions by the size of the population and expressing the result in percentage terms.

$$\text{Gross Rating Points (GRPs)} = \frac{\text{Impressions}}{\text{Population}} * 100\% = \frac{22}{5} * 100\% = 440$$

TRPs, by contrast, quantify the GRPs achieved by an advertisement or a campaign among targeted individuals within a larger population. For purposes of this example, let's assume that individuals A, B, and C comprise the targeted group. Individual A has received 10 exposures to the campaign; individual B, 5 exposures; and individual C, 0 exposures. Thus, the campaign has reached two out of three, or 66.67%, of targeted individuals. Among those reached, its average frequency has been 15/2, or 7.5. On this basis, we can calculate target rating points by either of the following methods.

$$\text{Target Rating Points (TRPs)} = \text{Reach (\%)} * \text{Average Frequency}$$

$$= 66.67\% * \frac{15}{2}$$

$$= 500$$

$$\text{Target Rating Points (TRPs)} = \frac{\text{Impressions (\#)}}{\text{Targets (\#)}} = \frac{15}{3} = 500$$

Data sources, complications, and cautions

Data on the estimated audience size (reach) of a media vehicle are typically made available by media sellers. Standard methods also exist for combining data from different media to estimate "net reach" and frequency.

Two different media plans can yield comparable results in terms of costs and total exposures but differ in reach and frequency measures. In other words, one plan can expose a larger audience to an advertising message less often, while the other delivers more exposures to each member of a smaller audience. Table 10.1 provides an example.

Table 10.1 Illustration of reach and frequency

	Reach	Average frequency*	Total exposures (Impressions, OTS)
Plan A	250,000	4	1,000,000
Plan B	333,333	3	1,000,000

* Average frequency is the average number of exposures made to each *individual who has received at least one exposure to a given advertisement or campaign*. To compare impressions across media, or even within classes of media, one must make a broad assumption: that there is some equivalency between the different types of impressions generated by each media classification. Nonetheless, marketers must still compare the "quality" of impressions delivered by different media.

For example, a billboard along a busy freeway and a subway advertisement can both yield the same number of impressions. Whereas the subway advertisement has a captive audience, members of the billboard audience are generally driving and concentrating on the road. As this example demonstrates, there may be differences in the quality of impressions. To account for these differences, media optimizers apply weightings to different media vehicles. When direct response data are available, they can be used to evaluate the relative effectiveness and efficiency of impression purchases in different media. Otherwise, this weighting might be a matter of judgment. A manager might believe, for example, that an impression generated by a TV commercial is twice as effective as one made by a magazine print advertisement.

Similarly, marketers often find it useful to define audience subgroups and generate separate reach and frequency statistics for each. Marketers might weight subgroups differently, just as they weight impressions delivered through different media differently.[1] This helps in evaluating whether an advertisement reaches its defined customer groups.

When calculating impressions, marketers often encounter an overlap of people who see an advertisement in more than one medium. Later in this text, we will discuss how to account for such overlap and estimate the percentage of people who are exposed to an advertisement multiple times.

10.2 Cost per thousand impressions (CPM) rates

Cost per thousand impressions (CPM) is the cost per 1,000 advertising impressions. This metric is calculated by dividing the cost of an advertising placement by the number of impressions (expressed in thousands) that it generates.

$$\text{Cost per Thousand Impressions (CPM) (\$)} = \frac{\text{Advertising Cost (\$)}}{\text{Impressions Generated (\# in Thousands)}}$$

CPM is useful in comparing the relative efficiency of different advertising opportunities or media and in evaluating the costs of overall campaigns.

Purpose: to compare the costs of advertising campaigns within and across different media.

A typical advertising campaign might try to reach potential consumers in multiple locations and through various media. The Cost per Thousand Impressions (CPM) metric enables marketers to make cost comparisons between these media, both at the planning stage and during reviews of past campaigns. (Technical people like to use *mille*—from Latin—for "thousand," hence the M in CPM.)

Marketers calculate CPM by dividing advertising campaign costs by the number of impressions (or opportunities-to-see) that are delivered by each part of the campaign.

As the impression counts are generally sizable, marketers customarily work with the CPM impressions. Dividing by 1,000 is an industry standard.

> **Cost per thousand impressions (CPM): The cost of a media campaign relative to its success in generating impressions or opportunities-to-see.**

Construction

To calculate CPM, marketers first state the results of a media campaign (gross impressions) in thousands. Second, they divide that result into the relevant media cost:

$$\text{Cost per Thousand Impressions (CPM) (\$)} = \frac{\text{Advertising Cost (\$)}}{\text{Impressions Generated (\# in Thousands)}}$$

Example An advertising campaign costs \$4,000 and generates 120,000 impressions. On this basis, CPM can be calculated as follows:

$$\text{Cost per Thousand Impressions} = \frac{\text{Advertising Cost}}{\text{Impressions Generated (Thousands)}}$$

$$= \frac{\$4,000}{(120,000/1,000)}$$

$$= \frac{\$4,000}{120} = \$33.33$$

Data sources, complications, and cautions

In an advertising campaign, the full cost of the media purchased can include agency fees and production of creative materials, in addition to the cost of media space or time. Marketers also must have an estimate of the number of impressions expected or delivered in the campaign at an appropriate level of detail. Internet marketers can usually easily access these data (see Chapter 11, "Online, email, and mobile metrics").

CPM is only a starting point for analysis. Not all impressions are equally valuable. Consequently, it can make good business sense to pay more for impressions from some sources than from others.

In calculating CPM, marketers should also be concerned with their ability to capture the full cost of advertising activity. Cost items typically include the amount paid to a creative agency to develop advertising materials, amounts paid to an organization that sells media, and internal salaries and expenses related to overseeing the advertisement.

Related metrics and concepts

Cost per Point (CPP): **The cost of an advertising campaign, relative to the rating points delivered. In a manner similar to CPM, CPP measures the cost per rating point for an advertising campaign by dividing the cost of the advertising by the rating points delivered.**

10.3 Reach, net reach, and frequency

Reach is the same as net reach; both of these metrics quantify the number or percentage of individuals in a defined population who are exposed to at least one exposure to an advertisement. Frequency measures the average number of times that each such individual sees the advertisement.

$$\text{Impressions (\#)} = \text{Reach (\#)} * \text{Frequency (\#)}$$

Net reach and frequency are important concepts in describing an advertising campaign. A campaign with a high net reach and low frequency runs the danger of being lost in a noisy advertising environment. A campaign with low net reach but high frequency can over-expose some audiences and miss others entirely. Reach and frequency metrics help managers adjust their advertising media plans to fit their marketing strategies.

Purpose: to separate total impressions into the number of people reached and the average frequency with which those individuals are exposed to advertising.

To clarify the difference between reach and frequency, let's review what we learned in Section 10.1. When impressions from multiple insertions are combined, the results are often called *gross impressions* or *total exposures*. When total impressions are expressed as a percentage of the population, this measure is referred to as gross rating points (GRPs). For example, suppose a media vehicle reaches 12% of the population. That vehicle will have a single-insertion reach of 12 rating points. If a firm advertised in 10 such vehicles, it would achieve 120 GRPs.

Now, let's look at the composition of these 120 GRPs. Suppose we know that the 10 advertisements had a combined net reach of 40% and an average frequency of 3. Then their gross rating points might be calculated as 40 * 3 = 120 GRPs.

Example A commercial is shown once in each of three time slots. Nielsen keeps track of which households have an opportunity to see the advertisement. The commercial airs in a market with only five households: A, B, C, D, and E. Time slots 1 and 2 both have a rating of 60 because 60% of the households view them. Time slot 3 has a rating of 20.

Time slot	Households with opportunity-to-see	Households with no opportunity-to-see	Rating points of time slot
1	A B E	C D	60
2	A B C	D E	60
3	A	B C D E	20
	G R P		140

$$GRP = \frac{\text{Impressions}}{\text{Population}} = \frac{7}{5} = 140\ (\%)$$

The commercial is seen by households A, B, C, and E but not D. Thus, it generates impressions in four out of five households, for a reach (%) of 80%. In the four households reached, the commercial is seen a total of seven times. Thus, its average frequency can be calculated as 7/4, or 1.75. On this basis, we can calculate the campaign's gross rating points as follows:

$$GRP = \text{Reach (\%)} * \text{Average Frequency (\#)} = \frac{4}{5} * \frac{7}{4} = 80\% * 1.75 = 140(\%)$$

Unless otherwise specified, simple measures of overall audience size (such as GRPs or impressions) do not differentiate between campaigns that expose larger audiences fewer times and those that expose smaller audiences more often. In other words, these metrics do not distinguish between reach and frequency.

Net reach and *reach* refer to the unduplicated audience of individuals who have been exposed at least once to the advertising in question. Reach can be expressed as either the number of individuals who have seen the advertisement or the percentage of the population that has seen the advertisement.

> **Reach:** The number of people or percentage of population exposed to an advertisement.

Frequency is calculated by dividing gross impressions by reach. Frequency is equal to the average number of exposures received by individuals who have been exposed to at least one impression of the advertising in question. Frequency is calculated *only* among individuals who have been exposed to this advertising. On this basis:

$$\text{Total Impressions} = \text{Reach} * \text{Average Frequency}$$

> **Average frequency:** The average number of impressions per reached individual.

Media plans can differ in reach and frequency but still generate the same number of total impressions.

> **Net reach:** This term is used to emphasize the fact that the reach of multiple advertising placements is not calculated through the gross addition of all individuals reached by each of those placements. Occasionally, the word Net is eliminated, and the metric is called simply Reach.

Example Returning to our prior example of a 10-insertion media plan in a market with a population of five people, we can calculate the reach and frequency of the plan by analyzing the following data. In the following table, 1 represents an opportunity-to-see, and 0 signifies that an individual did not have an opportunity to see a particular insertion.

Insertion	Individual					Impressions	Rating points (impressions/ population)
	A	B	C	D	E		
1	1	1	0	0	1	3	60
2	1	1	0	0	1	3	60
3	1	1	0	1	0	3	60
4	1	1	0	1	0	3	60
5	1	1	0	1	0	3	60
6	1	0	0	1	0	2	40
7	1	0	0	1	0	2	40
8	1	0	0	0	0	1	20
9	1	0	0	0	0	1	20
10	1	0	0	0	0	1	20
Totals	**10**	**5**	**0**	**5**	**2**	**22**	**440**

Reach is equal to the number of people who saw at least one advertisement. Four of the five people in the population (A, B, D, and E) saw at least one advertisement. Consequently, reach (#) = 4.

$$\text{Average Frequency} = \frac{\text{Impressions}}{\text{Reach}} = \frac{22}{4} = 5.5$$

When multiple vehicles are involved in an advertising campaign, marketers need information about the overlap among these vehicles as well as sophisticated mathematical procedures in order to estimate reach and frequency. To illustrate this concept, the following two-vehicle example can be useful. Overlap can be represented by a graphic known as a Venn diagram (see Figure 10.1).

Figure 10.1 Venn diagram illustration of net reach

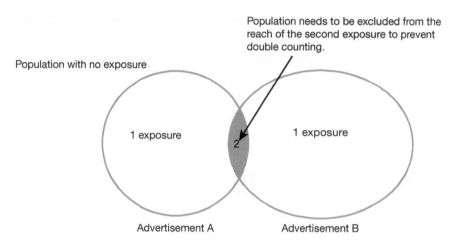

Example As an illustration of overlap effects, let's look at two examples. *Aircraft International* magazine offers 850,000 impressions for one advertisement. A second magazine, *Commercial Flying Monthly*, offers 1 million impressions for one advertisement.

Example 1: Marketers who place advertisements in both magazines should not expect to reach 1.85 million readers. Suppose that 10% of *Aircraft International* readers also read *Commercial Flying Monthly*. On this basis, net reach = (850,000 * .9) + 1,000,000 = 1,765,000 unique individuals. Of these, 85,000 (10% of *Aircraft International* readers) have received two exposures. The remaining 90% of *Aircraft International* readers have received only one exposure. The overlap between two different media types is referred to as *external overlap*.

Example 2: Marketers often use multiple insertions in the same media vehicle (such as the July and August issues of the same magazine) to achieve frequency. Even if the estimated audience size is the same for both months, not all of the same people will read the magazine each month. For purposes of this example, let's assume that marketers place insertions in two different issues of *Aircraft International* and that only 70% of readers of the July issue also read the August issue. On this basis, net reach is not merely 850,000 (the circulation of each issue of *Aircraft International*) because the groups viewing the two insertions are not precisely the same. Likewise, net reach is not 2 * 850,000, or 1.7 million, because the groups viewing the two insertions are also not completely disparate. Rather, net reach = 850,000 + (850,000 * 30%) = 1,105,000.

The reason: Thirty percent of readers of the August issue did not read the July issue and so did not have the opportunity to see the July insertion of the advertisement. These readers—and only these readers—represent incremental viewers of the advertisement in August, and so they must be added to Net Reach. The remaining 70% of August readers were exposed to the advertisement twice. Their total represents internal overlap or duplication.

Data sources, complications, and cautions

Although we've emphasized the importance of reach and frequency, the impressions metric is typically the easiest of these numbers to establish. Impressions can be aggregated on the basis of data originating from the media vehicles involved in a campaign. To determine net reach and frequency, marketers must know or estimate the overlap between audiences for different media or for the same medium at different times. It is beyond the capability of most marketers to make accurate estimates of reach and frequency without access to proprietary databases and algorithms. Full-service advertising agencies and media buying companies typically offer these services.

Assessing overlap is a major challenge. Although overlap can be estimated by performing customer surveys, it is difficult to do this with precision. Estimates based on managers' judgment occasionally must suffice.

10.4 Frequency response functions

Frequency response functions help marketers to model the effectiveness of multiple exposures to advertising. We discuss three typical assumptions about how people respond to advertisements: linear response, learning curve response, and threshold response.

In a linear response model, people are assumed to react equally to every exposure to an advertisement. The learning curve response model assumes that people are initially slow to respond to an advertisement and then respond more quickly for a time, until ultimately they reach a point at which their response to the message tails off. In a threshold response function, people are assumed to show little response until a critical frequency level is reached. At that point, their response immediately rises to maximum capacity.

Frequency response functions are not technically considered metrics. Understanding how people respond to the frequency of their exposure to advertising, however, is a vital part of media planning. Response models directly determine calculations of effective frequency and effective reach, metrics discussed in Section 10.5.

Purpose: to establish assumptions about the effects of advertising frequency.

Let's assume that a company has developed a message for an advertising campaign and that its managers feel confident that appropriate media for the campaign have been selected. Now they must decide: How many times should the advertisement be placed? The company wants to buy enough advertising space to ensure that its message is effectively conveyed, but it also wants to ensure that it doesn't waste money on unnecessary impressions.

To make this decision, a marketer will have to make an assumption about the value of frequency. This is a major consideration: What is the assumed value of repetition in advertising? Frequency response functions help us to think through the value of frequency.

Frequency response function: The expected relationship between advertising outcomes (usually in unit sales or dollar revenues) and advertising frequency.

There are a number of possible models for the frequency response functions used in media plans. A selection among these for a particular campaign will depend on the product advertised, the media used, and the judgment of the marketer. Three of the most common models are described next.

Linear response: The assumption behind a linear response function is that each advertising exposure is equally valuable, regardless of how many other exposures to the same advertising have preceded it.

Learning curve response: The learning curve model, or S curve model, rests on the assumption that a consumer's response to advertising follows a progression: The first few times an advertisement is shown, it does not register with its intended audience. As repetition occurs, the message permeates its audience and becomes more effective as people absorb it. Ultimately, however, this effectiveness declines, and diminishing returns set in. At this stage, marketers believe that individuals who want the information already have it and can't be influenced further; others simply are not interested.

Threshold response: The assumption behind this model is that advertising has no effect until its exposure reaches a certain level. At that point, its message becomes fully effective. Beyond that point, further advertising is unnecessary and would be wasted.

These are three common ways to value advertising frequency. Any function that accurately describes the effect of a campaign can be used. Typically, however, only one function will apply to a given situation.

Construction

Frequency response functions are most useful if they can be used to quantify the effects of incremental frequency. To illustrate the construction of the three functions described in this section, we have tabulated several examples.

Tables 10.2 and 10.3 show the assumed incremental effects of each exposure to a certain advertising campaign. Suppose that the advertisement will achieve maximum effect (100%) at eight exposures. By analyzing this effect in the context of various response functions, we can determine when and how quickly it takes hold.

Under a linear response model, each exposure below the saturation point generates one-eighth, or 12.5%, of the overall effect.

The learning curve model is more complex. In this function, the incremental effectiveness of each exposure increases until the fourth exposure and declines thereafter.

Under the threshold response model, there is no effect until the fourth exposure. At that point, however, 100% of the benefit of advertising is immediately realized. Beyond that point, there is no further value to be obtained through incremental advertising. Subsequent exposures are wasted.

The effects of these advertising exposures are tabulated cumulatively in Table 10.3. In this display, maximum attainable effectiveness is achieved when the response to advertising reaches 100%.

Table 10.2 Example of the effectiveness of advertising

Exposure frequency	Linear	Learning, or S, curve	Threshold value
1	0.125	0.05	0
2	0.125	0.1	0
3	0.125	0.2	0
4	0.125	0.25	1
5	0.125	0.2	0
6	0.125	0.1	0
7	0.125	0.05	0
8	0.125	0.05	0

Table 10.3 Assumptions: cumulative advertising effectiveness

Exposure frequency	Linear	Learning, or S, curve	Threshold value
1	12.5%	5%	0%
2	25.0%	15%	0%
3	37.5%	35%	0%
4	50.0%	60%	100%
5	62.5%	80%	100%
6	75.0%	90%	100%
7	87.5%	95%	100%
8	100.0%	100%	100%

We can plot cumulative effectiveness against frequency under each model (see Figure 10.2). The linear function is represented by a simple straight line. The threshold assumption rises steeply at four exposures to reach 100%. The cumulative effects of the learning curve model trace an S-shaped curve.

> **Frequency response function; linear: Under this function, the cumulative effect of advertising (up to the saturation point) can be viewed as a product of the frequency of exposures and effectiveness per exposure.**

Frequency Response Function; Linear (I) = Frequency (#) * Effectiveness per Exposure (I)

Stated another way, in a threshold response function, if frequency is greater than or equal to the threshold level of effectiveness, then the advertising campaign is 100% effective. If frequency is less than the threshold, there is no effect.

Figure 10.2 Illustration of cumulative advertising effectiveness

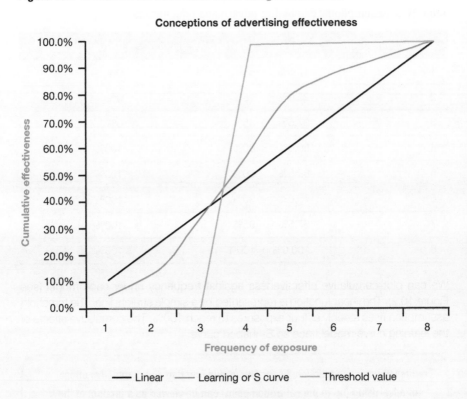

Conceptions of advertising effectiveness

—— Linear —— Learning or S curve —— Threshold value

Data sources, complications, and cautions

A frequency response function can be viewed as the structure of assumptions made by marketers in planning for the effects of an advertising campaign. In making these assumptions, a marketer's most useful information can be derived from an analysis of the effects of prior ad campaigns. Functions validated with past data, however, are most likely to be accurate if the relevant circumstances (such as media, creative, price, and product) have not significantly changed.

In comparing the three models discussed in this section, the linear response function has the benefit of resting on a simple assumption. It can be unrealistic, however, because it is hard to imagine that every advertising exposure in a campaign will have the same effect.

The learning curve has intuitive appeal. It seems to capture the complexity of life better than a linear model. Under this model, however, challenges arise in defining and predicting an advertisement's effectiveness. Three questions emerge: At what point does the curve begin to ramp up? How steep is the function? When does it tail off? With considerable research, marketers can make these estimates. Without it, however, there will always be the concern that the learning curve function provides a spurious level of accuracy.

Any implementation of the threshold response function hinges on a firm's estimate of where the threshold lies. This has important ramifications. If the firm makes a conservative estimate, setting the tipping point at a high number of exposures, it may pay for ineffective and unneeded advertising. If it sets the tipping point too low, it may not buy enough advertising media, and its campaign may fail to achieve the desired effect. In implementation, marketers may find that there is little practical difference between using the threshold model and the more complicated learning curve model.

Related metrics and concepts

Wear-in: The frequency required for a given advertisement or campaign to achieve a minimum level of effectiveness.

Wear-out: The frequency at which a given advertisement or campaign begins to lose effectiveness or even yield a negative effect.

10.5   Effective reach and effective frequency

The concept of effective frequency rests on the assumption that for an advertisement or a campaign to achieve an appreciable effect, it must attain a certain number of exposures to an individual within a specified time period.

Effective reach is defined as the number of people or the percentage of the audience that receives an advertising message with a frequency equal to or greater than the effective frequency. That is, effective reach is the population receiving the minimum effective exposure to an advertisement or campaign.

Purpose: to assess the extent to which advertising audiences are being reached with sufficient frequency.

Many marketers believe their messages require repetition to "sink in." Advertisers, like parents and politicians, therefore repeat themselves. But repetition must be monitored for effectiveness. Toward that end, marketers apply the concepts of effective frequency and effective reach. The assumptions behind these concepts run as follows: The first few times people are exposed to an ad, it may have little effect. It is only when more exposures are achieved that the message begins to influence its audience.

With this in mind, in planning and executing a campaign, an advertiser must determine the number of times that a message must be repeated in order to be useful. This number is the effective frequency. In concept, this is identical to the threshold frequency in the threshold response function discussed in Section 10.4. A campaign's effective frequency depends on many factors, including market circumstances, media used, type of ad, and campaign. As a rule of thumb, however, an estimate of three exposures per purchase cycle is used surprisingly often.

> Effective frequency: The number of times a certain advertisement must be exposed to a particular individual in a given period to produce a desired response.
>
> Effective reach: The number of people or the percentage of the audience that receives an advertising message with a frequency equal to or greater than the effective frequency.

Construction

Effective reach can be expressed as the number of people who have seen a particular advertisement or the percentage of the population that has been exposed to that advertisement at a frequency greater than or equal to the effective frequency.

$$\text{Effective Reach (\#, \%)} = \text{Individuals Reached with Frequency Equal to or Greater Than Effective Frequency}$$

Example An advertisement on the internet was believed to need three exposures before its message would sink in. Population data showed the distribution in Table 10.4.

Table 10.4 Number of exposures of advertisement

Number of exposures	Population
0	140,000
1	102,000
2	64,000
3	23,000
4 or more	11,000
Total	**340,000**

Because the effective frequency is 3, only those who have seen the advertisement three or more times have been effectively reached. The effective reach is thus 23,000 + 11,000 = 34,000.

In percentage terms, the effective reach of this advertisement is 34,000/340,000 = 10% of the population.

Data sources, complications, and cautions

The internet has provided a significant boost to data gathering in this area. Although even online campaigns can't be totally accurate with regard to the number of advertisements served to each customer, data on this question from online campaigns are far superior to those available in most other media.

Where data can't be tracked electronically, it's difficult to know how many times a customer has been in a position to see an advertisement. Under these circumstances, marketers make estimates on the basis of known audience habits and publicly available resources, such as TV ratings.

Although test markets and split-cable experiments can shed light on the effects of advertising frequency, marketers often lack comprehensive, reliable data on this question. In these cases, they must make—and defend—assumptions about the frequency needed for an effective campaign. Even where good historical data are available, media planning should not rely solely on past results because every campaign is different.

Marketers must also bear in mind that effective frequency attempts to quantify the *average* customer's response to advertising. In practice, some customers need more information and exposure than others.

10.6　Share of voice

> Share of voice quantifies the advertising presence that a specific product or brand enjoys. It is calculated by dividing the brand's advertising by total market advertising, and it is expressed as a percentage.
>
> $$\text{Share of Voice (\%)} = \frac{\text{Brand Advertising (\$, \#)}}{\text{Total Market Advertising (\$, \#)}}$$
>
> For purposes of share of voice, there are at least two ways to measure "advertising": in terms of dollar spending or in unit terms, through impressions or gross rating points (GRPs). By any of these measures, share of voice represents an estimate of a company's advertising, as compared to that of its competitors.

Purpose: to evaluate the comparative level of advertising committed to a specific product or brand.

Advertisers want to know whether their messages are breaking through the noise in the commercial environment. Toward that end, share of voice offers one indication of a brand's advertising strength, relative to the overall market.

There are at least two ways to calculate share of voice. The classic approach is to divide a brand's advertising dollar spend by the total advertising spend in the marketplace.

Alternatively, share of voice can be based on the brand's share of GRPs, impressions, effective reach, or similar measures. (See earlier sections in this chapter for more details on basic advertising metrics.)

Construction

> Share of voice: The percentage of advertising in a given market that a specific product or brand enjoys.

$$\text{Share of Voice (\%)} = \frac{\text{Brand Advertising (\$, \#)}}{\text{Total Market Advertising (\$, \#)}}$$

Data sources, complications, and cautions

When calculating share of voice, a marketer's central decision revolves around defining the boundaries of the market. One must ensure that these boundaries are meaningful to the intended customer. If a firm's objective is to influence internet users, for example, it would not be appropriate to define advertising presence solely in terms of print media. Share of voice can be computed at a company level, but brand- and product-level calculations are also common.

In executing this calculation, a company should be able to measure its total advertising spend fairly easily. Determining the ad spending for the market as a whole can be fraught with difficulty, however. Complete accuracy will probably not be attainable. It is important, however, that marketers take account of the major players in their market. External sources such as annual reports and press clippings can shed light on competitors' ad spending. Publications such as Leading National Advertisers (LNA) can also provide useful data. These services sell estimates of competitive purchases of media space and time. They generally do not report actual payments for media, however. Instead, costs are estimated on the basis of the time and space purchased and on published "rate cards" that list advertised prices. In using these estimates, marketers must bear in mind that rate cards rarely cite the discounts available in buying media. Without accounting for these discounts, published media spending estimates can be inflated. Marketers are advised to deflate them by the discount rates they themselves receive on advertising.

A final caution: Some marketers might assume that the price of advertising is equal to the value of that advertising. This is not necessarily the case. With this in mind, it can be useful to augment a dollar-based calculation of share of voice with one based on impressions.

10.7   Advertising elasticity of demand

In this section we examine advertising elasticity, which represents the responsiveness of sales to advertising.

$$\text{Advertising Elasticity of Demand, AED (I)} = \frac{\text{Change in Quantity Demanded (\%)}}{\text{Change in Spending on Advertising (\%)}}$$

We also discuss how the optimal level of advertising spending, as given by the Dorfman–Steiner theorem, relates to contribution margins, and the advertising/sales ratio.

Purpose: to understand the responsiveness of demand to advertising.

In Chapter 8, "Pricing strategy," we considered the price elasticity of demand, which represents the responsiveness of consumer demand (that is, sales) to a change in price. Advertising elasticity of demand is a similar concept that represents the change in consumer demand from an increase or a decrease in advertising. Price elasticities are almost always negative and less than 1.0, meaning that a given percentage change in price will result in a greater percentage change in sales—in the opposite direction of the price change. Advertising elasticities are almost always positive and less than 1.0; a given percentage increase in advertising spending will cause an increase in sales, but the percentage increase in sales will be less than the percentage increase in advertising.

Armed with an estimate of consumers' responsiveness to advertising, we can calculate the profit-maximizing amount to spend on advertising. We can do this by comparing the incremental contribution margin resulting from the change in sales revenue caused by the change in advertising spending and compare this incremental contribution margin generated by the advertising to the marginal cost of the advertising.

Construction

The advertising elasticity of demand is simply the change in demand from a change in advertising spending. This can be calculated by fitting an equation estimating advertising response as a function of advertising spending. To do this, you are likely to use historical data, the results of an advertising test, or both.

The formula for advertising elasticity of demand is

$$\text{Advertising Elasticity of Demand, AED (I)} = \frac{\text{Change in Quantity Demanded (\%)}}{\text{Change in Spending on Advertising (\%)}}$$

Unlike price elasticity of demand, advertising elasticity is almost certainly positive as increased spending on advertising should lead to greater demand. Greater elasticity means that demand is more responsive to advertising. When elasticity is higher, spending more on advertising is relatively more advantageous than when elasticity is lower.

Typically, managers fit a constant elasticity model to data. The fitted equation contains an estimate of advertising elasticity [the slope coefficient in the regression of ln(Sales) on ln(Advertising)]. However, when only two points are available, the same formula noted for price elasticity in Chapter 8 can be applied to estimate the point elasticity of demand at current spending levels. This point elasticity can be helpful in determining whether the firm is over- or under-spending, as we shall show.

$$\text{Advertising Elasticity of Demand, Constant Elasticity (I)} = \frac{\ln\left(\frac{D_2}{D_1}\right)}{\ln\left(\frac{A_2}{A_1}\right)}$$

In this equation, D_1 is initial demand (sales in dollars), and D_2 is demand after change in advertising. A_1 is the initial level of advertising spending, and A_2 is the level of advertising spending after the change.

Example MCS Associates sells refilled printer ink cartridges. It does all of its advertising online, mainly through banner ads. MCS's marketer wants to know the advertising elasticity of demand and runs a test using different levels of advertising spend in two periods that are thought to be comparable. The marketer is thus willing to assume that any difference in sales is caused by the difference in advertising spending.

Let us assume that advertising elasticity of demand is constant.

Period 1: Advertising spending (A_1) is $10,000, and quantity demanded (D_1) is $300,000.

Period 2: Advertising spending (A_2) is $10,500, and quantity demanded (D_2) is $303,000.

Advertising elasticity of demand can be assessed based on the impact of the increased advertising between periods A and B. Given constant elasticity, we must use the following formula:

$$\text{Advertising Elasticity of Demand, AED (I)} = \frac{\ln\left(\frac{D_2(\$)}{D_1(\$)}\right)}{\ln\left(\frac{A_2(\$)}{A_1(\$)}\right)}$$

What should you spend on advertising?

After we know what the advertising elasticity of demand is, the key question becomes "Are we spending too much, too little, or about the right amount?" An academic paper from 1954 answers this question and introduces the Dorfman–Steiner theorem.[2] This theorem yields an optimal level of advertising compared to sales, given the contribution margin of the firm.

The contribution margin of the firm matters because some firms and industries have relatively high contribution margins. In such a case, most of the value generated by increased demand (that is, sales) is captured by the firm, and so the firm is willing to spend more on advertising to stimulate demand. When a firm has low contribution margins, the firm requires a greater boost in sales to justify any increased spending on advertising.

Dorfman–Steiner theorem

The optimal level of advertising spending comparing sales is as follows:

$$\frac{\text{Advertising (\$)}}{\text{Sales (\$)}} = \frac{\text{Price (\$)} - \text{Cost to Produce (\$)}}{\text{Price (\$)}} * \text{AED (I)}$$

$$\text{or Contribution Margin (\$)} * \text{AED (I)}$$

Example MCS Associates sells each cartridge at $10, and it costs $7.50 in variable costs to acquire the used cartridges, fill them, and accept and dispatch the order. Thus, the contribution margin is 25%. Assume that the advertising elasticity of demand (AED) is a constant elasticity of 0.204.

The optimal level of advertising with respect to sales will be when Advertising ($)/ Sales ($) equals 25% * AED, so 0.204 * 0.25 = 0.051. This implies that MCS Associates should spend 5.1% of sales on advertising.

Say that MCS spent $10,000 on advertising and had sales of $300,000, this is an advertising-to-sales ratio of 3.3%. This gave a profit of $65,000 because Sales ($300,000) * Contribution Margin (25%) = $75,000 less Advertising Spending ($10,000).

The Dorfman–Steiner theorem suggests the firm was under-advertising and would benefit from advertising more heavily. The extra contribution from sales would outweigh the additional advertising costs. In this example, the optimal level of advertising is at an advertising-to-sales ratio of 5.1%, which is around $17,055 spent on advertising. This generates $334,507 in sales and in such a scenario, profit equals $66,572.

Table 10.5 illustrates an interesting effect called the *flat-maximum principle*, which states that profit is often similar over a wide range of advertising spending. Increasing advertising from $10,000 to $17,055 means a 71% increase in advertising spending, but profits only increase by 2%. The extra contribution generated by the advertising is not much more than the extra cost of the advertising. The good news for managers is that this means if your advertising spending isn't massively far off optimal, you won't lose too much from not being at the perfect level. Of course, a less optimistic interpretation is that constant elasticities may be only rough estimates of sales responses to advertising.

Table 10.5 Advertising and profits

Advertising spending ($)	Sales ($)	Contribution margin ($)	Profit ($)	Advertising to sales ratio
	= Scaling Factor * Advertising Spend ^AED	= Sales * Contribution Margin (%)	= Contribution Margin Minus Advertising Spending	Advertising/ Sales
$10,000	$300,000	$75,000	$65,000	3.33%
$13,000	$316,489	$79,122	$66,122	4.11%
$16,000	$330,179	$82,545	$66,545	4.85%
$17,055	**$334,507**	**$83,627**	**$66,572**	**5.10%**
$19,000	$341,956	$85,489	$66,489	5.56%
$22,000	$352,335	$88,084	$66,084	6.24%

What if advertising is an investment?

Almost all accounting standards suggest treating advertising as a current-period expense. Doing so benefits the firm from a time value of money (taxes) perspective but reflects the idea that the benefits of advertising spending (as opposed to, say, investments in equipment) occur in the fiscal year in which the ad budget was spent.

This misses the purpose of much advertising, such as that designed to build a brand, which drives more sales in future periods. Often advertising has a carryover effect: Yesterday's spending has benefits for us today and will have benefits for us tomorrow. How is the optimal level of advertising impacted by the fact that advertising effects can carry on from one period to the next?

The interesting result is that the optimal advertising-to-spending ratio is unchanged by carryover effects, given the assumption of constant elasticity. When advertising has greater impact in the long term because of carryover effects, the level of total sales rises. This means that the optimal level of advertising also rises, but the ideal ratio between the two remains the same. The key thing to remember is that the amount you should spend on advertising rises where advertising has a greater long-term effect but the optimal level of advertising still has the same ratio to the level of sales. However, our main point is that advertising elasticities, contribution margins, and advertising-to-sales ratios are linked in a way that can give managers insights into whether the firms are spending too much or too little.

Data sources, complications, and cautions

A manager needs to be able to map out (or at least predict) demand at various levels of advertising to use advertising elasticity of demand. This can be challenging for many managers who may not have the right data or be able to run tests to estimate elasticity.

Applying the Dorfman–Steiner theorem also assumes that the variables behave in a predictable fashion. Using advertising elasticity to assess the appropriate advertising-to-sales ratio, it is often necessary to assume that elasticity is constant. This is the sort of assumption that is often easier for academic economists to make than for practicing managers. As such, the "scientific" determination of advertising-to-sales ratios has been less widely used than the apparent power of the technique might suggest.

If the effect of advertising is not smooth, the models are much harder to apply. For instance, say that the impact of advertising spending is lumpy, and you need to reach spending thresholds before advertising has any impact. In such cases, raising advertising spending a little may not increase sales at all. Raising spending by a large amount, however, might, for example, allow a new media channel to be used, thereby substantially increasing sales.

The Dorfman–Steiner theorem result best applies to stable markets with well-established brands. When categories are forming (or undergoing fundamental change), however, brands often spend more than is immediately profitable (even after considering carryover effects) in battling for position (standards wars, for example).

Advertising elasticity and optimal advertising can assist in thinking about advertising effectiveness. The idea is to help managers approach the problem of how much to advertise rather than provide them with an answer that must be applied slavishly.

10.8   Return on advertising spend (ROAS)

The metric **Return on Advertising Spend (ROAS) is often used to describe incremental revenue generated per ad campaign dollar.**

$$\text{Return on Advertising Spend (\%)} = \frac{\text{Incremental Revenue Generated by Advertising Campaign (\$)}}{\text{Cost of Advertising Campaign (\$)}}$$

Purpose: to assess the productivity of advertising in generating additional sales.

The Return on Advertising Spend (ROAS) metric is designed to show the effectiveness of advertising spending. ROAS is not the same as but shares some commonality with the return on investment (ROI) calculations discussed in Chapter 12, "Marketing and finance." ROAS uses revenue while ROI uses profit to measure return. ROAS is widely used and typically much easier to implement than the MROI (Marketing Return on Investment) metrics described in Chapter 12. We elaborate on the advantages and disadvantages of ROAS compared to MROI in Chapter 12.

Construction

To calculate ROAS, find the incremental revenue generated from the campaign. The estimate of incremental revenue should be divided by the dollar amount spent on the advertising campaign. When it is possible to identify creative, production, and media buying expenses with specific advertising campaigns, a full evaluation of MROI would also include those expenses in addition to the costs of the media placement.

$$\text{Return on Advertising Spend (\%)} = \frac{\text{Incremental Revenue Generated by Advertising Campaign (\$)}}{\text{Cost of Advertising Campaign (\$)}}$$

To emphasize that only incremental revenue should be counted, the formula can be rewritten as follows:

$$\text{Return on Advertising Spend (\%)} = \frac{\text{Actual Revenue in Period (\$) } - \text{ Expected Revenue in Period Without Advertising Campaign (\$)}}{\text{Cost of Advertising Campaign (\$)}}$$

Although ROAS refers to advertising, the same calculation can be used to evaluate any number of marketing tactics, such as promotions, sampling, and additional sales force calls.

Example Mercury Enterprises spent $1 million on a new advertising campaign. Mercury's management estimated that baseline sales would have been $8 million without the advertising campaign in the period. After implementing the campaign, Mercury saw revenue of $12 million in the period. The incremental revenue was $12 million − $8 million = $4 million.

$$\text{Return on Advertising Spend (\%)} = \frac{\$12 \text{ million} - \$8 \text{ million}}{\$1 \text{ million}} = \frac{\$4 \text{ million}}{\$1 \text{ million}} = 400\%$$

Data sources, complications, and cautions

A key advantage of ROAS is that it reflects incremental revenues and advertising costs, two variables for which marketers are typically responsible. Also, estimating ROAS by dividing the estimated incremental sales likely to be achieved by the estimated cost of the advertising campaign being considered is useful to deciding whether to launch a campaign. The very significant disadvantage of ROAS compared to the MROI metric is that the former does not reflect incremental profits, while the latter does.

That said, when price–cost margins are the same (that is, do not vary across campaigns being evaluated), the ROAS metric yields the same rank ordering of campaigns as MROI and is much easier to calculate. If marketers can establish a benchmark minimum ROAS that represents a profitable campaign, the ease of application for ROAS may outweigh the disadvantage of its not reflecting margins. Indeed, in many cases, managers may not have access to the precise margin estimates needed for good MROI calculations.

If a good estimate of margin on sales is available, the minimum ROAS level that is profitable—which we can call the *benchmark ROAS*—can be calculated as 1/ Margin on Sales.

For example, a product with a margin of 50% would require an ROAS of 200%, or $2 of incremental revenue generated for each $1 of the advertising campaign. Similarly, margins of 25% would require an ROAS of 400% to break even, and so on.

Since the ROAS measure is typically estimated for an advertising campaign, it is usually an average ROAS for the total spent on the entire campaign. This is likely to be different from the amount that any additional advertisement would generate.

Finding incremental revenue can be difficult but it is crucial not just to consider total revenue. For more on the challenge of setting a baseline and estimating incremental sales, see Section 9.1.

10.9   Equivalent media value from sponsorship

Equivalent Media Value is used to directly compare the visibility gained from sponsorship to the value of impressions generated. In essence, you estimate what equivalent advertising would have cost.

$$\text{Equivalent Media Value (\$)} = \text{Number of Impressions Created (\#)} \\ * \text{Estimated Value per Impression (\$)}$$

Sponsorship metrics

Measuring sponsorship faces all the classic problems of marketing measurement. The benefits gained from a successful sponsorship are diffuse, including many long-term benefits. When 3M sponsors the Super Bowl, the company expects something from it—but not necessarily a massive increase in sales during the next week. When Coca-Cola or Visa sponsors an event, it expects long-term benefits, but measuring these benefits is challenging. This section looks at a number of the ways marketers try to determine the value created by sponsorship.

Purpose: to estimate the value of marketing impressions generated from sponsorship activities.

Equivalent Media Value is used as a simple way to assess the value of sponsorship. It involves directly comparing sponsorship to advertising impressions and asking, "How much would it cost if we had to pay for this many impressions?" What is delivered by the sponsorship is thus assumed to be directly equivalent to advertising exposures, impressions, or "opportunities-to-see" (recall, all three are equivalent terms).

Construction

To calculate Equivalent Media Value, you need an estimate of the number of impressions created. This number of impressions is then multiplied by the estimated value of a single impression to come up with the Equivalent Media Value, or the value of impressions created through the sponsorship.

$$\text{Equivalent Media Value (\$)} = \text{Number of Impressions Created (\#)} \\ * \text{Estimated Value per Impression (\$)}$$

The estimated value per impression is often described on a CPM basis (that is, per thousand impressions). When you use a CPM basis, you need to ensure that the number of impressions is also expressed in thousands.

In a single sponsorship, different types of exposures may occur (for example, in a stadium, on television, on the radio). Each type of exposure has a different value per impression. This is a big concern unless you can provide a relatively accurate estimate of the value of each type. If you can provide such an estimate, then it is a simple matter to create a value per type of exposure and total the types to find the Equivalent Media Value of an entire sponsorship. It is important to note that not all exposures are of equal value. An exposure where a consumer is paying attention to the medium is likely more highly valued by marketers than an exposure (or opportunity-to-see) where a logo moves past the viewer's sightline at speed.

Example General Image Inc. sponsored an opera. In return for the sponsorship, the company's logo was prominently displayed on the program and on billboards announcing the event.

The value of a billboard impression was estimated at $1 CPM. If the company had paid for a share of an equivalent billboard, it would have paid $1 per thousand people who had the opportunity to see it. (See Section 10.1 for further discussion of impressions and opportunities-to-see.) The billboards were centrally displayed downtown, and it was estimated that they generated 400,000 opportunities-to-see.

The prominent placement on the program was seen by the 25,000 people who attended the opera. Given that these individuals likely paid significantly more attention to the program than they would have paid to a billboard, the CPM was a more substantial $4.

Thus, total Equivalent Media Value is

[Value from Billboards ($1 CPM) * Opportunities-to-See (400,000)] + [Value from Programs ($4 CPM) * Opportunities-to-See (25,000)]

Equivalent Media Value ($) = ($1 * 400) + ($4 * 25) = $500

Data sources, complications, and cautions

Clearly, there are a number of assumptions embedded in this metric. For the number of impressions, it is likely to be hard to find a figure that is defensible (see Section 10.2).

Marketers also take a number of approaches to estimating the value of an impression. For example, they might compare each impression to a media source for which there is a more active market (for example, billboard, online, magazine advertising).

10.10 Sponsorship ROI

Sponsorship ROI brings the cost of a sponsorship into consideration. As a traditional ROI calculation, sponsorship ROI compares the return (the incremental profit from the sponsorship) with the costs of the sponsorship.

$$\text{Sponsorship ROI (\%)} = \frac{\text{Incremental Profit from a Sponsorship (\$)}}{\text{Cost of Sponsorship (\$)}}$$

▶

> *Sponsorship ROI* is sometimes also used to describe a variety of other ways to look at the success of sponsorship. We discourage such loose use of terminology, however, as it can cause considerable confusion and limits marketers' ability to communicate with colleagues from a financial background.

Purpose: to consider the cost of a sponsorship compared to the profit generated.

Sponsorship ROI is basically the traditional Return on Investment calculations translated into a sponsorship context.

A key task in assessing a sponsorship might be to divide up the return on a sponsorship into direct returns and indirect returns. Direct returns might include such things as MillerCoors gaining beer "pouring rights" at a sports stadium. This is a valuable concession, and it is relatively easy to estimate the value of such a sponsorship. There are a certain number of ticket holders, a certain percentage of them will buy beer, and these sales have associated costs. To work out the direct return, you simply estimate how much beer, on average, each patron will buy and multiply that figure by the number buying to estimate revenue. There will be significant costs involved in generating this revenue (for example, the product, serving staff, materials). Estimating and subtracting these costs allows you to calculate the margin and the profit.

Indirect returns are much harder to value as they are similar to advertising. They generally generate impressions, so measures such as Equivalent Media Value might be used for indirect returns.

Construction

When used correctly, sponsorship ROI is very much like a standard return on investment calculation (see Section 10.2).

$$\text{Sponsorship ROI (\%)} = \frac{\text{Incremental Profit from a Sponsorship (\$)}}{\text{Cost of Sponsorship (\$)}}$$

This can be divided into direct and industry returns:

$$\text{Sponsorship ROI (\%)} = \frac{\text{Incremental Direct Returns (\$)} + \text{Incremental Indirect Returns (\$)}}{\text{Cost of Sponsorship (\$)}}$$

As with all other ROI calculations, it is important to include only relevant returns and costs. This means if the profit or costs are not attributable to the sponsorship (that is, if they would have occurred regardless of the sponsorship), they should not be included in the calculation.

For sponsorships there are often two types of returns:

- **Direct returns, such as the rights to sell the product:** For example, a beer sponsor might be awarded the pouring rights in the stadium. This has a value that is relatively easily calculable. It is part of the return to the sponsorship and should not be netted off against the costs.

- **Other more indirect returns in the form of benefits such as Equivalent Media Value:** These returns can be harder to calculate but are often a very significant part of—or may even be the majority of—the return on the sponsorship. To be a meaningful measure of return, the indirect benefits must be something that the firm values. Specifically, one implicit assumption that justifies the idea that indirect returns are true returns is that the company would have paid for what it gains if the sponsorship didn't provide it. Equivalent Media Value is valuable if you would have spent that amount on media. The sponsorship saves the media costs, giving a return that is valuable to the firm.

Example Local Brew sponsored the City Football team. This involved pouring rights estimated at $10 million and Equivalent Media Value estimated at $90 million. The cost of the sponsorship was $50 million.

$$\text{Sponsorship ROI (\%)} = \frac{\$10 \text{ million} + \$90 \text{ million} - \$50 \text{ million}}{\$50 \text{ million}}$$

$$= \frac{\$50 \text{ million}}{\$50 \text{ million}} = 100\%$$

Data sources, complications, and cautions

It can be hard to generate reliable estimates for much of the data in sponsorship ROI. There is no perfect solution to this. One should create consistent measures of, for example, the Equivalent Media Value generated. Ideally, these measures should be agreed to by all parties involved in the sponsorship.

Returns to sponsorship should be added together in the numerator of the equation. Netting off direct returns (such as the profit from pouring rights) from sponsorship costs has the effect of lessening the costs. Generally speaking, this increases the reported ROI, showing an overly positive picture of the success of the sponsorship. This could also cause a problem if the direct profits are greater than the costs (for example, if pouring rights are especially valuable). This would leave the cost of the sponsorship as negative, and the resulting calculation would be confusing.

Example In estimating sponsorship ROI, Local Brew netted off the direct pouring rights of $10 million from the costs so that the cost of the sponsorship was assessed as $40 million ($50 million − $10 million). It valued Equivalent Media Value at $90 million.

$$\text{Sponsorship ROI (\%)} = \frac{\$90 \text{ million} - \$40 \text{ million}}{\$40 \text{ million}} = \frac{\$50 \text{ million}}{\$40 \text{ million}} = 125\%$$

▶

The sponsorship looks more effective this way merely because of how the metric was calculated—and this is not appropriate.

This problem becomes even more obvious if the direct returns (for example, pouring rights) are larger in value. Imagine if the total benefits of the sponsorship were the same but came from direct pouring rights of $60 million and Equivalent Media Value of $40 million. The correct approach to the formula is to see $100 million as the return less the $50 million cost, divided by the cost of $50 million. This gives a 100% return (as in the earlier example).

When netting off the direct pouring rights, the return would be $50 million, as before, but it would come from a negative $10 million of costs ($50 million costs − $60 million pouring rights) subtracted from the $40 million Equivalent Media Value.. This gives a numerator of $50 million as before. However, the negative $10 million in cost now forms the denominator, which gives a negative ROI—and that is certainly not the case here.

$$\text{Sponsorship ROI (\%)} = \frac{\$40 \text{ million} - (-\$10 \text{ million})}{-\$10 \text{ million}} = \frac{\$50 \text{ million}}{-\$10 \text{ million}} = -500\%$$

Netting off direct returns from costs usually merely overstates the ROI, but when direct returns are very high, it can lead to gibberish results. Not netting off the direct returns leaves the same correct answer in all these circumstances. You should not net off the direct returns from costs.

Caution on the casual use of ROI

There are ways that marketers use the term ROI that are not faithful to the financial idea of return on investment. For example, the ANA/MASB survey on sponsorship metrics saw 55% of marketers assessing the ROI of their sponsorships on sales but this does not include the investment. Those working outside marketing will frequently not recognize measures such as increased sales as being true ROI calculations.[3] Sales are a perfectly reasonable aim of a sponsorship, but showing increased sales is not the same as showing ROI.

Further reading

Association of National Advertisers and Marketing Accountability Standards Board. (2018). *Improving Sponsorship Accountability Metrics*, themasb. org/wp-content/uploads/2018/07/ANA-MASB_Improving-Sponsorship-Accountability-Metrics.pdf.

Bendle, Neil Thomas, and Charan K. Bagga. (2016). "The Metrics That Marketers Muddle," *Sloan Management Review*, 3, 73–82.

Dorfman, Robert, and Peter O. Steiner. (1954). "Optimal Advertising and Optimal Quality," *American Economic Review*, 44, 826–836.

Farris, Paul W., David Reibstein, and Ervin Shames. (1998). "Advertising Budgeting: A Report from the Field," American Association of Advertising Agencies.

Forrester, J. W. (1959). "Advertising: A Problem in Industrial Dynamics," *Harvard Business Review*, 37(2), 100.

Tellis, G. J., and D. L. Weiss. (1995). "Does TV Advertising Really Affect Sales? The Role of Measures, Models, and Data Aggregation," *Journal of Advertising*, 24(3), 1.

Tull, Donald S., Van R. Wood, Dale Duhan, Tom Gillpatrick, Kim R. Robertson, and James G. Helgeson. (1986). "'Leveraged' Decision Making in Advertising: The Flat Maximum Principle and Its Implications," *Journal of Marketing Research*, 23(1), 25–32.

Online, email, and mobile metrics

11

Key concepts covered in this chapter:

- Impressions and pageviews

- Media display time

- Media interaction rate

- Clickthrough rates

- Cost per impression, cost per click, and cost of acquisition

- Visits, visitors, and abandonment

- Bounce rate

- Friends/followers/supporters, likes

- Downloads

- Email metrics

- Mobile metrics

Introduction

In this chapter, we focus on metrics used in web-based and other marketing efforts enabled by the widespread use of information technology. Digital marketing has experienced exceptional growth, and the ecosystem remains messy. With respect to metrics, many advertising media terms, such as *impressions*, are used to describe and evaluate web-based advertising; other terms, such as *clickthrough*, are unique to the web. Certain web-specific metrics are needed because the internet, like direct mail, serves not only as a communications medium but also as a direct sales channel that can provide real-time feedback on the effectiveness of advertising in generating customer interest and sales. Billboards with 800 numbers or website names and even radio ("tell them JACK sent you") are also examples of direct-response advertising.

The use of cell phones has an especially significant potential for marketers, as consumers can interact with a firm online around the time of purchase. Offers can also be made to consumers when they are in a location where they can buy, and this is also likely to increase effectiveness. Of course, cell phones also provide much more data on consumer activity, and the privacy implications are still being debated.

With respect to metrics, the internet provides an extremely rich source of data. Indeed, marketers working in this area often have a profusion of data sources, unlike many in traditional areas of marketing. Lots of data are useful only if marketers know what to do with it. This chapter describes some key metrics and their strengths and weaknesses.

	Metric	Construction	Considerations	Purpose
11.1	Pageviews	The number of times a web page is served.	Represents the number of web pages served.	Provide a top-level measure of the popularity of a website.
11.2	Media Display Time	The average time that media are displayed per viewer.	Can be heavily influenced by unusually long display times. How data are gathered is an important consideration.	Measure average viewing time of media.
11.2	Media Interaction Rate	The fraction of viewers interacting with the media.	The definition of interaction should exclude actions unrelated to the media (such as a mouse crossing the media to reach another part of the screen).	Measure the relative attractiveness of media and the ability to generate viewer engagement.
11.3	Clickthrough Rate	Number of clickthroughs as a fraction of the number of impressions.	An interactive measure of web advertising. Has great strengths, but clicks represent only a step toward conversion and are thus an intermediate advertising goal.	Measure the effectiveness of a web advertisement by counting those customers who are sufficiently intrigued to click through it.

	Metric	Construction	Considerations	Purpose
11.4	Cost per Click	Advertising cost divided by number of clicks generated.	Often used as a billing mechanism.	Measure or establish the cost-effectiveness of advertising.
11.4	Cost per Order	Advertising cost divided by number of orders generated.	More directly related to profit than cost per click but less effective in measuring the impact of pure advertising. An advertisement may generate strong clickthrough but yield weak conversion due to a disappointing product.	Measure or establish the cost-effectiveness of advertising.
11.4	Cost per Impression	Advertising cost, divided by number of customers acquired.	Useful for purposes of comparison to customer lifetime value. Helps marketers determine whether customers are worth the cost of acquisition.	Measure or establish the cost-effectiveness of advertising.
11.5	Visits	The number of times that visitors come to a website.	By measuring visits relative to pageviews, marketers can determine whether viewers are investigating multiple pages on a website.	Measure audience traffic on a website.
11.5	Visitors	The number of unique website visitors in a given period.	Useful in determining the type of traffic generated by a website—a few loyal adherents or many occasional visitors. The period over which this metric is measured can be an important consideration.	Measure the reach of a website.

Metric		Construction	Considerations	Purpose
11.5	Abandonment Rate	The rate of purchases started but not completed.	Can warn of weak design in an e-commerce site by measuring the number of potential customers who lose patience with a transaction process or are surprised and put off by "hidden" costs revealed toward its conclusion.	Measure one element of the close rate of an internet business.
11.6	Bounce Rate (website)	Fraction of website visitors who view only a single page.	Requires a clear definition of when a visit ends. Usually considers bounce rate with respect to visits rather than visitors.	Determine a site's relevance and ability to generate visitor interest.
11.7	Friends/ Followers/ Supporters	Number of individuals joining a social network.	Success depends on the target group and the social nature of the product. This metric is unlikely to reflect the ultimate aim of a marketing campaign.	Measure the size of a social network (though not likely engagement).
11.7	Likes	Number who have favored a post/site/ organization on social media.	Measures engagement with the liked entity. Can be used to understand what posts resonate most with consumers.	Understand the relative popularity of social media elements.
11.7	Value of a Like	A dollar value ascribed to each like, follower, and so on.	Beware of causal claims. Consumers usually like a product on a social network because they favor the product offline. Merely generating likes won't necessarily change purchase behavior.	Find a dollar value for a like. (Do not use as a benchmark for spending on social media.)

Metric	Construction	Considerations	Purpose
11.8 Downloads	Number of times an application or a file is downloaded.	Counts the times a file was downloaded, not the number of customers who downloaded a file. It is often useful to monitor downloads started but not completed.	Determine effectiveness in getting applications out to users.
11.9 Mobile Metrics	Revenues divided by the number of users.	May help to indicate how effective an app is at generating revenues, but cost figures are needed to establish profitability.	Examine the effectiveness of an app at generating revenue from its user base.
11.10 Email Clickthrough	The clickthrough rate is the percentage of times an email is clicked on.	Measures how effectively email gains attention.	Determine the effectiveness of email campaigns.

11.1 Impressions and pageviews

As noted in Section 10.1, impressions represent the number of opportunities that have been presented to people to see an advertisement. The best available measures of this figure use technology in an effort to judge whether a given advertisement was actually seen. But this is never perfect. Many recorded impressions are not actually perceived by the intended viewer. Consequently, some marketers refer to this metric as *opportunities-to-see*.

In applying this concept to internet advertising and publishing, pageviews represent the number of opportunities-to-see for a given web page. Every web page is composed of a variety of individual objects and files, which can contain text, images, audio, and video. The total number of these files requested in a given period is the number of hits a website or web server receives. Measuring hits has largely fallen into disuse because pages composed of many small files generate numerous hits per pageview, giving an overly positive view of consumer activity.

Purpose: to assess website traffic and activity.

To quantify the traffic a website generates, marketers monitor pageviews—the number of times a page on a website is accessed. In the early days of e-commerce, managers paid attention to the number of hits—or file requests—a website received. Because web pages are composed of numerous text, graphic, and multimedia files, the number of hits a page receives is a function not only of pageviews but also of the way those pages were composed by their web designer. As marketing on the internet became more sophisticated, better measures of web activity and traffic evolved. As hits can be influenced by web page design, this measure is not as helpful. Pageviews is a better measure of traffic.

The Pageviews metric aims to measure the number of times a page has been displayed to a user. It should be measured as close to the end user as possible. The best technology counts pixels returned to a server and confirms that a page was properly displayed. This pixel count technique[1] yields numbers closer to the end user than would a tabulation of requests to the server or of pages sent from the server in response to a request. Good measurement can mitigate the problems of inflated counts due to servers not acting on requests, files failing to serve on a user's machine, or users terminating the serving of ads.

> Pageviews: **The number of times a specific page has been displayed to users.**
> **This should be recorded as late in the page-delivery process as possible in**
> **order to get as close as possible to the user's opportunity-to-see. A page can**
> **be composed of multiple files.**

A further distinction needs to be made as to how many times an advertisement was viewed by unique visitors. A marketer is typically interested in how many people viewed an advertisement, and the technology used to serve different ads to different visitors is widely available. For example, two individuals entering a web page from two different countries might receive the page in their respective languages and will also probably receive different advertisements. One example of an advertisement that is commonly displayed differently to different visitors is an embedded link with a banner ad. Recognizing this potential for variation, advertisers want to know the number of times that their specific advertisement was displayed to visitors rather than just the site's number of pageviews.

Internet advertisers often perform their analyses in terms of *impressions*—sometimes called *ad impressions* or *ad views*—which represent the number of times an advertisement is served to visitors, giving them opportunities to see it. (Many of the concepts in this section are in line with the terms covered in Chapter 10, "Advertising and sponsorship metrics.") Of course, if a page carries multiple advertisements, the total number of all ad impressions will exceed the number of pageviews.

Major sites have an ad server involved in presenting advertisements. The ad server can control who sees what and may serve different ads to different visitors or multiple ads to a single visitor. This can get surprisingly complex, and technical issues—such as the page refreshing—may complicate the data. Given the variety of ways an advertisement can be seen, it can be challenging to reconcile the data between a site and an ad server.

There can be considerable controversy about the serving of advertisements. The Media Rating Council defines a viewable impression as an impression that might have been viewed from an impression that was served for such a short period of time or in which so few of the pixels served that it should not count as an impression.[2]

Construction

Hits: **A count of the number of files served to visitors on the web. Because pages often contain multiple files, Hits is a function not only of pages visited but also of the number of files on each page. We detail this metric given its historical significance, but hits are more relevant to technicians responsible for planning server capacity than to marketers interested in measuring visitor activity.**

$$\text{Hits (\#)} = \text{Pageviews (\#)} * \text{Files on the Page (\#)}$$

Example If a website served three files per page and generated 300,000 pageviews, Hits would total 3 * 300,000 = 900,000.

Pageviews: **The number of pageviews can be easily calculated by dividing the number of hits by the number of files on the page.**

$$\text{Pageviews (\#)} = \frac{\text{Hits (\#)}}{\text{Files on Page (\#)}}$$

Example There are 250,000 hits on a website that serves five files each time a page is accessed. Pageviews = 250,000/5 = 50,000.

Data sources, complications, and cautions

Pageviews, page impressions, and ad impressions are measures of the responses of a web server to page and ad requests from users' browsers, filtered to remove robotic activity and error codes prior to reporting. These measures are recorded as close as possible to the user's opportunity to see the page or ad to most accurately capture the opportunities.[3]

For very simple websites, a count of ad impressions can be derived from pageviews if the percentage of pageviews that contain the ad in question is known. For example, if 10% of pageviews receive the advertisement for a luxury car, then the impressions for that car ad will equal 10% of pageviews. Simple websites that serve the same advertisement to all web users are easy to monitor, but for most marketers working in major firms, life is more challenging. They typically work with ad servers that have their own reporting systems to cope with the measurement problems.

The impression-based metrics quantify opportunities-to-see; they do not take into account the number of ads actually seen or the quality of what is shown. In particular, these metrics do not account for the following:

- Whether the message appeared to a specific, relevant, defined audience.
- Whether the people to whom the pages appeared actually looked at them.
- Whether the advertisement was clearly visible. The term "below the fold," borrowed from the newspaper world, is used to describe advertisements on a page that are not visible in the initial display of the page. Generally, if visitors must scroll to see the advertisement, they are less likely to be influenced by it.
- Whether those who looked at the page had any recall of the page's content or of any advertising messages contained on it after the event.

Despite the use of the term *impression*, these measures do not tell a business manager about the effect that an advertisement has on potential customers—that is, whether the advertisement actually made an impression on the potential customer. Marketers can't be sure of the effect that pageviews have on visitors.

Finally, pageview results often consist of data that include duplicate showings to the same visitor. For this reason, the term *gross impressions* may be used instead to highlight what is often a key point—that opportunities-to-see may be delivered to the same viewer on multiple occasions.

11.2 Media display time and interaction rate

Marketers use the Media Display Time metric to monitor how long their advertisements are holding the attention of potential customers.

$$\text{Average Media Display Time (\#)} = \frac{\text{Total Media Display Time (\#)}}{\text{Total Media Impressions (\#)}}$$

Media Display Time provides an important way of tracking the success of Internet advertising.

Marketers use the Media Interaction Rate metric to assess the effectiveness of a single media advertisement in generating engagement from its viewers.

$$\text{Media Interaction Rate (\%)} = \frac{\text{Total Media Impressions with Interactions (\#)}}{\text{Total Media Impressions (\#)}}$$

Media Interaction Rate provides an important way of tracking the success of Internet advertising in that it monitors the fraction of impressions that generate interaction on the part of the viewer.

Purpose: to determine how an advertisement engages viewers.

Rich media is a term used for interactive media that allow consumers to be more actively engaged than they might be with a billboard, a TV advertisement, or even a static display web advertisement. Rich media (or just media) metrics and audience interaction metrics are very similar in principle to other advertising metrics. Marketers want to track whether an advertisement is effective at grabbing and maintaining the attention of potential customers, and so they track how long people spend viewing an advertisement as a proxy for how interested they are in the content of the advertisement. The Media Display Time metric shows how long, on average, people spend engaged with the media.

The Media Interaction Rate metric tracks how actively involved potential consumers are with an advertisement. The big advantage of media is the ability of viewers to interact with it. Marketers using media can get a much better idea of potential customers' reactions to an advertisement simply because these interactions are counted. They can monitor whether potential customers are simply passively "viewing" the media on their screens or are actively engaged by taking some traceable action. A user who interacts is showing evidence of being more actively engaged and is thus probably more likely to move toward purchase.

Construction

> Average media display time: The average time that viewers spent with the media of an advertisement. For this metric, the marketer needs the total amount of time spent with the media and the total number of times that the media was displayed. It is a simple matter to create an average time in seconds spent with the media by dividing the total amount of time in seconds spent by the total number of impressions.
>
> $$\text{Average Media Display Time (\#)} = \frac{\text{Total Media Display Time (\#)}}{\text{Total Media Impressions (\#)}}$$

> Media interaction rate: The number of impressions of an advertisement that were interacted with divided by the total number of impressions of that advertisement. This metric tells marketers how successful any advertisement was at getting potential customers to engage with it in some way (for example, rolling the mouse over, clicking, deliberately starting a video). As an example, a media advertisement that was displayed 100 times with an interaction rate of 15% would mean that 15 of the impressions resulted in some kind of interaction, and 85 resulted in no interaction.

$$\text{Media Interaction Rate (\%)} = \frac{\text{Total Media Impressions with Interactions (\#)}}{\text{Total Media Impressions (\#)}}$$

Data sources, complications, and cautions

With many web-based metrics, data often seem abundant to marketers who come from the offline world. However, there are several measurement issues a marketer must address in order to convert the abundance of data into useful metrics (that is, to information and eventually to knowledge). For example, marketers usually cut off display times at some upper bound; for example, if a piece of media has been displayed for five minutes, a marketer may think it is safe to assume that the viewer has probably gone to make a cup of coffee or been otherwise distracted. The question of how long a displayed piece of media was actually viewed has some similarities to the question offline marketers face with respect to whether an offline advertisement was viewed. A slight advantage here goes to the online media in that most displays of media begin because of an active request of the viewer, whereas no such action is required offline.

Media display time, because it usually occurs for only short periods, can be influenced by unusual events. For example, if five people see a media display for 1 second each, and one person sees it for 55 seconds, the (average) media display time is 10 seconds. There is no way to distinguish this average display time from the average time generated by six moderately interested viewers each viewing the advertisement for 10 seconds. Such is the case with any average.

Marketers should clearly understand how the data were gathered and should be especially aware of any changes in the way the data were gathered. Changes in the way the data are gathered and in how the metric is constructed may be necessary for technological reasons but will limit the usefulness of the metric as longitudinal comparisons (that is, over time) lose their validity. At a minimum, a marketer must be aware of and account for measurement changes when interpreting such a metric.

Data for the Media Interaction Rate are typically available. Indeed, the metric itself might be reported as part of a standard reporting package. One important decision that has to be made in generating the metric is what counts as an interaction. The answer depends on the potential actions that the viewers could take, which in turn depends on the precise form of the advertisement. What counts as an interaction usually has some lower bound. For example, an interaction is counted only if the visitor spends more than one second with a mouse over the impression. (This guideline is designed to exclude movements of the mouse unrelated to the advertisement, such as moving the mouse over the advertisement to another part of the page.)

As is true of any advertising, marketers should not forget the goal of their advertising. Interaction is unlikely to be an end in itself. As such, a larger interaction rate, which might be secured by gimmicks that appeal to people who will never buy the product, may be no better than a smaller rate if the larger rate doesn't move the visitor closer to a sale (or some other high-order objective).

Media interaction time: The total amount of time that a visitor spends interacting with an advertisement. This is an accumulation of the total time spent interacting per visit on a single page. On a visit to a page, a user might interact with the media for two interactions of two seconds each and so have an interaction time of four seconds.

Video interactions: Video metrics are very similar to media metrics. Indeed, video can be classified as media, depending on the way it is served to the viewer. Similar principles apply, and a marketer should track how long viewers engage with the video (that is, the amount of time the video plays), what viewers do with the video (for example, pause it, mute it), and the total and specific interactions with the video (which show evidence of attention to the video). Such metrics are then summarized across the entire pool of visitors (for instance, the average visit might have led to the video being played for 12 seconds).

11.3   Clickthrough rates

The clickthrough rate is the percentage of impressions that lead a user to click on an ad. It describes the fraction of impressions that motivate users to click on a link, causing a redirect to another web location.

$$\text{Clickthrough Rate (\%)} = \frac{\text{Clickthroughs (\#)}}{\text{Impressions (\#)}}$$

Most Internet-based businesses use clickthrough metrics. Although these metrics are useful, they should not dominate all marketing analysis. Unless a user clicks on a "Buy Now" button, clickthroughs measure only one step along the path toward a final sale.

Purpose: to capture customers' initial response to websites.

Most commercial websites are designed to elicit some sort of action, whether it be to buy a book, read a news article, watch a music video, or search for a flight. People generally don't visit a website with the intention of viewing advertisements, just as people rarely watch TV with the purpose of consuming commercials. As marketers, we want to know the reaction of a web visitor. Under current technology, it is nearly impossible to fully quantify the emotional reaction to a site and the effect of that site on a firm's brand. One piece of information that is easy to acquire, however, is the clickthrough rate. The clickthrough rate measures the proportion of impressions that led to an initiated action with respect to an advertisement that redirected the visitor to another page, where the visitor might purchase an item or learn more about a product or service. Here we have discussed clicking on an advertisement (or link), but other interactions are possible. The consumer may access via a variety of smart technologies.

Construction

Clickthrough rate: **The number of times a click is made on an advertisement divided by the total impressions (the times an advertisement was served).**

$$\text{Clickthrough Rate (\%)} = \frac{\text{Clickthroughs (\#)}}{\text{Impressions (\#)}}$$

Clickthroughs: **If you have the clickthrough rate and the number of impressions, you can calculate the absolute number of clickthroughs by multiplying the clickthrough rate by the impressions.**

$$\text{Clickthroughs (\#)} = \text{Clickthrough Rate (\%)} * \text{Impressions (\#)}$$

Example There are 1,000 clicks (the more commonly used shorthand for clickthroughs) on a website that serves up 100,000 impressions. The clickthrough rate is 1%.

$$\text{Clickthrough Rate (\%)} = \frac{1,000}{100,000} = 1\%$$

If the same website had a clickthrough rate of 0.5%, there would have been 500 clicks:

$$\text{Clickthroughs (\#)} = 100,000 * 0.5\% = 500$$

If a different website had a 1% clickthrough rate and served up 200,000 impressions, there would have been 2,000 clicks:

$$\text{\# of Clicks} = 1\% * 200,000 = 2,000$$

Data sources, complications, and cautions

The number of impressions is a necessary input for the calculation of clickthrough rate. On the very simplest websites, this is likely to be the same as pageviews; every time the page is accessed, it shows the same details. On more sophisticated sites, different advertisements can be shown to different viewers, meaning the number of impressions of the advertisement cannot simply be estimated from the number of pageviews. The good news is that this metric is usually available as part of a reporting package. For clickthrough rate, you also need clicks, and the server can easily record the number of times the link was clicked (see Figure 11.1).

Figure 11.1 Clickthrough process

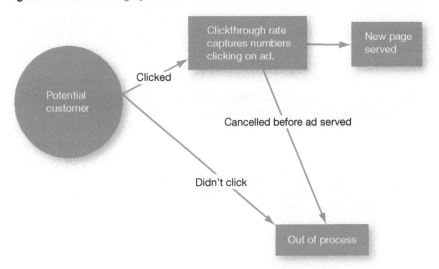

Remember that the clickthrough rate is expressed as a percentage. Although high clickthrough rates might in themselves be desirable and might help validate an ad's appeal, companies are also interested in the total number of people who clicked through. Imagine a website with a clickthrough rate of 80%. It might seem like a highly successful website until management discovers that only 20 people visited the site. Rather than see the 80% clickthrough rate as healthy, markets might do better to compare the resulting 16 potential customers who clicked through with management's stated objective of 500 clickthroughs.

Also remember that a click is a very weak signal of interest. Individuals who click on an ad might move on to something else even before the new page is loaded. A user might click on an advertisement by accident, or the page might take too long to load, prompting the user to click it. This problem has become significant with the increase in richer media advertisements. Marketers should understand whether their customers are using devices that are able to quickly display the requested file. Using large video files is likely to increase the number of people abandoning the process before the ad is served, especially if the potential customers have relatively slow connections.

As with impressions, try to ensure that you understand the measures. If the measure is of clicks (the requests received from client machines to the server to send a file), then there may be a number of breakage points between the click and the impressions of the ad generated from a returned pixel count. Large discrepancies should be understood: What role is played by technical problems (such as the size/design of the advertisement), and what is the role of weak interest from clickers?

Clicks are the number of times an advertisement was interacted with, not the number of customers who clicked. An individual visitor can click on an ad several times—either in a single session or across multiple sessions. You need to investigate your web analytics package to get a deeper understanding such as how many times an ad was clicked on by someone using the same browser. Furthermore, sophisticated websites can control the number of times they show a specific advertisement to the same customer. (A customer who logs onto a site can be tracked, which gives a marketer more information on what the person sees.) Finally, the clickthrough rate must be interpreted relative to an appropriate baseline. Clickthrough rates for banner ads are very low and continue to fall. In contrast, clickthrough rates for buttons that simply take visitors to the next page on a site should be much higher. An analysis of how clickthrough rates change as visitors navigate through various pages can help identify "dead end" pages that visitors rarely move beyond.

One can test the effectiveness of various web page designs by serving different pages randomly. The random serving of pages, when done correctly, allows a marketer to assume that those viewing the page are similar, and any differences in reaction can thus be attributed to differences in the web design.

It is possible to test a range of different sites and variations of content on the sites easily. The tests used for this are commonly known as A/B tests, or multivariate tests when there is more than one difference. Many tools that are available to help run these tests (for example, Unbounce) are affordable for a wide variety of organizations. In general, best practice is to test to find the best version of a web page or advertisement possible.

One useful approach is to classify metrics such as clickthroughs as micro-conversions on the path to the macro-conversion—an eventual purchase. The aim of a firm is not to generate clickthroughs (the micro-conversions), but the micro-conversions are a necessary stage in attaining the final aim, the macro-conversion. Describing them as macro- and micro-conversions helps keep the focus on the macro-conversion—the ultimate goal. It is still important to realize that failing on micro goals tends to mean you will ultimately fail on the macro goal.

11.4 Cost per impression, cost per click, and cost per order

The Cost per Impression, Cost per Click, and Cost per Order metrics measure the average cost of impressions, clicks, and customers. All of them are calculated in the same way—as the ratio of cost to the number of resulting impressions, clicks, or customers.

$$\text{Cost per Impression (\$)} = \frac{\text{Advertising Cost (\$)}}{\text{Number of Impressions (\#)}}$$

$$\text{CPM (\$)} = \frac{\text{Advertising Cost (\$)}}{\text{Number of Impressions in Thousands (\#)}}$$

$$\text{Cost per Click (\$)} = \frac{\text{Advertising Cost (\$)}}{\text{Number of Clicks (\#)}}$$

$$\text{Cost per Order (\$)} = \frac{\text{Advertising Cost (\$)}}{\text{Orders (\#)}}$$

These metrics provide a starting point for assessing the effectiveness of a company's Internet advertising and can be used for comparison across advertising media and vehicles.

Purpose: to assess the cost-effectiveness of Internet marketing.

In this section, we present three common ways of measuring the cost-effectiveness of Internet advertising. Each has benefits, depending on the perspective and end goal of the advertising activity.

Cost per Impression gives the cost to offer potential customers one opportunity to see an advertisement. CPM is the more commonly used version of Cost per Impression. It is the same metric but using per thousand impressions as the denominator. (For some reason technical people like to use *mille*, the Latin for "thousand," hence the M in CPM.)

Cost per Click gives the average amount spent to get an advertisement clicked. Cost per Click has a big advantage over Cost per Impression in that it tells something about how effective the advertising was. Clicks provide a way to measure attention and interest. An advertisement may look inexpensive in that it has a relatively low CPM. Of course, if an advertisement isn't relevant, it will end up with few clicks and therefore a high cost per click. Badly targeted advertisements can be very expensive, as measured by Cost per Click. If the main purpose of an ad is to generate a click, then Cost per Click is the preferred metric.

Cost per Order gives the average cost to acquire an order. If the main purpose of an ad is to generate sales, then Cost per Order is the preferred metric.

A certain number of web impressions need to be achieved to generate a reasonable number of orders, and the quality and placement of the advertisement will affect both click(through) rates and the resulting cost per click (see Figure 11.2).

Figure 11.2 The order acquisition process

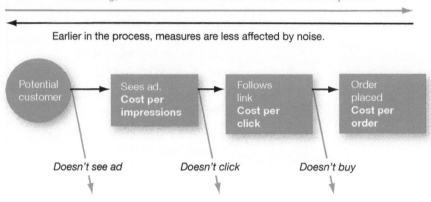

Further along, measures are better tied to overall business objectives.

Earlier in the process, measures are less affected by noise.

Potential customer → Sees ad. **Cost per impressions** → Follows link **Cost per click** → Order placed **Cost per order**

Doesn't see ad

Doesn't click

Doesn't buy

Customer out of process

Construction

The formulas are essentially the same for the metrics Cost per Impression, Cost per Click, and Cost per Order: Just divide the advertising cost by the appropriate number of impressions, clicks, or orders.

Cost per impression: Derived from advertising cost and the number of impressions. Cost per impression is typically expressed as cost per thousand impressions (CPM) in order to make the numbers easier to manage. (For more on CPM, refer to Section 10.2.)

$$\text{Cost per Impression (\$)} = \frac{\text{Advertising Cost (\$)}}{\text{Number of Impressions (\#)}}$$

Cost per click: Calculated by dividing the advertising cost by the number of clicks generated by the advertisement.

$$\text{Cost per Click (\$)} = \frac{\text{Advertising Cost (\$)}}{\text{Number of Clicks (\#)}}$$

Cost per order: The cost to generate an order. The precise form of this cost depends on the industry and is complicated by product returns and multiple sales channels. That said, the basic formula is

$$\text{Cost per Order (\$)} = \frac{\text{Advertising Cost (\$)}}{\text{Orders (\#)}}$$

Example An Internet retailer spent $24,000 on online advertising and generated 1.2 million impressions.

$$\text{Cost per Impression (\$)} = \frac{\$24,000}{1,200,000} = \$0.02$$

This led to 20,000 clicks.

$$\text{Cost per Click (\$)} = \frac{\$24,000}{20,000} = \$1.20$$

Only 1 in 10 of the clicks resulted in a purchase.

$$\text{Cost per Order (\$)} = \frac{\$24,000}{2,000} = \$12.00$$

This last metric is also called Cost per Purchase.

> Cost per customer acquired: **Divide the advertising cost by the number of new customers who make an order. Refer to Chapter 5, "Customer profitability," for more on defining customer and acquisition costs.**

Data sources, complications, and cautions

The Internet has provided greater availability of advertising data. Consequently, Internet advertising metrics are likely to rely on data that is more readily obtainable than data from conventional channels. The Internet can provide more information about how customers move through the system and how individual customers behave at the purchase stage of the process.

The calculations and data we have discussed in this section are often used in contracts compensating advertisers. Companies may prefer to compensate media and ad agencies on the basis of new customers acquired instead of impressions, although the agencies may be less happy as this pushes more risk onto the agency. The agency may find its efforts limited by the lack of appeal of the client's products rather than the agency's efforts to produce interesting advertising and get it widely distributed.

Search engines

Search engine payments help determine the placement of links on search results pages. An important search engine metric is Cost per Click, and it is generally the basis for establishing the search engine placement fee. Search engines can provide plenty of data to analyze the effectiveness of a campaign. In order to reap the benefits of a great site, a firm needs to get people to visit it. Previously we discussed how firms measure traffic. Search engines help firms create that traffic.

Although a strong brand helps drive traffic to a firm's site, including the firm's web address in all of its offline advertising might not be sufficient to increase traffic. In order to generate additional traffic, firms often turn to search engines. EMarketer estimated that social network spending reached $16.1 billion in 2019. Furthermore, $350 billion was spent on paid media in 2019 overall in the United States. Digital spending accounted for a significant 36.8% of this total.[4]

Paid search marketing (also known as *search engine marketing*) is essentially paying for the placement of ads on search engines across the Internet. The ads are typically small portions of text (much like newspaper want ads) made to look like the results of an unpaid or organic search. Payment is usually made only when someone clicks on the ad. It is possible to pay more per click in return for better placement on the search results page. Advertisers can bid to be displayed whenever someone searches for specified keyword(s). In this case, companies bid on the basis of Cost per Click. Bidding a higher amount per click gets you placed higher. However, there is an added complexity: If the ad fails to generate several clicks, its placement will be lowered in comparison to competing ads, despite a higher Cost per Click bid.

The measures for testing search engine effectiveness are largely the same as those used in assessing other Internet advertising.

Cost per Click

Cost per Click is widely quoted and used by search engines in charging for their services. Marketers use Cost per Click to build their budgets for search engine payments.

Search engines ask for a "maximum Cost per Click," which is a ceiling whereby marketers impose the maximum amount they are willing to pay for an individual click. A search engine typically auctions the placement of links and only charges for a click at a rate just above the next highest bid. This means the maximum Cost per Click that a company would be willing to pay can be considerably higher than the average Cost per Click it ends up paying.

Marketers often talk about the concept of daily spend on search engines: the total spent on paid search engine advertising during one day. In order to control spending, search engines allow marketers to specify maximum daily spends. When the maximum is reached, the advertisement doesn't show again until the next 24-hour period.

Daily spend can be thought of as the product of average cost per click and the number of clicks:

$$\text{Daily Spend (\$)} = \text{Average Cost per Click (\$)} * \text{Number of Clicks (\#)}$$

Example Andrei, the Internet marketing manager of an online music retailer, decides to set a maximum price of $0.10 a click. At the end of the week, he finds that the search engine provider has charged him a total of $350 for 1,000 clicks per day. His average cost per click is thus the cost of the advertising divided by the number of clicks generated:

$$\text{Cost per Click (\$)} = \frac{\text{Cost per Week}}{\text{Clicks per Week}}$$

$$= \frac{\$350}{7,000}$$

$$= \$0.05 \text{ a Click}$$

His average daily spend is $350/7, or $50 per day. This is average daily spend, which is not to be confused with daily spend limit.

Ad rank

Ad rank is the position of an advertisement served on a Pay per Click (PPC) basis on a search engine. The rank depends on the amount bid for each keyword as well as the relevance of the keywords, which determines the quality and ranking.

Search engines typically use auctions to establish prices for the search terms they sell and have the great advantage of having a relatively efficient market; all users have access to the information and can be in the same virtual location. Search engines tend to adopt a variant on the second price auction. Buyers pay only the amount needed for their requested placement; as such, search engine marketers can control the price they are willing to pay. The trick therefore is to know how much is reasonable for your firm to pay per click, which ultimately is a managerial judgment based on the benefits you expect to receive (for example, customers generated).

Search engine optimization

Search engine optimization involves efforts to get your website to rank more highly on search engines' organic (unpaid) search results. There is little reason not to try to improve your ranking on organic search. In practice, successful search engine optimization involves considerable skill and knowledge of how the rankings are constructed. The search engines have a variety of algorithms for ranking sites. Possibly the most famous is Google's PageRank, which works by counting the number and quality of links to a page to arrive at a rough estimate of how important the website is.

11.5 Visits, visitors, and abandonment

Visits measures the number of sessions on the website. Visitors measures the number of people making those visits. When an individual goes to a website on Tuesday and then again on Wednesday, this should be recorded as two visits from one visitor in the week. Visitors are sometimes referred to as "unique visitors." Visitors and Unique Visitors are the same metric.

Abandonment usually refers to shopping carts. The total number of shopping carts used in a specified period is the sum of the number abandoned and the number that resulted in complete purchases. The abandonment rate is the ratio of the number of abandoned shopping carts to the total.

Purpose: to understand website user behavior.

Websites can easily track the number of pages requested. As we saw in Section 11.1, the Pageviews metric can be useful but is far from a complete metric. We can do better. In addition to counting the number of pageviews a website delivers, firms also often count the number of times someone visits the website and the number of people requesting those pages.

To get a better understanding of traffic on a website, companies attempt to track the number of visits. A visit (known as a "session" in Google Analytics) can consist of a single pageview or multiple pageviews, and one individual can make multiple visits to a website. Visits captures the number of times individuals request a page from a website for the first time (that is, the first request triggers the visit). Subsequent requests from the same individual do not count as visits unless they occur after a specified timeout period. The exact specification of what constitutes a visit requires this accepted standard for a timeout period, usually set at 30 minutes, which is the number of minutes of inactivity from the time of entering the page to the time of requesting a new page.

In addition to tracking visits, firms also attempt to track the number of individual visitors to their websites. The Visitors (or Unique Visitors) metric captures the number of individuals requesting pages from the firm's website server during a given period. Google Analytics refers to these individuals as "users." Because a visitor can make multiple visits in a specified period, the number of visits is greater than the number of visitors. A visitor is sometimes referred to as a unique visitor or unique user to clearly convey the idea that each visitor is counted only once.

The number of users or visitors must be measured over a time period, such as the number of visitors in a given month.

Pageviews and visits are related. By definition, a visit is a series of pageviews grouped together in a single session, so the number of pageviews exceeds the number of visits.

Consider the metrics Visitors, Visits, Pageviews, and Hits as a series of concentric ovals, as shown in Figure 11.3. In this view, the number of visitors must be less than or equal to the number of visits, which must be less than or equal to the number of pageviews, which must be equal to or less than the number of hits. (Refer to Section 11.1 for details of the relationship between hits and pageviews.)

Another way to consider the relationship between Visitors, Visits, Pageviews, and Hits is to consider an example of a visitor entering the website of an online newspaper (see Figure 11.4). Suppose that the visitor enters the site on Monday, Tuesday, and Friday. In her visits, she looks at a total of 20 pageviews. Those pages are made up of a number of different graphic files, word files, and banner ads.

The ratio of pageviews to visitors is sometimes referred to as the *average pages per visit*. Marketers track this average to monitor how the average visit length changes over time.

It is possible to dig even deeper and track the paths visitors take. This path is called the *clickstream*.

Clickstream: The path of a user through the Internet.

Figure 11.3 Relationship of hits to pageviews to visits to visitors

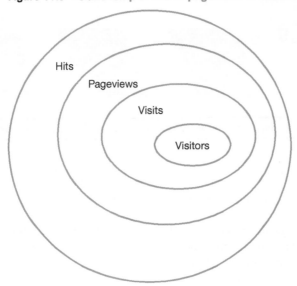

Figure 11.4 Example of online newspaper visitor

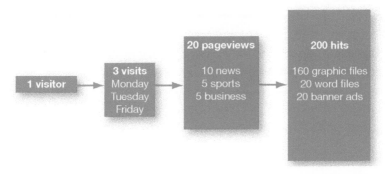

The clickstream refers to the sequence of clicked links the user makes. By using the clickstream on his or her own site, a marketer tracking at this level can help the firm identify the most and least appealing pages (see Figure 11.5).

The analysis of clickstream data often yields significant customer insights. What path is a customer most likely to take prior to purchase? Is there a way to make the most popular paths even easier to navigate? Should the unpopular paths be changed or even eliminated? Do purchases come at the end of lengthy or short sessions? At what pages do sessions end?

Figure 11.5 A clickstream documented

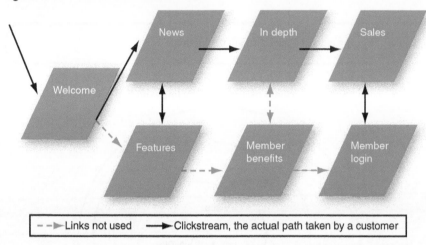

A portion of the clickstream that deserves considerable attention is the subset of clicks associated with the use of shopping carts. A shopping cart is a piece of software on a server that allows visitors to select items for eventual purchase. Although shoppers in brick-and-mortar stores rarely abandon their carts, abandonment of virtual shopping carts is quite common. Savvy marketers count how many of the shopping carts used in a specified period result in a completed sales versus how many were abandoned. The ratio of the number of abandoned shopping carts to the total is the abandonment rate.

Construction

Visits and visitors: Your analytics system will probably report these figures. Cookies can help servers track unique visitors, but this data is never 100% accurate (see the next section).

Example An online comics retailer found that of the 25,000 customers who loaded items into their electronic baskets, only 20,000 actually purchased:

$$\text{Purchases Not Completed} = \text{Purchases Initiated} - \text{Purchases Completed}$$

$$= 25,000 - 20,000 = 5,000$$

$$\text{Abandonment Rate (\%)} = \frac{\text{Carts Not Completed (\#)}}{\text{Customer Baskets Initiated (\#)}} = \frac{5,000}{25,000}$$

$$= 20\% \text{ abandonment rate}$$

Google Analytics uses Sessions as the denominator in this equation. This means that each consumer can convert more than once by visiting more than once. Be careful to understand which denominator your data represent.

Data sources, complications, and cautions

Visits can be estimated from log file data. Visitors are much more difficult to measure.

Companies often encourage users to register on their websites so they can gain a better understanding of their users. Often consumers aren't keen to do so—perhaps because they see registering as a hassle or as limiting their privacy. Indeed, marketers rarely know for certain that a user is unique. Instead, they consider visits from new browsers evidence of a new user and return visits from the same browser as returning visitors. This means a user who uses different devices will often show as two different users. Similarly, different people may show as the same user (for instance, when a family shares a computer).

To decide whether a visitor is a returning visitor or a new user, companies often employ cookies. A cookie is a file downloaded onto the computer of a person surfing the web that contains identifying information. When the browser returns, the web server reads the cookie and recognizes the visitor as someone who has been to the website previously. More advanced sites use cookies to offer customized content, and shopping carts make use of cookies to distinguish one shopping cart from another. For example, Amazon, eBay, and easyJet all make extensive use of cookies to personalize the web views to each customer. As users become more sophisticated, many are trying to protect their anonymity by using VPNs and by not allowing cookies or deleting them regularly. If visitors accept cookies, then at least the browser that was used for a visit can be identified. If customers do not accept cookies, this is much harder, and it can be a significant problem for a marketer's operations.

> **Cookie:** A small file that a website puts on the hard drive of a visitor for the purpose of future identification.

These metrics can be distorted by automatic activity (such as "bots") that aim to classify web content. To prevent this, estimates of visitors, visits, and other traffic statistics are usually filtered to remove this activity by eliminating known IP addresses for "bots," by requiring registration or cookies, or by using panel data.

Consultants may be able to help quantify your activity. For example, Nielsen, among other services, runs a panel in the United States and a number of other major economies.[5]

11.6   Bounce rate (website)

> **Bounce Rate is a measure of the effectiveness of a website in encouraging visitors to continue their visit. It is expressed as a percentage and represents the proportion of visits that end on the first page of the website that the visitor sees.**
>
> $$\text{Bounce Rate (\%)} = \frac{\text{Visits That Access Only a Single Page (\#)}}{\text{Total Visits to the Website (\#)}}$$
>
> **A High Bounce Rate metric typically indicates that a website isn't doing a good job of attracting the continuing interest of visitors.**

Purpose: to determine the effectiveness of the website at generating the interest of visitors.

Bounce Rate is a commonly reported metric that reflects the effectiveness of websites at drawing the continuing attention of visitors. The assumption behind the usefulness of the metric is that the owner of the website wants visitors to visit more than just the landing page. For most sites, this is a reasonable assumption. For example, sites that are seeking to sell goods want visitors to go to other pages to view the goods and ultimately make a purchase. Bounce Rate is also a measure of how effective the company is at generating relevant traffic. The more a website is relevant to the traffic coming to it, the lower the Bounce Rate. This becomes particularly important when traffic is generated through paid search. Money spent to generate traffic for whom the website is not relevant (as reflected in a high Bounce Rate) is money wasted. The Bounce Rate is a particularly useful measure with respect to the entry pages to websites. An entry page with a very low Bounce Rate may be thought of as doing its job of driving traffic to other pages, but the actual rate depends on a number of factors. As Google Analytics explains, "Evaluate and adjust factors that might contribute to your bounce rate, like site layout and navigation. Use only your past performances as a rubric, and try to improve your current bounce rate relative to your previous data. Provide enough time between changes to collect enough data to evaluate the impact the changes may be having on your users and their behaviors. Try using Content Experiments to help you."[6] A content experiment, similar to an A/B test, involves showing different pages to different visits (ideally randomly selected) and seeing which page performs best.

A low Bounce Rate is often a prerequisite for a successful e-commerce presence.

Construction

Bounce rate: **The number of visits that access only a single page of a website divided by the total number of visits to the website.**

$$\text{Bounce Rate (\%)} = \frac{\text{Visits That Access Only a Single Page (\#)}}{\text{Total Visits to the Website (\#)}}$$

Data sources, complications, and cautions

Data to construct the Bounce Rate metric, or even the metric itself, usually come from a website's host as part of the normal reporting procedure. Given how common it is that Bounce Rate is reported by default, it is a metric that is difficult to ignore. Construction of the metric requires a precise definition of when a visit ends. Leaving the site may be based on closing the window, hitting the Back button, or being timed out. (Google Analytics counts session timeouts.) After a timeout, a new session is usually started if the visitor returns to the website. A lower timeout period results in increased bounce rates, all else equal.

Reports may use the term *visitors* instead of *visits*. You should be clear what data are actually reported. Visits are much easier to track than visitors because when the same visitor makes return visits, especially to different entry pages, it can be difficult to connect the return visit to the original visitor. As such, visits is more likely than visitors to be used to calculate Bounce Rate.

This metric can also be defined and constructed for individual landing pages within a site. Indeed, the Bounce Rate for each landing page allows for more precise diagnosis of problem areas on a website. One must interpret Bounce Rate for a page, however, in light of the purpose of the page. For some pages, such as directions pages, where people go to find out specific information, a high Bounce Rate is to be expected.

The value of the Bounce Rate metric depends on the objective of the organization. Informational sites may develop a strong bond with their users through frequent short interactions, such as when the users check sports scores. Such an organization may be comfortable if many users do not visit other parts of the site and may not be too concerned about a high Bounce Rate. However, most companies are likely to want their Bounce Rate to be low and to actively monitor this important metric.

One of the most challenging problems in marketing (online, offline, and online to offline) is the problem of attribution. A consumer is likely to have been reached by multiple marketing actions prior to his or her purchase, and it can be impossible to say definitively which touchpoint generated a sale. Indeed, all touchpoints may have had vital contributions to generating a sale. For advertisers using a mix of online and offline media, it is especially difficult to categorize the cause-and-effect relationships between advertising and sales. Search ads might receive too much credit for an order if the customer has also been influenced by the fact that the consumer earlier saw the firm's billboard advertisement. Conversely, search ads might receive too little credit for offline sales where the consumer's interest was previously piqued by the search ad. Similarly, social media can sometimes play a big role in sales, assisting the final conversion but usually not as the last referral source clicked before a purchase. Given this, social media doesn't always get the credit it deserves for driving sales.

Attribution is challenging, but various assumptions are made. When all items influencing a purchase are online, a firm can attribute the sale in a number of ways.

With *last-click attribution*, full credit for a sale is given to the final touchpoint prior to purchase. With *first-click attribution*, full credit for a sale is given to the initial touchpoint—that is, the first contact on the customer's path to purchase. With *linear attribution*, the credit is shared equally between all touchpoints involved in the path to purchase. Clearly, it is hard to defend any of these assumptions as perfectly capturing what happens in the real world, but understanding the assumptions is necessary in determining whether the assumptions are useful approximations of reality even if they never perfectly capture reality.

Google Analytics

The tools Google has made available can help you understand the success of your marketing on a wide range of platforms. Google supplies an extensive range of assistance to those wishing to use Google Analytics. This material, which includes graded courses to work through, is supplied at the Google Analytics Academy, analyticsacademy.withgoogle.com/explorer.

11.7   Social media metrics: friends/followers/supporters/likes

> Friends/Followers/Supporters is a very simple metric that measures the number of individuals who join an organization's social network.
>
> Friends (#) is the number of friends of an entity registered on a social network. A high number of friends signifies an active interest in the owner of the page. If a brand has a high number of friends, this indicates a stronger brand with a loyal customer base.
>
> Likes is a similarly simple metric that measures the number of individuals who have favored a post/page/organization by clicking the "like" button.
>
> Likes (#) is the number of individuals favoring a social networking post/page. Both Friends/Followers/Supporters and Likes measure engagement by people on social media.

Purpose: to determine the effectiveness of a social networking presence.

Marketers want people to care about their brands and products. Various measures of engagement with a brand's social media presence indicate users' level of care.

We use the term *friends* to encompass followers, supporters, and other similar concepts. Friends are members of a social networking site who register that they know, like, and/or support the owner of the social networking page. For instance, a strong brand might have many customers who want to publicly signal their love of the brand. Social networking sites offer great benefits in allowing companies to develop customer relationships and can help a company identify and communicate with committed customers.

Likes are ways that individuals on social media show they favor a post or a page. They click on a like button for a page, comment, brand, and so on. Like is an extremely low commitment activity, and some people like many things in a day. It seems, however, a reasonable assumption that generally a larger number of likes is indicative of greater appeal.

Construction

The Friends and Likes metrics are supplied by a social network.

> Friends (#): The number of friends of the entity registered on a social network.
>
> Likes (#): The number of individuals favoring a social networking post/page.

> **Cost per friend (Like):** **The cost to the organization per friend recruited or Like generated.**
>
> $$\text{Cost per Friend (\$)} = \frac{\text{Total Costs to Provide Social Networking Presence (\$)}}{\text{Number of Friends (\#)}}$$
>
> $$\text{Cost per Like (\$)} = \frac{\text{Total Costs to Provide Social Networking Presence (\$)}}{\text{Number of Likes (\#)}}$$

Often the direct costs of having a social networking site are very low. This should not, however, lead a marketer to conclude that the cost is effectively zero. A site has to be designed, staff have to update the site, and marketers have to devise strategies. Remember when calculating the cost of having a social network presence that the cost should include all costs incurred in the provision of the social network presence.

> **Outcomes per friend:** **The precise downstream outcomes gained by the presence of friends. It is often very hard to track and attribute outcomes ("Did we sell more ketchup?") to specific social networking actions. This does not mean that an active social networking presence is not a vital part of an Internet marketing strategy; when designing a presence, the ultimate objective of the company needs to be borne in mind. For example, friends are often recruited to "vote" in polls. The percentage of friends participating is a simple example of an Outcome per Friend metric but is probably not the ultimate objective.**

Data sources, complications, and cautions

Success in recruiting friends is likely to depend heavily on the group of people who identify with the entity (for example, individuals, brands, companies, other groups). In the case of brands, some customer segments are more reluctant to reveal their brand loyalty than others, and therefore two brands of equivalent strength may have very different levels of social network presence. Similarly, the product involved is likely to influence the likelihood of registering as a friend at the social networking site. It is easy to think of some vitally important but more private products that are relied upon by their users but are less likely to gain public expressions of support than brands that are more related to public consumption.

It is very hard to objectively judge the effectiveness of social networking activities. Generally, having more followers or likes is an excellent sign of customer engagement. The more customers who have an ongoing relationship with a brand that they are willing to publicly support, the more likely the brand is to have strong customer awareness and loyalty. It is worth noting, however, that Friends and Likes, as with many other metrics, are most often intermediate metrics rather than an aim of an organization. It is unlikely that most organizations exist with the explicit objective of generating Friends. As such, it is rarely sufficient to report the number of Friends as a successful outcome of a marketing strategy without any additional information. This concern is only increased by the widespread practice of selling Friends and Followers on social media. Likes need to be tied to the objectives of the firm and should not just be a way of soothing the vanity of the marketer.

It is often appropriate to construct metrics around the downstream outcomes and cost-effectiveness of such strategies. A marketer would be well advised to pay attention to the costs and ultimate benefits of social networking presence as well as the clear potential to engage with customers.

The number of social networking posts that are engaged with may indicate successful engagement. A firm might therefore measure the number of posts that generate response divided by the total number of posts to give some idea of engagement with the social network.

Marketers may attempt to put a dollar value on social media. It is possible to calculate the value of a like as the difference between the value of someone who doesn't like a brand (for example) and someone who does. Value of a Like (or Value of a Follow) is sometimes calculated by subtracting the value of an individual consumer who did not choose to like (or follow) a brand from the value of an individual who did. It is important to note that it would be incorrect to argue that this difference is the value attributable to the social media strategy. It is unlikely that the social media strategy caused the entire difference in value observed between those choosing to like the brand and those not doing so. There are likely a number of other factors.

There are, thus, two major caveats that we have seen with the use of the Value of a Like metric, which leads to concern that Value of a Like can cause more harm than good. First, value to a firm should be the profit generated by the consumer and not revenue. Assessing Value of a Like as the revenue coming from consumers who like the firm overstates the value of a social media strategy as it ignores all the other costs of servicing these customers. Second, it is important to understand that this metric is not the amount that the organization can spend in order to secure a like (follower). Those who interact (positively) with a firm on social media are likely to already be positively predisposed to the firm. Encouraging other members of the public, who don't have the same prior positive predisposition, by, for example, rewarding those who follow a brand on social media, is unlikely to change the new recruits' purchase behaviors to resemble that of the more avid followers who followed without the incentive. When the difference in value is not caused by the social media strategy, it would be a mistake to use this as a benchmark for social media spending. Therefore, although Value of a Like is potentially an interesting number, the practical benefits of the metric are more limited than they might first appear.

Related metrics and concepts

Advocacy is exhibited when a consumer positively supports a brand or firm. The consumer might post a review of a brand or just give it a positive rating. The primary benefits of advocacy go to the brand or firm being advocated for, but other benefits exist. The subsidiary benefits of advocacy can go both ways. A retailer can benefit from consumers who advocate for a brand that is stocked in its store. Such advocacy can drive traffic to the retailer. Similarly, advocacy for the retailer helps the suppliers whose brands are sold in the retailer's stores to improve their sales.

Advocacy (#, %): The number of positive reviews a brand receives. This metric can also be expressed as a percentage by dividing the number of reviews that are positive by the total number of reviews.

11.8   Downloads

Monitoring downloads is a way of tracking engagement with the organization. The Downloads metric measures the number of times that an application or file is downloaded.
Downloads reflect the success of organizations at getting their applications distributed to users.

Purpose: to determine effectiveness in getting applications out to users.

Downloads—for applications for mobile phones, for MP3-style devices, and computers—are a common way for marketers to gain a presence with consumers.

Apps for iPhones, software trials, spreadsheets, ring tones, white papers, pictures, and widgets are examples of downloads. Such downloads typically provide benefit to a consumer in return for a presence on the device of the user. For instance, a weather app might be branded with the website of a particular TV channel and provide updates on atmospheric conditions. A consumer packaged goods company might supply an app that suggests recipes that use its products in novel ways.

Construction

The Downloads metric is supplied by analytics software.

> Downloads (#): **The number of times that an application or file is downloaded.**

Data sources, complications, and cautions

Downloads is a simple count of the number of times an application or a file is downloaded, regardless of who requested the download. It does not distinguish 10 identical downloads to a given individual from 10 separate downloads to 10 separate individuals, although these two situations may have dramatically different outcomes. In this way, Downloads is akin to Impressions, where a given number of impressions can be obtained through a variety of combinations of reach and frequency (see Section 10.3). Using your analytics package to see the number of downloads in unique sessions versus the total downloads should help you get a better feel for how many downloads were made by the same person. (Technically, this is often measured as downloads made by the same browser.)

A consideration in the counting of downloads is how to handle downloads that are started but not completed. One alternative is to keep track of both downloads started and downloads completed; another alternative is to pick one or the other (starts or completions) and use that measure consistently. As always, it is imperative for the user to know which convention was used in construction of the metric.

A further challenge is that downloads often raise problems in standard web analytics packages. This is because they often don't fire a pageview when they provide a file (for example, a .pdf, .doc, or .xls file). This means downloads can't be tracked as pages are. Downloads instead need to be tracked with event tracking, and event tracking involves code that creates a virtual pageview when an event is triggered.

11.9   Mobile metrics

> **Mobile metrics may be classified into metrics that are akin to website metrics and other metrics that focus on apps. Average Revenue per User (ARPU) is a widely used metric for app marketers.**
>
> $$\text{Average Revenue per User (\$)} = \frac{\text{Total Revenue (\$)}}{\text{Number of Users (\#)}}$$

Many issues in mobile marketing are similar to those in marketing aimed at users on computers. (*Mobile* relates to marketing using platforms optimized for use on handheld and other portable devices.) Mobile site metrics are similar to website metrics and can use web analytics packages such as the specialized mobile version of metrics on Google Analytics. These metrics allow you to better understand the users' interactions and experience with the mobile site. While the metrics may be similar to traditional website measures, one would expect the results to differ by channel to reflect, for example, the relative strengths of desktop and mobile search. Mobile marketing might lead to fewer sales on the devices but might have a greater role in providing support to the sale, such as downloads of coupons or store maps. (Clearly there may be challenges attributing credit for sales between the mobile site, the website, and the brick-and-mortar store.)

Your analytics package is likely to be able to tell you where your traffic is coming from (for example, 80% desktop and 20% mobile). Given the problems with making attributions, this is only a useful—but clearly far from complete—view of the reliance of your marketing on various platforms (the environment the software runs on).

The second strand of mobile marketing might be the use of apps. Ensuring that apps are downloaded is an element of mobile marketing. Once you have an installed user base, you will want to check how you are acquiring customers, how they use the app, and how long customers stay with you.

A marketer should be aware of the percentage of customers using mobile payments. Marketers should also monitor mobile coupons used. The principles are similar to those in the non-mobile world, but the data from mobile devices are rich and relatively clean. For example, people usually operate only their own personal phone, whereas people are more likely to share computers.

Construction

Here we highlight a selection of metrics related to mobile apps.

Session length: The length of time a user spends on an app.

$$\text{Average Session Length (\#)} = \frac{\text{Total Length of Time on App (\#)}}{\text{Number of Sessions (\#)}}$$

Active users (monthly/daily): The count of users who use the app during a given period (for example, a month, a day).

New User Acquisition and Retention Rate are similar to the metrics highlighted in Chapter 5. Retention can often be for a much shorter period in the world of mobile games, so it may be more appropriate to measure retention by the day rather than by the year.

Average revenue per user: The effectiveness of a marketer at gaining revenue from each user. Clearly, the importance of this metric depends on the purpose of the app. An app that is designed to build a brand or facilitate usage of a product may have no revenue associated with it, but this does not mean it is not a valuable part of the marketing strategy.

$$\text{Average Revenue per User (\$)} = \frac{\text{Total Revenue (\$)}}{\text{Number of Users (\#)}}$$

Store visits: A number of emerging applications meld the online and offline worlds. For example, store visits can be estimated using location-based tracking on mobile phones. This is anonymized data, so you can estimate the number of consumers who went to the stores—not which customers went there. When you have the number of consumers going into a store, you can compare this to an online action (for example, the number who downloaded a coupon) to assess how effectively the online strategy drives offline actions (for example, visits to stores).

$$\text{Online to Offline Conversion (\%)} = \frac{\text{Estimated Store Visits (\#)}}{\text{Online Actions (\#)}}$$

Data sources, complications, and cautions

Many of the key bits of data needed to assess mobile metrics come from analytics packages, such as Google's Mobile Analytics package.

While many of these concepts are the same across platforms, it is worth noting just how quickly the mobile market changes. In many areas, you might expect to see a payback to an investment in a few years. In mobile marketing, payback often needs to be much quicker. If a downloaded app doesn't pay back in weeks, it may never do so. The active lives of users of mobile apps may be quite short, meaning churn is likely to be extremely high. Indeed, you probably want to measure on a much shorter period to make any retention-related metrics more meaningful.

11.10 Email metrics

Monitoring email response is an important way of judging the success of email campaigns, individual emails, and lists.

Email metrics tend to measure the response of consumers to the email. Does the email lead to an action? For example, is an email opened?

$$\text{Email Open Rate (\%)} = \frac{\text{Emails Opened (\#)}}{\text{Emails Delivered (\#)}}$$

▶

> Bounce Rate in email marketing is a measure of the quality of the list and is essentially independent of consumer action. This is a notable difference from the Bounce Rate metric for measuring a website, which is based on the action the website generates from consumers.

Purpose: to determine the effectiveness of email campaigns.

Despite the popularity of search, email marketing retains a prominent place in the marketing efforts of many firms. Text marketing can follow similar principles. Many of these metrics appear similar to website metrics as they have a similar purpose. The metrics are focused on measuring the level of activity that is generated by the marketer's actions.

The simplest metric is email open rate, which is the percentage of emails that get opened. Clearly emails that don't get opened are relatively unlikely to motivate any further action.

Clickthrough Rate is similar to the search metrics and represents the percentage of emails that are clicked on. These might typically bring the consumer through to a website, where they could buy a product.

Email can annoy people, and unsubscribes capture the percentage of subscribers who ask to be removed from a list. All else equal, a list with a high unsubscribe rate is a worse list than one with a low unsubscribe rate. (However, a list on which consumers continue to receive email but aren't motivated to any action is not especially useful.)

Construction

Email open rate: The percentage of email delivered that gets opened.

$$\text{Email Open Rate (\%)} = \frac{\text{Emails Opened (\#)}}{\text{Emails Delivered (\#)}}$$

Email clickthrough rate: The percentage of email delivered that gets clicked on.

$$\text{Email Clickthrough Rate (\%)} = \frac{\text{Emails Clicked (\#)}}{\text{Emails Delivered (\#)}}$$

Email unsubscribe rate: The percentage of any list of email subscribers that opt out of the list in any given period.

$$\text{Email Unsubscribe Rate (\%)} = \frac{\text{Requests to Be Unsubscribed (\#)}}{\text{Total Subscribers at Beginning of Period (\#)}}$$

Bounce rate: The percentage of emails that can't be delivered. One notable complication is that Bounce Rate for email has a different definition than Bounce Rate for websites. For email, Bounce Rate records the quality of the list rather than any action on the part of the recipient in respect to the email. An older, poorer-quality list is likely to have a higher Bounce Rate as a percentage of recipients will have abandoned their old email addresses. Investigating the data further can help a marketer know more about the source of failure (for example, did the recipient's server accept the email before bouncing it back, perhaps because the email address has reached its maximum size?)

$$\text{Email Bounce Rate (\%)} = \frac{\text{Number of Emails Not Delivered (\#)}}{\text{Total Emails Sent (\#)}}$$

Cost per engagement (CPE): A similar metric to the other "cost per" metrics already discussed that measures an essential facet of a campaign. The marketer must define exactly what an engagement is, as it can be essentially whatever the marketer decides, based on the goals of the campaign. A marketer trying to gain email newsletter signups might pay a third party on a Cost per Engagement basis (that is, pay only for signups). Clearly, the third parties must be willing to work closely with marketers to establish the definition of engagement and associated tracking mechanisms.

$$\text{Cost per Engagement (\$)} = \frac{\text{Cost of Activity (\$)}}{\text{Number of Engagements (\#)}}$$

Data sources, complications, and cautions

The rules on what consumer information can be retained by marketers vary by country. In many parts of the world, a user must consent to receive email before a marketer is allowed to send it. The Direct Marketing Association (thedma.org) and American Marketing Association (www.ama.org) have helpful resources available.

There can be a considerable difference between emails sent and delivered, given abandoned email addresses, bounced emails, and full inboxes. Even emails that are delivered may be filtered away from the recipient's attention. Users may implement spam and other filtering, which can lead to reduced email response rates that have nothing to do with the effectiveness of the creative message sent. The recipients may simply never see a message, in which case it cannot have an effect even if the message is powerful.

The effect of a campaign can be monitored by tagging URLs in emails. It is then possible to see whether the message drives traffic to the site and which sites have traffic that results in conversions.

For example, one email creative might offer "Buy One, Get One Free," while the other creative offers "Two for the Price of One." Sending these emails randomly to the email list allows a marketer to assume that the recipients of each email were similar. Armed with this assumption, the marketer can then determine which creative is more effective, based upon which one is more frequently opened and clicked on.

Email opens and clicks can be used in testing different emails. When using an A/B test, a marketer sends out two types of email. In general, when testing, you should limit the differences between the emails as the differences constitute what is being tested. If you vary many things between the two emails, you need more advanced stats to tease out the effects. And sometimes teasing out the effects is simply impossible. For example, if two changes always occur together, it is impossible to assess the effect of each change independently.

Email marketing relies on the quality of email lists. The quality of lists, for a specific task, can be tested by observing the open and click rates for a message sent to several lists. Even high-quality lists may gain little response if an offer sent is inappropriate to the members of the list.

Further reading

Google Analytics Academy, analyticsacademy.withgoogle.com/explorer.

Marketing and finance

12

Key concepts covered in this chapter:

- Net profit and return on sales (ROS)

- Return on investment (ROI)

- Economic profit (a.k.a. EVA®)

- Project metrics: payback, NPV, IRR

- Marketing ROI (MROI or ROMI)

- Total shareholder returns

- Price to earnings (PE) ratio

- Market to book ratio

Introduction

As marketers progress in their careers, it becomes increasingly necessary to coordinate their plans with other functional areas. Sales forecasts, budgeting, and estimating returns from proposed marketing initiatives are often the focus of discussions between marketing and finance. For marketers with little exposure to basic finance metrics, a good starting point is to gain a deeper understanding of rate of return. *Return* is generally associated with profit—or at least positive cash flow. Return also implies that something has left (in order to have come back): cash outflow. Almost all business activity requires some cash outflow. Sales cost money that is returned only when bills are paid. In this chapter, we provide a brief overview of some of the more commonly employed measures of profitability and profits. Understanding how these metrics are constructed and used by finance to rank various projects will make it easier to develop marketing plans that meet the appropriate criteria.

The first section covers net profits and Return on Sales (ROS). Next, we look at Return on Investment (ROI), the ratio of net profit to amount of investment. Another metric that accounts for the capital investment required to earn profits is Economic Profits (also known as Economic Value Added [EVA]), or Residual Income. Because EVA and ROI provide snapshots of the per-period profitability of firms, they are not appropriate for valuing projects spanning multiple periods. For multi-period projects, three of the most common metrics are Payback, Net Present Value (NPV), and Internal Rate of Return (IRR).

Next, we discuss the frequently mentioned but rarely defined measure Marketing Return on Investment. Although it is a well-intentioned effort to measure marketing productivity, consensus definitions and measurement procedures for Marketing ROI (MROI), also known as Return on Marketing Investment (ROMI), have yet to emerge. The chapter ends with two sections on financial markets and metrics that combine financial market data with financial accounting data. These are useful when working with colleagues outside marketing, because of their relevance to the financial goals of for-profit firms.

	Metric	Construction	Considerations	Purpose
12.1	Net Profit	Sales revenue less total costs.	Revenue and costs can be defined in a number of ways, leading to confusion in profit calculations.	The basic profit equation.
12.1	Return on Sales (ROS)	Net profit as a percentage of sales revenue.	Acceptable level of return varies between industries and business models. Many models can be described as high volume/low return or vice versa.	Show the percentage of revenue that is being captured in profits.
12.1	Earnings Before Interest, Taxes, Depreciation, and Amortization (EBITDA)	Earnings before the subtraction of interest charges, taxes, and non-cash charges (depreciation and amortization).	Strips out the effect of accounting and financing policies from profits. Ignores important factors, such as depreciation of assets.	Rough measure of operating cash flow.

	Metric	Construction	Considerations	Purpose
12.2	Return on Investment (ROI)	Net profits over the investment needed to generate the profits.	Often meaningless in the short term. Variations such as Return on Assets and Return on Investment Capital analyze profits with respect to different inputs.	Describe how well assets are being used.
12.3	Economic Profit (a.k.a. Economic Value Added [EVA])	Net Operating Profit After Tax (NOPAT) less the cost of capital.	Requires a cost of capital to be provided/calculated.	Show profit made in dollar terms to make a clearer distinction between the sizes of returns than with a percentage calculation.
12.4	Payback	The length of time taken to return the initial investment.	Favors projects with quick returns more than long-term success.	Calculate return.
12.4	Net Present Value (NPV)	The value of a stream of future cash flows after accounting for the time value of money.	The discount rate used is the vital consideration and should account for the risk of the investment, too.	Summarize the value of cash flows over multiple periods.
12.4	Internal Rate of Return (IRR)	The discount rate at which the NPV of an investment is zero.	IRR does not describe the magnitude of return; $1 on $10 is the same as $1 million on $10 million.	An IRR is typically compared to a firm's hurdle rate. If IRR is higher than hurdle rate, invest; if lower, pass.

▶

Metric	Construction	Considerations	Purpose
12.5 Marketing Return on Investment (MROI or ROMI)	Incremental financial impact attributable to marketing divided by the marketing spending.	Marketers need to establish an accurate baseline to be able to meaningfully estimate incremental financial effects of marketing.	Evaluate productivity of various marketing efforts. The percentage term helps compare across plans of varying magnitude.
12.6 Total Shareholder Returns (TSR)	Changes in share price plus dividends received in period.	A key metric for looking at financial performance.	Measures how effective a firm is at making money for shareholders.
12.7 Price to Earnings (PE) Ratio	Compares share price to reported earnings.	Significant challenges exist in combining earnings with share price.	Shows financial markets' assessment of a firm's growth prospects.
12.7 Market to Book Ratio	A firm's market value divided by its accounting book value.	Has been used as a proxy for reliance on intangible assets marketers often strive to create, such as brands, number of customers, retention rates.	Show value not being captured in the financial accounts.

12.1 Net profit and return on sales

Net Profit measures the profitability of ventures after accounting for all costs. Return on Sales (ROS) is net profit as a percentage of sales revenue.

$$\text{Net Profit (\$)} = \text{Sales Revenue (\$)} - \text{Total Costs (\$)}$$

$$\text{Return on Sales ROS (\%)} = \frac{\text{Net Profit (\$)}}{\text{Sales Revenue (\$)}}$$

ROS is an indicator of profitability and is often used to compare the profitability of companies and industries of differing sizes. Significantly, ROS does not account for the capital (investment) used to generate the profit.

Earnings Before Interest, Taxes, Depreciation, and Amortization (EBITDA) is a rough measure of operating cash flow that reduces the effect of accounting, financing, and tax policies on reported profits.

$$\text{EBITDA (\$)} = \text{Net Profit (\$)} + \text{Interest Payments (\$)} + \text{Taxes (\$)} + \text{Depreciation and Authorization Charges (\$)}$$

Purpose: to measure levels and rates of profitability.

How does a company decide whether it is successful or not? Probably the most common way is to look at the net profits of the business. Given that companies are collections of projects and markets, individual areas can be judged based on how successful they are at adding to the corporate net profit. Not all projects are of equal size, however, and one way to adjust for size is to divide the profit by sales revenue. The resulting ratio is Return on Sales (ROS), the percentage of sales revenue that gets "returned" to the company as net profits, after all the related costs of the activity are deducted.

Construction

Net Profit measures the fundamental profitability of a business. It is the revenues of the activity less the costs of the activity. The main complication is in more complex businesses, when overhead needs to be allocated across divisions of the company (see Figure 12.1). Almost by definition, overheads are costs that cannot be directly tied to any specific product or division. A classic example is the cost of headquarters staff.

Net profit: A measure that calculates net profit for a unit (such as a company or division) by subtracting all costs, including a fair share of total corporate overheads, from the gross revenues.

$$\text{Net Profit (\$)} = \text{Sales Revenue (\$)} - \text{Total Costs (\$)}$$

Figure 12.1 Profits = revenues less costs

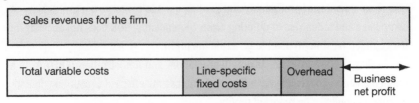

Simple view of business—revenues and costs

Return on sales (ROS): **Net profit as a percentage of sales revenue.**

$$\text{Return on Sales ROS (\%)} = \frac{\text{Net Profit (\$)}}{\text{Sales Revenue (\$)}}$$

Earnings before interest, taxes, depreciation, and amortization (EBITDA): **A popular measure of financial performance. It is used to assess the "operating" profit of the business. It provides a rough way of calculating how much cash the business is generating and is even sometimes called the "operating cash flow." EBITDA can be calculated by adding back the costs of interest, depreciation, and amortization charges and any taxes incurred.**

$$\text{EBITDA (\$)} = \text{Net Profit (\$)} + \text{Interest Payments (\$)} + \text{Taxes Incurred (\$)}$$
$$+ \text{Depreciation and Amortization Charges (\$)}$$

EBITDA can be useful because it removes factors that change the view of performance, depending on the accounting and financing policies of the business. Supporters argue that it reduces management's ability to change the profits they report by their choice of accounting rules and the way they generate financial backing for the company. This metric excludes from consideration expenses related to decisions such as how to finance the business (debt or equity) and over what period to depreciate fixed assets. EBITDA is typically closer to actual cash flow than is NOPAT (discussed later in the chapter).

Data sources, complications, and cautions

Although it is theoretically possible to calculate profits for any subunit, such as a product or region, often the calculations are rendered suspect by the need to allocate overhead costs. Because overhead costs often don't come in neat packages, their allocation among the divisions or product lines of the company can often be more art than science.

For Return on Sales, it is worth bearing in mind that a "healthy" figure depends on the industry and capital intensity (the assets per sales dollar). Return on Sales is similar to Margin (%) except that ROS accounts for overheads and other fixed costs that are often ignored when calculating Margin (%) or Contribution Margin (%). (Refer to Section 3.1.)

Related metrics and concepts

> **Net operating profit after tax (NOPAT): A measure that deducts relevant income taxes but excludes some items that are deemed to be unrelated to the main ("operating") business.**

12.2   Return on investment

> **Return on Investment (ROI) is one way of considering profits in relation to capital invested.**
>
> $$\text{Return on Investment (ROI) (\%)} = \frac{\text{Net Profit (\$)}}{\text{Investment (\$)}}$$
>
> **Return on Assets (ROA), Return on Net Assets (RONA), Return on Capital (ROC), and Return on Invested Capital (ROIC) are similar measures that vary in terms of how "investment" is defined.**
>
> **Marketing not only influences net profits but also can affect investment levels. New plants and equipment, inventories, and accounts receivable are three of the main categories of investments that can be affected by marketing decisions.**

Purpose: to measure per-period rates of return on dollars invested in an economic entity.

Return on Investment (ROI) and related metrics—Return on Assets (ROA), Return on Net Assets (RONA), Return on Capital Employed (ROCE), and Return on Invested Capital (ROIC)—provide a snapshot of profitability adjusted for the size of the investment assets tied up in the enterprise. Marketing decisions have obvious potential connection to the numerator of ROI (profits), but these same decisions often influence asset usage and capital requirements (for example, receivables and inventories). Marketers should understand the position of their company and the returns expected. ROI is often compared to expected (or required) rates of return on dollars invested.

Construction

For a single-period review, just divide the return (net profit) by the resources that were committed (investment):

$$\text{Return on Investment (\%)} = \frac{\text{Net Profit (\$)}}{\text{Investment (\$)}}$$

Data sources, complications, and cautions

Averaging profits and investments over periods such as one year can disguise wide swings in profits and assets, especially inventories and receivables. This is especially true for seasonal businesses (such as some construction materials and toys). In such businesses, it is important to understand these seasonal variations to relate quarterly and annual figures to each other.

ROI is often used to represent returns over a specified period of time. Later in this chapter we introduce Marketing Return on Investment (MROI), which is typically assessed on a specific marketing campaign.

Related metrics and concepts

Return on Assets (ROA), Return on Net Assets (RONA), Return on Capital Employed (ROCE), and Return on Invested Capital (ROIC) are commonly used variants of ROI. They are also calculated using net profit as the numerator, but they have different denominators. The relatively subtle distinctions between these metrics are beyond the scope of this book. Some differences lie in whether payables are subtracted from working capital and how borrowed funds and stockholder equity are treated.

Whenever you use financial accounting data, it is worth remembering that the formal objective of external financial reporting is not to provide a dollar value for any entity,[1] but to give background information in a standardized format. Therefore, the asset figures recorded in the financial accounts may differ substantially from an economic view of assets that a marketer might take.

12.3   Economic profit—EVA

> **Economic profit has many names, some of them trademarked as "brands." Economic Value Added (EVA) is Stern Stewart's trademark. Stern Stewart deserves credit for popularizing this measure of net operating profit after tax adjusted for the cost of capital.**
>
> Economic Profit (\$) = Net Operating Profit After Tax (NOPAT) (\$)
> − Cost of Capital (\$)
>
> Cost of Capital (\$) = Capital Employed (\$) * WACC (%)

> Unlike percentage measures of return (for example, ROS or ROI), Economic Profit is a dollar metric. It reflects not only the rate of profitability but also the size of the business (sales and assets).

Purpose: to measure dollar profits while accounting for required returns on capital invested.

Economic Profit, sometimes called Residual Income or the proprietary Economic Value Added (EVA),[2] is different from Accounting Profit in that Economic Profit also considers the cost of invested capital: the opportunity cost (see Figure 12.2). Like the discount rate for NPV calculations, this charge should also account for the risk associated with the investment.

Marketers are increasingly being made aware of how some of their decisions influence the amount of capital invested or assets employed. First, sales growth almost always requires additional investment in fixed assets, receivables, or inventories. Economic Profit helps determine whether these investments are justified by the profit earned. Second, the marketing improvements in supply chain management and channel coordination often show up in reduced investments in inventories and receivables. In some cases, even if sales and profit fall, the investment reduction can be worthwhile. Economic profit is a metric that helps assess whether these trade-offs are being made correctly.

Figure 12.2 EVA is after-tax profit minus a charge for capital usage

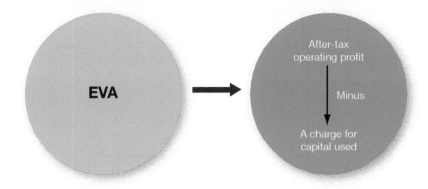

Construction

Economic Profit/EVA can be calculated in three stages:

1. Determine NOPAT.
2. Calculate the cost of capital by multiplying capital employed by the weighted average cost of capital.[3]
3. Subtract the cost of capital from NOPAT.

$$\text{Economic Profit (\$) = Net Operating Profit After Tax (NOPAT) (\$) – Cost of Capital (\$)}$$

$$\text{Cost of Capital (\$) = Capital Employed (\$) * WACC (\%)}$$

> **Economic profit:** A measure of profit in dollar terms. If profits are less than the cost of capital, the firm has lost value. Where economic profit is positive, value has been generated.

Example A company has profits—NOPAT—of $145,000. It has a straightforward capital structure, with half of the capital supplied by shareholders. This equity expects a 12% return on the risk the shareholders are taking by investing in this company. The other half of the capital comes from a bank at a charge of 6%. Therefore,

$$\text{Weighted Average Cost of Capital (WACC) = Equity (12\% * 50\%)}$$
$$\text{+ Debt (6\% * 50\%) = 9\%}$$

The company employs total capital of $1 million. Multiplying the capital employed by the WACC gives us an estimate of the profit (return) required to cover the opportunity cost of capital used in the business:

$$\text{Cost of Capital = Capital Employed * WACC}$$
$$= \$1,000,000 * 9\%$$
$$= \$90,000$$

Economic profit is the surplus of profits over the expected return to capital.

$$\text{Economic Profit = NOPAT – Cost of Capital}$$
$$= \$145,000 – \$90,000$$
$$= \$55,000$$

Data sources, complications, and cautions

Economic Profit can give a different ranking for companies than does Return on Investment. This is especially true for companies, such as Walmart and Microsoft, that have experienced (achieved) high rates of growth in sales. Judging the historic results of the giant U.S. retailer Walmart by many conventional metrics would disguise its success. Although the rates of return are generally good, they hardly imply the rise to dominance that the company has achieved. Economic Profit reflects both Walmart's rapid sales growth and its adequate return on the capital invested. The Economic Profit metric shows the magnitude of profits after the cost of capital has been subtracted. It combines the idea of a return on investment with a sense of volume of profits. Simply put, Walmart achieved the trick of continuing to gain decent returns on a dramatically increasing pool of capital.

12.4　Evaluating multi-period investments

> **Multi-period investments are commonly evaluated with three metrics:**
>
> Payback (#) = The number of periods required to "pay back" or "return" the initial investment
>
> Net Present Value (NPV) ($) = The discounted value of future cash flows minus the initial investment
>
> Internal Rate of Return (IRR) (%) = The discount rate that results in an NPV of zero
>
> **These three metrics deal with economic consequences occurring at different points in time.**

Purpose: to evaluate investments with financial consequences spanning multiple periods.

"Investment" is a word businesspeople like. It has all sorts of positive connotations of future success and wise stewardship. However, because not all investments can be pursued, those available must be ranked against each other. Also, some investments are not attractive even if we have enough cash to fund them. In a single period, the return on any investment is merely the net profits produced in the time considered divided by the capital invested. Evaluation of investments that produce returns over multiple periods requires a more complicated analysis—one that considers both the magnitude and timing of the returns.

> **Payback (#):** The time (usually years) required to generate the (undiscounted) cash flow to recover the initial investment.
>
> **Net present value (NPV) ($):** The present (discounted) value of future cash inflows minus the present value of the investment and any associated future cash outflows.
>
> **Internal rate of return (IRR) (%):** The discount rate that results in a net present value of zero for a series of future cash flows after accounting for the initial investment.

Construction

Payback

Payback is the number of years required for an investment to return the initial investment. Projects with a shorter payback period are regarded more favorably because they allow the resources to be reused quickly. Also, generally speaking, the shorter the payback period, the less uncertainty is involved in receiving the returns. Of course, the main flaw with payback period analysis is that it ignores all cash flows after the payback period. As a consequence, projects that are attractive but that do not produce immediate returns will be penalized with this metric.

Example Harry is considering buying a small chain of hairdressing salons. He estimates that the salons will produce a net income of $15,000 a year for at least five years. Harry's payback on this investment is $50,000/$15,000, or 3.33 years.

Net present value

Net Present Value (NPV) is the discounted value of the cash flows associated with a project.

The present value of a dollar received in a given number of periods in the future is

$$\text{Discounted Value (\$)} = \frac{\text{Cash Flow (\$)} * 1}{[1 + \text{Discount Rate (\%)}]^{\wedge} \text{Period (\#)}}$$

This is easiest to see when set out in spreadsheet form.

A 10% discount rate applied to $1 received now and in each of the next three years reduces in value over time, as shown in Table 12.1.

Table 12.1 Discounting nominal values

	Year 0	Year 1	Year 2	Year 3
Discount Formula	1	1/(1 + 10%) ^ 1	1/(1 + 10%) ^ 2	1/(1 + 10%) ^ 3
Discount Factor	1	90.9%	82.6%	75.1%
Undiscounted Cash Flows	$1.00	$1.00	$1.00	$1.00
Present Value	$1.00	$0.91	$0.83	$0.75

Spreadsheets make it easy to calculate the appropriate discount factors.

Example Harry wants to know the dollar value of his business opportunity. Although he is confident about the success of the venture, all future cash flows have a level of uncertainty. After receiving a friend's advice, Harry decides a 10% discount rate on future cash flows is about right.

He enters all the cash flow details into a spreadsheet (see Table 12.2).[4] Harry works out the discount factor using the formula and his discount rate of 10%:

$$\text{Discounted Value} = \frac{\text{Cash Flow} * 1}{(1 + \text{Discount Rate}) \char`\^ \text{Year}}$$

$$\text{For Year 1 Cash Flows} = \frac{\$15,000 * 1}{(1 + 10\%) \char`\^ 1} = \frac{\$15,000 * 1}{110\%}$$

$$= \$15,000 * 90.9\% = \$13,636$$

Table 12.2 Discounted cash flow (10% discount rate)

	Year 0	Year 1	Year 2	Year 3	Year 4	Year 5	Total
Investment	($50,000)						($50,000)
Income		$15,000	$15,000	$15,000	$15,000	$15,000	$75,000
Undiscounted Cash Flow	($50,000)	$15,000	$15,000	$15,000	$15,000	$15,000	$25,000
Discount Formula	1/(1+ DR)^0	1/(1+ DR)^1	1/(1+ DR)^2	1/(1+ DR)^3	1/(1+ DR)^4	1/(1+ DR)^5	
Discount Factor	100.0%	90.9%	82.6%	75.1%	68.3%	62.1%	
Present Value	($50,000)	$13,636	$12,397	$11,270	$10,245	$9,314	$6,862

The NPV of Harry's project is $6,862. Of course, the NPV is lower than the sum of the undiscounted cash flows. NPV accounts for the fact that, on a per-dollar basis, cash flows received in the future are less valuable than cash in hand.

Internal rate of return

The internal rate of return is the percentage return made on an investment over a period of time. The internal rate of return is a feature supplied on most spreadsheets.

> **Internal rate of return (IRR): The discount rate for which the net present value of the investment is zero.**

The IRR is especially useful because it can be compared to a company's hurdle rate. The hurdle rate is the necessary percentage return to justify a project. Thus, a company might decide only to undertake projects with a return greater than 12%. Projects that have an IRR greater than 12% get the green light; all others are thrown in the bin.

Example In Harry's case, we can see that IRR is an easy calculation to perform by using a software package: Simply enter the values given in the relevant periods on the spreadsheet (see Table 12.3).

Year 0—now—is when Harry makes the initial investment; each of the next five years sees a $15,000 return. Applying the IRR function gives a return of 15.24%.

Table 12.3 Five-year cash flow

Cell ref	A	B	C	D	E	F	G
1		Year 0	Year 1	Year 2	Year 3	Year 4	Year 5
2	Cash flows	($50,000)	$15,000	$15,000	$15,000	$15,000	$15,000

In Microsoft Excel, the function is = IRR(B2:G2). This function tells Excel to perform an IRR on the range B2 (cash flow for year 0) to G2 (cash flow for year 5). The result in this case is 15.24%.

IRR and NPV are related

Remember that the Internal Rate of Return is the percentage discount rate at which the Net Present Value of the operation is zero. Thus, companies using a hurdle rate are really saying that they will only accept projects where the net present value is positive at the discount rate they specify as the hurdle rate. That is, they will accept projects only if the IRR is greater than the hurdle rate.

Data sources, complications, and cautions

Payback and IRR calculations require estimates of cash flows. The cash flows are the monies received and paid out that are associated with the project per period, including the initial investment. Topics that are beyond the scope of this book include the time frame over which forecasts of cash flows are made and how to handle the "terminal value" (the value associated with the opportunity at the end of the last period).[5] Net present value calculations require the same inputs as payback and IRR plus one other: the *discount rate.* Typically, the discount rate is decided at the corporate level. This rate has a dual purpose to compensate for the following:

- The time value of money
- The risk inherent in the activity

A general principle to employ is that the riskier the project, the greater the discount rate to use. Considerations for setting the discounts rates are beyond the scope of this book. We can simply observe that, ideally, separate discount rates would be assessed for each individual project because risk varies by activity. A government contract might be a fairly certain project, but an investment by the same company in buying a fashion retailer could carry a lot of risk. The same concern occurs when companies set a single hurdle rate for all projects assessed using IRR analysis.

Cash flows and net profits

In our examples, cash flow equals profit, but in many cases, they are different.

A note for users of spreadsheet programs

Microsoft Excel has an NPV calculator, which can be very useful in calculating NPV. The formula to use is NPV (rate, value1, value2, etc.) where the rate is the discount rate and the values are the cash flows by year, so year 1 = value1, year 2 = value2, and so on.

The calculation starts in period 1, and the cash flow for that period is discounted. If you are using the convention of having the investment in the period before (that is, period 0), you should not discount it but add it back outside the formula. Therefore, Harry's returns discounted at 10% would be

$$= \text{NPV(rate, value1, value2, value3, value4, value5)}$$
$$= \text{NPV(10\%, 15000, 15000, 15000, 15000, 15000)}$$

This is equal to \$56,861.80 minus the initial investment of \$50,000, or an NPV of \$6,861.80, as demonstrated fully in the example.

12.5 Marketing return on investment

Marketing Return on Investment (MROI), also known as Return on Marketing Investment (ROMI), is a relatively new metric. It is not like the other ROI metrics because marketing is not the same kind of investment. Marketing spending is typically expensed in the current period in accounting records, which means current accounting practices do not classify most marketing expenditures as an investment. Whereas investment tends to be money that is tied up in plants and inventories, marketing funds are typically risked.

There are many variations in the way this metric has been used, and although no authoritative sources for defining it exist, we believe the consensus of usage refers to MROI as the dollar-denominated estimate of the incremental financial value to

▶

the entity generated by identifiable marketing expenditures, less the cost of those expenditures as a percentage of the same expenditures:

$$\text{Marketing Return on Investment (MROI) (\%)} = \frac{\text{Incremental Financial Value Created by Marketing (\$)} - \text{Cost of Marketing (\$)}}{\text{Cost of Marketing (\$)}}$$

There are many ways to estimate the financial value generated by marketing. The most commonly employed method is to estimate incremental contribution margin, net of marketing, generated by marketing divided by the marketing spend.

Purpose: to measure the rate at which spending on marketing contributes to profits.

Marketers are under more and more pressure to "show a return" on their activities. However, it is often unclear exactly what this means. Certainly, marketing spending is often not treated as an "investment" in current accounting practice. There is usually no tangible asset—nor even a predictable (quantifiable) result to show for the spending—but marketers still want to emphasize that their activities contribute to financial health. Some might argue that marketing should be considered an expense, and the focus should be on whether it is a necessary expense. Marketers, however, typically believe that many of their activities generate lasting results and therefore should be considered investments in the future of the business.[6]

Marketing return on investment (MROI) or return on marketing investment (ROMI): The incremental financial value attributable to marketing (net of marketing spending), divided by the marketing "invested" or risked.

Construction

A necessary step in calculating MROI is the estimation of the incremental financial value attributable to marketing. This incremental value can be the total attributable to marketing or the marginal value attributable to a new marketing initiative. The following example and Figure 12.3 should help clarify the difference:

Y_0 = Baseline financial value (with $0 marketing spending)

Y_1 = Financial value at marketing spending level X_1

Y_2 = Financial value at marketing spending level X_2

In this case, the difference between X_1 and X_2 represents the cost of an incremental marketing budget item that is to be evaluated, such as an advertising campaign or a trade show.

Three important marketing calculations can be illustrated with Figure 12.3.

Financial value attributable to marketing $= Y_2 - Y_0$: **The increase in financial value attributable to the entire marketing budget (equal to financial value with marketing minus baseline financial value).**

Marketing return on investment (MROI) $= [(Y_2 - Y_0) - X_2]/X_2$: **The financial value created by all marketing activities divided by the cost of those activities.**

Return on incremental marketing investment (ROIMI) $= [(Y_2 - Y_1) - (X_2 - X_1)]/(X_2 - X_1)$: **The incremental financial value due to the incremental marketing spending divided by the amount of incremental spending.**

Figure 12.3 Evaluating the return to marketing

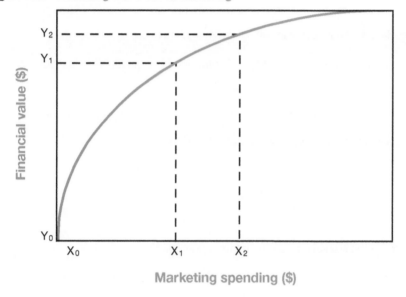

For some industries, revenue-based metrics might be useful but must be interpreted differently. (See the Return on Advertising Spend metric in Section 10.8.) MROI and ROIMI, as shown in the following examples, are generally more direct measures of marketing's effect on firm profits.

$$\text{Marketing Return on Investment (MROI) (\%)} = \frac{\text{Incremental Financial Value Created by Marketing (\$)} - \text{Cost of Marketing (\$)}}{\text{Cost of Marketing (\$)}}$$

Example A farm equipment company was considering a direct mail campaign to remind customers to have tractors serviced before spring planting. The campaign was expected to cost $1,000 and to increase revenues from $45,000 to $50,000. Baseline revenues for tractor servicing (with no marketing) were estimated at $25,000. The direct mail campaign was in addition to the regular advertising and other marketing activities and would cost $6,000. The firm planned to use contribution to assess financial value; the contribution on tractor servicing revenues (after parts and labor) averaged 60%.

Example Each of the metrics in this section can be calculated from the information in the example. First, calculate the financial value with marketing and direct mail:

$$Y_2 = \text{Revenue (\$50,000)} * \text{Contribution Margin (60\%)} = \$30,000$$

Calculate the financial value with all the marketing except the direct mail:

$$Y_1 = \text{Revenue (\$45,000)} * \text{Contribution Margin (60\%)} = \$27,000$$

Calculate financial value with no marketing:

$$Y_0 = \text{Revenue (\$25,000)} * \text{Contribution Margin (60\%)} = \$15,000$$

Calculate the financial value attributable to marketing:

$$Y_2 - Y_0 = \$30,000 - \$15,000 = \$15,000$$

Calculate the financial value attributable to the direct mail:

$$Y_2 - Y_1 = \$30,000 - \$27,000 = \$3,000$$

Calculate the Marketing Return on Investment (MROI):

[Incremental Financial Value Attributable to Marketing ($)
− Cost of Marketing ($)]/Cost of Marketing ($)

($15,000 − $7,000)/$7,000 = 114%

If the direct mail campaign were not used, the MROI would be

($12,000 − $6,000)/$6,000 = 100%

Therefore,

$$\text{Return on Incremental Marketing Investment (ROIMI), the direct mail} = \frac{\$3,000 - \$1,000}{\$1,000} = 200\%$$

Data sources, complications, and cautions

The first piece of information needed for MROI is the cost of the marketing campaign, program, or budget. Although defining which costs belong in marketing can be problematic, a bigger challenge is estimating the incremental revenue, contribution, and net profits attributable to marketing. This is similar to the distinction between baseline and lift discussed in Section 9.1. Farris and his colleagues[7] outline five ways that financial returns are often assessed; see Table 12.4.

Table 12.4 Approaches to measuring financial return

Valuation Method	Financial return assessed
Comparable Costs	Cost savings for achieving equivalently valuable contacts
Funnel Conversions	Future-period incremental sales and profits based on estimated conversion rates
Baseline Lift	Current-period incremental sales and profits
Customer Equity	Changes in customer lifetime value
Marketing Assets	Changes in brand and firm valuations

We suggest that it is important to understand the approach being used and to ensure that it is appropriate for the situation.

A further complication of estimating MROI concerns how to deal with important interactions between different marketing programs and campaigns. The return on many marketing "investments" is likely to show up as an increase in the responses received for other types of marketing. For example, if direct mail solicitations show an increase in response because of television advertising, we could and should calculate that those positive outcomes had something to do with the TV campaign. As an interaction, however, the return on advertising would depend on what was being spent on other programs. The function is not a simple linear return to the campaign costs.

For budgeting, one key element to recognize is that maximizing the MROI would probably reduce spending and profits. Marketers typically encounter diminishing returns, with each incremental dollar yielding lower and lower incremental MROI, and so low levels of spending will tend to have very high return rates. Maximizing MROI might lead to reduced marketing and eliminating campaigns or activities that are, on balance, profitable, even if the return rates are not as high as the first campaigns chosen. This issue is similar to the distinction between ROI (%) and EVA ($) discussed in Sections 12.2 and 12.3. Additional marketing activities or campaigns that bring down average percentage returns but increase overall profits can be quite sensible. So, using MROI or any percentage measure of profit to determine overall budgets is questionable. Of course, merely eliminating programs with a negative MROI is almost always a good idea. Still, maximizing long-term profits is often not simply a matter of shifting funds from low-ROI activities to high-ROI activities because there may well be strategic considerations not fully captured in the ROI measures themselves. Examples are brand building and new customer acquisition versus the need for short-term sales, balancing push and pull efforts to support distribution channels, and targeting market segments that are of strategic importance.

The previous discussion intentionally does not deal with any carryover effect (that is, a marketing effect on sales and profits that extends into future periods). When marketing spending is expected to have effects beyond the current period, other techniques are needed, including Payback, Net Present Value, and Internal Rate of Return (discussed earlier in this chapter). Also, Customer Lifetime Value (see Section 5.3) provides a more disaggregated approach to evaluating marketing spending and is designed to acquire long-lived customer relationships.

All of the above discussion is based on referring to the "R" in MROI as "return of profit" resulting from marketing expenditures. The reality is that several firms today are now using *return* in various different dimensions other than just profit contributions. While this can be confusing, part of the reason for it might be that the immediate profits are less obvious, costs are unknown, or the associated incremental revenue is not easy to determine. Hence, many are referring to "return" per dollar spent as a way to judge achieving some interim stage in the purchase funnel, as described below.

Related metrics and concepts

Media exposure return on marketing investment

In an attempt to evaluate the value of marketing activities such as sponsorships, marketers often commission research to gauge the number and quality of media exposures achieved. (See Section 10.9 for the related metric Equivalent Media Impressions from Sponsorship.) These exposures are then valued (often using "rate cards" to determine the cost of equivalent advertising space/time), and a "return" is calculated by dividing the estimated value by the costs:

$$\text{Media Exposure Return on Marketing Investment (MEROMI) (\%)} = \frac{\substack{\text{Estimated Value of Media Exposures} \\ \text{Achieved (\$) — Cost of Marketing Campaign,} \\ \text{Sponsorship, or Promotion (\$)}}}{\substack{\text{Cost of Marketing Campaign, Sponsorship,} \\ \text{or Promotion (\$)}}}$$

This is most appropriate where there isn't a clear market rate for the results of the campaign and so marketers want to be able to illustrate the equivalent cost for the result for a type of campaign that has an established market rate.

Example A travel portal decides to sponsor a car at a Formula 1 event. It assumes that the logo it puts on the car will gain the equivalent of 500,000 impressions and will cost 10,000,000 yen. The cost per impression is thus 10 million yen/500,000 = 20 yen per impression. This can be compared to the costs of other marketing campaigns.

Because MROI has been used in so many different contexts (incremental versus marginal or total spending, short term versus long term, and with the "R" expressed not just in terms of profit but as some level in the purchase funnel), MROI can be confusing. Farris and colleagues[8] suggest that for clarification, all expressions of MROI should be expressed as follows: "Our analysis measured a (*total, incremental, or marginal*) MROI of (*scope of spending*) using (*valuation method*) over *time period*."

A key difference between MROI and Return on Advertising Spend (ROAS) is that advertising costs should not be subtracted from the incremental revenue for any advertising campaign before calculating ROAS. Such a subtraction may seem intuitive when calculating ROAS for those used to MROI, but this causes confusion as the advertising revenue in ROAS does not have other costs subtracted. ROAS captures the increase generated by advertising, so while MROI would be negative if the marketing expenditure were unprofitable, for ROAS to be negative, the campaign would have to decrease sales. Any campaign that generates even one extra sale regardless of advertising cost will have a positive ROAS, but whether the campaign was profitable depends on the precise level of incremental sales, the profit margin on those incremental sales, and the advertising cost. As such one can expect MROI levels to be very significantly less than ROAS levels. They are quite different metrics and should not be used interchangeably.

12.6   Financial market measures

The use of financial market metrics as indicators of marketing performance relies on the assumption that financial markets give an accurate view of the worth (market capitalization) of a firm. More specifically, market capitalization is the value of a firm to its owners, also known as market value of equity.

Total Shareholder Returns (TSR) measures a company's value creation for its shareholders.

Total Shareholder Returns in Period (%)

$$= \frac{\text{Share Price at End of Period (\$) } - \text{ Share Price at Beginning of Period (\$)} + \text{Dividends Paid in Period (\$)}}{\text{Share Price Beginning of Period (\$)}}$$

Abnormal Returns is the difference in returns compared to some expected level of returns.

Abnormal Return in a Period ($, %)

$= \text{Actual Return in a Period (\$, \%) } - \text{ Expected Return in a Period (\$, \%)}$

Purpose: *to measure marketing impact on the stock price.*

As marketers advance in their careers, especially if they become chief marketing officers (CMOs), they are likely to want to understand as best as possible how marketing might affect the stock price. Here we give some key metrics frequently employed by colleagues in the finance disciplines.

Construction

Market capitalization (or market value of equity)

Market capitalization is a measure of the value that shareholders own. In an efficient market, this capitalization equals the projected future (that is, appropriately discounted) cash flows.

The value of an individual share is found directly from reports from the New York Stock Exchange, NASDAQ, London FTSE, Tokyo Nikkei, TSX (Canada), and other markets. Market capitalization is often reported; when it isn't, it can be calculated by multiplying the number of shares in the firm by the price of each individual share:

$$\text{Market Capitalization (\$)} = \text{Share Price (\$)} * \text{Number of Shares (\#)}$$

Total shareholder returns (TSR)

TSR is a measure of a shareholder's gain over a specified period (often a year). To calculate TSR, find the change in share price over a period in dollar terms, add to this any dividends paid out to the shareholders, and divide all by the share price at the period's beginning.

$$\text{Total Shareholder Returns (TSR) in Period (\%)}$$

$$= \frac{\substack{\text{Share Price at End of Period (\$)} - \text{Share Price at Beginning of Period (\$)} \\ + \text{Dividends Paid in Period (\$)}}}{\text{Share Price Beginning of Period (\$)}}$$

Example Xilin's firm had a share price of $1.20 at the beginning of 2019, and by the end of the year the price was $1.40. The firm had also distributed 10 cents per share in dividends.

$$\text{TSR (\%)} = \frac{(\$1.40 - \$1.20) + \$0.10}{\$1.20} = \frac{\$0.30}{\$1.20} = 25\%$$

Abnormal returns

Events happen that may be within the marketer's control (such as a new product launch) or not (such as spillover from a health scare about a competitor's product). A marketer may want to understand whether the change in financial market valuations after such an event is unusual (that is, abnormal). Abnormal returns can be good or bad, depending on whether the returns are higher or lower than expected.

An actual return in dollar terms is simply the stock price at the end of the period less the stock price at the beginning of the period. In percentage terms, just divide the change by the stock price at the beginning of the period. Then create a model that shows an expected return for the period. Models of expected returns take into account reasonable market factors. For example, if the share price of all firms in the industry increased by 5%, one might expect the share price of a particular company in that industry to have increased by 5%. This expected return can be compared to what actually happened:

> Abnormal Return in a Period ($, %)
> = Actual Return in a Period ($, %) − Expected Return in a Period ($, %)

The next step is to model whether the abnormal return is significantly different from what was expected or whether it is simply a normal random fluctuation. The basic idea is that we expect some variation by chance, and it is only when returns are dramatically different from expected that we call the returns significantly different.

Data sources, complications, and cautions

Market capitalization is the value of the owners' equity at any given point, but throughout a period, a firm might issue, buy back, split, or merge shares. Don't forget to adjust for such changes. Furthermore, firms may issue shares with different rights, and so these may also differ in value.

Many marketers find it difficult to accept the argument that financial markets are sufficiently efficient to incorporate all available information and give good predictions about the impact of marketing actions on future earnings. When markets are thought to be less efficient, any metric that uses them loses value.

How you choose what returns are "normal" directly affects estimates of "abnormal" returns. Furthermore, even if an estimate of abnormal return assessment is accurate, we may question whether any associated event was the cause of the estimated abnormal return.

The time window assessed for abnormal returns can make a big difference. A very short window may miss genuine changes if the market takes a longer time to respond. Longer windows typically also increase noise in the data as other events happen (for example, competitor actions, macroeconomic news), thereby also reducing confidence that any changes in returns are tied to the event being studied.

12.7 Combined market and accounting measures

Price to Earnings (PE) Ratio measures what an investor must pay for a share compared to its earnings. Higher PE ratios are often interpreted as implying that a firm has good prospects.

$$\text{Price to Earnings (PE) Ratio (\$)} = \frac{\text{Price of Single Share (\$)}}{\text{Earnings per Share (\$)}}$$

Market to Book Ratio compares what the financial markets think a firm is worth with what is recorded in the financial accounting records.

$$\text{Market to Book Ratio (I)} = \frac{\text{Market Value of Equity (\$)}}{\text{Book Value of Equity (\$)}}$$

Mixing financial accounting and financial market measures creates potential challenges.

Purpose: to measure firm worth in terms of earnings and market price.

Earnings is a single-period accounting measure, whereas the market price, in an efficient market, reflects all future earnings expected to be gained by a firm. A high Price to Earnings (PE) Ratio thus may suggest that a larger stream of earnings is expected in the future.

Market to Book Ratio compares financial markets valuations (assumed to be forward looking) with financial accounting records (which are generally backward looking). Proponents thus suggest that this measure shows when value has been created but has yet to be recorded in the financial accounts. There are very significant caveats associated with Market to Book Ratio, so we caution against using it—at least to measure performance.

Construction

Earnings per share (EPS) ratio: A measure calculated by dividing a company's reported earnings by the number of shares outstanding. This data is contained in the financial accounts.

$$\text{Earnings per Share (EPS) (\$)} = \frac{\text{Earnings of Company (\$)}}{\text{Number of Shares Outstanding (\$)}}$$

> **Price to earnings (PE) ratio:** The market price per share divided by the earnings per share.
>
> $$\text{Price to Earnings (PE) Ratio (\$)} = \frac{\text{Price of Single Share (\$)}}{\text{Earnings per Share (\$)}}$$

Example Kleen-it declared earnings of $400 million. Each of its 100 million shares cost $40 at year end. Earnings per share were $400 million/$100 million = $4 per share.

The PE Ratio at year end was $40/$4 = 10.

> **Market to book ratio:** A measure of the market value of the equity of a firm (taken from stock market reports) divided by the book value of the owners' equity reported in the financial accounts. (This value of equity is the assets of the firm less its liabilities.) High values suggest that value has been created and noticed by the market but not yet recorded in the financial accounts.
>
> $$\text{Market to Book Ratio (I)} = \frac{\text{Market Value of Equity (\$)}}{\text{Book Value of Equity (\$)}}$$

Example BronzeWorks had a market value of equity of $2 million. The financial accounts showed assets of $3 million and liabilities of $2 million, leaving a book value of equity of $1 million.

$$\text{Market to Book Ratio (I)} = \frac{\$2 \text{ million}}{\$3 \text{ million} - \$2 \text{ million}} = 2$$

The next year BronzeWorks invested $500,000 in marketing. This left $500,000 less in the bank, so assets were $2.5 million. Liabilities stayed the same. The share price, however, rose to $2.75.

$$\text{Market to Book Ratio (I)} = \frac{1 \text{ million} * \$2.75}{\$2.5 \text{ million} - \$2 \text{ million}} = \frac{\$2.75 \text{ million}}{\$500,000} = 5.5$$

The Market to Book Ratio increased, but the reasons are messy because of both (1) reduced assets, given accounting rules require expensing of the vast majority of marketing investments, and (2) increased share price.

> **Price to book ratio: A measure that can be thought of as the Market to Book Ratio at the individual share level.**
>
> $$\text{Price to Book Ratio (I)} = \frac{\text{Market Value of a Single Share (\$)}}{\text{Book Value of a Single Share (\$)}}$$

Example BronzeWorks shares traded at $2. Owners' equity was Assets ($3 million) − Liabilities ($2 million) = $1 million. There were 1 million shares outstanding, meaning each share represented $1 of equity.

$$\text{Price to Book Ratio (I)} = \frac{\text{Market Value of a Single Share (\$)}}{\text{Book Value of a Single Share (\$)}} = \frac{\$2}{\$1} = 2$$

> **Tobin's q: A measure used by academics that is similar to Market to Book Ratio.**
>
> $$\text{Tobin's q (I)} = \frac{\text{Market Value of Assets (\$)}}{\text{Replacement Cost of Assets (\$)}}$$
>
> The market value of assets is the value of the equity plus the value of preferred stock and debt. The replacement cost of assets is hard to estimate, so accounting-based measures use book values as approximations (typically "Total Assets" from the financial accounts).
>
> Accounting Based Approximation of Tobin's q (I)
>
> $$= \frac{\text{Market Value of Equity (\$)} + \text{Preferred Stock (\$)} + \text{Debt (\$)}}{\text{Total Assets (\$)}}$$
>
> Book value understates replacement value for marketing-intensive firms. This means Tobin's q is typically higher for marketing-intensive firms than for comparably successful non-marketing-intensive firms. This makes accounting-based approximations of Tobin's q problematic for measuring performance.[9]

Data sources, complications, and cautions

Share price, in efficient markets, is often assumed to be an unbiased estimate of suitably discounted future cash flows, the value of which will accrue to the shareholders. Of course, how efficient financial markets actually are is a matter of ongoing debate.

Financial accounting numbers (such as earnings and book value) come from regular periodic reports, but the market value of equity can be a real-time value. Make sure to compare market and book values for the same time periods.

Accounting numbers are problematic for marketers, given that nearly all investments in marketing are expensed (that is, treated as costs). For example, brands are often omitted from financial accounting records when created by internal investments. If fewer assets are recorded, but all liabilities are recorded, then reported equity will be less at the same level of performance. We would expect Price to Earnings Ratio and Market to Book Ratio to be higher for firms that invest heavily in marketing.

Further reading

Bendle, Neil Thomas, and Moeen Naseer Butt. (2018). "The Misuse of Accounting-Based Approximations of Tobin's q in a World of Market-Based Assets," *Marketing Science*, 37(3), 484–504.

Farris, Paul W., Dominique M. Hanssens, James D. Lenskold, and David J. Reibstein. (2015). "Marketing Return on Investment: Seeking Clarity for Concept and Measurement," *Applied Marketing Analytics*, 1(3), 267–282.

Hawkins, D. I., Roger J. Best, and Charles M. Lillis. (1987). "The Nature and Measurement of Marketing Productivity in Consumer Durables Industries: A Firm Level Analysis," *Journal of the Academy of Marketing Science*, 1(4), 1–8.

The marketing metrics x-ray and testing

13

13.1 The marketing metrics x-ray

Our purpose in this chapter is to give some examples of how marketing metrics can augment and complement traditional financial metrics when used to assess firm and brand performance. In particular, marketing metrics can serve as leading indicators of problems, opportunities, and future financial performance. Just as x-rays and MRIs are designed to provide deeper views of our bodies, marketing metrics can show problems (and opportunities) that would otherwise be missed.

Put your money where your metrics are

Table 13.1 shows common summary financial information for two hypothetical companies: Boom and Cruise. Income statement data from five years provide the basis for comparing the companies on several dimensions.

On which firm would you bet your grandparent's savings?
We have used this example with MBA students and executives many times. Usually, we say to them, "Assume that your grandparent wants to buy a partnership in one of these firms, using limited retirement savings. If these financial statements were the *only* data you had available or could obtain, which firm would you recommend?" These data are the metrics traditionally used to evaluate firm performance.

Table 13.1 shows that gross margins and profits are the same for both firms. Although Boom's sales and marketing spending are growing faster, its return on sales (ROS) and return on investment (ROI) are declining. If this decline continues, Boom will be in trouble. In addition, Boom's marketing-to-sales ratio is increasing faster than Cruise's. Is this a sign of inefficient marketing?

Table 13.1 Financial statements (all $ in thousands)

	Boom				
	Year 1	Year 2	Year 3	Year 4	Year 5
Revenue	$833	$1,167	$1,700	$2,533	$3,919
Margin Before Marketing	$125	$175	$255	$383	$588
Marketing	$100	$150	$230	$358	$563
Profit	$25	$25	$25	$25	$25
Margin (%)	15%	15%	15%	15%	15%
Marketing/Sales	12%	13%	14%	14%	14%
ROS	3.0%	2.1%	1.5%	1.0%	0.6%
Year-on-Year Revenue Growth	—	40%	46%	50%	53%
CAGR Revenue from Year 1	—	40%	43%	45%	47%
Invested Capital	$500	$520	$552	$603	$685
ROI	5.0%	4.8%	4.8%	4.1%	3.6%
	Cruise				
	Year 1	Year 2	Year 3	Year 4	Year 5
Revenue	$1,320	$1,385	$1,463	$1,557	$1,670
Margin Before Marketing	$198	$208	$219	$234	$251
Marketing	$173	$183	$194	$209	$226
Profit	$25	$25	$25	$25	$25
Margin (%)	15%	15%	15%	15%	15%
Marketing/Sales	13%	13%	13%	13%	14%
ROS	1.9%	1.8%	1.7%	1.6%	1.5%
Year-on-Year Revenue Growth	—	5%	6%	6%	7%
CAGR Revenue from Year 1	—	5%	5%	6%	6%
Invested Capital	$500	$501	$503	$505	$507
ROI	5.0%	5.0%	5.0%	5.0%	4.9%

On the basis of the information in Table 13.1, most people choose Cruise. Cruise is doing more with less. It's more efficient. Its trend in ROS looks much better, and Cruise has maintained a fairly consistent ROI of about 5%. About the only things Boom has going for it are size and growth of the "top line" (sales revenue). Let's look more deeply at the marketing metrics x-ray.

Using the marketing metrics x-ray

Table 13.2 presents the results of our marketing metrics x-ray of Boom and Cruise. It shows the number of customers each firm is serving and separates them into "old" (existing) customers and "new" customers.

This table allows us to see not only the rate at which the firms have acquired new customers but also their retention (loyalty) rates. Boom's spending on marketing now looks a lot better because we can see that spending was used to generate new customers and keep old ones. In addition, Boom acquires new customers at a lower cost than Cruise. And although Cruise's customers spend more, Boom's customers stay around longer. Perhaps we should order another set of x-rays to examine customer profitability and lifetime value?

Table 13.3 uses the information from Table 13.2 to calculate some additional customer metrics. Under an assumption of constant margins and retention rates and a 15% discount rate, we can calculate the customer lifetime value (CLV) for the customers of each firm and compare this CLV with what the firms are spending to acquire the customers. The CLV represents the discounted margins a firm will earn from its customers over their period of buying from the firm. Refer to Section 5.3 for details about the estimation of CLV and the process for using the number to value the customer base as an asset. The asset value is merely the number of ending customers times their remaining lifetime value. For these examples, we have assumed that all marketing is used to acquire new customers, so the customer acquisition cost is obtained by dividing marketing spending by the new customers in a given period.

Boom's aggressive marketing spending looks even better in this light. The difference between the CLV and acquisition cost is only $3.71 for Cruise but is $48.21 for Boom. From the viewpoint of the customer asset value at the end of Year 5, Boom is worth almost five times as much as Cruise.

Table 13.4 gives us even more information on customers. Customer satisfaction is much higher for Boom, and Boom's customers are more willing to recommend the firm to others. As a consequence, we might expect Boom's acquisition costs to decline in the future. In fact, with such a stable and satisfied customer base, we could expect that brand equity (refer to Section 4.4) measures would be higher, too.

Table 13.2 Comparing firms on customer metrics

Metric	Boom					Cruise				
	Year 1	Year 2	Year 3	Year 4	Year 5	Year 1	Year 2	Year 3	Year 4	Year 5
New Customers (Thousands)	1.33	2.00	3.07	4.77	7.50	1.86	1.97	2.09	2.24	2.43
Total Customers (Thousands)	3.33	4.67	6.80	10.21	15.67	3.86	4.05	4.28	4.55	4.88
Sales/Customer	$250	$250	$250	$250	$250	$342	$342	$342	$342	$342
Marketing/New Customer	$75	$75	$75	$75	$75	$93	$93	$93	$93	$93
Retention Rate	—	80%	80%	80%	80%	—	54%	54%	54%	54%

Table 13.3 Customer profitability of the two firms

Customer Value Metric	Boom	Cruise
Customer CLV	$123.21	$96.71
Customer Acquisition Cost	$75.00	$93.00
Customer Count (Thousands)	15.67	4.88
Customer Asset Value (Thousands)	$1,344	$222

Table 13.4 Customer attitudes and awareness of the two firms

Metric	Boom					Cruise				
	Year 1	Year 2	Year 3	Year 4	Year 5	Year 1	Year 2	Year 3	Year 4	Year 5
Awareness	30%	32%	31%	31%	33%	20%	22%	22%	23%	23%
Top of Mind	17%	18%	20%	19%	20%	12%	12%	11%	11%	10%
Satisfaction	85%	86%	86%	87%	88%	50%	52%	52%	51%	53%
Willingness to Recommend	65%	66%	68%	67%	69%	42%	43%	42%	40%	39%

Hiding problems in the marketing baggage?

The income statement for another example firm, Prestige Luggage, is depicted in Table 13.5. The company seems to be doing quite well. Unit and dollar sales are growing rapidly. Margins before marketing are stable and quite robust. Marketing spending and marketing-to-sales ratios are growing, but so is the bottom line. So what is not to like?

Table 13.5 Prestige Luggage income

	Statement			
	Year 1	Year 2	Year 3	Year 4
Sales Revenue (Thousands)	$14,360	$18,320	$23,500	$30,100
Unit Sales (Thousands)	85	115	159	213
Market Share (Unit)	14%	17%	21%	26%
Gross Margin	53%	53%	52%	52%
Marketing	$1,600	$2,143	$2,769	$3,755
Profit	$4,011	$5,317	$7,051	$9,227
ROS	27.9%	29.0%	30.0%	30.7%
Marketing/Sales	11.1%	11.7%	11.8%	12.5%

Using the marketing metrics x-ray

Let's take a deeper look at what's going on with Prestige Luggage by examining the company's retail customers. When we do, we'll get a better view of the marketing mechanics that underlie the seemingly pleasant financials in Table 13.5.

Table 13.6 shows that Prestige Luggage's sales growth comes from two sources: an expanding number of outlets stocking the brand and an increase (more than four-fold) in price promotions. (Refer to Chapter 7, "Channel management," for distribution measures.) Still, there are plenty of outlets that do not stock the brand. So there may be room to grow.

Table 13.7 reveals that although the overall sales are increasing, they are not keeping pace with the number of stores stocking the brand. (Sales per retail store are already declining.) Also, the promotional pricing by the manufacturer seems to be encouraging individual stores' inventories to grow. Soon, retailers may become irritated that the GMROII (Gross Margin Return on Inventory Investment) has declined considerably. *Future sales may continue to slow further and put pressure on retail margins.* If retailer dissatisfaction causes some retailers to drop the brand from their assortment, manufacturer sales will decline precipitously.

Table 13.6 Prestige Luggage marketing and channel metrics

	Year 1	Year 2	Year 3	Year 4
Retail Dollar Sales (Thousands)	$24,384	$27,577	$33,067	$44,254
Retail Unit Sales (Thousands)	87	103	132	183
Number Stocking Outlets	300	450	650	900
Price Premium	30.0%	22.3%	15.1%	8.9%
ACV Distribution**	30%	40%	48%	60%
% Sales on Deal	10%	13%	20%	38%
Advertising Spending (Thousands)	$700	$693	$707	$721
Promotion Spending (Thousands)	$500	$750	$1,163	$2,034

** ACV = All Commodity Volume, a measure of distribution coverage (refer to Section 7.1).

Table 13.7 Luggage manufacturer retail profitability metrics

	Year 1	Year 2	Year 3	Year 4
Retail Margin $	$9,754	$11,169	$13,557	$18,366
Retail Margin %	40%	41%	41%	42%
Retail Inventory (Thousands)	15	27	54	84
Inventory per Store	50	60	83	93
Sales/Outlet (Thousands)	$81	$61	$51	$49
Stores per Point of AVC %	10	11	14	15
GMROII	385%	260%	170%	155%

In addition, the broadening of distribution and the increase of sales on deal suggest a possible change in how potential consumers view the previously exclusive image of the Prestige Luggage brand. The firm might want to order another set of x-rays to see if and how consumer attitudes about the brand have changed. Again, if these changes are by design, then maybe Prestige Luggage is okay. If not, then Prestige Luggage should be worried that its established strategy is falling apart. Add that to the possibility that some retailers are using deep discounts to unload inventory after they've dropped the brand, and we see that Prestige Luggage faces a vicious cycle from which it may never recover.

Some things you can't make up, and this example is one. The actual company was "pumped up" through a series of price promotions, distribution was expanded, and sales grew rapidly. Shortly after being bought by another company looking to add to its luxury goods portfolio of brands, the strategy unraveled. Many stores dropped the line, and it took years to rebuild the brand and sales.

These two examples illustrate the importance of digging behind the financial statements using tools such as the marketing x-ray. More numbers, in and of themselves, are only part of the answer. The ability to see patterns and meaning behind the numbers is even more important.

Smoking more, but enjoying it less?

Table 13.8 displays marketing metrics reported by a big tobacco company aimed at analyzing the trends in competition by lower-priced discount brands. A declining market size, stagnant company market share, and growing share of firm sales accounted for by discount brands combined to paint a baleful picture of the future. The firm was replacing premium sales with discount brand sales. To top it off, the advertising and promotion budgets had almost doubled. In the words of Erv Shames, former CEO of General Foods and president of Kraft, it would be easy to conclude that the marketers had "run out of ideas" and were resorting to the bluntest of instruments: price.

Table 13.8 Market trends for discount brands and spending: Big Tobacco Company

Year	1987	1992
Market Size (Units)	4,000	3,850
Company Unit Share	25%	24%
Unit Sales	1,000	924
Premium Brand Units	925	774
Discount Brand Units	75	150
Advertising & Promotion Spend	$600	$1,225

Table 13.9 Additional metrics

Year	1987	1992
Revenue (Thousands)	$1,455	$2,237
Average Unit Price	$1.46	$2.42
Average Premium Price	$1.50	$2.60
Average Discount Price	$0.90	$1.50
Operating Profit (Thousands)	$355	$550

The picture looks much brighter, however, after examining the metrics in Table 13.9. It turns out that in the same five years during which discount brands had become more prominent, sales revenue and operating income had both grown by over 50%. The reason is clear: Prices had almost doubled, even though a large portion of these price increases had been "discounted back" through promotions. Overall, the net impact on the firm's bottom line was positive.

Now you might be thinking that the messages in Table 13.9 are so obvious that no one would ever find the metrics in Table 13.8 to be as troubling as we made them out to be. In fact, our experience in teaching a case that contains all these metrics is that experienced marketers from all over the world tend to focus on the metrics in Table 13.8 and pay little or no attention to the additional metrics—even when they are given the same level of prominence.

The situation described by the two tables is a close approximation to the actual market conditions just before the now-famous "Marlboro Friday." Top management took action because they were concerned that the series of price increases that led to the attractive financials in 1992 would not be sustainable because the higher premium prices gave competitive discount brands more latitude to cut prices. On what later became known as "Marlboro Friday" (April 2, 1993), Phillip Morris cut Marlboro prices by $0.40 a pack, reducing operating earnings by almost 40%. The stock price tumbled by 25%.

Note the contrast between this example and the preceding example. Prestige Luggage was increasing promotion expenditures to expand distribution. Prices were falling, while promotion, or sales on deal, were increasing—an ominous sign. Marlboro, on the other hand, was constantly raising the price and then discounting back—a very different strategy.

Marketing dashboards

The presentation of metrics in the form of management dashboards has received a substantial amount of attention in the past several years. The basic notion seems to be that the manner of presenting complex data can influence management's ability to recognize key patterns and trends. Would a dashboard, which provides a graphical depiction of information, make it easier for managers to pick up the ominous trends?

The metaphor of an automobile dashboard is appropriate because there are numerous metrics that could be used to measure a car's operation. The dashboard is meant to provide a *reduced set* of the *vital measures* in a form that is *easy for the operator to interpret and use*. Unfortunately, although all automobiles have the same key metrics, it is not as universal across all businesses. The set of appropriate and critical measures may differ across businesses.

Figure 13.1 presents a dashboard for the Prestige Luggage example above of five critical measures over time. It reveals strong sales growth while maintaining margins even though selling less expensive items. Disturbingly, however, the returns for the retailer (GMROII) have fallen precipitously, and store inventories have grown. Sales per store have similarly dropped. The price premium that Prestige Luggage can command has fallen, and more of the company's sales are on deal. This should provide a foreboding picture for the company and should raise concerns about the ability to maintain distribution.

Figure 13.1 Prestige Luggage: marketing management dashboard

Revenue and margins

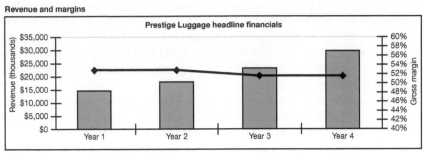

The financial metrics look healthy; revenue showing good growth while margins are almost unchanged.

Manufacturer prices to store prices

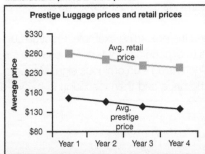

Prestige Luggage is selling less expensive items.

Store inventory and GMROII

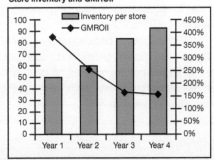

Prestige Luggage is making diminishing returns for retailer.

Distribution

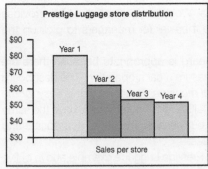

Prestige Luggage is moving into smaller stores.

Pricing and promotions

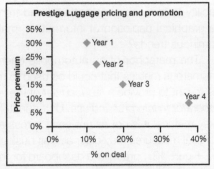

Prestige Luggage is becoming reliant on promotion.

Summary: marketing metrics + financial metrics = deeper insight

Dashboards, scorecards, and what we have termed x-rays are collections of marketing and financial metrics that management believes are important indicators of business health. Dashboards are designed to provide depth of marketing understanding concerning the business. Many specific metrics may be considered important—or even critical—in any given marketing context. We do not believe it is generally possible to provide unambiguous advice on which metrics are most important or which management decisions are contingent on the values and trends in certain metrics. These recommendations would have to be of the "if, then" form, such as "If relative share is greater than 1.0 and market growth is higher than change in GDP, then invest more in advertising." Although such advice might be valuable under many circumstances, our aims were more modest—simply to provide a resource for marketers to achieve a deeper understanding of the diversity of metrics that exist.

Our examples, Boom versus Cruise, Prestige Luggage, and Big Tobacco, show how selected marketing metrics can allow deeper insights into the financial future of companies. In situations such as these, it is important that a full array of marketing and financial metrics inform the decision. Examining a complete set of x-rays does not necessarily make the decisions any easier. (The Big Tobacco example is debated by knowledgeable industry observers to this day!) However, it does help ensure a more comprehensive diagnosis.

13.2 The value of information

How much should you spend on gaining information—such as through market research? Imagine that a firm has three potential marketing strategies: bold, moderate, and cautious. There are three possible moods that, collectively, the target consumers are in: excited (40% chance), happy (40% chance), or cynical (20% chance). The firm has to decide how much to spend to learn the mood of the target consumers.

The cautious strategy will earn $2 million in profit whatever mood the consumers are in. The bold strategy will resonate with excited consumers (earning $10 million), perform decently with happy consumers (earning $2 million), but alienate cynical consumers (losing $8 million). The moderate strategy will do pretty well with excited ($5 million) and happy consumers ($3 million), plus it only loses $1 million when paired with cynical consumers.

Given this, what is the value of perfect information about the mood of the target consumers?

First, we calculate how much we can expect to earn with no further information. This is the maximum of the expected values of the three strategies, where expected value is the probability weighted average of the outcome values.

$$\text{Expected Value, Bold: } 40\% * \$10 \text{ million} + 40\% * \$2 \text{ million} + 20\% * -\$8 \text{ million}$$
$$= \$3.2 \text{ million}$$

$$\text{Expected Value, Moderate: } 40\% * \$5 \text{ million} + 40\% * \$3 \text{ million} + 20\% *$$
$$-\$1 \text{ million} = \$3 \text{ million}$$

$$\text{Expected Value, Cautious: Whatever the consumers' mood} = \$2 \text{ million}$$

Thus, without any additional information on the consumers' mood, we'd choose the bold strategy because its expected value ($3.2 million) is the highest.

If market research could give us perfect information, it would allow us to pick the best strategy to pair with the consumers' mood: bold with excited (earning $10 million), moderate with happy (earning $3 million), and cautious with cynical (earning $2 million). With perfect information, we would expect a profit of

$$\text{Expected Value with Perfect Information}$$
$$40\% * \$10 \text{ million} + 40\% * \$3 \text{ million} + 20\% * \$2 \text{ million} = \$5.6 \text{ million}$$

Because the expected value with perfect information is $5.6 million and the expected value without additional information is $3.2 million, the expected value of the perfect information is the difference between the two, or $2.4 million. This quantity is an upper bound on the value of any actual information the firm can collect. In the real world, the value of any imperfect information the firm can collect must be less than this upper bound.

These calculations assume that marketers care only about expected value when, in fact, risk is also a concern. Firms typically prefer a certain $10 million to a 50% chance of gaining $20 million and 50% chance of gaining nothing, even though the expected values are the same. This is known as *risk aversion*. If you are risk averse, you might want to pay for information that reduces the range of outcomes that you face, even if this doesn't change the expected value—a consideration not taken into account in the calculation of the expected value of perfect information.

Individual decision makers are also often loss averse. Decision makers who are loss averse are willing to reduce the expected value of a decision in order to limit potential losses. Unlike risk aversion, loss aversion is often viewed by economists as poor decision making. Marketers who know they will be fired if they lose money in the above scenario might select the cautious strategy, which, although it has the lowest expected value, never loses money. The actual value of perfect information to risk-averse and loss-averse decision makers is usually higher than the expected value of perfect information because the information not only improves expected value but decreases risk/loss.

In summary, the value of information and so the usefulness of market research and testing vary with the precise situation at hand. Since reality is decidedly more complicated than our illustrative example, allocating data collection and analytical resources is an important management decision. Estimating the value of information requires specific quantitative inputs, which are often assumptions. Unfortunately, managers may be sufficiently unsure of these inputs that they are unable or unwilling to quantify these estimates. Even in such instances, however, it may be worthwhile to develop an intuitive appreciation of when additional information is likely to be most valuable. Table 13.10 should be useful in making qualitative comparisons of situations in which managers are uncertain about the value of collecting further data to refine their choices.

Table 13.10 Quick guide to the value of information

Criterion	Information is most valuable when
Potential financial consequences of decision	Large difference between the consequences of the best and worst alternatives
Uncertainty of future outcomes	High degree of uncertainty
Ability of information to change decision	Information is likely to change the decision (a combination of powerful information and close initial decision)
Validity of metrics	Metrics are valid indicators of market outcome
Reliability of data	When the sample size is large and measurement error is small

13.3 Testing

Testing usually underpins successful marketing. When you are not sure which advertising copy to use, which marketing mix elements to emphasize, or even which product variants to offer, testing can help. When testing, you should consider the precision (known as *reliability*) of the test. Testing an advertisement on one person will be unreliable as each person has idiosyncrasies. Increasing the number of respondents in the test increases your confidence that the responses are typical of the group being tested. You must also consider the validity of your test: Are you testing the right group? Are you asking the right question? If you test an advertisement on bank managers, for example, the information you get may not be valid for estimating how your target market, college athletes, will react.

With side-by-side A/B testing, two versions of an advertisement are created and tested against each other. Online it is easy to serve randomly selected visitors different versions of the advertisement. Randomly selecting which visitors get which advertisement ensures that there is no systematic difference between who gets which advertisement, suggesting that any observed difference is driven by the advertisement. Online it is usually relatively cheap to create and test new versions of advertisements. That said, even online testing is not free, and in general the cost of any testing can be high.

The more versions of an advertisement we create and test, the greater the chance of finding excellent copy. Unfortunately, creating and testing versions reduces the money available to spend on deploying whichever version wins the test. The Gross model is designed to help managers make this trade-off.

The Gross model

The Gross model, named after Irwin Gross, advises how much of the budget should be spent on creating (and testing) advertising copy. The number of alternative copies you should be willing to develop depends on the variability of the effectiveness of the advertisements. If some advertisements are highly effective, but most are ineffective, you will want to spend relatively heavily on developing and testing copy. The potential upside is high, and you want to develop many versions in order to get a great version. If, however, all advertisements perform relatively similarly, the difference between what you already have and what you can gain with further development is quite limited. In that case, it is better to spend less on developing new copy and spend more of the budget showing the currently best advertisement.

In the Gross model, the effectiveness of an advertising campaign (Z) is the amount spent on buying media (D) multiplied by the effectiveness of the best advertisement created (E):

$$Z = E * D$$

If we assume that advertising effectiveness is linear—that is, each piece of spending is equally effective—this is a simple model. Unfortunately, advertising often takes multiple views to gain any traction and eventually loses effectiveness; recall the S curve described in Chapter 10, "Advertising and sponsorship metrics." This means E varies with the amount spent on media (D), making the model more difficult to use.

The amount spent on media (D) is the total budget (B) less the fixed costs of copy testing (C_F) and the total costs of each new advertisement. This is the number of advertisements (N) developed multiplied by the average cost to develop an advertisement (C) plus the marginal (extra) costs to test each advertisement (C_S):

$$D = B - C_F - N(C + C_S)$$

O'Connor and her colleagues[1] applied this formula using the historical distribution of advertising effectiveness and concluded that 20% to 30% of media budgets (B) should be spent on developing and testing, and the rest (D) should be spent on deployment. Of course, this rule of thumb may vary significantly depending on context.

Should you test another advertisement?

The original Gross model was designed to help managers decide how many advertisements to create and test. The general conclusion was that firms tended to spend too little on creating and testing alternative versions (perhaps because this budget item is often called "non-working" media expense).

We will consider a slightly different question: Should the firm develop an additional advertising copy execution or use all of the remaining budget to air the current best copy?

Let B be the total budget to create, test, and deploy the best testing advertising. Let C be the cost to develop and test a new version of the advertisement—that is, the expenditure incurred when commissioning a new piece of copy. Because tests are never perfectly reliable or valid, we propose a "vaguely right" adjustment factor (A). The formula for the adjustment factor is Reliability * Validity (an approach similar to that proposed by Irwin Gross). As the reliability and validity of the tests approach 1, the adjustment factor approaches 1. As A gets higher—that is, whenever the validity and reliability of the test gets lower—each test is less useful at predicting real-world performance. The intuition is that with low reliability and validity, the test would need to indicate a higher probability of increased effectiveness before we would spend the money for the test. In our model, we use A = 2, which means the test would need to indicate an expected return two times (2X) the cost before we would deem it acceptable. This 2X would, for example, result from reliability of 70% and validity of 70%.

We can now estimate how much lift we need to expect to gain from a new version of an advertisement to make commissioning it worthwhile. This break-even lift is the cost of commissioning the new version as a percentage of the free budget multiplied by the adjustment factor. If we have a budget of $2.25 million, and the cost to develop and test each version is $40,000, then developing a new version costs 1.8% of the budget. If the adjustment factor is 2, we must expect to gain at least 2 * 1.8% = 3.6% performance lift to make commissioning a new version of the advertisement worthwhile (see Table 13.11). Of course, this approach means that each time we spend money for a copy test, the remaining budget is also reduced, and the next copy decision will represent a higher percentage of the budget and, therefore, require a higher percentage expected increase in sales to justify undertaking the test.

Table 13.11 (Break-even) lift needed to commission new piece of copy

Free Budget to Buy Media or Develop and Test Versions (B)	$2,250,000
Cost to Develop and Test New Version (C)	$40,000
Developing and Testing as % of Budget (D = C/B)	1.8%
Adjustment Factor for Lack of Test Reliability and Validity (A)	2
Expected Lift That Justifies Testing New Version (JT = A*D)	3.6%

Will a new version of the advertisement give sufficient lift to make creating it worthwhile? The challenge in answering this question is that we don't know any version's effectiveness before it has been created and tested.

The expected value of the new version is the chance of getting a new version of a certain quality multiplied by the outcome when we get a new version of that quality. There are two broad outcomes. The new version is equal to or of worse quality than our best current advertisement. When this is the case, the new version has no value at all. When the new version is of higher quality, then lift is the additional value coming from the new version.

We make the assumption that each version of an advertisement has a quality score between 1 and 10, and a quality of 10 is twice as effective—in some way defined by the firm—as 5 and so on. For our example, we assume that there is a uniform distribution of quality for versions of the advertisement. If we have 10 levels of quality, 1–10, each is equally likely. (Note that one of the advantages of this model is that you can specify any distribution of advertisement quality that you wish; just change the distribution in Table 13.12.)

The lift from the new version is the quality of the new version minus the quality of the current version divided by the quality of the current version. We know the quality of our current version—what we will deploy if we end testing—and so can create an expected lift from a new version. If this exceeds the expected lift needed to justify commissioning a new version (refer to Table 13.11), we should do so; otherwise, we should stop testing and deploy our current version. Table 13.12 shows us that with a current version quality 8, we should continue testing, but it is a very close call. (To read Table 13.12, note that the current advertisement scores an 8. Looking across shows us that a new version that scores 8 or less will not provide an effectiveness lift. A new advertisement that generates a score of 9 will improve lift by 12.5%.)

Table 13.12 Expected lift from new advertisement

Quality of current version (QCur)			8
Quality of new version (QNew)	Chance of occurring (CO)	Lift from new version (LV)**	LV * CO
1	10%	0	0
2	10%	0	0
3	10%	0	0
4	10%	0	0
5	10%	0	0
6	10%	0	0
7	10%	0	0
8	10%	0	0
9	10%	12.5%	1.25%
10	10%	25.0%	2.5%
Expected Lift from New Version (ENew)			**3.75%**

** Lift from New Version = IF(QNew>QCur, (QNew-QCur)/QCur, 0)

Whether you should continue creating versions depends on the quality of your current version. Table 13.13 shows the expected lift at each quality of current version. When you have only a low-quality current version, developing new copy has a huge expected value as you are likely to get copy that will substantially increase the effectiveness of your media spending. You should stop testing if you have a current version of quality 9; the expected benefits of continuing to commission versions are less than the cost of doing so. If you already have a version of quality 10, there is no possible benefit to further testing.

This model contains a number of assumptions—for example, that the version of an advertisement can be neatly scored, and the quality translates predictably into relative sales results. Furthermore, we assume that each new copy comes from the same distribution; this somewhat implies that the agency isn't giving you its best ideas first. This need not be true. You might get progressively worse ideas each time you go to the agency. Despite the challenges in getting a perfect model, we think the method is most valuable as a general illustration of how to think about the value of information in a management decision context that includes uncertainty, financial consequences, and ability of imperfect data to inform a decision.

Table 13.13 Expected lift from new version, given current version score

Quality of current version (QCur)	Expected lift from new version (ENew)	Decision (Test if ENew > JT)
1	450.0%	Test As > 3.6%
2	180.0%	Test As > 3.6%
3	93.3%	Test As > 3.6%
4	52.5%	Test As > 3.6%
5	30.0%	Test As > 3.6%
6	16.7%	Test As > 3.6%
7	8.6%	Test As > 3.6%
8	3.75%	Test As > 3.6%
9	1.1%	Don't Test As < 3.6%
10	0.0%	Don't Test As < 3.6%

Further reading

Ambler, Tim, Flora Kokkinaki, and Stefano Puntonni. (2004). "Assessing Marketing Performance: Reason for Metric Selection," *Journal of Marketing Management,* 20, 475–498.

McGovern, Gail, David Court, John A. Quelch, and Blair Crawford. (2004). "Bringing Customers into the Boardroom," *Harvard Business Review,* 82(11), 70–80, 148.

Meyer, C. (1994). "How the Right Measures Help Teams Excel," *Harvard Business Review,* 72(3), 95.

O'Conner, Fina Colarelli, Thomas R. Willemain, and James MacLachlan. (1996). "The Value of Competition among Agencies in Developing Ad Campaigns: Revisiting Gross's Model," *Journal of Advertising,* 25(1), 51–62.

System of metrics

14

> *"There are three kinds of economists: those who can count and those who can't."*

Unknown source

14.1 Modeling firm performance

To better understand the factors contributing to overall firm success, managers and analysts often decompose return on assets (ROA) into the product of two ratios, with each ratio reflecting a different aspect of the business. One popular approach for this decomposition is the DuPont model, which states

$$\text{ROA} = \frac{\text{Net Profit}}{\text{Sales}} \times \frac{\text{Sales}}{\text{Assets}}$$

The first ratio in this simplified DuPont model is called either the *profit margin* or *return on sales*. It measures profits as a percentage of sales. To the extent that marketers create products that customers value, claim that value through intelligent pricing, drive down costs by paying attention to manufacturing and channel costs, and optimize their marketing spending, marketers can increase the firm's return on sales. The second ratio in the DuPont model is known as *asset turnover*. Asset turnover can be thought of as the number of dollars of sales each dollar of assets generates. Here the job of marketers is even more focused—on generating dollars of sales but with an eye toward managing assets such as inventory and receivables captured in the denominator.

Notice that the DuPont model is an identity.[1] It is always true, regardless of the values of the various ratios. It is always true mostly because we have defined the ratios in such a way to make it always true. So it makes no sense to argue with or take exception to the DuPont model.

But if it is simply an equation that is true by definition, what good is it? The DuPont model is useful to the extent that the decomposition of ROA into the two component ratios helps firms maximize ROA by focusing (separately) on the two components. It is also useful in that it reminds marketers that their job is not simply to generate sales but to generate profitable sales and to do so efficiently (with respect to assets used).

The DuPont model has demonstrated its usefulness in practice. A Google search resulted in 4.4 million results for "DuPont model" compared to 2.9 million results for "DuPont Chemicals." In some circles, the company is now more famous for its model than its chemicals.

Figure 14.1 illustrates how the DuPont model is often expanded to include components affecting the two input ratios.

Figure 14.1 An extended DuPont model (adapted from www.12manage.com/ methods_dupont_model.html)

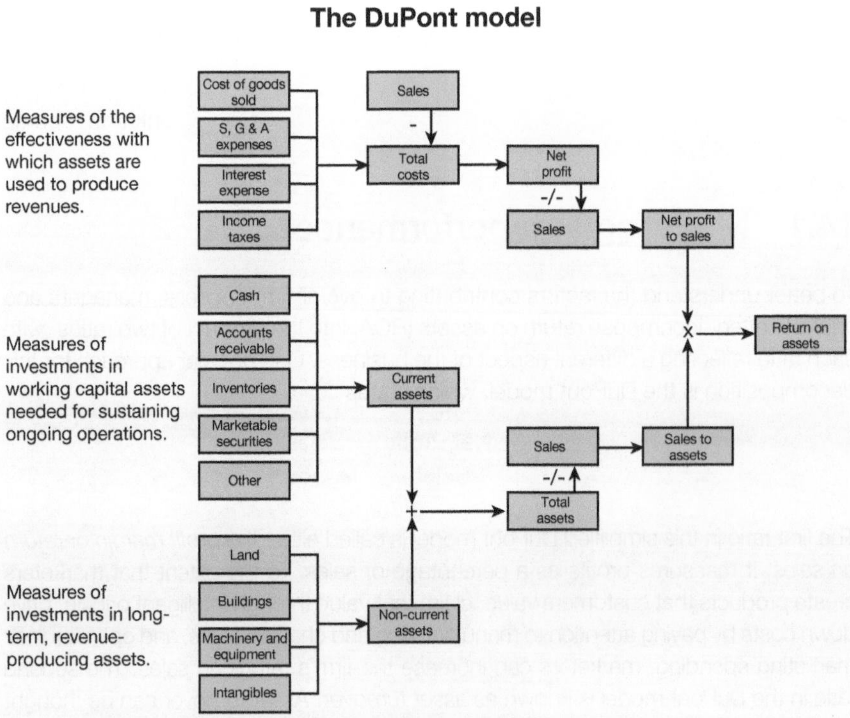

The DuPont model

Notice that the three rightmost columns of boxes in Figure 14.1 represent the DuPont model. The two leftmost columns of boxes represent a particular method of breaking apart net profit and total assets into smaller components. Our purpose here is not to critique this representation of the components of firm performance but simply to offer a few observations. First, we note that the decompositions of total costs, current assets, and non-current assets should be familiar to most readers. The categories of components used are consistent with what one finds on income statements (where total costs appears) and balance sheets (where total assets appears). Second, we note that the assets that marketing creates (brands and customer relationships, for example) get lumped together as intangibles, signaling that they are difficult to measure (which we agree with), and perhaps an afterthought or "other" category (which we disagree with). Many intangibles are not captured in accounting records, so it is important to clarify what exactly this number represents.

Finally, and most importantly, we observe that although total costs, current assets, and non-current assets all get broken out into smaller, well-understood components, sales does not. It is as if *Costs* and *Assets* deserve a lot of attention but the components of sales do not. This is perhaps not surprising since this particular model was designed by finance and accounting executives. As marketers, however, much of our focus is on how sales are generated. We also care about costs and asset utilization, of course, but we care more about sales and the components of sales. Figure 14.1 reflects the inward focus of a firm whose success depended on making things, minimizing costs, and using assets efficiently. For today's firms whose success depends at least as much on marketing and sales as production, we need a different model. We need our own "DuPont model," with at least the same amount of detail and clarity for breaking down the components of sales as the commonly used breakdowns of costs and assets.

Of course, as we begin to think about *how* to break down sales into its components, we quickly come to understand why there is no commonly used breakdown across different types of businesses. As all marketers know, there are multiple ways to decompose or break down sales simply because several entities (most of them outside the firm) are involved in the creation of revenue: sales force, customers, dealers, and even our competition. With a multitude of insightful ways to break down sales, it is no wonder there is not one commonly accepted way.

To illustrate, Figure 14.2 shows four (of many) separate and valid ways to break down sales into smaller components:

- Sales = Number Salespersons * Avg. Sales/Salesperson
- Sales = Number Dealers * Avg. Sales/Dealer
- Sales = Our Dollar Share * Total Market Sales
- Sales = Number Customers * Sales per Customer

As with the DuPont model, each of four ways to compute sales is an identity. Sales will always equal the number of customers times the average sales per customer. But even though these are identities, they can still lead to valuable insights, as we demonstrate in this section.

Figure 14.2 A sales model

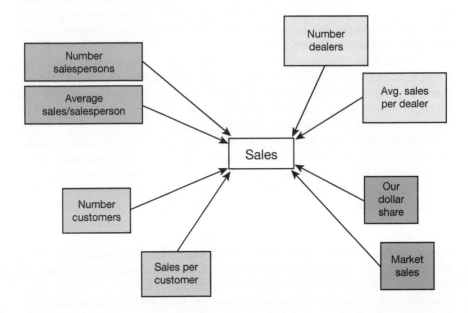

We also point out that there are other ways to break down sales. Figure 14.2 simply illustrates four ways. Also know that the components of sales in the outer ring in Figure 14.2 can themselves be decomposed. For example, Sales per Customer can be calculated as Purchases per Customer (per Period) * Average Sales per Purchase. And, not unexpectedly, there are multiple ways to decompose each of the outer-ring components. For example, Sales per Customer can also be decomposed into Units Purchased per Customer * Average Price per Unit. Decomposing the components of sales can be thought of as expanding the diagram in Figure 14.2 outward. We might also think of expanding the model "upward," with separate pages (decompositions) for each product or each customer group or each vendor.

14.2   Three reasons for using systems of identities in marketing

There are three primary reasons for formulating marketing DuPont-like component models of your marketing decisions and objectives:

- Decomposing the metric of interest into components can make it possible to identify problems and opportunities for improvement in more detail. For example, did shares drop because our sales were down or because competitors' sales were up? If our sales were down, was that due to fewer customers buying, lower unit sales per customer, lower average prices, or some combination of the above? Decomposition may also help by separating identities (which follow from the definitions used) from empirical relationships (which reflect how a complicated world actually works). Although identities are easy (just arithmetic), empirical relationships require difficult judgments about the form of the relationship, causality, and the future.

- Decomposing metrics may also allow us to estimate, indirectly, other component metrics that are difficult to measure directly. Using multiple identities can help eliminate measurement error with multiple "checks" on the value of any specific metrics. In the same way, individual marketing metrics may be regarded as part of a network or "web" of relationships. If each link in the network is valid, even if individual values are estimated with error, the entire structure will be more robust.

- Selecting and organizing the right network of marketing metrics often helps formulate models of marketing mix decisions. As with using the DuPont model, using models with interim components can make such models and dashboards more managerially transparent and help managers make and monitor the effects of their decisions.

Decomposing for diagnostic purposes

As mentioned previously, a primary purpose for using one or more identities to decompose any marketing metric of interest is to gain a deeper understanding of (or at least a different perspective on) the reasons for changes and differences observed. Although identities may be developed with a view to understanding the sources of changes and differences, they do not require calibration or estimation. They are true by definition, and we will designate these with an (ID).

An example of an identity is the relationship between sales, quantity, and price:

$$\text{Sales} = \text{Quantity} * \text{Price (ID)}$$

If we witness declining sales, the identity helps us see, first, whether the decline was due to declining quantity or price or both. Next, it helps us understand that if quantity declined, price increased, and sales declined, then quantity must have declined by a larger percentage than the price increased.

In contrast to identities are empirical relationships—relationships between variables for which the exact equation is not known and/or for which the relationship holds only imperfectly. Empirical relationships are required, for example, to help us decide whether we should increase or decrease prices. We designate these with an (EM). For example, we might consider the relationship between quantity sold to be a direct, linear function of price charged:

$$\text{Quantity} = b * \text{Price} + \text{Error (EM)}$$

This empirical relationship between quantity and price necessarily contains an error to account for measuring price or quantity imperfectly or influences on quantity sold other than price (our competitors' prices, for example). Also note that the parameter b in this empirical relationship is, itself, a parameter. It is an unknown constant—one that we might, for example, be able to estimate from available data. But one of the key differences between an identity (ID) and empirical relationships (EM) is that empirical relationships are more flexible. They apply to the tough and important questions such as "How many more units will we sell if we lower the price by $1?"

Dashboards of metrics often reflect underlying management logic about how marketing works to influence sales and profits. Dashboards include both identities and empirical relationships. As illustrated in Figure 14.2, sales can be decomposed many ways. Some of the components of sales might themselves be decomposed using one or more identities. Each firm needs to identify its primary performance measures. This is what should appear on their dashboards. There should be the capability to drill down on each of these performance measures (using identities) to diagnose and explain changes across time. But if dashboards are to be more than monitoring devices, we should have some idea of causal connections (for example, step on the brake to slow down the vehicle, step on the accelerator to make it go faster). Before long, dashboards can become complicated as we start to take into consideration the multiple effects of some of the variables (for example, step on the accelerator to make the car go faster, and the fuel gauge drops). Sometimes we also need a system of metrics to help infer (or forecast) values that are difficult to measure directly (for example, how much farther can we drive before the gas tank is empty?)

Eliminating error by harnessing the law of large (and not-so-large) numbers

There is a classic story of a physics professor whose final exam asked students to explain how to use a barometer to measure the height of a building. In addition to the "obvious" answer to measure the barometric pressures at the top and bottom of the building and use the difference to calculate the building's height, the professor purportedly received several other creative answers. Drop the barometer from the top of the building, time how long it takes to hit the ground, and use the appropriate physics formula to infer the height. Tie the barometer to a string, lower it to the ground, and measure the length of the string. Measure the length of the shadow cast by the building, the length of the shadow cast by the barometer, and the height of the barometer and use proportions to calculate the height of the building. By far the most creative solution purportedly offered was to knock on the door of the building's janitor and offer to give the janitor the barometer in exchange for revealing the height of the building.

The multiple ways to calculate sales shown in Figure 14.2 are similar to the multiple ways students came up with to measure the height of the building. Rather than argue over which single method to use, we propose to look for a way to use them all. When faced with a dilemma of which of two methods to use, why not do both? For the barometer problem, why not use several different methods and then combine the many estimates into one final estimate—perhaps by doing something as simple as taking the average of the estimates. If we wanted to do a little bit better, we could calculate a weighted average with weights depending on some measure of how "accurate" each estimate was. We might put more weight on the string-based estimate and less on the estimate from timing the fall of the barometer if we thought our watch and wind made the timing-based estimate less accurate. The relative weight to put on the janitor's estimate would depend on our confidence in the estimate. If the janitor claims to "know" the height, we should give the estimate more weight than if the janitor admits the number is something of a guess.

Using the average of the estimates instead of any one of the estimates takes advantage of the law of large (and not-so-large) numbers. The average is expected to be closer to the true value and become closer the more estimates that we have to average together. Ideally, we want "independent" estimates such as might be the case with the barometer example (unless, of course, the janitor got his number using the string method).

In the barometer example, we are mostly interested in measuring the height of the building. In our example, marketers are probably just as interested in the measuring components as we are in measuring sales itself. In fact, it often is the case that a firm has a good handle on sales and would like to get a better measure of some of the components, such as share or the sales per customer or any of the other metrics in the outer ring or outer-outer ring. In extreme cases, a firm may have no separate measure of one of the components and will have to "back into it" based on the measurements of all the others. (In the barometer example, use the height of the building and the length of the barometer's shadow to estimate the length of the building's shadow—to measure how far away the building is, for example, without having to travel to the building.)

What this means is that every initial estimate (and the associated standard deviation) will combine to determine our final estimates. Our estimate of the length of the string will be used to help revise our estimate of the time it took the barometer to hit the ground and the length of the building's shadow and vice versa. We think it is easy to see that the more separate estimates and identities we have in the model, the more confident we are with the final estimate.

Whereas the carpenters' adage is to measure twice and cut once, here we say measure many times and many ways and put them all together in a systematic, logical way. Use not only a square to check for a right angle but also measure 3 feet and 4 feet along each side and check to see if the diagonal measures 5 feet. That's the idea behind the proposed process for fine-tuning a system of marketing metrics.

Using identities to estimate metrics that are difficult to measure directly

> "Decomposition involves figuring out how to compute something very uncertain from other things that are a lot less uncertain or at least easier to measure."[2]

Marketing models can often make use of our ability to infer missing variables through construction of the appropriate identity. First, let's take an example from the physical world and use that to draw a parallel to marketing problems. Directly calculating the average depth of your local swimming pool would involve a series of complicated and difficult measurements (either measuring the depth repeatedly while moving across the length and width of the pool or somehow capturing the curve of the bottom with a functional form and using calculus and algebra). An indirect method might be easier: Record the volume of water required to fill the pool and divide by the pool's surface area.

Marketers are also often interested in estimating the values that are conceivably directly measurable yet might be more efficiently estimated from combinations of other metrics. An example is a firm's average Share of Requirements or Share of Wallet, either in dollars or in units. Measuring this directly would require a database of customer purchases that included its own firm purchases and all other purchases in the same category. Further, the customers included in the database would need to be representative of the entire category or weighted in an appropriate way. Instead of using a direct measurement, marketers might find it easier and more efficient to estimate share of requirements from the equation included in Sections 2.3 and 2.5:

$$\text{Share of Requirements (\%)} = \frac{\text{Market Share (\%)}}{\text{Penetration Share (\$, \#)} * \text{Usage Index (\$, \#)}}$$

The latter three variables might be directly measurable from reported sales, a count of known customers, and an estimate of the degree to which the firm's own customers are heavy or light users of the category. Of course, the metric estimated in this manner is an average and will not give insight into the variation in customer loyalty behavior represented by the metric.

14.3   Marketing mix models: monitoring relationships between marketing decisions and objectives

As Neil Borden, Sr., the author of the term "marketing mix" noted over half a century ago, "Several characteristics of the marketing environment make it difficult to predict and control the effect of marketing actions."[3] A system of marketing identities can help with this problem by providing integrated frameworks and structures for monitoring the outcomes from marketing decisions. Marketing models must often trade off comprehensiveness with comprehensibility, completeness with simplicity.

The complexities include these: First, several potential marketing actions may affect sales and profits. These potential actions include pricing, price promotion, advertising, personal selling, and distribution changes, to name just a few. Second, the effects of any one of these actions on sales, even holding all of the other actions equal, are often nonlinear. The infamous S-curve is an example of this non-linearity: A little advertising produces no effect, somewhat more stimulates sales, and at some point effectiveness diminishes and disappears altogether. Third, the effects of one marketing decision often depend on other marketing decisions. For example, the effects of advertising on sales depend not only on the product design but also on price and product availability. Fourth, there are "feedback" and lagged effects in marketing. Over time, our investments in advertising might build brand equity that allows our brand to charge higher prices. Or, if competitors introduce a better product and sales fall to the point that salespeople are earning too little, the same salespeople may resign or spend less time on a particular product line, causing sales to fall again.

The potential complexity resulting from specifying a large number of marketing mix elements, non-linearities of effects, interactions among elements, lagged and feedback effects, and competitive behavior is mind numbing. Further, these potential complexities seem to be limited only by the imagination—and marketing people are (by definition?) creative! It is simply not possible, we assert, to capture all of these complexities with any empirical model.

In the face of such potential for complexity, it is important that marketers find approaches that will help them, in the words of Arnold Zellner, keep it sophisticatedly simple (KISS—we know you thought it stood for something else).[4] Careful selection of marketing metrics frameworks that are constructed around a few important identities has several benefits. One is that they enable us to specify the most important interactions and feedback loops at the level of structural identities instead of empirical relationships.

Let's begin by distinguishing between marketing decisions (actions), objectives (for example, profits), and intervening metrics that help us understand the connections. A simple marketing mix model might be the following: Profits = f(Unit Price, Advertising, Sales Force, and Trade Promotion), which written out in English means profits are a function of unit price, advertising, sales force, and trade promotion (see Figure 14.3).

Many marketers would reject the model in Figure 14.3 as not sufficiently detailed as concerns the multiple effects of marketing mix decisions. A $1 increase in unit price, for example, would result in a $1 increase in unit margin while, probably, decreasing unit sales. Estimating the empirical relationship between unit price and unit sales separately and then making use of identities involving unit price, unit cost, and unit sales to calculate gross profit (as illustrated in Figure 14.4) is generally preferred. Thus, we separate what can be calculated (using an identity) from what *must* be estimated (using an empirical relationship). Similarly, knowing the causal effect of advertising, sales force, and trade promotion spending on unit sales allows the marketer to calculate the effect on profits and determine whether an increase or a decrease is justified (see Figure 14.4). The usefulness rests on the assumption that we will do a better job of understanding marketing mix effects by separating those that must be empirically estimated from others that are governed by accounting identities.

Figure 14.3 Empirical relationships between marketing decisions and objectives

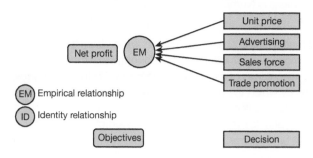

Figure 14.4 Empirical relationship with components of marketing outcomes

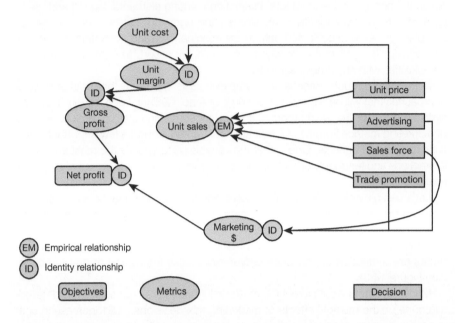

Marketing mix models are used to estimate the effects of marketing levers on marketing objectives and make decisions about how to allocate resources. One of the most frequently applied marketing mix models is the one underlying simulated test markets and depicted in Figure 14.5. With only minor variations, these models are used to forecast new product sales. (See Section 4.1 for more detail.) The structure of this model is straightforward, even if some would argue that it is not simple. Forecast unit sales are calculated in a multiplicative identity from the metrics below. The multiplicative nature of the identity captures the most significant interactions of the marketing mix without resorting to (even more) complex equations. It is, we assert, more managerially transparent and useful because of this well-structured system of metrics that defines and separates identities from empirical relationships.

Forecast Unit Sales = Number of Consumer Prospects * Awareness * Availability * (Trial Rate * Trial Units + Repeat Rate * Repeat Units)

The input estimates for the components are obtained from the results of the simulated test, surveys, management judgment, and/or empirical models.

One of the advantages of the model in Figure 14.5 is that it also provides clear and separate paths by which the different marketing mix elements are believed to impact unit sales. Advertising affects consumer awareness but not availability. Of course, in reality, everything affects everything, but the KISS structure affords a transparency and utility that might be destroyed if management didn't impose the discipline of focusing on the most important empirical relationships that the identity relationships suggest.

Figure 14.5 Simulated test markets combine empirical and identity relationships

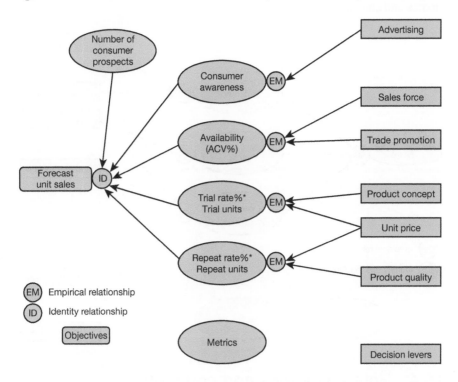

In the case of the new product forecasting model in Figure 14.5, we have decomposed (defined) the forecast sales to be a function of the metrics listed. The way we choose to decompose the objective may be more or less suitable for separating marketing mix empirical effects. For example, breaking down a shared goal into share of requirements, usage index, and penetration share would not have an obvious relationship to individual mix elements. Everything would still affect everything. So, not every identity will be helpful in a model of marketing mix effects.

Also, depending on how the data are collected, some identities may be strongly suggested by the data, even if they are not directly measured. For example, in consumer packaged goods markets, data on distribution (see Section 7.1) and channel promotion activity (incremental sales lift %; see Section 9.1) are regularly collected and reported to marketing managers. The availability of these two metrics strongly suggests the need for a third metric, "preference," to create an attractive identity that may be useful in separating empirical effects and allowing for important interactions. Figure 14.6 shows how marketers might be able to "back into" values of preference by combining Share, Lift %, and Distribution metrics. Of course, this approach means that the marketers are *defining* preference in a way that is consistent with relative choice under scenarios of equal Distribution and Lift %.

Figure 14.6 Empirical relationship with marketing components and intermediate metrics and constructs

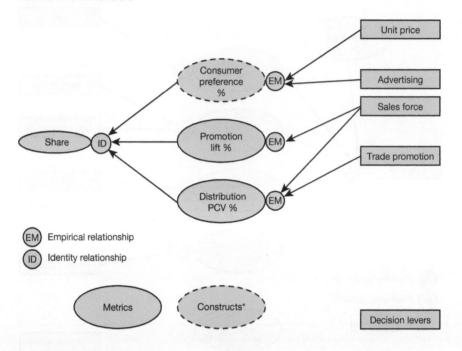

14.4 Related metrics and concepts

By definition, accounting identities always hold. It is simply a matter of getting the correct values for the component parts. Other identities, such as those in theoretical models of finance and economics, are true "in theory" or assuming certain conditions. For example, as discussed in Sections 8.3 and 8.4, at profit-maximizing levels of price, this identity should be true:

Margin on Sales [(Price – Variable Cost)/Price] = 1/absolute value of price
elasticity for constant elasticity demand

or

Price = Variable Cost + ½ (Maximum Willingness to Pay – Variable Cost)
for linear demand functions

These identities identify relationships that are unlikely to be precise but are vaguely right.

Conclusion

"Metrics should be necessary (i.e., the company cannot do without them), precise, consistent, and sufficient (i.e., comprehensive) for review purposes."[5]

Understanding metrics allows marketers to choose the right input data to get meaningful information. They should be able to pick and choose from a variety of metrics, depending on the circumstances, and create a dashboard of the most vital metrics to aid in managing their business. After reading this book, we hope you agree that no one metric is going to give a full picture. It is only when you can use multiple viewpoints—known as *triangulating* because you come at the problem from different angles—that you are likely to obtain anything approaching a full picture.

> "*Results measures tell us where we stand in efforts to achieve goals but not how we go there or what to do differently.*"[6]

Marketing metrics are needed to give a complete picture of a business's health. Financial metrics focus on dollars and periods of time, telling us how profits, cash, and assets are changing. However, we also need to understand what is happening with our customers, products, prices, channels, competitors, and brands.

The interpretation of marketing metrics requires knowledge and judgment. This book helps give you the knowledge so that you can better understand how metrics are constructed and what they measure. Knowing the limitations of individual metrics is important. In our experience, businesses are usually complex, requiring multiple metrics to capture different facets in order to tell you what is going on.

Because of the complexity, marketing metrics often raise as many questions as they answer. Certainly, they rarely provide easy answers about what managers should do. Having a set of metrics based on a limited, faulty, or outmoded view of the business can also blind you. Such a set of metrics can falsely reassure you that the business is fine when in fact trouble is developing. Like the ostrich with his head in the sand, it might be more comfortable to know less. We recommend that you guard against the classic problem of measuring what you can easily measure regardless of whether doing so is helpful to your business. It is better to consider what metrics will be useful for your business and work to find a way to access them.

We also recommend that you spend time considering how to communicate metrics. The message in metrics is useful only if it is received. When you are communicating about metrics, take time to help the listener turn the information into knowledge. Perhaps determine whether you can make a clear visual representation of the information that highlights the key message of the metric.

We don't expect that a command of marketing metrics will make your job easier. We do expect that such knowledge will help you do your job better.

Further reading

Hubbard, Douglas W. (2007). *How to Measure Anything: Finding the Value of "Intangibles" in Business*, John Wiley & Sons.

Bibliography

Aaker, David A. (1991). *Managing Brand Equity*, The Free Press.

Aaker, David A. (1996). *Building Strong Brands*, The Free Press.

Aaker, David A., and James M. Carman. (1982). "Are You Over Advertising?" *Journal of Advertising Research*, 22, 57–70.

Aaker, David A., and Kevin Lane Keller. (1990). "Consumer Evaluations of Brand Extensions," *Journal of Marketing*, 54, 27.

Abela, Andrew, Bruce H. Clark, and Tim Ambler. (2004). "Marketing Performance Measurement, Performance, and Learning," working paper.

Abraham, Magid H., and Leonard M. Lodish. (1990). "Getting the Most Out of Advertising and Promotion," *Harvard Business Review*, 68(3), 50–58.

Ailawadi, Kusum, and Paul W. Farris. (2017). "Managing Multi- and Omni-Channel Distribution: Metrics and Research Directions," *Journal of Retailing*, 93(1), 120–135.

Ailawadi, Kusum L., and Paul W. Farris. (2020). *Getting Multi-Channel Distribution Right*, Wiley.

Ailawadi, Kusum, Paul Farris, and Ervin Shames. (1999). "Trade Promotion: Essential to Selling through Resellers," *Sloan Management Review*, Fall.

Ailawadi, Kusum, Donald Lehmann, and Scott Neslin. (2003). "Revenue Premium as an Outcome Measure of Brand Equity," *Journal of Marketing*, 67(4), 1–17.

Ambler, Tim, and Chris Styles. (1995). "Brand Equity: Toward Measures That Matter," working paper No. 95-902, London Business School, Centre for Marketing.

Barwise, Patrick, and John U. Farley. (2003). "Which Marketing Metrics Are Used and Where?" Marketing Science Institute, (03-111) working paper.

Bendle, Neil T., and C. K. Bagga. (2017). "The Confusion About CLV in Case-Based Teaching Materials," *Marketing Education Review*, 27(1), 27–38.

Bendle, Neil T., C. K. Bagga, and M. A. Nastasoiu. (2019). "Forging a Stronger Academic-Practitioner Partnership: The Case of Net Promoter Score (NPS)," *Journal of Marketing Theory and Practice*, 27(2), 210–226.

Bendle, Neil Thomas, and Moeen Naseer Butt. (2018). "The Misuse of Accounting-Based Approximations of Tobin's q in a World of Market-Based Assets," *Marketing Science*, 37(3), 484–504.

Berger, Paul D., Bruce Weinberg, and Richard C. Hanna. (2003). "Customer Lifetime Value Determination and Strategic Implications for a Cruise-Ship Line," *Database Marketing and Customer Strategy Management*, 11(1), 40–52.

Blattberg, Robert C., and Stephen J. Hoch. (1990). "Database Models and Managerial Intuition: 50% Model + 50% Manager," *Management Science*, 36(8), 887–899.

Borden, Neil H. (1964). "The Concept of the Marketing Mix," *Journal of Advertising Research*, 4, 2–7.

Bruno, Hernan, Unmish Parthasarathi, and Nisha Singh, Eds. (2005). "The Changing Face of Measurement Tools Across the Product Lifecycle," in *Does Marketing Measure Up? Performance Metrics: Practices and Impact*, Marketing Science Conference Summary, No. 05-301.

Christen, Markus, Sachin Gupta, John C. Porter, Richard Staelin, and Dick R. Wittink. (1994). "Using Market-Level Data to Understand Promotion Effects in a Nonlinear Model," *Journal of Marketing Research*, 34(3), 322–334.

Clark, Bruce H., Andrew V. Abela, and Tim Ambler. (2004). "Return on Measurement: Relating Marketing Metrics Practices to Strategic Performance," working paper.

Dekimpe, Marnik G., and Dominique M. Hanssens. (1995). "The Persistence of Marketing Effects on Sales," *Marketing Science*, 14, 1–21.

Dolan, Robert J., and Hermann Simon. *Power Pricing: How Managing Price Transforms the Bottom Line*, The Free Press.

Farris, Paul W., David Reibstein, and Ervin Shames. (1998). *Advertising Budgeting: A Report from the Field*, American Association of Advertising Agencies.

Farris, Paul W., Dominique M. Hanssens, James D. Lenskold, and David J. Reibstein. (2015). "Marketing Return on Investment: Seeking Clarity for Concept and Measurement," *Applied Marketing Analytics*, 1(3), 267–282.

Forrester, Jay W. (1961). "Advertising: A Problem in Industrial Dynamics," *Harvard Business Review*, March–April, 110.

Forrester, Jay W. (1965). "Modeling of Market and Company Interactions," in Peter D. Bennet, ed., *Marketing and Economic Development*, American Marketing Association, pp. 353–364.

Gregg, Eric, Paul W. Farris, and Ervin Shames. (2004). "Perspective on Brand Equity," Darden School Technical Notes, UVA-M-0668.

Greyser, Stephen A. (1980). "Marketing Issues," *Journal of Marketing*, 47, 89–93.

Gupta, Sunil, and Donald R. Lehmann. (2003). "Customers as Assets," *Journal of Interactive Marketing*, 17(1), 9–24.

Hauser, John, and Gerald Katz. (1998). "Metrics: You Are What You Measure," *European Management Journal*, 16(5), 517–528.

Interactive Advertising Bureau. (2004). *Interactive Audience Measurement and Advertising Campaign Reporting and Audit Guidelines*, Version 6.0b.

Kaplan, R. S., and V. G. Narayanan. (2001). "Measuring and Managing Customer Profitability." *Journal of Cost Management*, 15(5), 5–15.

Keiningham, Timothy, Bruce Cooil, Tor Wallin Andreassen, and Lerzan Aksoy. (2007). "A Longitudinal Examination of Net Promoter and Firm Revenue Growth," *Journal of Marketing*, 71(3), 39–51.

Little, John D. C. (1970). "Models and Managers: The Concept of a Decision Calculus," *Management Science*, 16(8), b-466–b-484.

Lodish, Leonard M. (1997). "J.P. Jones and M.H. Blair on Measuring Advertising Effects: Another Point of View," *Journal of Advertising Research*, 37(5), 75–79.

Marn, Michael V., Eric V. Roegner, and Craig C. Zawada. (2004). *The Price Advantage*, John Wiley & Sons.

McGovern, G. J., D. Court, J. A. Quelch, and B. Crawford. (2004). "Bringing Customers into the Boardroom," *Harvard Business Review*, 82(11), 70–80.

Meyer, Christopher. (1994). "How the Right Measures Help Teams Excel," *Harvard Business Review*, 72(3), 95.

Much, James G., Lee S. Sproull, and Michal Tamuz. (1989). "Learning from Samples of One or Fewer," *Organizational Science*, 2(1), 1–12.

Murphy, Allan H., and Barbara G. Brown. (1984). "A Comparative Evaluation of Objective and Subjective Weather Forecasts in the United States," *Journal of Forecasting*, 3, 369–393.

Peppers, D., and M. Rogers. (1997). *Enterprise One to One: Tools for Competing in the Interactive Age*, Currency Doubleday.

Pfeifer, P. E., Mark E. Haskins, and Robert M. Conroy. (2005). "Customer Lifetime Value, Customer Profitability, and the Treatment of Acquisition Spending," *Journal of Managerial Issues*, 17(1), 11–25.

Poundstone, William. (1993). *Prisoner's Dilemma*, Doubleday.

Rangan, V. Kasturi, and Marie Bell. (1994). *Nestle Refrigerated Foods: Contadina Pasta & Pizza (A)*. Harvard Business School.

Reichheld, Frederick F. (2006). *The Ultimate Question: Driving Good Profits and True Growth*, Harvard Business School Publishing Corporation.

Reichheld, Frederick F., and Earl W. Sasser, Jr. (1990). "Zero Defections: Quality Comes to Services," *Harvard Business Review*, 68(5), 105–111.

Sheth, Jagdish N., and Rajendra S. Sisodia. (2002). "Marketing Productivity Issues and Analysis," *Journal of Business Research*, 55, 349–362.

Tellis, Gerald J., and Doyle L. Weiss. (1995). "Does TV Advertising Really Affect Sales? The Role of Measures, Models, and Data Aggregation," *Journal of Marketing Research*, 24(3), 1–12.

Wilner, Jack D. (1998). *Seven Secrets to Successful Sales Management*, CRC Press.

Zellner, A., H. Kuezenkamp, and M. McAleer. (2001). *Simplicity, Inference and Modeling (Keeping It Sophisticatedly Simple)*, Cambridge University Press.

Zoltners, Andris A., Prabhakant Sinha, and Greggor A. Zoltners. (2001). *The Complete Guide to Accelerating Sales Force Performance*, AMACON.

Endnotes

Chapter 1

1. Word Reference, www.wordreference.com.
2. Bartlett, John. (1992). *Bartlett's Familiar Quotations*, 16th ed.
3. Hauser, John, and Gerald Katz. (1998). "Metrics: You Are What You Measure," *European Management Journal*, 16(5), 517–528.
4. Kaplan, Robert S., and David P. Norton. (1996). *Balanced Scorecard*, Harvard Business School Press.
5. Brady, Diane, with David Kiley and Bureau Reports. (2004, December 13). "Making Marketing Measure Up," *Business Week*, 112–113.
6. Strictly speaking, all the numbers contain some error. For example, share might be estimated from retail sales to consumers or from shipments to retailers.
7. Barwise, Patrick, and John U. Farley. (2003). "Which Marketing Metrics Are Used and Where?" Marketing Science Institute working paper.
8. Ambler, Tim, Flora Kokkinaki, and Stefano Puntoni. (2004). "Assessing Marketing Performance: Reasons for Metrics Selection," *Journal of Marketing Management*, 20, 475–498.
9. Watt, James H., and Sjef van den Berg. (1995). *Research Methods for Communication Science*, Allyn & Bacon, p. 11.
10. Armstrong, J. Scott. (1974). "Eclectic Research and Construct Validation," in Jagdish N. Sheth (Ed.), *Models of Buyer Behavior: Conceptual, Quantitative, and Empirical* (pp. 3–14), Harper & Row.

Chapter 2

1. Report: Walmart Continues To Gain Market Share In Most Categories by Sarah Mahoney @mahoney_sarah, January 24, 2019 Accessed July 8th, 2020 in Marketing Daily https://www.mediapost.com/publications/article/331054/report-walmartcontinues-to-gain-market-share-in.html
2. "Running Out of Gas," *Business Week*, March 28, 2005.
3. MASB Common Language Dictionary, "Three-Firm Concentration Ratio," marketing-dictionary.org/t/three-firm-concentration-ratio/.
4. Check the Marketing Evaluations, Inc., website for more detail: www.qscores.com.
5. Claritas provides the Prizm analysis. For more details, visit www.claritas.com.
6. Reichheld, Fred. (2006). *The Ultimate Question: Driving Good Profits and True Growth*, Harvard Business School Publishing.
7. Reichheld, Fred. (2003). "The One Number You Need to Grow," *Harvard Business Review*, 81(12), 46–54.
8. Keiningham, Timothy, Bruce Cooil, Tor Wallin Andreassen, and Lerzan Aksoy. (2007). "A Longitudinal Examination of Net Promoter and Firm Revenue Growth," *Journal of Marketing*, 71(3), 39–51.

9. For more on net promoter and the implications for academia and practice, see Bendle, N. T., C. K. Bagga, and M. A. Nastasoiu. (2019). "Forging a Stronger Academic-Practitioner Partnership: The Case of Net Promoter Score (NPS)," *Journal of Marketing Theory and Practice*, 27(2), 210–226.

10. Thanks to Dr. Manuel Garcia-Garcia of New York University Stern School of Business and to neuroscience student Pasha Davoudian from Neuroscience University of Virginia for their invaluable guidance and assistance with this section.

11. McClure, Samuel M., Jian Li, Damon Tomlin, Kim S. Cypert, Latané. M. Montague, and P. Read Montague. (2004). "Neural Correlates of Behavioral Preference for Culturally Familiar Drinks," Neuron, 44(2), 379–387.

12. Another key study on the role of the reward system in predicting consumer behavior is Knutson, Rick B., G. E. Wimmer, D. Prelec, and G. Loewenstein. (2007). "Neural Predictors of Purchases," *Neuron*, 53(1), 147–156.

13. Teixeira, Thales, Michel Wedel, and Rik Pieters. (2012). "Emotion-Induced Engagement in Internet Video Advertisements," *Journal of Marketing Research*, 49, 144–159.

14. Trabulsi, Julia, Manuel Garcia-Garcia, and Michael E. Smith. (2015). "Consumer Neuroscience: A Method for Optimizing Marketing Communication," *Journal of Cultural Marketing Strategy*, 1(1), 80–89.

15. Varan, Duane, Annie Lang, Patrick Barwise, Rene Weber, and Steven Bellman. (2015). "How Reliable Are Neuromarketers' Measures of Advertising Effectiveness: Data from Ongoing Research Holds No Common Truth Among Vendors," *Journal of Advertising Research*, 55(2), 176–191.

Chapter 3

1. "Running Out of Gas," *Business Week*, March 28, 2005.

2. This formula should be familiar if we consider that the supplier selling price is merely the cost to that layer of the chain. So this becomes Selling Price = Cost/(1 − Margin %). This is the same as Sale ($) = Cost ($) + Margin ($).

3. Those familiar with basic economics use the term *marginal* cost to refer to the cost of an additional unit of output. In this linear cost model, marginal cost is the same for all units and is equal to the variable cost per unit.

4. Both contribution per unit ($) and contribution margin (%) are closely related to unit margin ($) and margin (%). The difference is that contribution margins (whether unit or percentage based) result from a more careful separation of fixed and variable costs.

Chapter 4

1. Rangan, V. Kasturi, and Marie Bell. (1995). *Nestle Refrigerated Foods: Contadina Pasta & Pizza (A)*. Harvard Business School.

2. Kusum Ailawadi, Donald Lehmann, and Scott Neslin. (2003). "Revenue Premium as an Outcome Measure of Brand Equity," *Journal of Marketing*, 67(4), 1–17.

3. Ibid.

4. Young and Rubicam can be found at yr.com/BAV. Accessed 02/12/2020.

5. Simon, Julian. (1969). "'Product Differentiation': A Meaningless Term and an Impossible Concept," *Ethics*, 79(2), 131–138.

6. Orme, B. (2010, 2019). *Getting Started with Conjoint Analysis: Strategies for Product Design and Pricing Research*. Fourth Edition, Madison, Wis.: Research Publishers LLC. https://www.sawtoothsoftware.com/download/techpap/interpca.pdf.

Chapter 5

1. Bell Canada. (2018). Annual Report, www.bce.ca/investors/AR-2018/2018-bce.annual-report.pdf.
2. State Farm Mutual Automobile Insurance Company. https://www.statefarm.com/about-us/company-overview/company-profile/fast-facts
3. "Selected Orders of the Public Service Commission of Wisconsin," Volumes 59-60 (1974, 1975). By Public Service Commission of Wisconsin, 132.
4. Wikipedia. "Atlanta Braves Home Attendance," http://en.wikipedia.org/wiki/Major_League_Baseball_attendance_records.
5. eBay, "Unaudited Supplemental Operating Data," ebay.q4cdn.com/610426115/files/doc_downloads/financials_and_metrics/Q4/Q4'19-Metrics.pdf.
6. Thanks to Gerry Allan, President, Anametrica, Inc. (developer of web-based tools for managers) for his work on this section.
7. Pfeifer, P. E., M. E. Haskins, and R. M. Conroy. (2005). "Customer Lifetime Value, Customer Profitability, and the Treatment of Acquisition Spending," *Journal of Managerial Issues*, 17(1), 11–25.
8. Kaplan, R. S., and V. G. Narayanan. (2001). "Measuring and Managing Customer Profitability," *Journal of Cost Management*, 15(5), 5–15.
9. Peppers, D., and M. Rogers. (1997). *Enterprise One to One: Tools for Competing in the Interactive Age*, Currency Doubleday.
10. Berger, P. D., B. Weinberg, and R. Hanna. (2003). "Customer Lifetime Value Determination and Strategic Implications for a Cruise-Ship Line," *Database Marketing and Customer Strategy Management*, 11(1), 40–52.
11. Gupta, Sunil, and Donald R. Lehmann. (2003). "Customers as Assets," *Journal of Interactive Marketing*, 17(1), 9–24.

Chapter 6

1. Material in Sections 6.1–6.5 is based on Eric Larson, *Note on Sales Force Metrics*, Darden MBA 2005.
2. Zoltners, Andris A., Prabhakant Sinha, and Greggor A. Zoltners. (2001). *The Complete Guide to Accelerating Sales Force Performance*, AMACON.
3. Wilner, Jack D. (1998). *Seven Secrets to Successful Sales Management*, CRC Press, pp. 35–36, 42.
4. For more on these total allocations, see Zoltners, Andris A., Prabhakant Sinha, and Greggor A. Zoltners. (2001). *The Complete Guide to Accelerating Sales Force Performance*, AMACON.
5. Ibid.
6. Dolan, Robert J., and Benson P. Shapiro. *Milford Industries (A)*, Harvard Business School, Case 584-012.
7. Zoltners, Andris A., Prabhakant Sinha, and Greggor A. Zoltners. (2001). *The Complete Guide to Accelerating Sales Force Performance*, AMACON.
8. Jones, Eli, Carl Stevens, and Larry Chonko. (2005). *Selling ASAP: Art, Science, Agility, Performance*, South Western, p. 176.

Chapter 7

1. Product category volume is also known as weighted distribution.

Chapter 8

1. Dolan, Robert J., and Hermann Simon. (1996). *Power Pricing: How Managing Price Transforms the Bottom Line*, The Free Press, p. 4.
2. Barwise, Patrick, and John U. Farley. (2003). "Which Marketing Metrics Are Used and Where?" Marketing Science Institute working paper.
3. Constant elasticity functions are also called *log linear* because they can be expressed as log Q = log A + elasticity * log (p).
4. In graphing such relationships, economists often plot price on the vertical axis and quantity demanded on the horizontal axis. When reviewing a graph, managers are advised to always check the axis definitions.
5. If price elasticity is expressed in shorthand as a positive number, then we do not need the negative sign in the formula that follows.
6. For more information, see www.ftc.gov/tips-advice/competition-guidance/guide-antitrust-laws/price-discrimination-robinson-patman.
7. Ibid.
8. Poundstone, William. (1993). *Prisoner's Dilemma*, Doubleday.

Chapter 9

1. In this context, we use the term *permanent* with some flexibility, recognizing that even long-term arrangements must be subject to change in response to market and industry dynamics.
2. Often, contribution can be used as a proxy for profits.
3. Distribution for coupons is used in the sense of postage and insertion costs rather than retail and inventory logistics.
4. For a richer discussion, see Ailawadi, Farris, and Shames, *Sloan Management Review*, Fall 1999.
5. Roegner, E. V., M. V. Marn, and C. C. Zawada. (2005). "Pricing," *Marketing Management*, 14(1), 23–28.
6. The following are the two main types of injury contemplated by the act: (a) Price discrimination might be used as a predatory pricing tactic, setting prices below cost to certain customers to harm competition at the supplier's level. Antitrust authorities use the same standards applied to predatory pricing claims under the Sherman Act and the FTC Act to evaluate allegations of price discrimination used for this purpose. (b) Secondary line competitive injury occurs when a seller charges competing buyers different prices for the same "commodity" or discriminates in the provision of "allowances" such as compensation for advertising and other services. This kind of price discrimination can hurt competition by giving favored customers an edge in the market that has nothing to do with their superior efficiency. However, in the United States, price discrimination is generally lawful, particularly if it reflects the different costs of dealing with diverse buyers or results from a seller's attempts to meet a competitor's prices or services. Clearly this is not intended to be a legal opinion, and legal advice should be sought for a company's individual circumstances.

Chapter 10

1. Farris, Paul W. (2003). "Getting the Biggest Bang for Your Marketing Buck," *Measuring and Allocating Marcom Budgets: Seven Expert Points of View*, Marketing Science Institute Monograph.
2. Dorfman, Robert, and Peter O. Steiner. (1954). "Optimal Advertising and Optimal Quality," *American Economic Review*, 44, 826–836.
3. For more on the misuse of ROI, see Bendle, Neil Thomas, and Charan K. Bagga. (2016). "The Metrics That Marketers Muddle," *Sloan Management Review*, 3, 73–82.

Chapter 11

1. The pixel count technique is also known as *client-side tagging, beacon, and 1 × 1 clear pixel technology*.
2. See the Media Rating Council for its latest guidance at http://mediaratingcouncil.org/.
3. The Interactive Advertising Bureau gives the following definition of *ad impression*: "A measurement of response from an ad delivery system to an ad request from the user's browser, which is filtered from robotic activity and is recorded at a point as late as possible in the process of delivery of the creative material to the user's browser — therefore closest to actual opportunity to see by the user." See Interactive Advertising Bureau. (2004). *Interactive Audience Measurement and Advertising Campaign Reporting and Audit Guidelines*.
4. eMarketer. (2019). *US Total Media Ad and Marketing Spending, by Media and Format, 2018 and 2019*. chart-na1.emarketer.com/226158/us-total-media-ad-marketing-spending-by-media-format-2018-2019-billions-change. Data are from the January 2019 Winterberry Group report titled "Outlook for Data Driven Marketing: First Look 2019."
5. "Consumer Panels," www.nielsen.com/us/en/solutions/capabilities/consumer-panels/.
6. "Bounce Rate," support.google.com/analytics/answer/1009409?hl=en.

Chapter 12

1. For more details on giving background information to aid in understanding a firm's value, see FASB. (2010). *Statement of Financial Accounting Concepts*, No. 8, objective 7.
2. Economic Value Added (EVA) is a trademark of Stern Stewart.
3. The weighted average cost of capital (WACC) is the percentage return expected by capital sources. This finance concept is better left to specialist texts, but to give a simple example, if one-third of a firm's capital comes from the bank at 6% and two-thirds from shareholders who expect a 9% return, then the WACC is the weighted average 8%. The WACC will be different for different companies, depending on their structure and risks.
4. Excel has a function to do this quickly, as explained at the end of the section. However, it is important to understand what the calculation is doing.
5. A terminal value in a simple calculation might be assumed to be zero or some simple figure for the sale of the enterprise. More complex calculations consider future cash flows; where this is done, ask about assumptions and importance. If the estimated terminal value is a significant area of the analysis, why have you curtailed the full analyses at this point?

6. Hawkins, Del I., Roger J. Best, and Charles M. Lillis. (1987). "The Nature and Measurement of Marketing Productivity in Consumer Durables Industries: A Firm Level Analysis," *Journal of the Academy of Marketing Science*, 1(4), 1–8.
7. Farris, Paul W., Dominique M. Hanssens, James D. Lenskold, and David J. Reibstein. (2015). "Marketing Return on Investment: Seeking Clarity for Concept and Measurement," *Applied Marketing Analytics*, 1(3), 267–282.
8. Ibid.
9. Bendle, Neil Thomas, and Moeen Naseer Butt. (2018). "The Misuse of Accounting-Based Approximations of Tobin's q in a World of Market-Based Assets," *Marketing Science*, 37(3), 484–504.

Chapter 13

1. O'Conner, Fina Colarelli, Thomas R. Willemain, and James MacLachlan. (1996). "The Value of Competition among Agencies in Developing Ad Campaigns: Revisiting Gross's Model," *Journal of Advertising*, 25(1), 51–62.

Chapter 14

1. An identity is "an equality satisfied by all values of the variables for which the expression involved in the equality are defined." *American Heritage Dictionary*, 2nd ed., Houghton Mifflin, 1982.
   In finance, economics, and accounting, an identity is "an equality that must be true regardless of the value of its variables, or a statement that by definition (or construction) must be true." Where an accounting identity applies, any deviation from the identity signifies an error in formulation, calculation, or measurement. en.wikipedia.org/wiki/Accounting_identity#cite_note-0.
2. Hubbard, Douglas W. (2007). *How to Measure Anything: Finding the Value of "Intangibles" in Business*, John Wiley & Sons.
3. Borden, Neil H. (1964). "The Concept of the Marketing Mix," *Journal of Advertising Research*, 4, 2–7.
4. Zellner, A., H. Kuezenkamp, and M. McAleer. (2001). *Simplicity, Inference and Modeling (Keeping It Sophisticatedly Simple)*, Cambridge University Press.
5. Ambler, Tim. (2000). *Marketing and the Bottom Line: The New Metrics of Corporate Wealth*, Prentice Hall.
6. Meyer, Christopher. (1994). "How the Right Measures Help Teams Excel," *Harvard Business Review*, 72(3), 95.

Index